FTCE Middle Grades Integrated Curriculum

Teacher Certification Exam

By: Sharon Wynne, M.S.
Southern Connecticut State University

"And, while there's no reason yet to panic, I think it's only prudent that we make preparations to panic."

XAMonline, INC.
Boston

To obtain permission(s) to use the material from this work for any purpose including workshops or seminars, please submit a written request to:

XAMonline, Inc.
25 First St. Suite 106
Cambridge MA 02141
Toll Free 1-800-509-4128
Email: info@xamonline.com
Web www.xamonline.com
Fax: 1-781-662-9268

Library of Congress Cataloging-in-Publication Data

Wynne, Sharon A.
Middle Grades Integrated Curriculum: Teacher Certification / Sharon A. Wynne. -2nd ed.
ISBN 978-1-60787-009-8
1. Middle Grades Integrated Curriculum. 2. Study Guides. 3. FTCE
4. Teachers' Certification & Licensure. 5. Careers

Disclaimer:
The opinions expressed in this publication are the sole works of XAMonline and were created independently from the National Education Association, Educational Testing Service, or any State Department of Education, National Evaluation Systems or other testing affiliates.

Between the time of publication and printing, state specific standards as well as testing formats and website information may change that is not included in part or in whole within this product. Sample test questions are developed by XAMonline and reflect similar content as on real tests; however, they are not former tests. XAMonline assembles content that aligns with state standards but makes no claims nor guarantees teacher candidates a passing score. Numerical scores are determined by testing companies such as NES or ETS and then are compared with individual state standards. A passing score varies from state to state.

Printed in the United States of America

FTCE: Middle Grades Integrated Curriculum
ISBN: 978-1-60787-009-8

Table of Contents

DOMAIN II. GENERAL SCIENCE

DOMAIN IV. **ENGLISH**

Great Study and Testing Tips!

What to study in order to prepare for the subject assessments is the focus of this study guide but equally important is *how* you study.

You can increase your chances of truly mastering the information by taking some simple, but effective steps.

Study Tips:

1. Some foods aid the learning process. Foods such as milk, nuts, seeds, rice, and oats help your study efforts by releasing natural memory enhancers called CCKs (*cholecystokinin*) composed of *tryptophan*, *choline*, and *phenylalanine*. All of these chemicals enhance the neurotransmitters associated with memory. Before studying, try a light, protein-rich meal of eggs, turkey, and fish. All of these foods release the memory enhancing chemicals. The better the connections, the more you comprehend.

Likewise, before you take a test, stick to a light snack of energy boosting and relaxing foods. A glass of milk, a piece of fruit, or some peanuts all release various memory-boosting chemicals and help you to relax and focus on the subject at hand.

2. Learn to take great notes. A by-product of our modern culture is that we have grown accustomed to getting our information in short doses (i.e. TV news sound bites or USA Today style newspaper articles.)

Consequently, we've subconsciously trained ourselves to assimilate information better in neat little packages. If your notes are scrawled all over the paper, it fragments the flow of the information. Strive for clarity. Newspapers use a standard format to achieve clarity. Your notes can be much clearer through use of proper formatting. A very effective format is called the *"Cornell Method."*

> Take a sheet of loose-leaf lined notebook paper and draw a line all the way down the paper about 1-2" from the left-hand edge.
>
> Draw another line across the width of the paper about 1-2" up from the bottom. Repeat this process on the reverse side of the page.

Look at the highly effective result. You have ample room for notes, a left hand margin for special emphasis items or inserting supplementary data from the textbook, a large area at the bottom for a brief summary, and a little rectangular space for just about anything you want.

3. **Get the concept then the details.** Too often we focus on the details and don't gather an understanding of the concept. However, if you simply memorize only dates, places, or names, you may well miss the whole point of the subject.

A key way to understand things is to put them in your own words. If you are working from a textbook, automatically summarize each paragraph in your mind. If you are outlining text, don't simply copy the author's words.

Rephrase them in your own words. You remember your own thoughts and words much better than someone else's, and subconsciously tend to associate the important details to the core concepts.

4. **Ask Why?** Pull apart written material paragraph by paragraph and don't forget the captions under the illustrations.

Example: If the heading is "Stream Erosion", flip it around to read "Why do streams erode?" Then answer the questions.

If you train your mind to think in a series of questions and answers, not only will you learn more, but it also helps to lessen the test anxiety because you are used to answering questions.

5. **Read for reinforcement and future needs.** Even if you only have 10 minutes, put your notes or a book in your hand. Your mind is similar to a computer; you have to input data in order to have it processed. *By reading, you are creating the neural connections for future retrieval.* The more times you read something, the more you reinforce the learning of ideas.

Even if you don't fully understand something on the first pass, *your mind stores much of the material for later recall.*

6. **Relax to learn so go into exile.** Our bodies respond to an inner clock called biorhythms. Burning the midnight oil works well for some people, but not everyone.

If possible, set aside a particular place to study that is free of distractions. Shut off the television, cell phone, and pager and exile your friends and family during your study period.

If you really are bothered by silence, try background music. Light classical music at a low volume has been shown to aid in concentration over other types. Music that evokes pleasant emotions without lyrics is highly suggested. Try just about anything by Mozart. It relaxes you.

7. Use arrows not highlighters. At best, it's difficult to read a page full of yellow, pink, blue, and green streaks. Try staring at a neon sign for a while and you'll soon see that the horde of colors obscure the message.

A quick note, a brief dash of color, an underline, and an arrow pointing to a particular passage is much clearer than a horde of highlighted words.

8. Budget your study time. Although you shouldn't ignore any of the material, ***allocate your available study time in the same ratio that topics may appear on the test.***

Testing Tips:

1. **Get smart, play dumb. Don't read anything into the question.** Don't make an assumption that the test writer is looking for something else than what is asked. Stick to the question as written and don't read extra things into it.

2. **Read the question and all the choices *twice* before answering the question.** You may miss something by not carefully reading, and then re-reading both the question and the answers.

If you really don't have a clue as to the right answer, leave it blank on the first time through. Go on to the other questions, as they may provide a clue as to how to answer the skipped questions. If later on, you still can't answer the skipped ones . . . ***Guess.*** The only penalty for guessing is that you *might* get it wrong. Only one thing is certain; if you don't put anything down, you will get it wrong!

3. **Turn the question into a statement.** Look at the way the questions are worded. The syntax of the question usually provides a clue. Does it seem more familiar as a statement rather than as a question? Does it sound strange?

By turning a question into a statement, you may be able to spot if an answer sounds right, and it may also trigger memories of material you have read.

4. **Look for hidden clues.** It's actually very difficult to compose multiple-foil (choice) questions without giving away part of the answer in the options presented.

In most multiple-choice questions you can often readily eliminate one or two of the potential answers. This leaves you with only two real possibilities and automatically your odds go to Fifty-Fifty for very little work.

5. **Trust your instincts.** For every fact that you have read, you subconsciously retain something of that knowledge. On questions that you aren't really certain about, go with your basic instincts. **Your first impression on how to answer a question is usually correct.**

6. **Mark your answers directly on the test booklet.** Don't bother trying to fill in the optical scan sheet on the first pass through the test.

7. **Watch the clock!** You have a set amount of time to answer the questions. Don't get bogged down trying to answer a single question at the expense of 10 questions you can more readily answer.

DOMAIN I. MATHEMATICS

COMPETENCY 1.0 KNOWLEDGE OF NUMBER SENSE, CONCEPTS, AND OPERATIONS

Skill 1.1 Apply ratio and proportion to solve real-world problems.

A **ratio** is a comparison of 2 numbers. If a class had 11 boys and 14 girls, the ratio of boys to girls could be written one of 3 ways:

11:14 or 11 to 14 or $\frac{11}{14}$

The ratio of girls to boys is:

14:11, 14 to 11 or $\frac{14}{11}$

Ratios can be reduced when possible. A ratio of 12 cats to 18 dogs would reduce to 2:3, 2 to 3 or $2/3$.

Note: Read ratio questions carefully. Given a group of 6 adults and 5 children, the ratio of children to the entire group would be 5:11.

A **proportion** is an equation in which a fraction is set equal to another. To solve the proportion, multiply each numerator times the other fraction's denominator. Set these two products equal to each other and solve the resulting equation. This is called **cross-multiplying** the proportion.

Example: $\frac{4}{15}=\frac{x}{60}$ is a proportion.

To solve this, cross multiply.

$(4)(60)=(15)(x)$

$240=15x$

$16=x$

Example: $\frac{x+3}{3x+4}=\frac{2}{5}$ is a proportion.

To solve, cross multiply.

$$5(x+3)=2(3x+4)$$
$$5x+15=6x+8$$
$$7=x$$

Example: $\frac{x+2}{8}=\frac{2}{x-4}$ is another proportion.

To solve, cross multiply.

$$(x+2)(x-4)=8(2)$$
$$x^2-2x-8=16$$
$$x^2-2x-24=0$$
$$(x-6)(x+4)=0$$
$$x=6 \text{ or } x={}^-4$$

Proportions can be used to solve word problems whenever relationships are compared. Some situations include scale drawings and maps, similar polygons, speed, time and distance, cost, and comparison shopping.

Example: Which is the better buy, 6 items for $1.29 or 8 items for $1.69?

Find the unit price.

$$\frac{6}{1.29}=\frac{1}{x} \qquad \frac{8}{1.69}=\frac{1}{x}$$
$$6x = 1.29 \qquad 8x = 1.69$$
$$x = 0.215 \qquad x = 0.21125$$

Thus, 6 items for $1.29 is the better buy.

Example: A car travels 125 miles in 2.5 hours.. How far will it go in 6 hours?

Write a proportion comparing the distance and time.

$\frac{miles}{hours}$ $\frac{125}{2.5} = \frac{x}{6}$

$2.5x = 750$

$x = 300$

Thus, the car can travel 300 miles in 6 hours.

Example: The scale on a map is $\frac{3}{4}$ inch = 6 miles. What is the actual distance between two cities if they are $1\frac{1}{2}$ inches apart on the map?

Write a proportion comparing the scale to the actual distance.

scale actual

$\frac{\frac{3}{4}}{1\frac{1}{2}} = \frac{6}{x}$

$\frac{3}{4}x = 1\frac{1}{2} \times 6$

$\frac{3}{4}x = 9$

$x = 12$

Thus, the actual distance between the cities is 12 miles.

Skill 1.2 Solve real-world problems that involve percents, decimals, fractions, or numbers expressed in scientific and exponential notation.

Percent = per 100 (written with the symbol %). Thus 10% $= \frac{10}{100} = \frac{1}{10}$.

Decimals = deci = part of ten. To find the decimal equivalent of a fraction, use the denominator to divide the numerator as shown in the following example.

Example: Find the decimal equivalent of $\frac{7}{10}$.

Since 10 cannot divide into 7 evenly

$\frac{7}{10} = 0.7$

The **exponent form** is a shortcut method to write repeated multiplication. Basic form: b^n, where b is called the base and n is the exponent. b and n are both real numbers. b^n implies that the base b is multiplied by itself n times.

Examples: $3^4 = 3 \times 3 \times 3 \times 3 = 81$

$2^3 = 2 \times 2 \times 2 = 8$

$(^-2)^4 = (^-2) \times (^-2) \times (^-2) \times (^-2) = 16$

$^-2^4 = ^-(2 \times 2 \times 2 \times 2) = ^-16$

Key exponent rules:

For 'a' nonzero, and 'm' and 'n' real numbers:

1) $a^m \cdot a^n = a^{(m+n)}$ Product rule

2) $\frac{a^m}{a^n} = a^{(m-n)}$ Quotient rule

3) $\frac{a^{-m}}{a^{-n}} = \frac{a^n}{a^m}$

When 10 is raised to any power, the exponent tells the numbers of zeroes in the product.

Example: $10^7 = 10{,}000{,}000$

Caution: Unless the negative sign is inside the parentheses and the exponent is outside the parentheses, the sign is not affected by the exponent.

$(^-2)^4$ implies that -2 is multiplied by itself 4 times.

$^-2^4$ implies that 2 is multiplied by itself 4 times, then the answer is negated.

Scientific notation is a more convenient method for writing very large and very small numbers. It employs two factors. The first factor is a number between 1 and 10. The second factor is a power of 10. This notation is a "shorthand" for expressing large numbers (like the weight of 100 elephants) or small numbers (like the weight of an atom in pounds).

Recall that:

$10^n = (10)^n$ Ten multiplied by itself n times.

$10^0 = 1$ Any nonzero number raised to power of zero is 1.

$10^1 = 10$

$10^2 = 10\times10 = 100$

$10^3 = 10\times10\times10 = 1000$ (kilo)

$10^{-1} = 1/10$ (deci)

$10^{-2} = 1/100$ (centi)

$10^{-3} = 1/1000$ (milli)

$10^{-6} = 1/1{,}000{,}000$ (micro)

Example: Write 46,368,000 in scientific notation.

1) Introduce a decimal point and decimal places.
46,368,000 = 46,368,000.0000

2) Make a mark between the two digits that give a number between -9.9 and 9.9.
$4 \wedge 6{,}368{,}000.0000$

3) Count the number of digit places between the decimal point and the $\wedge$ mark. This number is the 'n'-the power of ten.

So, $46{,}368{,}000 = 4.6368\times10^7$

Example: Write 0.00397 in scientific notation.

1) Decimal place is already in place.

2) Make a mark between 3 and 9 to get a one number between -9.9 and 9.9.

3) Move decimal place to the mark (3 hops).

$0.003 \wedge 97$

Motion is to the right, so n of 10^n is negative.

Therefore, $0.00397 = 3.97 \times 10^{-3}$

Word problems involving percents can be solved by writing the problem as an equation, then solving the equation. Keep in mind that **"of" means "multiplication"** and **"is" means "equals."**

Example: The Ski Club has 85 members. Eighty percent of the members are able to attend the meeting. How many members attend the meeting?

Restate the problem.	What is 80% of 85?
Write an equation.	$n = 0.8 \times 85$
Solve.	$n = 68$

Sixty-eight members attend the meeting.

Example: There are 64 dogs in the kennel. Forty-eight are collies. What percent are collies?

Restate the problem.	48 is what percent of 64?
Write an equation.	$48 = n \times 64$
Solve.	$\frac{48}{64} = n$
	$n = \frac{3}{4} = 75\%$

75% of the dogs are collies.

Example: The auditorium was filled to 90% capacity. There were 558 seats occupied. What is the capacity of the auditorium?

Restate the problem. 90% of what number is 558?
Write an equation. $0.9n = 558$
Solve. $n = \frac{558}{.9}$
$n = 620$

The capacity of the auditorium is 620 people.

Example: Shoes cost $42.00. Sales tax is 6%. What is the total cost of the shoes?

Restate the problem. What is 6% of 42?
Write an equation. $n = 0.06 \times 42$
Solve. $n = 2.52$

Add the sales tax to the cost. $42.00 + $2.52 = $44.52

The total cost of the shoes, including sales tax, is $44.52.

An alternative method would be to multiply $42.00 by 1.06.

$42.00 x 1.06 = $44.52 (cost including sales tax)[SA1]

COMMON EQUIVALENTS

$\frac{1}{2} = 0.5 = 50\%$
$\frac{1}{3} = 0.333 = 33\frac{1}{3}\%$
$\frac{1}{4} = 0.25 = 25\%$
$\frac{1}{5} = 0.2 = 20\%$
$\frac{1}{6} = 0.1667 = 16\frac{2}{3}\%$
$\frac{1}{8} = 0.125 = 12\frac{1}{2}\%$
$\frac{1}{10} = 0.1 = 10\%$
$\frac{2}{3} = 0.6667 = 66\frac{2}{3}\%$
$\frac{5}{6} = 0.833 = 83\frac{1}{3}\%$
$\frac{3}{8} = 0.375 = 37\frac{1}{2}\%$
$\frac{5}{8} = 0.625 = 62\frac{1}{2}\%$
$\frac{7}{8} = 0.875 = 87\frac{1}{2}\%$
$1 = 1.0 = 100\%$

Skill 1.3 Apply number concepts including primes, factors, and multiples to build number sequences.

A numeration system is a set of numbers represented a by a set of symbols (numbers, letters, or pictographs). Sets can have different bases of numerals within the set. Instead of our base 10, a system may use any base set from 2 on up. The position of the number in that representation defines its exact value. Thus, the numeral 1 has a value of ten when represented as "10". Early systems, such as the Babylonian, used position in relation to other numerals or column position for this purpose since they lacked a zero to represent an empty position.

A base of 2 uses only 0 and 1.

Decimal Binary Conversion		
Decimal	Binary	Place Value
1	1	2^0
2	10	2^1
4	100	2^2
8	1000	2^3

Thus, 9 in Base 10 becomes 1001 in Base 2.

9+4 = 13 (Base 10) becomes 1001 + 100 = 1101 (Base 2).
Fractions, ratios and other functions alter in the same way.
Computers use a base of 2 but combine it into 4 units called a byte to function in base 16 (hexadecimal). A base of 8 (octal) was also used by older computers.

Prime numbers are numbers that can only be factored into 1 and the number itself. When factoring into prime factors, all the factors must be numbers that cannot be factored again (without using 1). Initially numbers can be factored into any 2 factors. Check each resulting factor to see if it can be factored again. Continue factoring until all remaining factors are prime. This is the list of prime factors. Regardless of which way the original number was factored, the final list of prime factors will always be the same.

Example: Factor 30 into prime factors.

Divide by 2 as many times as you can, then by 3, then by other successive primes as required.

2 · 2 · 2 · 2 · 2 · 2 · 2 · 2 · 2 · 2 · 2 · 2 · 2 · 2 · 2

[SA2]

Factor 30 into any 2 factors.

5 · 6	Now factor the 6.
5 · 2 · 3	These are all prime factors.

Factor 30 into any 2 factors.

3 · 10	Now factor the 10.
3 · 2 · 5	These are the same prime factors even though the original factors were different.

Example: Factor 240 into prime factors.

Factor 240 into any 2 factors.

24 · 10	Now factor both 24 and 10.
4 · 6 · 2 · 5	Now factor both 4 and 6.
2 · 2 · 2 · 3 · 2 · 5	These are prime factors.

This can also be written as $2^4 \cdot 3 \cdot 5$

Skill 1.4 Categorize numbers by their memberships in the various subsets of the real number system.

Rational numbers can be expressed as the ratio of two integers, $\frac{a}{b}$ where b ≠ 0, for example $\frac{2}{3}$, $-\frac{4}{5}$, $5 = \frac{5}{1}$.

The rational numbers include integers, fractions and mixed numbers, terminating and repeating decimals. Every rational number can be expressed as a repeating or terminating decimal and can be shown on a number line.

Integers are positive and negative whole numbers and zero.
...-6, -5, -4, -3, -2, -1, 0, 1, 2, 3, 4, 5, 6, ...

Whole numbers are natural numbers and zero.
0, 1, 2, 3, ,4 ,5 ,6 ...

Natural numbers are the counting numbers.
1, 2, 3, 4, 5, 6, ...

Irrational numbers are real numbers that cannot be written as the ratio of two integers. These are infinite non-repeating decimals.
Examples: $\sqrt{5} = 2.2360..$, pi =Π = 3.1415927...

A **fraction** is an expression of numbers in the form of x/y, where ***x*** is the numerator and ***y*** is the denominator, which cannot be zero.

Example: $\frac{3}{7}$ 3 is the numerator; 7 is the denominator

If the fraction has common factors for the numerator and denominator, divide both by the common factor to reduce the fraction to its lowest form.

Example:

$$\frac{13}{39} = \frac{1 \times 13}{3 \times 13} = \frac{1}{3}$$ Divide by the common factor 13

A **mixed** number has an integer part and a fractional part.

Example: $2\frac{1}{4}$, $^{-}5\frac{1}{6}$, $7\frac{1}{3}$

Skill 1.5 Identify the use of the field properties of the real number system in real-world situations and apply operations of real numbers.

Addition of whole numbers

Example: At the end of a day of shopping, a shopper had $24 remaining in his wallet. He spent $45 on various goods. How much money did the shopper have at the beginning of the day?

The total amount of money the shopper started with is the sum of the amount spent and the amount remaining at the end of the day.

```
  24
+ 45
----
  69 ——→  The original total was $69.
```

Example: A race took the winner 1 hr. 58 min. 12 sec. on the first half of the race and 2 hr. 9 min. 57 sec. on the second half of the race. How much time did the entire race take?

```
  1 hr. 58 min. 12 sec.
+ 2 hr.  9 min. 57 sec.     Add these numbers
-----------------------
  3 hr. 67 min. 69 sec.
+ 1 min -60 sec.            Change 60 seconds to 1 min.
  3 hr. 68 min.  9 sec.
+ 1 hr.-60 min.      .      Change 60 minutes to 1 hr.
-----------------------
  4 hr.  8 min.  9 sec.  ←final answer
```

Subtraction of Whole Numbers

Example: At the end of his shift, a cashier has $96 in the cash register. At the beginning of his shift, he had $15. How much money did the cashier collect during his shift?

The total collected is the difference of the ending amount and the starting amount.

```
  96
- 15
----
  81 ——→  The total collected was $81.
```

Multiplication of whole numbers

Multiplication is one of the four basic number operations. In simple terms, multiplication is the addition of a number to itself a certain number of times. For example, 4 multiplied by 3 is the equal to 4 + 4 + 4 or 3 + 3 + 3 +3. Another way of conceptualizing multiplication is to think in terms of groups. For example, if we have 4 groups of 3 students, the total number of students is 4 multiplied by 3. We call the solution to a multiplication problem the product.

The basic algorithm for whole number multiplication begins with aligning the numbers by place value with the number containing more places on top.

```
  172
x  43  ——►  Note that we placed 122 on top because it has more
            places than 43 does.
```

Next, we multiply the ones' place of the second number by each place value of the top number sequentially.

```
 (2)
  172       {3 x 2 = 6, 3 x 7 = 21, 3 x 1 = 3}
x  43  ——►  Note that we had to carry a 2 to the hundreds' column
  516       because 3 x 7 = 21. Note also that we add, not
            multiply, carried numbers to the product.
```

Next, we multiply the number in the tens' place of the second number by each place value of the top number sequentially. Because we are multiplying by a number in the tens' place, we place a zero at the end of this product.

```
 (2)
  172
x  43  ——►  {4 x 2 = 8, 4 x 7 = 28, 4 x 1 = 4}
  516
 6880
```

Finally, to determine the final product we add the two partial products.

```
  172
x  43
  516
+6880
 7396  ——►  The product of 172 and 43 is 7396.
```

Example: A student buys 4 boxes of crayons. Each box contains 16 crayons. How many total crayons does the student have?

The total number of crayons is 16 x 4.

$$\begin{array}{r} 16 \\ \times\ 4 \\ \hline 64 \end{array} \longrightarrow$$ Total number of crayons equals 64.

Division of whole numbers

Division, the inverse of multiplication, is another of the four basic number operations. When we divide one number by another, we determine how many times we can multiply the divisor (number divided by) before we exceed the number we are dividing (dividend). For example, 8 divided by 2 equals 4 because we can multiply 2 four times to reach 8 (2 x 4 = 8 or 2 + 2 + 2 + 2 = 8). Using the grouping conceptualization we used with multiplication, we can divide 8 into 4 groups of 2 or 2 groups of 4. We call the answer to a division problem the quotient.

If the divisor does not divide evenly into the dividend, we express the leftover amount either as a remainder or as a fraction with the divisor as the denominator. For example, 9 divided by 2 equals 4 with a remainder of 1 or 4 ½.

The basic algorithm for division is long division. We start by representing the quotient as follows.

$14\overline{)293} \longrightarrow$ 14 is the divisor and 293 is the dividend.
This represents 293 ÷ 14.

Next, we divide the divisor into the dividend starting from the left.

$$\begin{array}{r} 2 \\ 14\overline{)293} \end{array} \longrightarrow$$ 14 divides into 29 two times with a remainder.

Next, we multiply the partial quotient by the divisor, subtract this value from the first digits of the dividend, and bring down the remaining dividend digits to complete the number.

$$\begin{array}{r} 2 \\ 14\overline{)293} \\ -28\downarrow \\ \hline 13 \end{array} \longrightarrow$$ 2 x 14 = 28, 29 – 28 = 1, and bringing down the 3 yields 13.

Finally, we divide again (the divisor into the remaining value) and repeat the preceding process. The number left after the subtraction represents the remainder.

$$\begin{array}{r} 20 \\ 14\overline{)293} \\ \underline{-28} \\ 13 \\ \underline{-0} \\ 13 \end{array}$$

→ The final quotient is 20 with a remainder of 13. We can also represent this quotient as 20 13/14.

Example: Each box of apples contains 24 apples. How many boxes must a grocer purchase to supply a group of 252 people with one apple each?

The grocer needs 252 apples. Because he must buy apples in groups of 24, we divide 252 by 24 to determine how many boxes he needs to buy.

$$\begin{array}{r} 10 \\ 24\overline{)252} \\ \underline{-24} \\ 12 \\ \underline{-0} \\ 12 \end{array}$$

→ The quotient is 10 with a remainder of 12.

Thus, the grocer needs 10 boxes plus 12 more apples. Therefore, the minimum number of boxes the grocer can purchase is 11.

Example: At his job, John gets paid $20 for every hour he works. If John made $940 in a week, how many hours did he work?

This is a division problem. To determine the number of hours John worked, we divide the total amount made ($940) by the hourly rate of pay ($20). Thus, the number of hours worked equals 940 divided by 20.

```
     47
 20)940
   -80
    140
   -140
      0  ——→  20 divides into 940, 47 times with no
              remainder.
```

John worked 47 hours.

Addition and Subtraction of Decimals

When adding and subtracting decimals, we align the numbers by place value as we do with whole numbers. After adding or subtracting each column, we bring the decimal down, placing it in the same location as in the numbers added or subtracted.

Example: Find the sum of 152.3 and 36.342.

```
   152.300
 +  36.342
   188.642
```

Note that we placed two zeroes after the final place value in 152.3 to clarify the column addition.

Example: Find the difference of 152.3 and 36.342.

```
     2 910          (4)11(12)
   152.300           152.300
 -  36.342  ——→   -   36.342
        58           115.958
```

Note how we borrowed to subtract from the zeroes in the hundredths' and thousandths' place of 152.300.

Multiplication of Decimals

When multiplying decimal numbers, we multiply exactly as with whole numbers and place the decimal moving in from the left the total number of decimal places contained in the two numbers multiplied. For example, when multiplying 1.5 and 2.35, we place the decimal in the product 3 places in from the left (3.525).

Example: Find the product of 3.52 and 4.1.

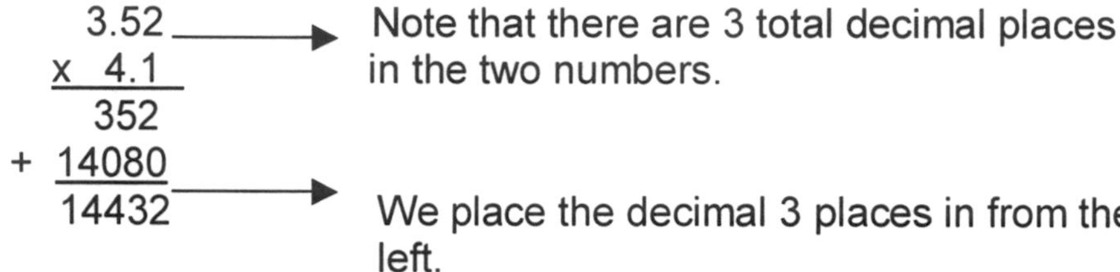

3.52
x 4.1
352
+ 14080
14432
Note that there are 3 total decimal places in the two numbers.
We place the decimal 3 places in from the left.

Thus, the final product is 14.432.

Example: A shopper has 5 one-dollar bills, 6 quarters, 3 nickels, and 4 pennies in his pocket. How much money does he have?

5 x \$1.00 = \$5.00

3 \$0.25	\$0.05	\$0.01
x 6	x 3	x 4
\$1.50	\$0.15	\$0.04

Note the placement of the decimals in the multiplication products. Thus, the total amount of money in the shopper's pocket is:

\$5.00
1.50
0.15
+ 0.04
\$6.69

Division of Decimals

When dividing decimal numbers, we first remove the decimal in the divisor by moving the decimal in the dividend the same number of spaces to the right. For example, when dividing 1.45 into 5.3 we convert the numbers to 145 and 530 and perform normal whole number division.

Example: Find the quotient of 5.3 divided by 1.45.
Convert to 145 and 530.

Divide.

```
     3                  3.65
145)530   ---->   145)530.00   ----> Note that we insert
  - 435              - 435             the decimal to continue
     95                950             division.
                     - 870
                       800
```

Because one of the numbers divided contained one decimal place, we round the quotient to one decimal place. Thus, the final quotient is 3.7.

Addition and subtraction of fractions

Key Points

1. You need a common denominator in order to add and subtract reduced and improper fractions.

Example: $\frac{1}{3}+\frac{7}{3}=\frac{1+7}{3}=\frac{8}{3}=2\frac{2}{3}$

Example: $\frac{4}{12}+\frac{6}{12}-\frac{3}{12}=\frac{4+6-3}{12}=\frac{7}{12}$

2. Adding an integer and a fraction of the same sign results directly in a mixed fraction.

Example: $2+\frac{2}{3}=2\frac{2}{3}$

Example: $^{-}2-\frac{3}{4}={}^{-}2\frac{3}{4}$

3. Adding an integer and a fraction with different signs involves the following steps.

-get a common denominator
-add or subtract as needed
-change to a mixed fraction if possible

Example: $2-\frac{1}{3}=\frac{2\times3-1}{3}=\frac{6-1}{3}=\frac{5}{3}=1\frac{2}{3}$

Example: Add $7\frac{3}{8}+5\frac{2}{7}$

Add the whole numbers; add the fractions and combine the two results:

$$7\frac{3}{8}+5\frac{2}{7}=(7+5)+(\frac{3}{8}+\frac{2}{7})$$

$$=12+\frac{(7\times3)+(8\times2)}{56} \quad \text{(LCM of 8 and 7)}$$

$$=12+\frac{21+16}{56}=12+\frac{37}{56}=12\frac{37}{56}$$

Example: Perform the operation.

$$\frac{2}{3}-\frac{5}{6}$$

We first find the LCM of 3 and 6 which is 6.

$$\frac{2\times 2}{3\times 2}-\frac{5}{6}\rightarrow\frac{4-5}{6}=\frac{^-1}{6}$$ (Using method A)

Example: $^-7\frac{1}{4}+2\frac{7}{8}$

$$^-7\frac{1}{4}+2\frac{7}{8}=(^-7+2)+(\frac{^-1}{4}+\frac{7}{8})$$

$$=(^-5)+\frac{(^-2+7)}{8}\ =(^-5)+(\frac{5}{8})$$

$$=(^-5)+\frac{5}{8}=\frac{^-5\times 8}{1\times 8}+\frac{5}{8}=\frac{^-40+5}{8}$$

$$=\frac{^-35}{8}={}^-4\frac{3}{8}$$

Divide 35 by 8 to get 4, remainder 3.

Caution: Common error would be

$$^-7\frac{1}{4}+2\frac{7}{8}={}^-7\frac{2}{8}+2\frac{7}{8}={}^-5\frac{9}{8}$$ Wrong.

It is correct to add -7 and 2 to get -5, but adding $\frac{2}{8}+\frac{7}{8}=\frac{9}{8}$ is wrong. It should have been $\frac{^-2}{8}+\frac{7}{8}=\frac{5}{8}$. Then,

$^-5+\frac{5}{8}={}^-4\frac{3}{8}$ as before.

Multiplication of fractions

Using the following example: $3\frac{1}{4}\times\frac{5}{6}$

1. Convert each number to an improper fraction.

$$3\frac{1}{4}=\frac{(12+1)}{4}=\frac{13}{4}$$

$\frac{5}{6}$ is already in reduced form.

2. Reduce (cancel) common factors of the numerator and denominator if they exist.

$\frac{13}{4}\times\frac{5}{6}$ No common factors exist.

3. Multiply the numerators by each other and the denominators by each other.

$$\frac{13}{4}\times\frac{5}{6}=\frac{65}{24}$$

4. If possible, reduce the fraction back to its lowest term.

$\frac{65}{24}$ Cannot be reduced further.

5. Convert the improper fraction back to a mixed fraction by using long division.

$$\frac{65}{24}=24\overline{)65}\quad \text{quotient } 2;\ \ 65-48=17 \qquad =2\frac{17}{24}$$

Summary of sign changes for multiplication:

a. $(+)\times(+)=(+)$

b. $(-)\times(+)=(-)$

c. $(+)\times(-)=(-)$

d. $(-)\times(-)=(+)$

Example: $7\frac{1}{3}\times\frac{5}{11}=\frac{22}{3}\times\frac{5}{11}$ Reduce like terms (22 and 11)

$=\frac{2}{3}\times\frac{5}{1}=\frac{10}{3}=3\frac{1}{3}$

Example: $^{-}6\frac{1}{4}\times\frac{5}{9}=\frac{^{-}25}{4}\times\frac{5}{9}$

$=\frac{^{-}125}{36}={}^{-}3\frac{17}{36}$

Example: $\frac{^{-}1}{4}\times\frac{^{-}3}{7}$ Negative times a negative equals positive.

$=\frac{1}{4}\times\frac{3}{7}=\frac{3}{28}$

Division of fractions:

1. Change mixed fractions to improper fraction.
2. Change the division problem to a multiplication problem by using the reciprocal of the number after the division sign.
3. Find the sign of the final product.
4. Cancel if common factors exist between the numerator and the denominator.
5. Multiply the numerators together and the denominators together.
6. Change the improper fraction to a mixed number.

Example: $3\frac{1}{5}\div 2\frac{1}{4}=\frac{16}{5}\div\frac{9}{4}$

$=\frac{16}{5}\times\frac{4}{9}$ Reciprocal of $\frac{9}{4}$ is $\frac{4}{9}$.

$=\frac{64}{45}=1\frac{19}{45}$

Example: $7\frac{3}{4} \div 11\frac{5}{8} = \frac{31}{4} \div \frac{93}{8}$

$= \frac{31}{4} \times \frac{8}{93}$ Reduce like terms.

$= \frac{1}{1} \times \frac{2}{3} = \frac{2}{3}$

Example: $\left(^{-}2\frac{1}{2}\right) \div 4\frac{1}{6} = \frac{^{-}5}{2} \div \frac{25}{6}$

$= \frac{^{-}5}{2} \times \frac{6}{25}$ Reduce like terms.

$= \frac{^{-}1}{1} \times \frac{3}{5} = \frac{^{-}3}{5}$

Example: $\left(^{-}5\frac{3}{8}\right) \div \left(\frac{^{-}7}{16}\right) = \frac{^{-}43}{8} \div \frac{^{-}7}{16}$

$= \frac{^{-}43}{8} \times \frac{^{-}16}{7}$ Reduce like terms.

$= \frac{43}{1} \times \frac{2}{7}$ Negative times a negative equals a positive.

$= \frac{86}{7} = 12\frac{2}{7}$

Properties are rules that apply for addition, subtraction, multiplication, or division of real numbers. These properties are:

Commutative: You can change the order of the terms or factors as follows.

For addition: $a + b = b + a$
For multiplication: $ab = ba$

Since addition is the inverse operation of subtraction and multiplication is the inverse operation of division, no separate laws are needed for subtraction and division.

Example: $5 + {}^-8 = {}^-8 + 5 = {}^-3$

Example: ${}^-2 \times 6 = 6 \times {}^-2 = {}^-12$

Associative: You can regroup the terms as you like.

For addition: $a + (b + c) = (a + b) + c$
For multiplication: $a(bc) = (ab)c$

This rule does not apply for division and subtraction.

Example: $({}^-2 + 7) + 5 = {}^-2 + (7 + 5)$
$5 + 5 = {}^-2 + 12 = 10$

Example: $(3 \times {}^-7) \times 5 = 3 \times ({}^-7 \times 5)$
${}^-21 \times 5 = 3 \times {}^-35 = {}^-105$

Identity:

Finding a number so that when added to a term results in that number (additive identity); finding a number such that when multiplied by a term results in that number (multiplicative identity).

For addition:	$a + 0 = a$	(zero is additive identity)
For multiplication:	$a \cdot 1 = a$	(one is multiplicative)

Example: $17 + 0 = 17$

Example: $^{-}34 \times 1 = {}^{-}34$
The product of any number and one is that number.

Inverse:

Finding a number such that when added to the number it results in zero; or when multiplied by the number results in 1.

For addition:	$a + (-a) = 0$
For multiplication:	$a \cdot (1/a) = 1$

($-a$) is the additive inverse of a; ($1/a$), also called the reciprocal, is the multiplicative inverse of a.

Example: $25 + {}^{-}25 = 0$

Example: $5 \times \frac{1}{5} = 1$ The product of any number and its reciprocal is one.

Distributive:

This technique allows us to operate on terms within a parenthesis without first performing operations within the parentheses. This is especially helpful when terms within the parentheses cannot be combined.

$a\,(b + c) = ab + ac$

Example: $6 \times ({}^{-}4 + 9) = (6 \times {}^{-}4) + (6 \times 9)$
$6 \times 5 = {}^{-}24 + 54 = 30$

To multiply a sum by a number, multiply each addend by the number, then add the products.

The Order of Operations are to be followed when evaluating algebraic expressions. Follow these steps in order:

1. Simplify inside grouping characters such as parentheses, brackets, square root, fraction bar, etc.

2. Multiply out expressions with exponents.

3. Do multiplication or division, from left to right.

4. Do addition or subtraction, from left to right.

Example: $3^3 - 5(b + 2)$

$= 3^3 - 5b - 10$

$= 27 - 5b - 10 = 17 - 5b$

Example: $2 - 4 \times 2^3 - 2(4 - 2 \times 3)$

$= 2 - 4 \times 2^3 - 2(4 - 6) = 2 - 4 \times 2^3 - 2(^-2)$

$= 2 - 4 \times 2^3 + 4 = 2 - 4 \times 8 + 4$

$= 2 - 32 + 4 = 6 - 32 = ^- 26$

Skill 1.6 Determine the greatest common factor or least common multiple in a given set of numbers.

GCF is the abbreviation for the greatest common factor. The GCF is the largest number that is a factor of all the numbers given in a problem. The GCF can be no larger than the smallest number given in the problem. If no other number is a common factor, then the GCF will be the number 1. To find the GCF, list all possible factors of the smallest number given (include the number itself). Starting with the largest factor (which is the number itself), determine if it is also a factor of all the other given numbers. If so, that is the GCF. If that factor does not work, try the same method on the next smaller factor. Continue until a common factor is found. That is the GCF. Note: There can be other common factors besides the GCF.

Example: Find the GCF of 12, 20, and 36.

The smallest number in the problem is 12. The factors of 12 are 1, 2, 3, 4, 6, and 12. The largest factor is 12, but it does not divide evenly into 20. Neither does 6, but 4 will divide into both 20 and 36 evenly. Therefore, 4 is the GCF.

Example: Find the GCF of 14 and 15.

Factors of 14 are 1, 2, 7, and 14. The largest factor is 14, but it does not divide evenly into 15. Neither does 7 or 2. Therefore, the only factor common to both 14 and 15 is the number 1, the GCF.

LCM is the abbreviation for least common multiple. The least common multiple of a group of numbers is the smallest number into which all of the given numbers will divide. The least common multiple will always be the largest of the given numbers or a multiple of the largest number.

Example: Find the LCM of 20, 30, and 40.

The largest number given is 40, but 30 will not divide evenly into 40. The next multiple of 40 is 80 (2 x 40), but 30 will not divide evenly into 80 either. The next multiple of 40 is 120. 120 is divisible by both 20 and 30, so 120 is the LCM (least common multiple).

Example: Find the LCM of 96, 16, and 24.

The largest number is 96. The number 96 is divisible by both 16 and 24, so 96 is the LCM.

Skill 1.7 Compare the relative values of fractions, decimals, percents, and other real numbers expressed in a variety of symbolic notations used in a real-world context.

Percent means parts of one hundred. Fractions, decimals and percents can be interchanged.

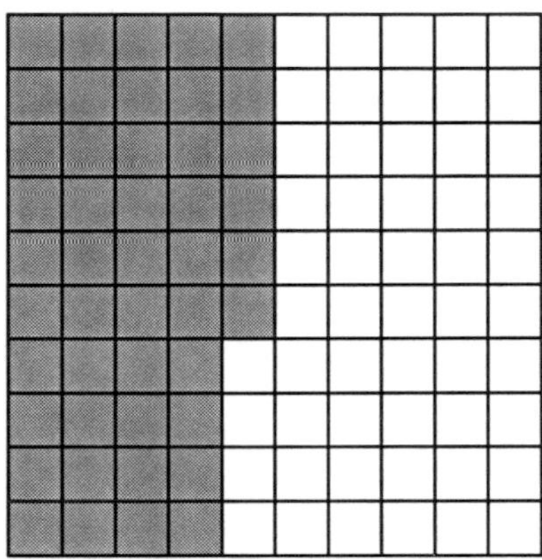

The shaded region represents 47 out of 100 or 0.47 or $\frac{47}{100}$ or 47%.

100% = 1

If a fraction can easily be converted to an equivalent **fraction** whose denominator is a power of 10 (for example, 10, 100, 1000), then it can easily be expressed as a **decimal** or **%.**

Examples: $\frac{1}{10}$ = 0.10 = 10%
$\frac{2}{5}$ = $\frac{4}{10}$ = 0.40 = 40%
$\frac{1}{4}$ = $\frac{25}{100}$ = 0.25 = 25%

Alternately, the **fraction** can be converted to a **decimal** and then a **percent** by dividing the numerator by the denominator, adding a decimal point and zeroes.

Example: $\frac{3}{8} = 8\overset{\displaystyle 0.375}{\overline{)3.000}}$ = 37.5%

To convert a fraction to a decimal, simply divide the numerator (top) by the denominator (bottom). Use long division if necessary.

If a decimal has a fixed number of digits, the decimal is said to be terminating. To write such a decimal as a fraction, first determine what place value the farthest right digit is in, for example: tenths, hundredths, thousandths, ten thousandths, hundred thousands, etc. Then drop the decimal and place the string of digits over the number given by the place value.

A **decimal** can be converted to a **percent** by multiplying by 100, or merely moving the decimal point two places to the right. A **percent** can be converted to a **decimal** by dividing by 100, or moving the decimal point two places to the left.

Examples: 0.375 = 37.5%
0.7 = 70%
0.04 = 4 %
3.15 = 315 %
84% = 0.84
3 % = 0.03
60% = 0.6
110% = 1.1
$\frac{1}{2}$% = 0.5% = 0.005

A **percent** can be converted to a **fraction** by placing it over 100 and reducing to simplest terms.

Example: Convert 0.056 to a fraction.

Multiplying 0.056 by $\frac{1000}{1000}$ to get rid of the decimal point:

$$0.056 \times \frac{1000}{1000} = \frac{56}{1000} = \frac{7}{125}$$

Example: Find 23% of 1000.

$$= \frac{23}{100} \times \frac{1000}{1} = 23 \times 10 = 230$$

Example: Convert 6.25% to a decimal and to a fraction.

$$6.25\% = 0.0625 = 0.0625 \times \frac{10000}{10000} = \frac{625}{10000} = \frac{1}{16}$$

An example of a type of problem involving fractions is the conversion of recipes. For example, if a recipe serves 8 people and we want to make enough to serve only 4, we must determine how much of each ingredient to use. The conversion factor, the number we multiply each ingredient by, is:

$$\text{Conversion Factor} = \frac{\text{Number of Servings Needed}}{\text{Number of Servings in Recipe}}$$

Example: Consider the following recipe.

3 cups flour
½ tsp. baking powder
2/3 cups butter
2 cups sugar
2 eggs

If the above recipe serves 8, how much of each ingredient do we need to serve only 4 people?

First, determine the conversion factor.

Conversion Factor = $\frac{4}{8} = \frac{1}{2}$

Next, multiply each ingredient by the conversion factor.

3 x ½ =	1 ½ cups flour
½ x ½ =	¼ tsp. baking powder
2/3 x ½ = 2/6 =	1/3 cups butter
2 x ½ =	1 cup sugar
2 x ½ =	1 egg

COMPETENCY 2.0 KNOWLEDGE OF DATA ANALYSIS AND PROBABILITY

Skill 2.1 Determine whether mean, median, or mode is the most appropriate measure of central tendency in a given situation

The arithmetic **mean** (or average) of a set of numbers is the *sum* of the numbers given, *divided* by the number of items being averaged.

Example: Find the mean. Round to the nearest tenth.
24.6, 57.3, 44.1, 39.8, 64.5
The sum is 230.3 ˜ 5
= 46.06, rounded to 46.1

The **median** of a set is the middle number. To calculate the median, the terms must be arranged in order. If there are an even number of terms, the median is the mean of the two middle terms.

Example 1: Find the median.

12. 14. 27. 3. 13. 7. 17. 12. 22. 6. 16

Rearrange the terms.
3, 6, 7, 12, 12, 13, 14, 16, 17, 22, 27
Since there are 11 numbers, the middle would be the sixth number or 13.

The **mode** of a set of numbers is the number that occurs with the greatest frequency. A set can have no mode if each term appears exactly one time. Similarly, there can also be more than one mode.

Example: Find the mode.

26, 15, 37, **26,** 35, **26,** 15

15 appears twice, but 26 appears 3 times, therefore the mode is 26.

The **range** is the difference between the highest and lowest value of data items.

The **variance** is the sum of the squares quantity divided by the number of items. (the lower case greek letter sigma squared (σ^2)represents variance).

$$\frac{Sx^2}{N} = \sigma^2$$

The larger the value of the variance the larger the spread

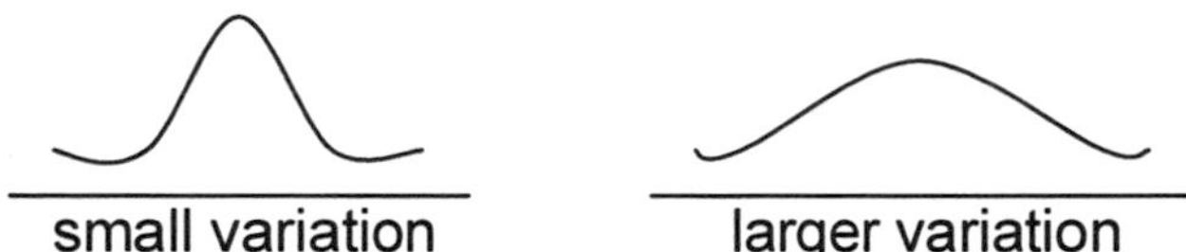

Standard deviation means the square root of the variance. The lower case Greek letter sigma (σ) is used to represent standard deviation.

$$\sigma = \sqrt{\sigma^2}$$

Most statistical calculators have standard deviation keys on them and should be used when asked to calculate statistical functions. It is important to become familiar with the calculator and the location of the keys needed.

Example: Given the ungrouped data below, calculate the mean, range, standard deviation and the variance.

15	22	28	25	34	38
18	25	30	33	19	23

Mean ($\overline{X}$) = 25.8333333
Range: $38 - 15 = 23$
standard deviation $(\sigma) = 6.6936952$
Variance $(\sigma^2) = 44.805556$

Different situations require different information. Information can be misleading if the data is not presented appropriately. If a data set contains one very high or very low value, the mean will not be representative; for ex., including the teacher's height in the mean height of a classroom. If the data are clustered around two numbers with a large gap between them, the median will not be representative; for ex. expressing the median height in a family of two parents and two small children. Modes are best used with categorical data. In other words, do not mix apples with oranges; for ex., a mode of the sale of men's shoe sizes would be helpful to a store for reordering stock of men's shoes. However, finding the mode of men and women's shoe sizes combined would not be a good indicator of the stock that needed to be reordered.

Consider the set of test scores from a math class: 0, 16, 19, 65, 65, 65, 68, 69, 70, 72, 73, 73, 75, 78, 80, 85, 88, and 92. The mean is 64.06 and the median is 71. Since there are only three scores less than the mean out of the eighteen score, the median (71) would be a more descriptive score.

Example: Is the mean, median, or mode the best measure of central tendency for the set 135, 135, 137, 190?

The mean is 149.25, the median is 136 and the mode is 135, therefore, the median or mode would be a better measure than the mean since they are both closer to most of the scores.

Example: The yearly salaries of the employees of Company A are $11,000, $12,000, $12,000, $15,000, $20,000, and $25,000. Which measure of central tendency would you use if you were a manager? If you were an employee trying to get a raise?

The mean is $15,833 The median is $13,500 The mode is $12,000
The manager would probably use the mean since it is the largest amount.

The employee would most likely use the mode since is the smallest.

Skill 2.2 Interpret information from graphical representations.

To make a **bar graph** or a **pictograph**, determine the scale to be used for the graph. Then determine the length of each bar on the graph or determine the number of pictures needed to represent each item of information. Be sure to include an explanation of the scale in the legend.

Example: A class had the following grades:
4 As, 9 Bs, 8 Cs, 1 D, 3 Fs.
Graph these on a bar graph and a pictograph.

Pictograph

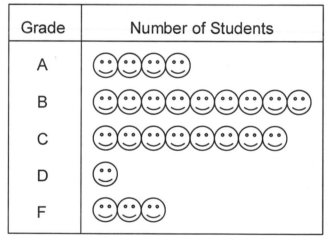

Grade	Number of Students
A	☺☺☺☺
B	☺☺☺☺☺☺☺☺☺
C	☺☺☺☺☺☺☺☺
D	☺
F	☺☺☺

Bar graph

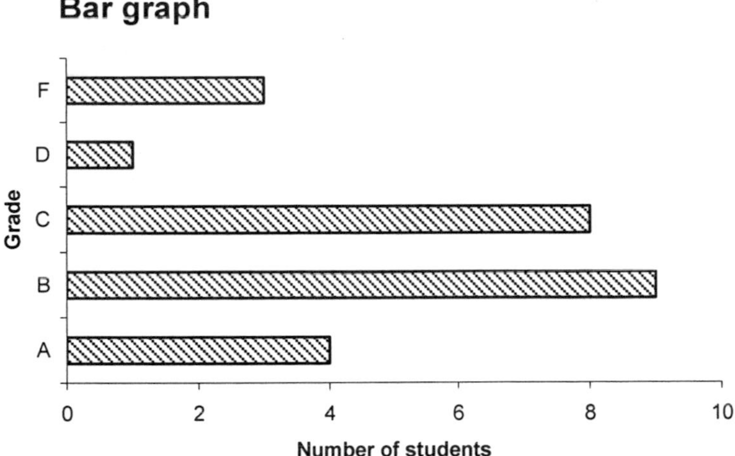

To make a **line graph**, determine appropriate scales for both the vertical and horizontal axes (based on the information to be graphed). Describe what each axis represents and mark the scale periodically on each axis. Graph the individual points of the graph and connect the points on the graph from left to right.

Example: Graph the following information using a line graph.

The number of National Merit finalists/school year

	'90-'91	'91-'92	'92-'93	'93-'94	'94-'95	'95-'96
Central	3	5	1	4	6	8
Wilson	4	2	3	2	3	2

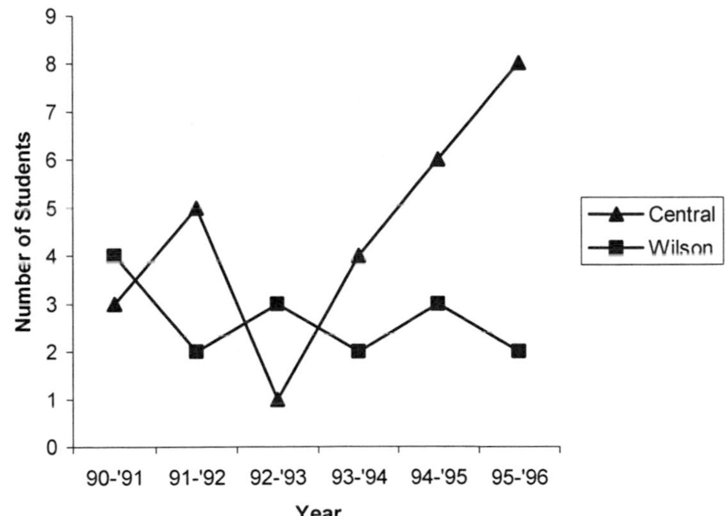

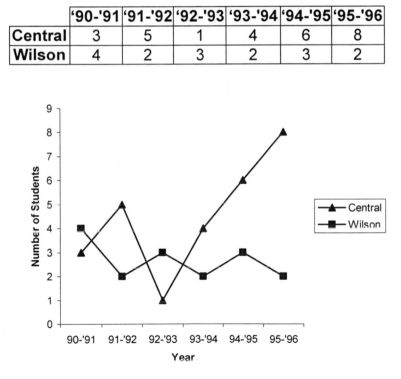

To make a **circle graph**, total all the information that is to be included on the graph. Determine the central angle to be used for each sector of the graph using the following formula:

$$\frac{\text{information}}{\text{total information}} \times 360^{\circ} = \text{degrees in central } \square$$

Lay out the central angles to these sizes, label each section and include its percent.

Example: Graph this information on a circle graph:

Monthly expenses:

Rent, $400
Food, $150
Utilities, $75
Clothes, $75
Church, $100
Misc., $200

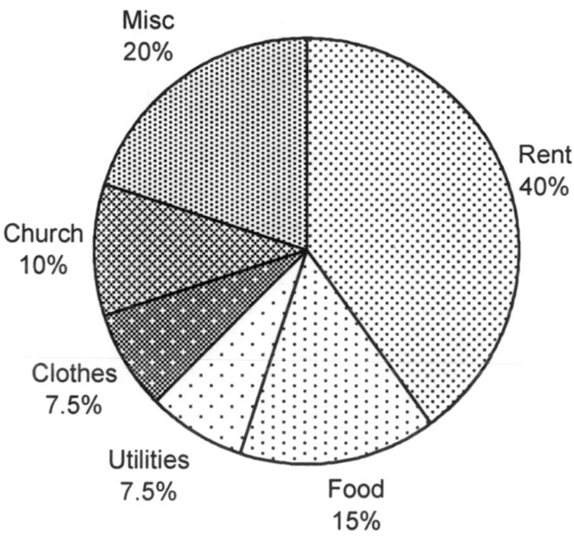

A **trend** line on a line graph shows the correlation between two sets of data. A trend may show positive correlation (both sets of data get bigger together) negative correlation (one set of data gets bigger while the other gets smaller), or no correlation.

An **inference** is a statement which is derived from reasoning. When reading a graph, inferences help with interpretation of the data that is being presented. From this information, a **conclusion** and even **predictions** about what the data actually means is possible.

Example: Katherine and Tom were both doing poorly in math class. Their teacher had a conference with each of them in November. The following graph shows their math test scores during the school year.

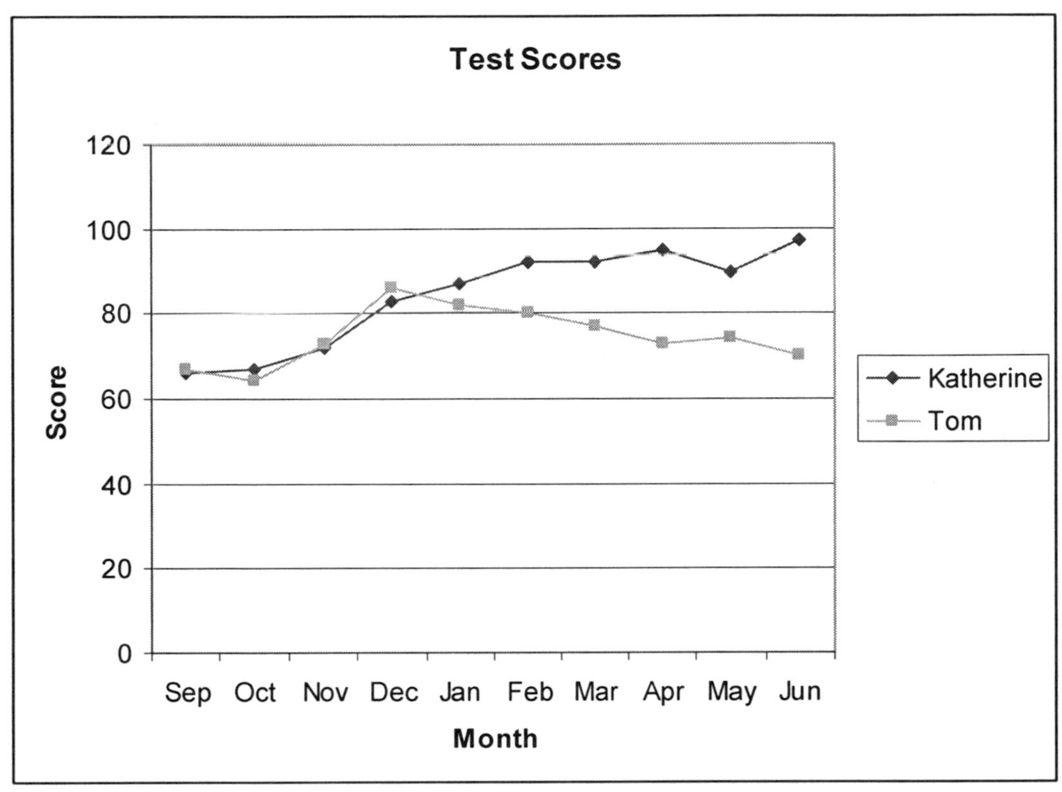

What kind of trend does this graph show?

This graph shows that there is a positive trend in Katherine's test scores and a negative trend in Tom's test scores.

What inferences can you make from this graph?

We can infer that Katherine's test scores rose steadily after November. Tom's test scores spiked in December but then began to fall again and became negatively trended.
What conclusion can you draw based upon this graph?

We can conclude that Katherine took her teacher's meeting seriously and began to study in order to do better on the exams. It seems as though Tom tried harder for a bit, but his test scores eventually slipped back down to the level where he began.

Skill 2.3 Apply experimental or theoretical probabilities to make conjectures based on data.

The absolute probability of some events cannot be determined. For instance, one cannot assume the probability of winning a tennis match is $\frac{1}{2}$ because, in general, winning and losing are not equally likely. In such cases, past results of similar events can be used to help predict future outcomes. The **relative frequency** of an event is the number of times an event has occurred divided by the number of attempts.

$$\text{Relative frequency} = \frac{\text{number of successful trials}}{\text{total number of trials}}$$

For example, if a weighted coin flipped 50 times lands on heads 40 times and tails 10 times, the relative frequency of heads is 40/50 = 4/5. Thus, one can predict that if the coin is flipped 100 times, it will land on heads 80 times.

Example: Two tennis players, John and David, have played each other 20 times.

John has won 15 of the previous matches and David has won 5.
(a) Estimate the probability that David will win the next match.
(b) Estimate the probability that John will win the next 3 matches.

Solution:

(a) David has won 5 out of 20 matches. Thus, the relative frequency of David winning is 5/20 or ¼. We can estimate that the probability of David winning the next match is ¼.

(b) John has won 15 out of 20 matches. The relative frequency of John winning is 15/20 or ¾. We can estimate that the probability of John winning a future match is ¾. Thus, the probability that John will win the next three matches is:

$$\frac{3}{4}\times\frac{3}{4}\times\frac{3}{4}=\frac{27}{64}$$

Skill 2.4 Determine the probability of occurrence or nonoccurrence of an event in a real-world context.

In probability, the **sample space** is a list of all possible outcomes of an experiment. For example, the sample space of tossing two coins is the set {HH, HT, TT, TH}, the sample space of rolling a six-sided die is the set {1, 2, 3, 4, 5, 6}, and the sample space of measuring the height of students in a class is the set of all real numbers {R}. **Probability** measures the chances of an event occurring. The probability of an event that *must* occur, a certain event, is **one.** When no outcome is favorable, the probability of an impossible event is **zero**

$$P(\text{event}) = \frac{\text{number of favorable outcomes}}{\text{number of possible outcomes}}$$

Example: Given one die with faces numbered 1 - 6, the probability of tossing an even number on one throw of the die is 3/6 or ½ since there are 3 favorable outcomes (even faces) and a total of 6 possible outcomes (faces).

Example: If a fair die is rolled.

a)Find the probability of rolling an even number
b)Find the probability of rolling a number less than three.

a)The sample space is

S = {1, 2, 3, 4, 5, 6} and the event representing even numbers is

E = {2, 4, 6}

Hence, the probability of rolling an even number is

$$p(E) = \frac{n(E)}{n(S)} = \frac{3}{6} = \frac{1}{2} \text{ or } 0.5$$

b)The event of rolling a number less than three is represented by

A = {1, 2}

Hence, the probability of rolling a number less than three is

$$p(A) = \frac{n(A)}{n(S)} = \frac{2}{6} = \frac{1}{3} \text{ or } 0.33$$

Example: A class has thirty students. Out of the thirty students, twenty-four are males. Assuming all the students have the same chance of being selected, find the probability of selecting a female. (Only one person is selected.)

The number of females in the class is

$$30 - 24 = 6$$

Hence, the probability of selecting a female is

$$p(\text{female}) = \frac{6}{30} = \frac{1}{5} \text{ or } 0.2$$

If A and B are **independent** events then the outcome of event A does not affect the outcome of event B or vice versa. The multiplication rule is used to find joint probability.

P(A and B) = P(A) x P(B)

Example: The probability that a patient is allergic to aspirin is .30. If the probability of a patient having a window in his/her room is .40, find the probability that the patient is allergic to aspirin and has a window in his/her room.

Defining the events: A = The patient being allergic to aspirin.
B = The patient has a window in his/her room.

Events A and B are independent, hence
p(A and B) = p(A) · p(B)
= (.30) (.40)
= .12 or 12%

Example: Given a jar containing 10 marbles, 3 red, 5 black, and 2 white. What is the probability of drawing a red marble and then a white marble if the marble is returned to the jar after choosing?

3/10 X 2/10 = 6/100 = 3/50

When the outcome of the first event affects the outcome of the second event, the events are **dependent.** Any two events that are not independent are dependent. This is also known as conditional probability.

Probability of (A and B) = P(A) × P(B given A)

Example: Two cards are drawn from a deck of 52 cards, without replacement; that is, the first card is not returned to the deck before the second card is drawn. What is the probability of drawing a diamond?

A = drawing a diamond first
B = drawing a diamond second

P(A) = drawing a diamond first
P(B) = drawing a diamond second

P(A) = 13/52 = ¼ P(B) = 12/52 = 4/17

(PA+B) = ¼ X 14/17 = 1/17

Example: A class of ten students has six males and four females. If two students are selected to represent the class, find the probability that

a)the first is a male and the second is a female.
b)the first is a female and the second is a male.
c)both are females.
d)both are males.

Defining the events: F = a female is selected to represent the class.
M = a male is selected to represent the class.

F/M = a female is selected after a male has been selected.

M/F = a male is selected after a female has been selected.

a) Since F and M are dependent events, it follows that
P(M and F) = P(M) · P(F/M)
$=\frac{6}{10}x\frac{4}{9}=\frac{3}{5}x\frac{4}{9}=\frac{12}{45}$

P(F/M) = $\frac{4}{9}$ instead of , $\frac{4}{10}$ since the selection of a male first changed the Sample Space from ten to nine students.

b) P(F and M) = P(F) · P(M/F)
$=\frac{4}{10}x\frac{6}{9}=\frac{2}{5}x\frac{2}{3}=\frac{4}{15}$

c) P(F and F) = p(F) · p(F/F)
$=\frac{4}{10}x\frac{3}{9}=\frac{2}{5}x\frac{1}{3}=\frac{2}{15}$

d) P(both are males) = p(M and M)
$=\frac{6}{10}x\frac{5}{9}=\frac{30}{90}=\frac{1}{3}$

Odds are defined as the ratio of the number of favorable outcomes to the number of unfavorable outcomes. The sum of the favorable outcomes and the unfavorable outcomes should always equal the total possible outcomes.

For example, given a bag of 12 red and 7 green marbles compute the odds of randomly selecting a red marble.

$$\text{Odds of red} = \frac{12}{19} : \frac{7}{19} \text{ or } 12{:}7.$$

$$\text{Odds of not getting red} = \frac{7}{19} : \frac{12}{19} \text{ or } 7{:}12.$$

In the case of flipping a coin, it is equally likely that a head or a tail will be tossed. The odds of tossing a head are 1:1. This is called even odds.

COMPETENCY 3.0 KNOWLEDGE OF ALGEBRA

Skill 3.1 Analyze and interpret relationships represented by tables, graphs, and rules.

A relationship between two quantities can be shown using a table, graph or rule. In this example, the rule y= 9x describes the relationship between the total amount earned, y, and the total amount of $9 sunglasses sold, x.

A table using this data would appear as:

number of sunglasses sold	1	5	10	15
total dollars earned	9	45	90	135

Each *(x,y)* relationship between a pair of values is called the coordinate pair and can be plotted on a graph. The coordinate pairs *(1,9), (5,45), (10,90)*, and *(15,135),* are plotted on the graph below.

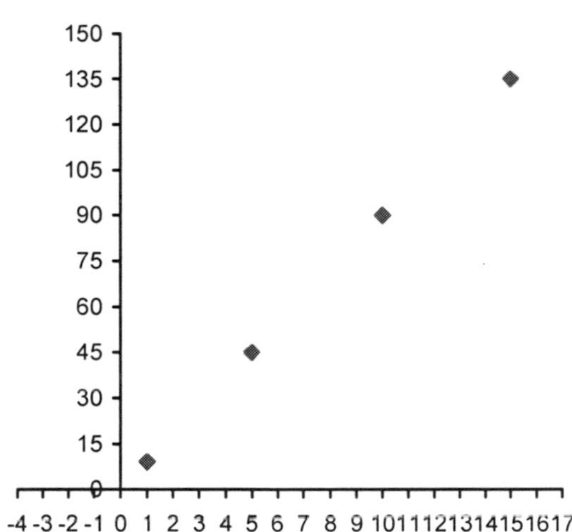

The graph above shows a linear relationship. A linear relationship is one in which two quantities are proportional to each other. Doubling *x* also doubles *y*. On a graph, a straight line depicts a linear relationship.

The function or relationship between two quantities may be analyzed to determine how one quantity depends on the other. For example, the function below shows a relationship between y and x: y=2x+1

The relationship between two or more variables can be analyzed using a table, graph, written description or symbolic rule. The function, y=2x+1, is written as a symbolic rule. The same relationship is also shown in the table below:

x	0	2	3	6	9
y	1	5	7	13	19

A relationship could be written in words by saying the value of y is equal to two times the value of x, plus one. This relationship could be shown on a graph by plotting given points such as the ones shown in the table above.

Another way to describe a function is as a process in which one or more numbers are input into an imaginary machine that produces another number as the output. If 5 is input, (x), into a machine with a process of x +1, the output, (y), will equal 6.

In real situations, relationships can be described mathematically. The function, y=x+1, can be used to describe the idea that people age one year on their birthday. To describe the relationship in which a person's monthly medical costs are 6 times a person's age, we could write y=6x. The monthly cost of medical care could be predicted using this function. A 20 year-old person would spend $120 per month (120=20*6). An 80 year-old person would spend $480 per month (480=80*6). Therefore, one could analyze the relationship to say: as you get older, medical costs increase $6.00 each year.

Another type of relationship is a nonlinear relationship. This is one in which change in one quantity does not affect the other quantity to the same extent. Nonlinear graphs have a curved line such as the graph below.

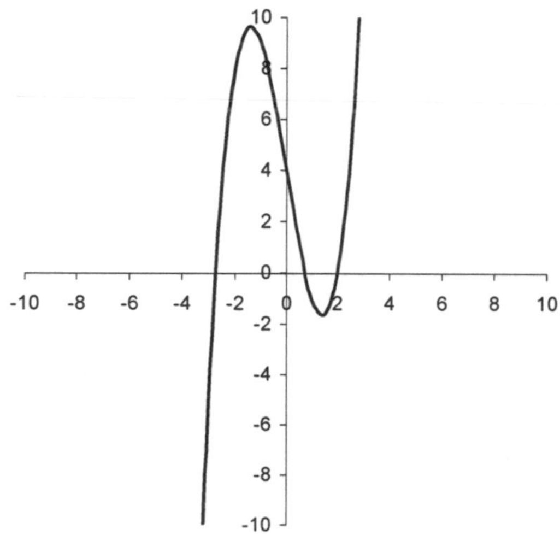

Skill 3.2 Analyze functional relationships expressed as rosters, rules, graphs, and mappings.

See Skill 3.1

Skill 3.3 Determine the solution set of a pair of linear equations or linear inequalities.

Procedure for solving algebraic equations.

Example: $3(x+3) = {}^{-}2x+4$ Solve for x.

1) Expand to eliminate all parentheses.

$3x+9 = {}^{-}2x+4$

2) Multiply each term by the LCD to eliminate all denominators.

3) Combine like terms on each side when possible.

4) Use the properties to put all variables on one side and all constants on the other side.

$\rightarrow 3x+9-9 = {}^{-}2x+4-9$ (subtract nine from both sides)

$\rightarrow 3x = {}^{-}2x-5$

$\rightarrow 3x+2x = {}^{-}2x+2x-5$ (add $2x$ to both sides)

$\rightarrow 5x = {}^{-}5$

$\rightarrow \frac{5x}{5} = \frac{{}^{-}5}{5}$ (divide both sides by 5)

$\rightarrow x = {}^{-}1$

Example: Solve: $3(2x+5)-4x = 5(x+9)$

$$6x+15-4x = 5x+45$$
$$2x+15 = 5x+45$$
$${}^{-}3x+15 = 45$$
$${}^{-}3x = 30$$
$$x = {}^{-}10$$

The solution **set of linear equations** is all the ordered pairs of real numbers that satisfy both equations, thus the intersection of the lines.

The solution set of a **pair of linear equations** is all the ordered pairs of real numbers that satisfy both equations, thus the intersection of the lines (see competency 17).

Equivalent or **dependent** equations are two equations that are represented by the same line; that is, one is a multiple of the other.

Example: $3x - 4y = 8$
$6x - 8y = 16$

Consistent equations are pairs of equations to which we can find a solution.

Example: $x + 3y = 5$
$2x - y = 15$

Inconsistent equations can be represented by parallel lines; that is, there are no values of x and y that satisfy both equations.

Example: $2x - y = 3$
$6x - 3y = 2$

There are two methods for solving linear equations: **linear combinations** and **substitution**.

In the **substitution** method, an equation is solved for either variable. Then, that solution is substituted in the other equation to find the remaining variable.

Example: (1) $2x + 8y = 4$
(2) $x - 3y = 5$

(2a) $x = 3y + 5$ — Solve equation (2) for x

(1a) $2(3y + 5) + 8y = 4$ — Substitute x in equation (1)
$6y + 10 + 8y = 4$ — Solve.
$14y = -6$
$y = \frac{-3}{7}$ — Solution

(2) $x - 3y = 5$
$x - 3(\frac{-3}{7}) = 5$ — Substitute the value of y.
$x = \frac{26}{7} = 3\frac{5}{7}$ — Solution

Thus the solution set of the system of equations is $(3\frac{5}{7}, \frac{-3}{7})$.

In the **linear combinations** method, one or both of the equations are replaced with an equivalent equation in order that the two equations can be combined (added or subtracted) to eliminate one variable.

Example:
(1) $4x + 3y = -2$
(2) $5x - y = 7$

(1) $4x + 3y = -2$
(2a) $15x - 3y = 21$ Multiply equation (2) by 3

$19x = 19$ Combining (1) and (2a)
$x = 1$ Solve.

To find *y*, substitute the value of *x* in equation 1 (or 2).

(1) $4x + 3y = -2$
$4(1) + 3y = -2$
$4 + 3y = -2$
$3y = -2$
$y = -2$

Thus the solution is $x = 1$ and $y = -2$ or the order pair (1, -2).

Example: Solve for x and y.

$$4x + 6y = 340$$
$$3x + 8y = 360$$

To solve by addition-subtraction:

Multiply the first equation by 4: $4(4x + 6y = 340)$

Multiply the other equation by $^{-}3$: $^{-}3(3x + 8y = 360)$

By doing this, the equations can be added to each other to eliminate one variable and solve for the other variable.

$$16x + 24y = 1360$$
$$-9x - 24y = {}^{-}1080$$
$$7x = 280$$
$$x = 40$$

solving for y, $y = 30$

Procedure for solving algebraic inequalities.

We use the same procedure used for solving linear equations, but the answer is represented in graphical form on the number line or in interval form.

Example: Solve the inequality, show its solution using interval form, and graph the solution on the number line.

$$\frac{5x}{8}+3\geq 2x-5$$

$$8\left(\frac{5x}{8}\right)+8(3)\geq 8(2x)-5(8)$$ Multiply by LCD = 8.

$$5x+24\geq 16x-40$$

$$5x+24-24-16x\geq 16x-16x-40-24$$ Subtract 16*x* and 24 from both sides of the equation.

$$^{-}11x\geq {}^{-}64$$

$$\frac{^{-}11x}{^{-}11}\leq\frac{^{-}64}{^{-}11}$$

$$x\leq\frac{64}{11}\ ;\ x\leq 5\frac{9}{11}$$

Solution in interval form: $\left(^{-}\infty,5\frac{9}{11}\right]$

Note: "] " means $5\frac{9}{11}$ is included in the solution.

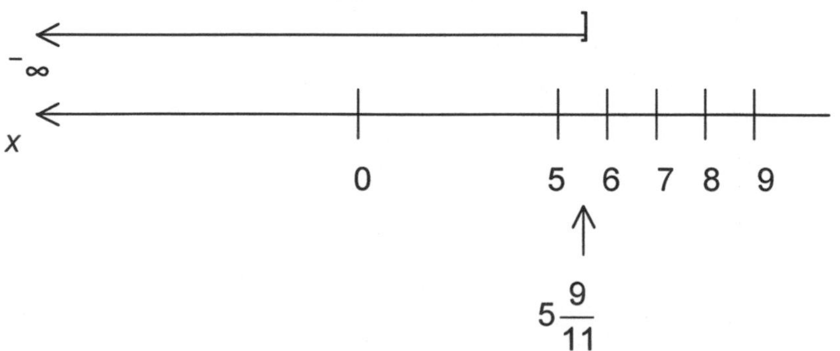

Example: Solve the following inequality and express your answer in both interval and graphical form.

$3x - 8 < 2(3x - 1)$

$3x - 8 < 6x - 2$ Distributive property.

$3x - 6x - 8 + 8 < 6x - 6x - 2 + 8$

Add 8 and subtract $6x$ from both sides of the equation.

$^{-}3x < 6$

$\frac{^{-}3x}{^{-}3} > \frac{6}{^{-}3}$ Note the change in direction of the equality.

$x > ^{-}2$

Graphical form:

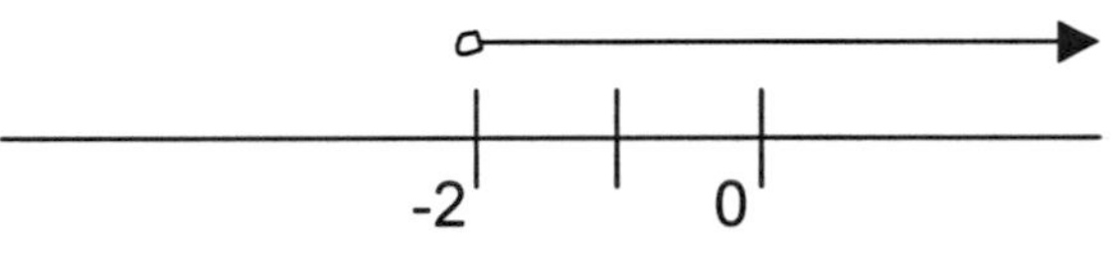

or

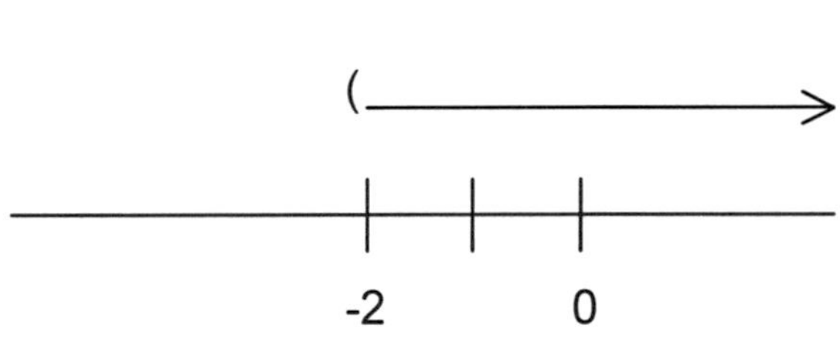

Interval form: $(^{-}2, \infty)$

Recall:

a) Using a parentheses or an open circle implies the point in not included in the answer.

b) Using a bracket or a closed circle implies the point is included in the answer.

Example: Solve: $6x + 21 < 8x + 31$

$^{-}2x + 21 < 31$

$^{-}2x < 10$

$x > ^{-}5$

Note that the inequality sign has changed.

Skill 3.4 Solve real-world problems using graphs, equations, or inequalities

Example: Mark and Mike are twins. Three times Mark's age plus four equals four times Mike's age minus 14. How old are the boys?

Since the boys are twins, their ages are the same. "Translate" the English into Algebra. Let x = their age

$3x + 4 = 4x - 14$

$18 = x$

The boys are each 18 years old.

Example: The YMCA wants to sell raffle tickets to raise $32,000. If they must pay $7,250 in expenses and prizes out of the money collected from the tickets, how many tickets worth $25 each must they sell?

Let $x =$ number of tickets sold
Then $25x =$ total money collected for x tickets

Total money minus expenses is greater than $32,000.

$25x - 7250 = 32,000$
$25x = 39350$
$x = 1570$

If they sell 1,570 tickets, they will raise $32,000.

Example: The Simpsons went out for dinner. All 4 of them ordered the aardvark steak dinner. Bert paid for the 4 meals and included a tip of $12 for a total of $84.60. How much was an aardvark steak dinner?

Let $x =$ the price of one aardvark dinner

So $4x =$ the price of 4 aardavark dinners

$4x = 84.60 - 12$

$4x = 72.60$

$x = \frac{72.60}{4} = \$18.15$ The price of one aardvark dinner.

Some word problems can be solved using a system (group) of equations or inequalities. Watch for words like greater than, less than, at least, or no more than which indicate the need for inequalities.

Example: Farmer Greenjeans bought 4 cows and 6 sheep for $1700. Mr. Ziffel bought 3 cows and 12 sheep for $2400. If all the cows were the same price and all the sheep were another price, find the price charged for a cow or for a sheep.

Let x = price of a cow
Let y = price of a sheep

Then Farmer Greenjeans' equation would be: $4x+6y=1700$
Mr. Ziffel's equation would be: $3x+12y=2400$

To solve by **addition-subtraction**:
Multiply the first equation by $^-2$: $^-2(4x+6y=1700)$
Keep the other equation the same : $(3x+12y=2400)$
By doing this, the equations can be added to each other to eliminate one variable and solve for the other variable.

$$\begin{array}{l} ^-8x-12y={}^-3400 \\ \underline{3x+12y=2400} \\ ^-5x \qquad = {}^-1000 \end{array}$$ Add these equations.

$x=200 \leftarrow$ the price of a cow was $200.
Solving for y, $y=150 \leftarrow$ the price of a sheep,$150.

To solve by **substitution**:

Solve one of the equations for a variable. (Try to make an equation without fractions if possible.) Substitute this expression into the equation that you have not yet used. Solve the resulting equation for the value of the remaining variable.

$4x+6y=1700$
$3x+12y=2400 \leftarrow$ Solve this equation for x.

It becomes $x=800-4y$. Now substitute $800-4y$ in place of x in the OTHER equation. $4x+6y=1700$ now becomes:

$$4(800-4y)+6y=1700$$
$$3200-16y+6y=1700$$
$$3200-10y=1700$$
$$^-10y={}^-1500$$

$y=150$, or $150 for a sheep.

Substituting 150 back into an equation for y, find x.

$$4x + 6(150) = 1700$$
$$4x + 900 = 1700$$
$$4x = 800 \text{ so } x = 200 \text{ for a cow.}$$

Example: Sharon's Bike Shoppe can assemble a 3 speed bike in 30 minutes or a 10 speed bike in 60 minutes. The profit on each bike sold is \$60 for a 3 speed or \$75 for a 10 speed bike. How many of each type of bike should they assemble during an 8 hour day (480 minutes) to make the maximum profit? Total daily profit must be at least \$300.

Let $x =$ number of 3 speed bikes.
$y =$ number of 10 speed bikes.

Since there are only 480 minutes to use each day,

$30x + 60y \leq 480$ is the first inequality.

Since the total daily profit must be at least \$300,

$60x + 75y \geq 300$ is the second inequality.

$30x + 65y \leq 480$ solves to $y \leq 8 - 1/2\,x$

$$60y \leq -30x + 480$$
$$y \leq -\frac{1}{2}x + 8$$

$60x + 75y \geq 300$ solves to $y \geq 4 - 4/5\,x$

$$75y + 60x \geq 300$$
$$75y \geq -60x + 300$$
$$y \geq -\frac{4}{5}x + 4$$

This problem can be solved by graphing these two inequalities.

Graph these 2 inequalities:

$$y \le 8 - 1/2x$$
$$y \ge 4 - 4/5x$$

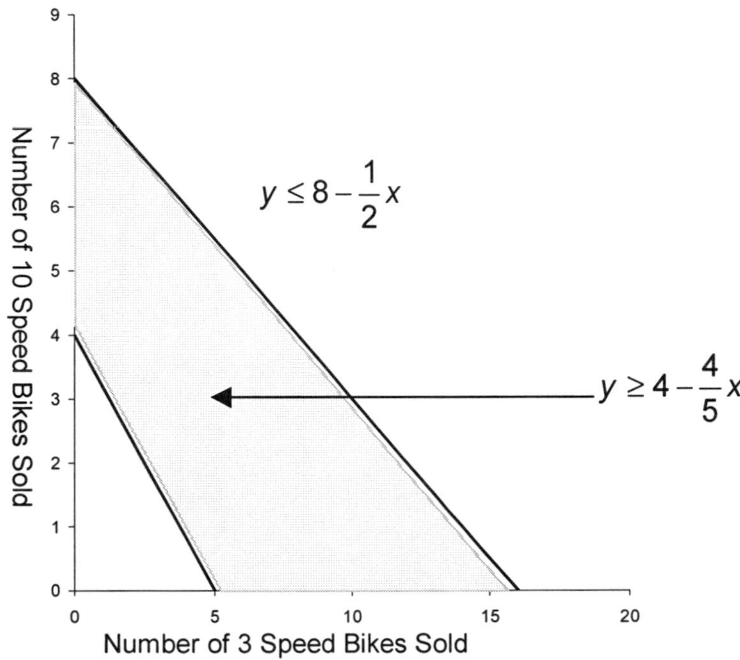

Realize that $x \ge 0$ and $y \ge 0$, since the number of bikes assembled can not be a negative number. Graph these as additional constraints on the problem. The number of bikes assembled must always be an integer value, so points within the shaded area of the graph must have integer values. The maximum profit will occur at or near a corner of the shaded portion of this graph. Those points occur at (0,4), (0,8), (16,0), or (5,0). Since profits are \$60/3-speed or \$75/10-speed, the profit would be :

$$(0,4) \quad 60(0) + 75(4) = 300$$
$$(0,8) \quad 60(0) + 75(8) = 600$$
$$(16,0) \quad 60(16) + 75(0) = 960 \leftarrow \text{Maximum profit}$$
$$(5,0) \quad 60(5) + 75(0) = 300$$

The maximum profit would occur if 16 3-speed bikes are made daily.

To graph an inequality, solve the inequality for y. This gets the inequality in **slope intercept form**, (for example: $y < mx + b$). The point (0,b) is the y-intercept and m is the line's slope.

If the inequality solves to $x \geq$ **any number**, then the graph includes a **vertical line**.

If the inequality solves to $y \leq$ **any number**, then the graph includes a **horizontal line**.

When graphing a linear inequality, the line will be dotted if the inequality sign is $<$ or $>$. If the inequality signs are either $\geq$ or $\leq$, the line on the graph will be a solid line. Shade above the line when the inequality sign is $\geq$ or $>$. Shade below the line when the inequality sign is $<$ or $\leq$. For inequalities of the forms $x >$ number, $x \leq$ number, $x <$ number, or $x \geq$ number, draw a vertical line (solid or dotted). Shade to the right for $>$ or $\geq$. Shade to the left for $<$ or $\leq$.

Remember: **Dividing or multiplying by a negative number will reverse the direction of the inequality sign.**

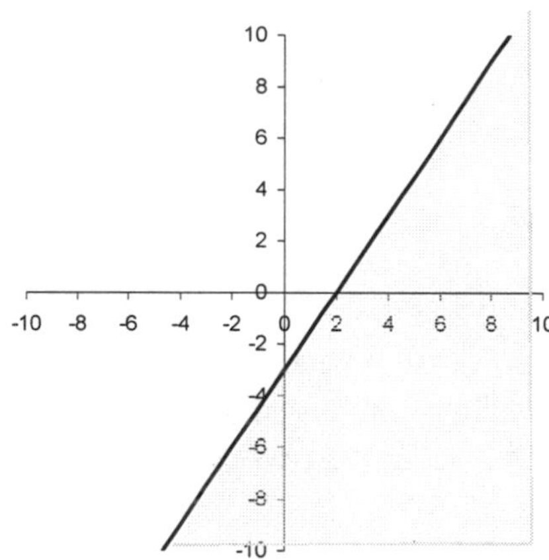

$$3x - 2y \geq 6$$
$$y \leq 3/2x - 3$$

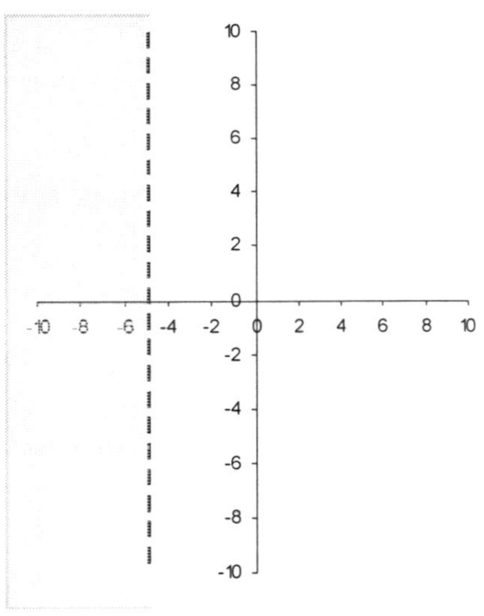

$$3x + 12 < -3$$

$$x < {}^{-}5$$

Example: Solve by graphing:

$x + y \le 6$

$x - 2y \le 6$

Solving the inequalities for y, they become:

$y \le {}^{-}x + 6$ (y intercept of 6 and slope = ${}^{-}1$)

$y \ge 1/2x - 3$ (y intercept of ${}^{-}3$ and slope = $1/2$)

A graph with shading is shown below:

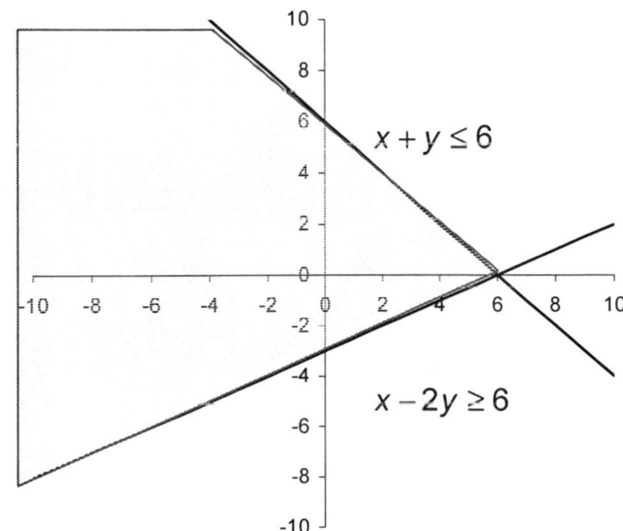

Skill 3.5 Generalize and/or extend patterns and relations to explain mathematical relationships.

Arithmetic Sequences

When given a set of numbers where the common difference between the terms is constant, use the following formula:

$a_n = a_1 + (n-1)d$ where

a_1 = the first term
a_n = the nth term (general term)
d = the common difference

Example: Find the 8th term of the arithmetic sequence 5, 8, 11, 14...

$a_n = a_1 + (n-1)d$
$a_1 = 5$ identify the 1st term
$d = 8 - 5 = 3$ find d
$a_n = 5 + (8-1)3$ substitute
$a_n = 26$

Example: Given two terms of an arithmetic sequence, find a_1 and d.

$a_4 = 21$ $a_6 = 32$
$a_n = a_1 + (n-1)d$ $a_4 = 21, n = 4$
$21 = a_1 + (4-1)d$ $a_6 = 32, n = 6$
$32 = a_1 + (6-1)d$

$21 = a_1 + 3d$ solve the system of equations
$32 = a_1 + 5d$

$32 = a_1 + 5d$
$\underline{-21 = -a_1 - 3d}$ multiply by −1
$11 = 2d$ add the equations

$5.5 = d$

$21 = a_1 + 3(5.5)$ substitute d = 5.5 into one of the equations
$21 = a_1 + 16.5$
$a_1 = 4.5$

The sequence begins with 4.5 and has a common difference of 5.5 between numbers.

Geometric Sequences

When using geometric sequences, consecutive numbers are compared to find the common ratio.

$r = \frac{a_{n+1}}{a_n}$ where
r = common ratio
a_n = the nth term

The ratio is then used in the geometric sequence formula:
$a_n = a_1 r^{n-1}$

Example: Find the 8th term of the geometric sequence 2, 8, 32, 128...

$r = \frac{a_{n+1}}{a_n}$ use common ratio formula to find ratio

$r = \frac{8}{2}$ substitute $a_n = 2$, $a_{n+1} = 8$

$r = 4$

$a_n = a_1 \bullet r^{n-1}$ use r = 4 to solve for the 8th term
$a_n = 2 \bullet 4^{8-1}$
$a_n = 32,768$

The following table represents the number of problems Mr. Rodgers is assigning his math students for homework each day, starting with the first day of class.

Day	1	2	3	4	5	6	7	8	9	10	11
Number of Problems	1	1	2	3	5	8	13				

If Mr. Rodgers continues this pattern, how many problems will he assign on the eleventh day?

If we look for a pattern, it appears that the number of problems assigned each day is equal to the sum of the problems assigned for the previous two days. We test this as follows:

Day 2 = 1 + 0 = 1
Day 3 = 1 + 1 = 2
Day 4 = 2 + 1 = 3
Day 5 = 3 + 2 = 5
Day 6 = 5 + 3 = 8
Day 7 = 8 + 5 = 13

Therefore, Day 8 would have 21 problems; Day 9, 34 problems; Day 10, 55 problems; and Day 11, 89 problems.

A sequence is a pattern of numbers arranged in a particular order. When a list of numbers is in a sequence, a pattern may be expressed in terms of variables. Suppose we have the sequence 8, 12, 16.... If we assign the variable *a* to the initial term, 8, and assign the variable *d* to the difference between the first two terms, we can formulate a pattern of a, $a + d$, $a + 2d$ ... $a + (n-1)d$. With this formula, we can determine any number in the sequence. For example, let's say we want to know what the 400th term would be. Using the formula,

$$a+(n-1)d =$$
$$8+(400-1)4 =$$
$$8+399(4) =$$
$$8+1596 = 1604$$

we determine that the 400th term would be 1604.

Suppose we have an equation $y = 2x + 1$. We construct a table of values in order to graph the equation to see if we can find a pattern.

x	y
-2	-3
-1	-1
0	1
1	3
2	5

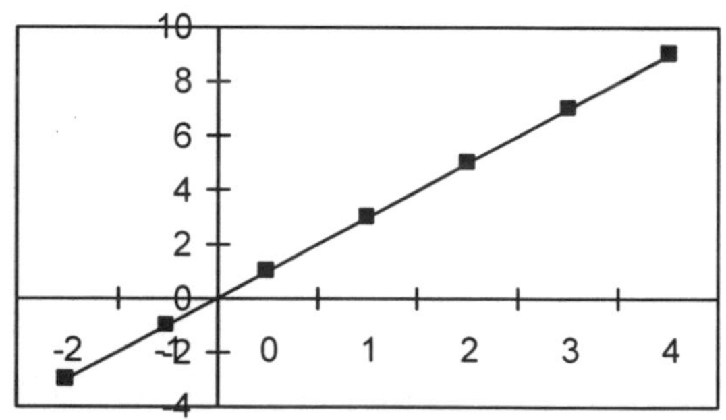

The pattern formed by the points is that they all lie on a line. We, therefore, can determine any solution of *y* by picking an *x*-coordinate and finding the corresponding point on the line. For example, if we want to know the solution of *y* when *x* is equal to 4, we find the corresponding point and see that *y* is equal to 9.

Mathematical Relationships

If two things vary directly, as one gets larger, the other also gets larger. If one gets smaller, then the other gets smaller too. If x and y vary directly, there should be a constant, c, such that $y = cx$. Something can also vary directly with the square of something else, $y = cx^2$.

If two things vary inversely, as one gets larger, the other one gets smaller instead. If x and y vary inversely, there should be a constant, c, such that $xy = c$ or $y = c/x$. Something can also vary inversely with the square of something else, $y = c/x^2$.

Example: If $30 is paid for 5 hours work, how much would be paid for 19 hours work?

This is direct variation and $30 = 5c, so the constant is 6 ($6/hour). So $y = 6(19)$ or y = $114.

This could also be done as a proportion:

$$\frac{\$30}{5} = \frac{y}{19}$$

$$5y = 570$$

$$y = 114$$

Example: On a 546 mile trip from Miami to Charlotte, one car drove 65 mph while another car drove 70 mph. How does this affect the driving time for the trip?

This is an inverse variation, since increasing your speed should decrease your driving time. Using the equation: rate $\times$ time = distance, rt = d.

65t = 546	and	70t = 546
t = 8.4	and	t = 7.8
slower speed, more time		faster speed, less time

Example: Consider the average monthly temperatures for a hypothetical location.

Month	Avg. Temp. (F)
Jan	40
March	48
May	65
July	81
Sept	80
Nov	60

Note that the graph of the average temperatures resembles the graph of a trigonometric function with a period of one year. We can use the periodic nature of seasonal temperature fluctuation to predict weather patterns.

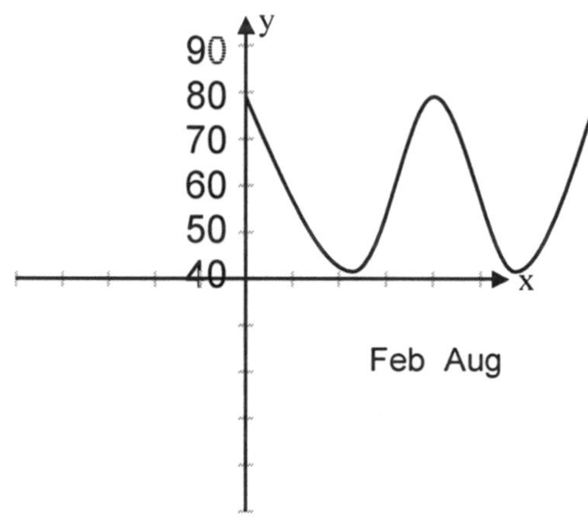

Skill 3.6 Translate between coordinate geometry representations and algebraic equations or inequalities.

Coordinate plane - A plane with a point selected as an origin, some length selected as a unit of distance, and two perpendicular lines that intersect at the origin, with positive and negative direction selected on each line. Traditionally, the lines are called x (drawn from left to right, with positive direction to the right of the origin) and y (drawn from bottom to top, with positive direction upward of the origin). Coordinates of a point are determined by the distance of this point from the lines, and the signs of the coordinates are determined by whether the point is in the positive or in the negative direction from the origin. The standard coordinate plane consists of a plane divided into 4 quadrants by the intersection of two axis, the *x*-axis (horizontal axis), and the *y*-axis (vertical axis).

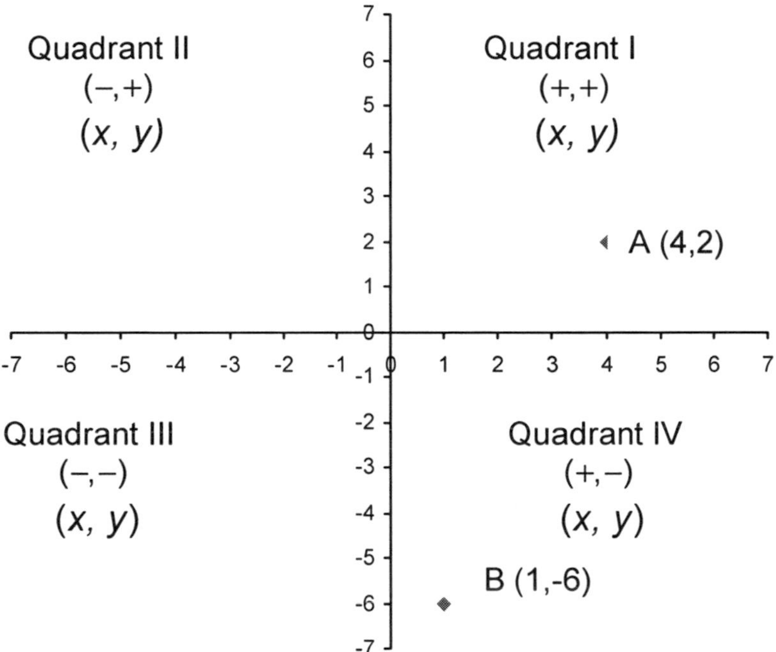

Coordinates - A unique **ordered pair** of numbers that identifies a point on the coordinate plane. The first number in the ordered pair identifies the position with regard to the x-axis while the second number identifies the position on the y-axis (*x* ,*y*)

In the coordinate plane shown above, point A has the ordered pair (4,2); point B has the ordered pair (1,-6).

Skill 3.7 Interpret or solve problems with algebraic expressions, equations, inequalities, or graphs.

A first degree equation has an equation of the form $ax+by=c$. To find the slope of a line, solve the equation for y. This gets the equation into **slope intercept form**, $y=mx+b$. **m is the line's slope.**

The y intercept is the coordinate of the point where a line crosses the y axis. To find the y intercept, substitute 0 for x and solve for y. This is the y intercept. In slope intercept form, $y=mx+b$, b is the y intercept.

To find the x intercept, substitute 0 for y and solve for x. This is the x intercept.

If the equation solves to **x = any number**, then the graph is a **vertical line**. It only has an x intercept. Its slope is **undefined**.

If the equation solves to **y = any number**, then the graph is a **horizontal line**. It only has a y intercept. Its slope is 0 (zero).

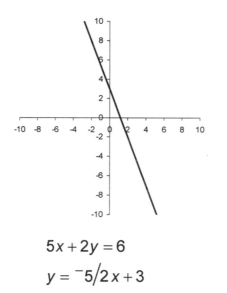

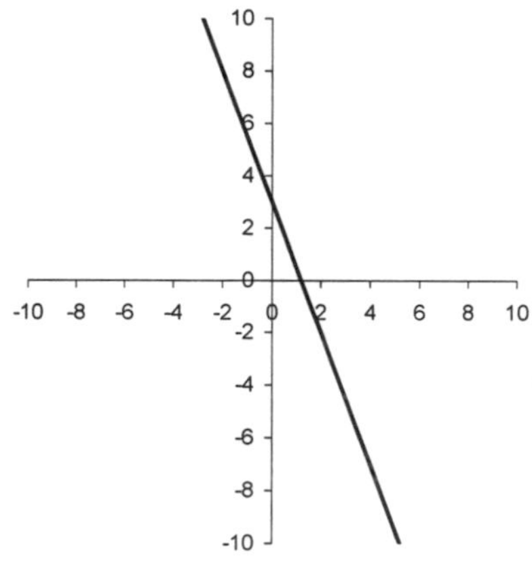

$$5x+2y=6$$

$$y={}^{-}5/2x+3$$

Slope – The slope of a line is the "slant" of a line. A downward left to right slant means a negative slope. An upward slant is a positive slope.
The formula for calculating the slope of a line with coordinates $(x_1, y_1) and (x_2, y_2)$ is:

$$\text{slope} = \frac{y_2 - y_1}{x_2 - x_1}$$

The top of the fraction represents the change in the y coordinates; it is called the **rise**. The bottom of the fraction represents the change in the x coordinates, it is called the **run.**

Example: Find the slope of a line with points at (2,2) and (7,8).

$\frac{(8)-(2)}{(7)-(2)}$ plug the values into the formula

$\frac{6}{5}$ solve the rise over run

$= 1.2$ solve for the slope

Example: One line passes through the points (-4, -6) and (4, 6); another line passes through the points (-5, -4) and (3, 8). Are these lines parallel, perpendicular or neither?

Find the slopes.

$$m = \frac{y_2 - y_1}{x_2 - x_1}$$

$$m_1 = \frac{6-(-6)}{4-(-4)} = \frac{6+6}{4+4} = \frac{12}{8} = \frac{3}{2}$$

$$m_2 = \frac{8-(-4)}{3-(-5)} = \frac{8+4}{3+5} = \frac{12}{8} = \frac{3}{2}$$

Since the slopes are the same, the lines are parallel.

Example: One line passes through the points (1, -3) and (0, -6); another line passes through the points (4, 1) and (-2, 3). Are these lines parallel, perpendicular or neither?

Find the slopes.

$$m = \frac{y_2 - y_1}{x_2 - x_1}$$

$$m_1 = \frac{-6-(-3)}{0-1} = \frac{-6+3}{-1} = \frac{-3}{-1} = 3$$

$$m_2 = \frac{3-1}{-2-4} = \frac{2}{-6} = -\frac{1}{3}$$

The slopes are negative reciprocals, so the lines are perpendicular.

Example: One line passes through the points (-2, 4) and (2, 5); another line passes through the points (-1, 0) and (5, 4). Are these lines parallel, perpendicular or neither?

Find the slopes.

$$m = \frac{y_2 - y_1}{x_2 - x_1}$$

$$m_1 = \frac{5-4}{2-(-2)} = \frac{1}{2+2} = \frac{1}{4}$$

$$m_2 = \frac{4-0}{5-(-1)} = \frac{4}{5+1} = \frac{4}{6} = \frac{2}{3}$$

Since the slopes are not the same, the lines are not parallel. Since they are not negative reciprocals, they are not perpendicular, either. Therefore, the answer is “neither.”

The **equation of a line from its graph** can be found by finding its slope and its y intercept.

$$Y - y_a = m(X - x_a)$$

(x_a, y_a) can be (x_1, y_1) or (x_2, y_2) If **m**, the value of the slope, is distributed through the parentheses, the equation can be rewritten into other forms of the equation of a line.

Example: Find the equation of a line through $(9, {}^-6)$ and $({}^-1, 2)$.

$$\text{slope} = \frac{y_2 - y_1}{x_2 - x_1} = \frac{2 - {}^-6}{{}^-1 - 9} = \frac{8}{{}^-10} = \frac{{}^-4}{5}$$

$$Y - y_a = m(X - x_a) \rightarrow Y - 2 = {}^-4/5(X - {}^-1) \rightarrow$$
$$Y - 2 = {}^-4/5(X + 1) \rightarrow Y - 2 = {}^-4/5\,X - 4/5 \rightarrow$$
$Y = {}^-4/5\ X + 6/5$ This is the slope-intercept form.

Multiplying by 5 to eliminate fractions, it is:

$5Y = {}^-4X + 6 \rightarrow 4X + 5Y = 6$ Standard form.

Example: Find the slope and intercepts of $3x + 2y = 14$.

$$3x + 2y = 14$$
$$2y = {}^-3x + 14$$
$$y = {}^-3/2\ x + 7$$

The slope of the line is ${}^-3/2$. The y intercept of the line is 7.

The intercepts can also be found by substituting 0 in place of the other variable in the equation.

To find the y intercept:
let $x = 0$; $3(0) + 2y = 14$
$0 + 2y = 14$
$2y = 14$
$y = 7$
(0,7) is the y intercept.

To find the x intercept:
let $y = 0$; $3x + 2(0) = 14$
$3x + 0 = 14$
$3x = 14$
$x = 14/3$
(14/3 ,0) is the x intercept.

Example: Sketch the graph of the line represented by $2x+3y=6$.

Let $x=0 \rightarrow 2(0)+3y=6$
$\rightarrow 3y=6$
$\rightarrow y=2$
$\rightarrow (0,2)$ is the y intercept.

Let $y=0 \rightarrow 2x+3(0)=6$
$\rightarrow 2x=6$
$\rightarrow x=3$
$\rightarrow (3,0)$ is the x intercept.

Let $x=1 \rightarrow 2(1)+3y=6$
$\rightarrow 2+3y=6$
$\rightarrow 3y=4$
$\rightarrow y=\frac{4}{3}$
$\rightarrow \left(1,\frac{4}{3}\right)$ is the third point.

Plotting the three points on the coordinate system, we get the following:

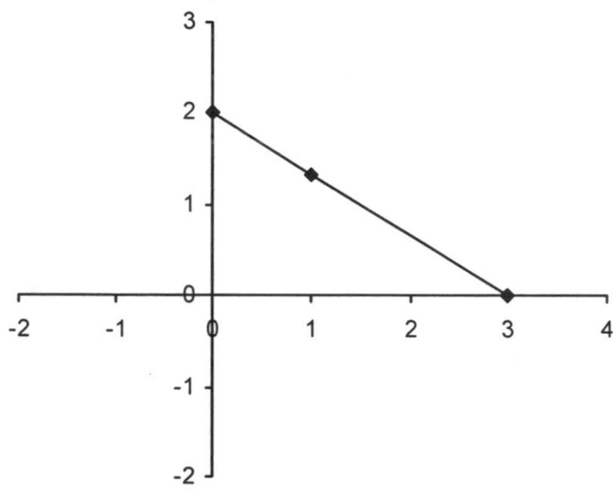

Midpoint Definition:

If a line segment has endpoints of (x_1, y_1) and (x_2, y_2), then the midpoint can be found using:

$$\left(\frac{x_1+x_2}{2}, \frac{y_1+y_2}{2}\right)$$

Example: Find the center of a circle with a diameter whose endpoints are (3,7) and $(^-4, ^-5)$.

$$\text{Midpoint} = \left(\frac{3+(^-4)}{2}, \frac{7+(^-5)}{2}\right)$$

$$\text{Midpoint} = \left(\frac{^-1}{2}, 1\right)$$

Example: Find the midpoint given the two points $\left(5, 8\sqrt{6}\right)$ and $\left(9, ^-4\sqrt{6}\right)$.

$$\text{Midpoint} = \left(\frac{5+9}{2}, \frac{8\sqrt{6}+(^-4\sqrt{6})}{2}\right)$$

$$\text{Midpoint} = \left(7, 2\sqrt{6}\right)$$

The length of a line segment is the **distance** between two different points, A and B. The formula for the length of a line is:

$$\text{length} = \sqrt{(x_1 - x_2)^2 + (y_1 - y_2)^2}$$

Example: Find the length between the points (2,2) and (7,8)

$= \sqrt{(2-7)^2 + (2-8)^2}$	plug the values into the formula
$= \sqrt{(-5)^2 + (-6)^2}$	calculate the x and y differences
$= \sqrt{25+36}$	square the values
$= \sqrt{61}$	add the two values
$= 7.81$	calculate the square root

COMPETENCY 4.0 KNOWLEDGE OF GEOMETRY

Skill 4.1 Solve real-world problems that involve the use of the Pythagorean theorem.

The Pythagorean Theorem states that given any right-angles triangle, $\square ABC$, the square of the hypotenuse is equal to the sum of the squares of the other two sides.

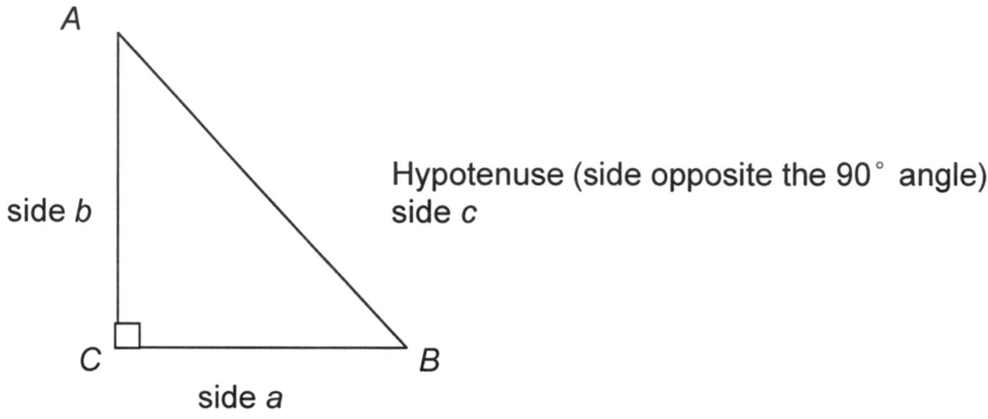

This theorem says that $(AB)^2 = (BC)^2 + (AC)^2$

or

$$c^2 = a^2 + b^2$$

Example: Find the area and perimeter of a rectangle if its length is 12 inches and its diagonal is 15 inches.

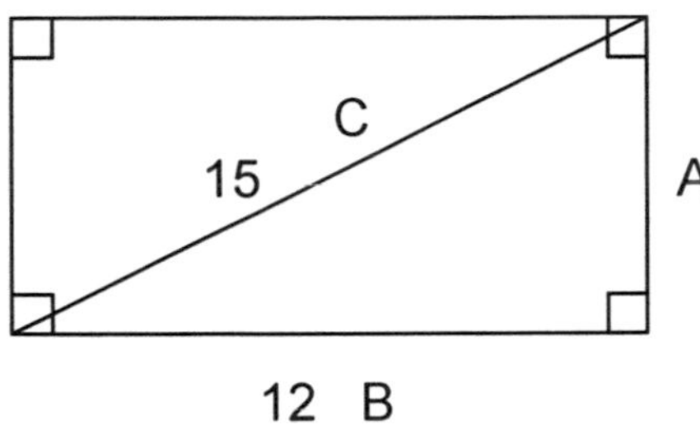

1. Draw and label sketch.

2. Since the height is still needed use Pythagorean formula to find missing leg of the triangle.

$$A^2 + B^2 = C^2$$
$$A^2 + 12^2 = 15^2$$
$$A^2 = 15^2 - 12^2$$
$$A^2 = 81$$
$$A = 9$$

Now use this information to find the area and perimeter.

$\text{A} = LW$	$\text{P} = 2(L + W)$	1. write formula
$\text{A} = (12)(9)$	$\text{P} = 2(12 + 9)$	2. substitute
$\text{A} = 108 \text{ in}^2$	$\text{P} = 42$ inches	3. solve

Example: Two old cars leave a road intersection at the same time. One car traveled due north at 55 mph while the other car traveled due east. After 3 hours, the cars were 180 miles apart. Find the speed of the second car.

Using a right triangle to represent the problem we get the figure:

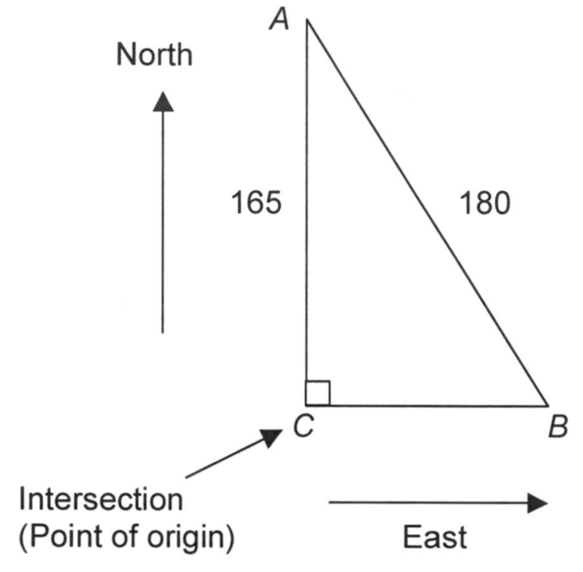

Traveling at 55 mph for 3 hours, the northbound car has driven (55)(3)=165 miles. This is the side *AC.*

We are given that the cars are 180 miles apart. This is side *AB*.

Since $\triangle ABC$ is a right triangle, then, by Pythagorean Theorem, we get:

$$(AB)^2 = (BC)^2 + (AC)^2 \quad \text{or}$$
$$(BC)^2 = (AB)^2 - (AC)^2$$

$$(BC)^2 = 180^2 - 165^2$$
$$(BC)^2 = 32400 - 27225$$
$$(BC)^2 = 5175$$

Take the square root of both sides to get:

$$\sqrt{(BC)^2} = \sqrt{5175} \approx 71.937 \text{ miles}$$

Since the east bound car has traveled 71.935 miles in 3 hours, then the average speed is:

$$\frac{71.937}{3} \approx 23.97 \text{ mph}$$

Skill 4.2 Apply geometric properties and relationships to solve real-world and other mathematics problems.

See Skill 5.2

Skill 4.3 Apply concepts and properties of transformational geometry.

A **transformation** is a change in the position, shape, or size of a geometric figure. **Transformational geometry** is the study of manipulating objects by flipping, twisting, turning and scaling. **Symmetry** is exact similarity between two parts or halves, as if one were a mirror image of the other.

There are four basic **transformational symmetries** that can be used: **translation, rotation, reflection,** and **glide reflection**. The transformation of an object is called its image. If the original object was labeled with letters, such as $ABCD$, the image may be labeled with the same letters followed by a prime symbol, $A'B'C'D'$.

A **translation** is a transformation that "slides" an object a fixed distance in a given direction. The original object and its translation have the same shape and size, and they face in the same direction.

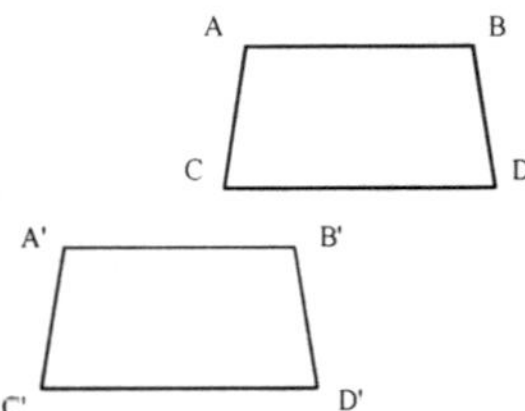

An example of a translation in architecture would be stadium seating. The seats are the same size and the same shape and face in the same direction.

A **rotation** is a transformation that turns a figure about a fixed point called the center of rotation. An object and its rotation are the same shape and size, but the figures may be turned in different directions. Rotations can occur in either a clockwise or a counterclockwise direction.

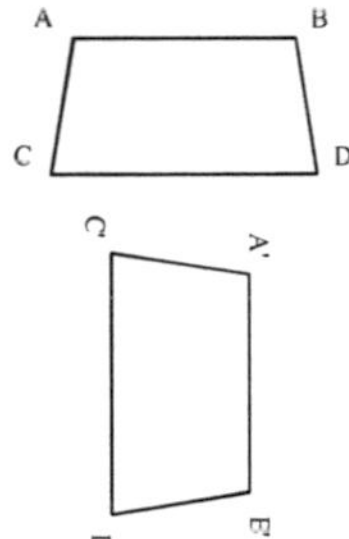

Rotations can be seen in wallpaper and art, and a Ferris wheel is an example of rotation.

An object and its **reflection** have the same shape and size, but the figures face in opposite directions.

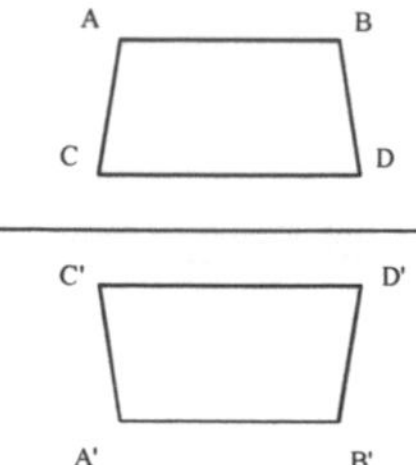

The line (where a mirror may be placed) is called the **line of reflection**. The distance from a point to the line of reflection is the same as the distance from the point's image to the line of reflection.

A **glide reflection** is a combination of a reflection and a translation.

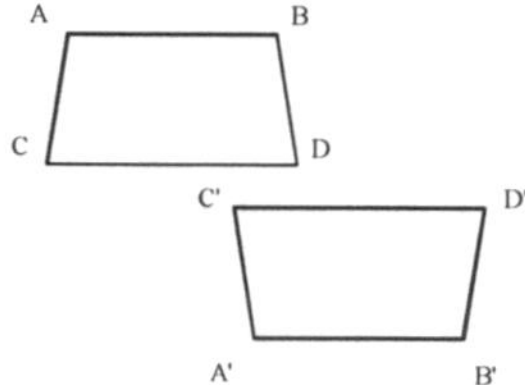

Objects that are **tangent** make contact at a single point or along a line without crossing. Understanding tangency is critical in the construction industry where architects and engineers must figure out how various elements will fit together. An example would be the building of a stair railing. The architect must determine the points of tangency between the banisters, which might even be curved, and the posts supporting the banisters.

Many types of flooring found in our homes are examples of **symmetry**: Oriental carpets, tiling, patterned carpet, etc. The human body is an example of symmetry, even though it is not usually perfect. If you split the torso down the middle, on each half, you will find one ear, one eye, one nostril, one shoulder, one arm, one leg, and so on, in approximately the same place.

Another type of transformation is **dilation**. Dilation is a transformation that "shrinks" or "makes it bigger."

Example: Using dilation to transform a diagram.

Starting with a triangle whose center of dilation is point P,

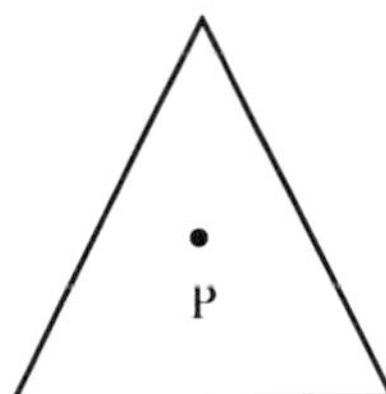

we dilate the lengths of the sides by the same factor to create a new triangle.

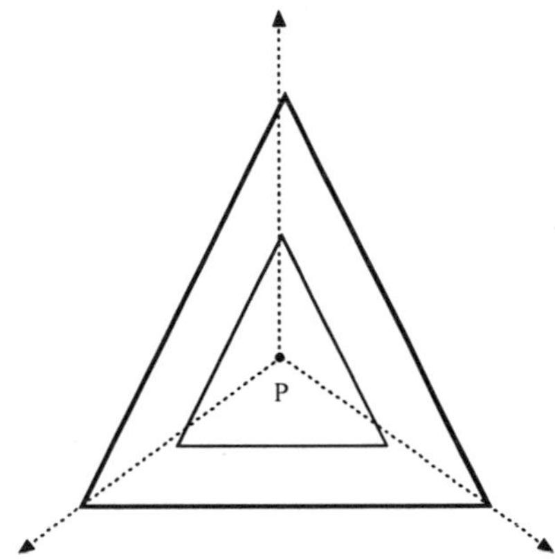

Skill 4.4 Apply properties of lines, angles, triangles, quadrilaterals, and circles in solving problems.

A point, a line and a plane are actually undefined terms since we cannot give a satisfactory definition using simple defined terms. However, their properties and characteristics give a clear understanding of what they are.

A **point** indicates place or position. It has no length, width or thickness.

• point A
A

A **line** is considered a set of points. Lines may be straight or curved, but the term line commonly denotes a straight line. Lines extend indefinitely.

A B line $\overleftrightarrow{AB}$

A **plane** is a set of points composing a flat surface. A plane also has no boundaries.

plane A

A **line segment** has two endpoints.

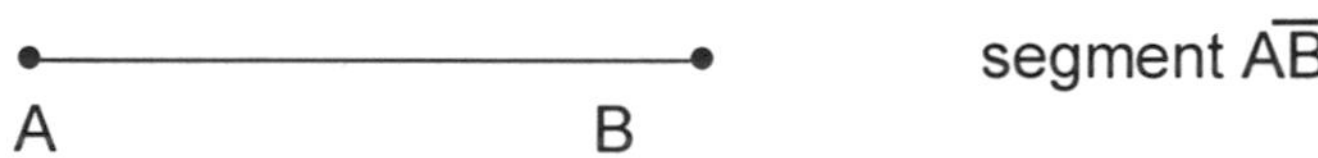

segment $\overline{AB}$

A **ray** has exactly one endpoint. It extends indefinitely in one direction.

ray $\overrightarrow{AB}$

An **angle** is formed by the intersection of two rays.

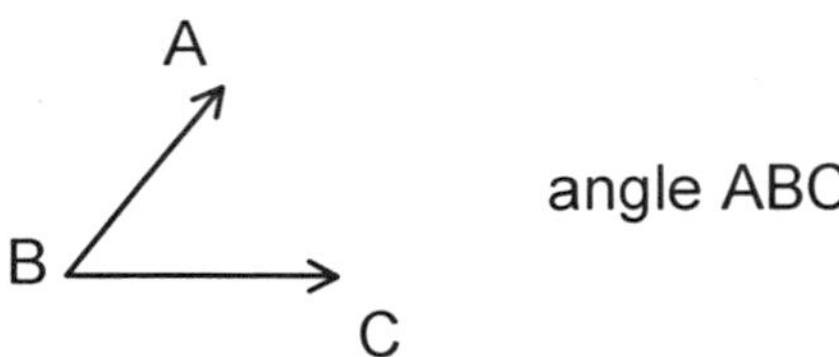

Angles are measured in degrees. $1^\circ = \frac{1}{360}$ of a circle.

A **right angle** measures 90°.

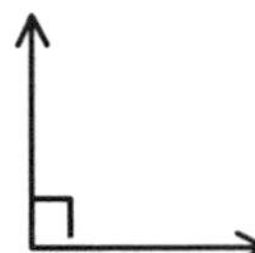

An **acute angle** measures more than 0° and less than 90°.

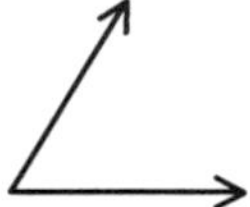

An **obtuse angle** measures more than 90° and less than 180°.

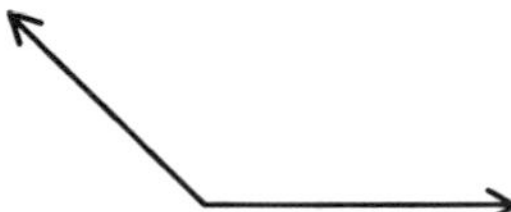

A **straight angle** measures 180°.

A **reflexive angle** measures more than 180° and less than 360°.

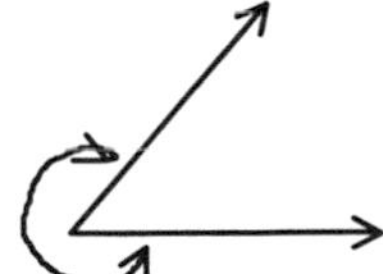

Angles can be classified in a number of ways. Some of those classifications are outlined here.

Adjacent angles have a common vertex and one common side but no interior points in common.

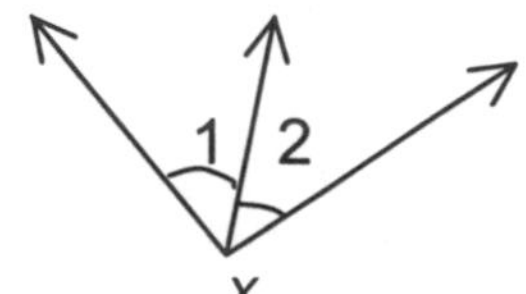

Complimentary angles add up to 90 degrees.

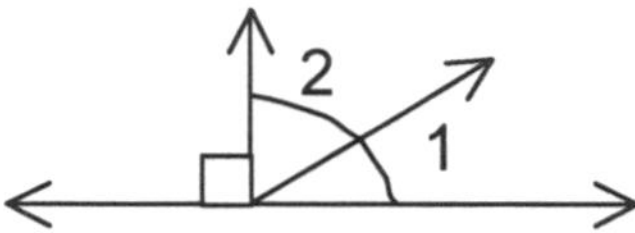

Supplementary angles add up to 180 degrees.

Vertical angles have sides that form two pairs of opposite rays.

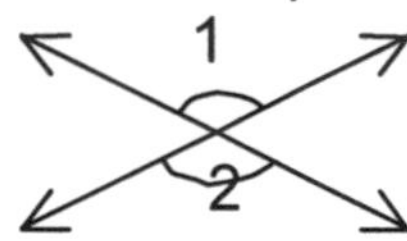

Corresponding angles are in the same corresponding position on two parallel lines cut by a transversal.

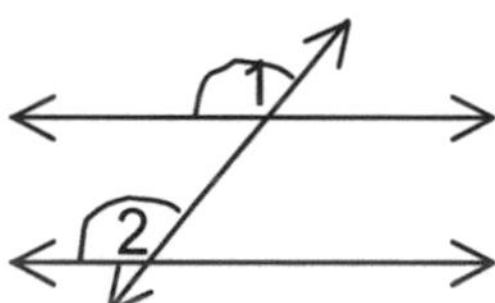

Alternate interior angles are diagonal angles on the inside of two parallel lines cut by a transversal.

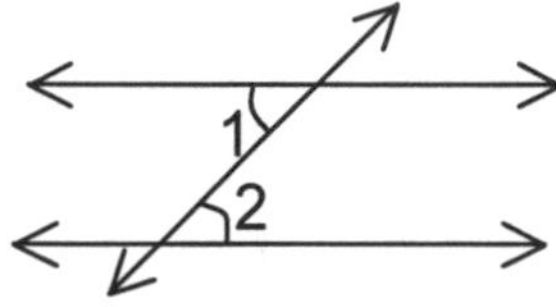

Alternate exterior angles are diagonal on the outside of two parallel lines cut by a transversal.

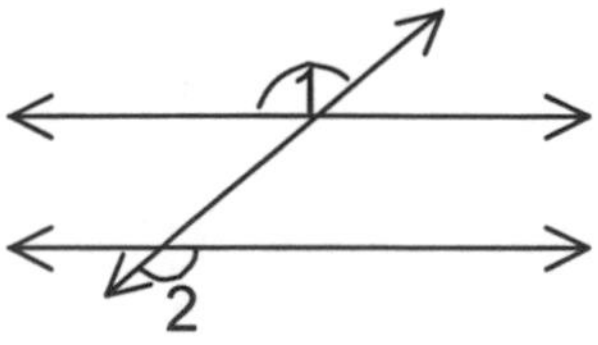

An infinite number of lines can be drawn through any point.

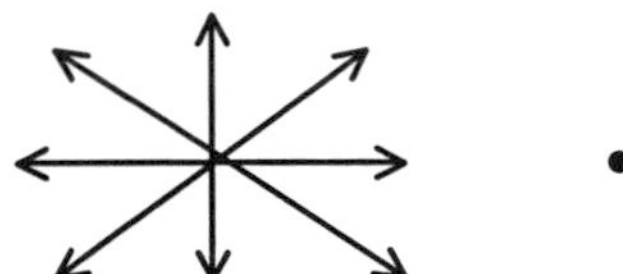

Exactly one line can be drawn through two points.

Perpendicular lines or planes form a 90 degree angle to each other. Perpendicular lines have slopes that are negative reciprocals.

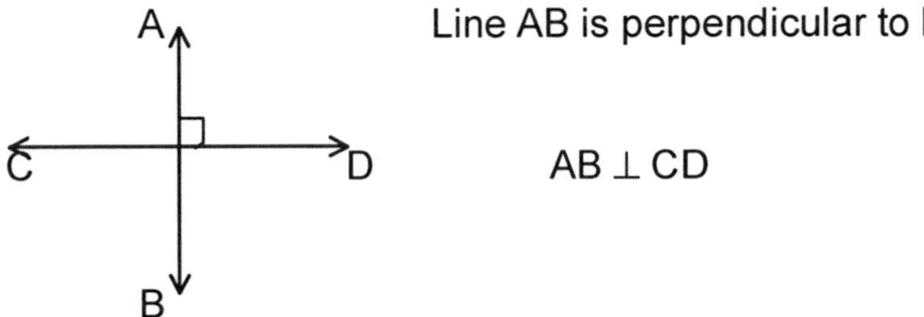

Line AB is perpendicular to line CD.

$AB \perp CD$

Parallel lines or planes do not intersect. Two parallel lines will have the same slope and are everywhere equidistant.

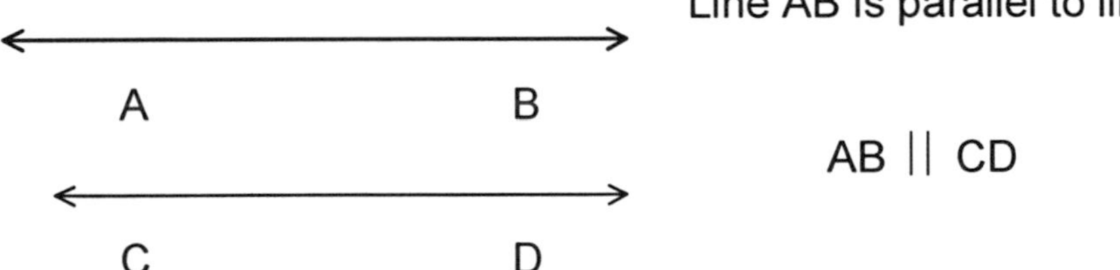

Line AB is parallel to line CD.

$AB \parallel CD$

See also Skill 5.2

Skill 4.5 Determine the measure of the interior and exterior angles of polygons.

The sum of the measures of the **interior angles** of a polygon can be determined using the following formula, where n represents the number of angles in the polygon.

$$\text{Sum of } \angle s = 180(n-2)$$

The measure of each angle of a regular polygon can be found by dividing the sum of the measures by the number of angles.

$$\text{Measure of } \angle = \frac{180(n-2)}{n}$$

Example: Find the measure of each angle of a regular octagon.

Since an octagon has eight sides, each angle equals:

$$\frac{180(8-2)}{8} = \frac{180(6)}{8} = 135^\circ$$

The sum of the measures of the **exterior angles** of a polygon, taken one angle at each vertex, equals 360°.

The measure of each exterior angle of a regular polygon can be determined using the following formula, where n represents the number of angles in the polygon.

$$\text{Measure of exterior } \angle \text{ of regular polygon} = 180 - \frac{180(n-2)}{n}$$

$$\text{or, more simply} = \frac{360}{n}$$

Example: Find the measure of the interior and exterior angles of a regular pentagon.

Since a pentagon has five sides, each exterior angle measures:

$$\frac{360}{5} = 72^\circ$$

Since each exterior angle is supplementary to its interior angle, the interior angle measures 180 – 72 or 108°.

The sum of the measures of the angles of a triangle is 180°.

Example: Can a triangle have two right angles?
No. A right angle measures 90°, therefore the sum of two right angles would be 180° and there could not be a third angle.

Example: Can a triangle have two obtuse angles?
No. Since an obtuse angle measures more than 90°, the sum of two obtuse angles would be greater than 180°.

Example: In a triangle, the measure of the second angle is three times the first. The third angle equals the sum of the measures of the first two angles. Find the number of degrees in each angle.

Let x = the number of degrees in the first angle
$3x$ = the number of degrees in the second angle
$x + 3x$ = the measure of the third angle

Since the sum of the measures of all three angles is 180°.

$$x + 3x + (x + 3x) = 180$$
$$8x = 180$$
$$x = 22.5$$
$$3x = 67.5$$
$$x + 3x = 90$$

Thus, the angles measure 22.5°, 67.5°, and 90°. Additionally, the triangle is a right triangle.

Two adjacent angles form a linear pair when they have a common side and their remaining sides form a straight angle. Angles in a linear pair are supplementary. An **exterior angle** of a triangle forms a linear pair with an angle of the triangle.

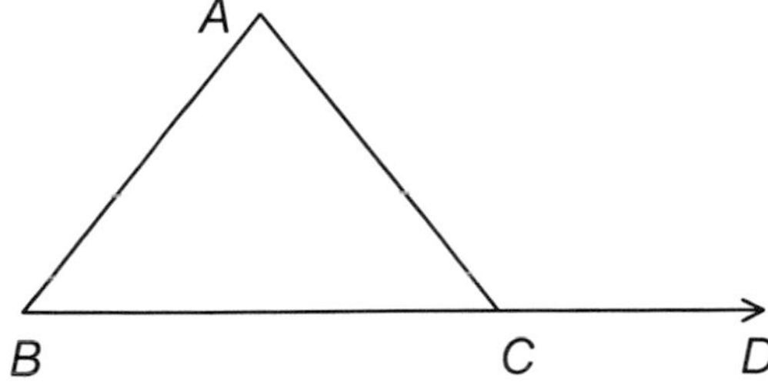

$\angle ACD$ is an exterior angle of triangle ABC, forming a linear pair with $\angle ACB$.

The measure of an exterior angle of a triangle is equal to the sum of the measures of the two non-adjacent interior angles.

Example: In triangle ABC, the measure of $\angle A$ is twice the measure of $\angle B$. $\angle C$ is 30° more than their sum. Find the measure of the exterior angle formed at $\angle C$.

Let x = the measure of $\angle B$
$2x$ = the measure of $\angle A$
$x + 2x + 30$ = the measure of $\angle C$

$$x + 2x + x + 2x + 30 = 180$$
$$6x + 30 = 180$$
$$6x = 150$$
$$x = 25$$
$$2x = 50$$

It is not necessary to find the measure of the third angle, since the exterior angle equals the sum of the opposite interior angles. Thus, the exterior angle at $\angle C$ measures 75°.

COMPETENCY 5.0 KNOWLEDGE OF MEASUREMENT

Skill 5.1 Solve problems involving units of measure and convert answers to a larger or smaller unit within either the metric or customary system.

Measurements of length (English system)

12 inches (in)	=	1 foot (ft)
3 feet (ft)	=	1 yard (yd)
1760 yards (yd)	=	1 mile (mi)

Measurements of length (Metric system)

kilometer (km)	=	1000 meters (m)
hectometer (hm)	=	100 meters (m)
decameter (dam)	=	10 meters (m)
meter (m)	=	1 meter (m)
decimeter (dm)	=	1/10 meter (m)
centimeter (cm)	=	1/100 meter (m)
millimeter (mm)	=	1/1000 meter (m)

Conversion of length from English to Metric

1 inch	=	2.54 centimeters
1 foot	≈	30.48 centimeters
1 yard	≈	0.91 meters
1 mile	≈	1.61 kilometers

Measurements of weight (English system)

28.35 grams (g)	=	1 ounce (oz)
16 ounces (oz)	=	1 pound (lb)
2000 pounds (lb)	=	1 ton (t) (short ton)
1.1 ton (t)	=	1 metric ton (t)

Measurements of weight (Metric system)

kilogram (kg)	=	1000 grams (g)
gram (g)	=	1 gram (g)
milligram (mg)	=	1/1000 gram (g)

Conversion of weight from English to metric

1 ounce	≈	28.35 grams
1 pound	≈	0.454 kilogram
1.1 ton	=	1 metric ton

Measurement of volume (English system)

8 fluid ounces (oz)	=	1 cup (c)
2 cups (c)	=	1 pint (pt)
2 pints (pt)	=	1 quart (qt)
4 quarts (qt)	=	1 gallon (gal)

Measurement of volume (Metric system)

kiloliter (kl)	=	1000 liters (l)
liter (l)	=	1 liter (l)
milliliter (ml)	=	1/1000 liter (ml)

Conversion of volume from English to metric

1 teaspoon (tsp)	≈	5 milliliters
1 fluid ounce	≈	29.56 milliliters
1 cup	≈	0.24 liters
1 pint	≈	0.47 liters
1 quart	≈	0.95 liters
1 gallon	≈	3.8 liters

Note: (') represents feet and (") represents inches.

Square units can be derived with knowledge of basic units of length by squaring the equivalent measurements.

1 square foot (sq. ft.) = 144 sq. in.
1 sq. yd. = 9 sq. ft.
1 sq. yd. = 1296 sq. in.

Example:
14 sq. yd. = _____ sq. ft.
$14 \times 9 = 126$ sq. ft.

Length

Example: A car skidded 170 yards on an icy road before coming to a stop. How long is the skid distance in kilometers?

Since 1 yard $\approx$ 0.9 meters, multiply 170 yards by 0.9.

$$170 \times 0.9 = 153 \text{ meters}$$

Since 1000 meters = 1 kilometer, divide 153 by 1000.

$$\frac{153}{1000} = 0.153 \text{ kilometers}$$

Example: The distance around a race course is exactly 1 mile, 17 feet, and $9\frac{1}{4}$ inches. Approximate this distance to the nearest tenth of a foot.

Convert the distance to feet.

1 mile = 1760 yards = 1760 $\times$ 3 feet = 5280 feet.

$$9\frac{1}{4} \text{ inches } = \frac{37}{4} \times \frac{1}{12} = \frac{37}{48} \approx 0.77083 \text{ feet}$$

So 1 mile, 17 feet and $9\frac{1}{4}$ inches = $5280 + 17 + 0.77083$ feet

$$= 5297.\underline{7}7083 \text{ feet.}$$

Now, we need to round to the nearest tenth digit. The underlined 7 is in the tenth place. The digit in the hundredth place, also a 7, is greater than 5, the 7 in the tenths place needs to be rounded up to 8 to get a final answer of 5297.8 feet.

Weight

Example: Zachary weighs 150 pounds. Tom weighs 153 pounds. What is the difference in their weights in grams?

153 pounds – 150 pounds = 3 pounds
1 pound = 454 grams
3(454 grams) = 1362 grams

Capacity

Example: Students in a fourth grade class want to fill a 3 gallon jug using cups of water. How many cups of water are needed?

1 gallon = 16 cups of water
3 gallons x 16 cups = 48 cups of water are needed.

Time

Example: It takes Cynthia 45 minutes to get ready each morning. How many hours does she spend getting ready each week?

45 minutes X 7 days = 315 minutes

$$\frac{\text{315 minutes}}{\text{60 minutes in an hour}} = \text{5.25 hours}$$

Skill 5.2 Solve real-world and other mathematics problems involving length, perimeter, weight/mass, capacity/volume, time, temperature, and angles, including their use in more complex situations.

The **perimeter** of any polygon is the sum of the lengths of the sides.

The **area** of a polygon is the number of square units covered by the figure.

FIGURE	AREA FORMULA	PERIMETER FORMULA
Rectangle	LW	$2(L+W)$
Triangle	$\frac{1}{2}bh$	$a+b+c$
Parallelogram	bh	sum of lengths of sides
Trapezoid	$\frac{1}{2}h(a+b)$	sum of lengths of sides

Perimeter

Example: A farmer has a piece of land shaped as shown below. He wishes to fence this land at an estimated cost of $25 per linear foot. What is the total cost of fencing this property to the nearest foot.

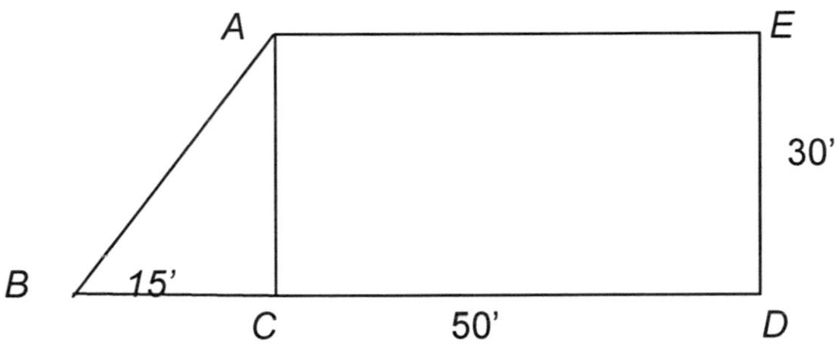

From the right triangle ABC, AC = 30 and BC = 15.

Since $(AB) = (AC)^2 + (BC)^2$
$(AB) = (30)^2 + (15)^2$

So $\sqrt{(AB)^2} = AB = \sqrt{1125} = 33.5410$ feet

To the nearest foot AB = 34 feet.

Perimeter of the piece of land is $= AB + BC + CD + DE + EA$

= 34 + 15 + 50 + 30 + 50 = 179 feet

cost of fencing = $25 x 179 = $4, 475.00

Area
Area is the space that a figure occupies. Example:

Example: What will be the cost of carpeting a rectangular office that measures 12 feet by 15 feet if the carpet costs \$12.50 per square yard?

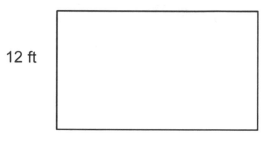

15 ft

The problem is asking you to determine the area of the office. The area of a rectangle is *length x width = A*
Substitute the given values in the equation $A = lw$

$A = (12 \text{ ft.})(15 \text{ ft.})$

$A = 180 \text{ ft.}$

The problem asked you to determine the cost of carpet at \$12.50 per square yard.

First, you need to convert 180 ft.^2 into yards^2.

1 yd. = 3 ft.

$$(1 \text{ yard})(1 \text{ yard}) = (3 \text{ feet})(3 \text{ feet})$$
$$1 \text{ yd}^2 = 9 \text{ ft } 2$$

Hence, $\dfrac{180 \text{ ft}^2}{1} = \dfrac{1 \text{ yd}^2}{9 \text{ ft}^2} = \dfrac{20}{1} = 20 \text{ yd}^2$

The carpet cost \$12.50 per square yard; thus the cost of carpeting the office described is \$12.50 x 20 = \$250.00.

Example: Find the area of a parallelogram whose base is 6.5 cm and the height of the altitude to that base is 3.7 cm.

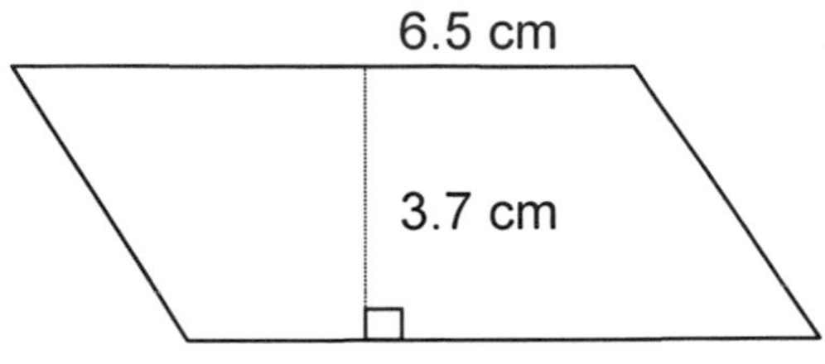

$A_{parallelogram} = bh$

$= (3.7)(6.5)$
$= 24.05 \text{ cm}^2$

Example: Find the area of this triangle.

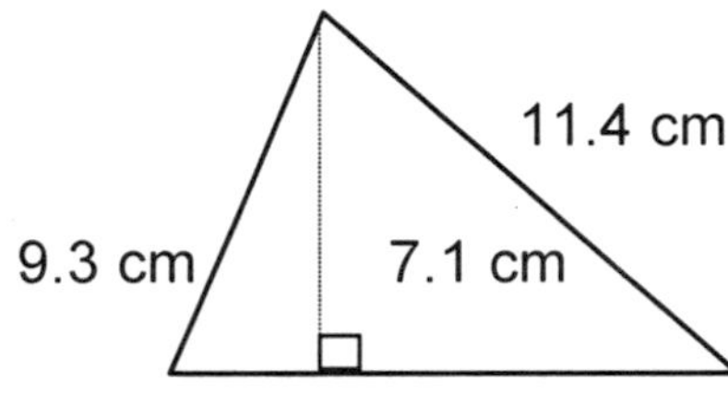

$A_{triangle} = \frac{1}{2}bh$
$= 0.5\ (16.8)\ (7.1)$
$= 59.64 \text{ cm}^2$

Example: Find the area of this trapezoid.

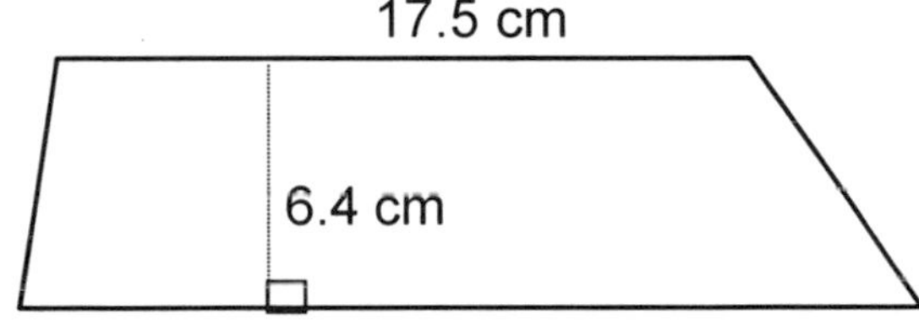

The area of a trapezoid equals one-half the sum of the bases times the altitude.

$A_{trapezoid} = \frac{1}{2}h(b_1 + b_2)$
$= 0.5\ (6.4)\ (17.5 + 23.7)$
$= 131.84 \text{ cm}^2$

The distance around a circle is the **circumference**. The ratio of the circumference to the diameter is represented by the Greek letter pi. $\Pi \sim 3.14 \sim \frac{22}{7}$.

The circumference of a circle is found by the formula $C = 2\Pi r$ or $C = \Pi d$ where r is the radius of the circle and d is the diameter.

The **area** of a circle is found by the formula $A = \Pi r^2$.

Example: Find the circumference and area of a circle whose radius is 7 meters.

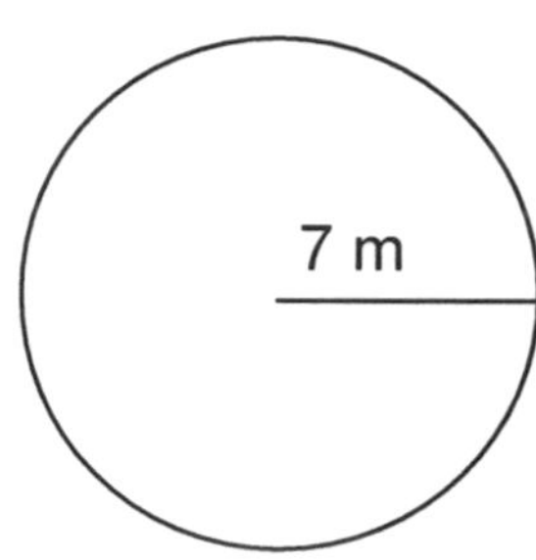

$C = 2\Pi r$	$A = \Pi r^2$
$= 2(3.14)(7)$	$= 3.14(7)(7)$
$= 43.96$ m	$= 153.86\ m^2$

Volume and **Surface area** are computed using the following formulas:

FIGURE	VOLUME	TOTAL SURFACE AREA
Right Cylinder	$\pi r^2 h$	$2\pi rh + 2\pi r^2$
Right Cone	$\frac{\pi r^2 h}{3}$	$\pi r\sqrt{r^2 + h^2} + \pi r^2$
Sphere	$\frac{4}{3}\pi r^3$	$4\pi r^2$
Rectangular Solid	LWH	$2LW + 2WH + 2LH$

FIGURE	LATERAL AREA	TOTAL AREA	VOLUME
Regular Pyramid	1/2Pl	1/2Pl+B	1/3Bh

P = Perimeter
h = height
B = Area of Base
l = slant height

Example: What is the volume of a shoe box with a length of 35 cms, a width of 20 cms and a height of 15 cms?

Volume of a rectangular solid
= Length x Width x Height
= 35 x 20 x 15
= 10500 cm^3

Example: A water company is trying to decide whether to use traditional cylindrical paper cups or to offer conical paper cups since both cost the same. The traditional cups are 8 cm wide and 14 cm high. The conical cups are 12 cm wide and 19 cm high. The company will use the cup that holds the most water.

Draw and label a sketch of each.

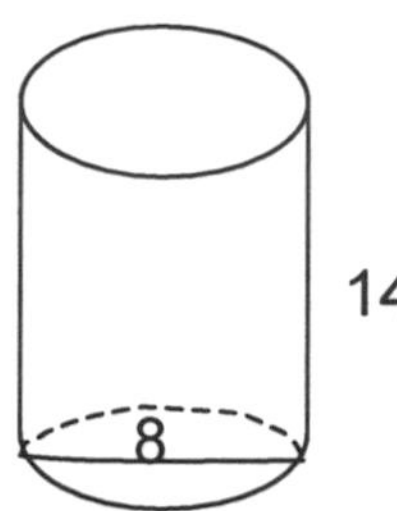

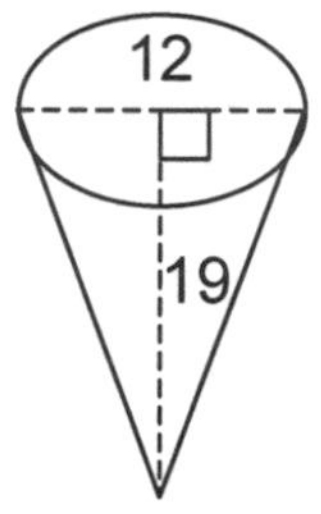

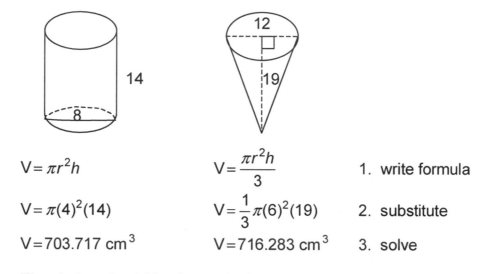

$V=\pi r^2 h$	$V=\dfrac{\pi r^2 h}{3}$	1. write formula
$V=\pi(4)^2(14)$	$V=\dfrac{1}{3}\pi(6)^2(19)$	2. substitute
$V=703.717\text{ cm}^3$	$V=716.283\text{ cm}^3$	3. solve

The choice should be the conical cup since its volume is more.

Example: How much material is needed to make a basketball that has a diameter of 15 inches? How much air is needed to fill the basketball?

Draw and label a sketch:

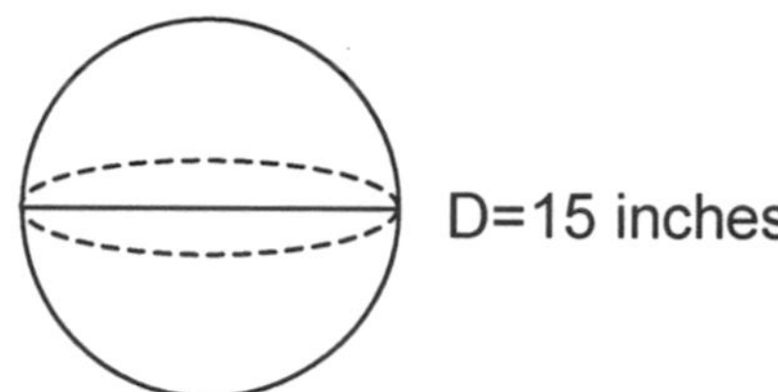

Total surface area	Volume	
$TSA=4\pi r^2$	$V=\dfrac{4}{3}\pi r^3$	1. write formula
$=4\pi(7.5)^2$	$=\dfrac{4}{3}\pi(7.5)^3$	2. substitute
$=706.9\text{ in}^2$	$=1767.1\text{ in}^3$	3. solve

Skill 5.3 Solve real-world problems by determining how a change in dimension affects other measurements.

Examining the change in area or volume of a given figure requires first to find the existing area given the original dimensions and then finding the new area given the increased dimensions.

Example: Given the rectangle below determine the change in area if the length is increase by 5 and the width is increased by 7.

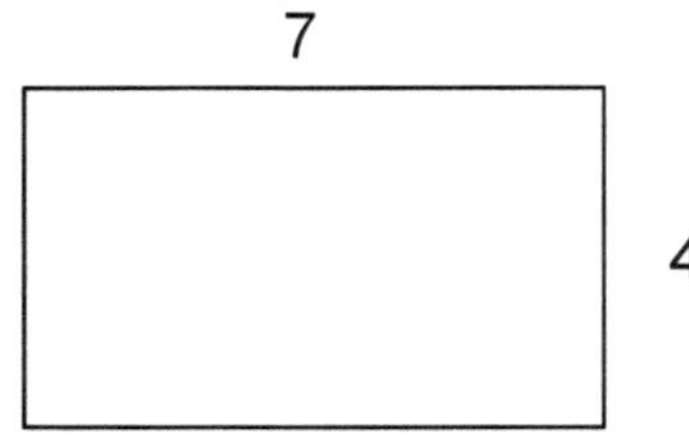

Draw and label a sketch of the new rectangle.

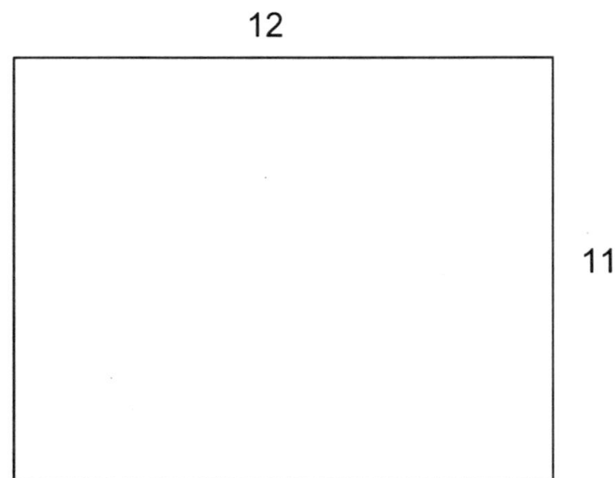

Find the areas.

Area of original = LW	Area of enlarged shape = LW
= (7)(4)	= (12)(11)
= 28 units^2	= 132 units^2

The change in area is 132 – 28 = 104 units^2.

Problems Involving Rates

Example: A class wants to take a field trip from New York City to Albany to visit the capital. The trip is approximately 160 miles. If they will be traveling at 50 miles per hour, how long will it take for them to get there (assuming traveling at a steady rate)?

Set up the equation as a proportion and solve:

$$\frac{160 \text{ miles}}{x \text{ hours}} = \frac{50 \text{ miles}}{1 \text{ hour}}$$

(160 miles)(1 hour) = (50 miles) (x hours)

$160 = 50x$

$x = 3.2$ hours

Example: A salesman drove 480 miles from Pittsburgh to Hartford. The next day he returned the same distance to Pittsburgh in half an hour less time than his original trip took, because he increased his average speed by 4 mph. Find his original speed.

Since distance = rate x time then time = $\frac{\text{distance}}{\text{rate}}$

original time $-$ 1/2 hour $=$ shorter return time

$$\frac{480}{x} - \frac{1}{2} = \frac{480}{x+4}$$

Multiplying by the LCD of $2x(x+4)$, the equation becomes:

$$480[2(x+4)] - 1[x(x+4)] = 480(2x)$$

$$960x + 3840 - x^2 - 4x = 960x$$

$$x^2 + 4x - 3840 = 0$$

$(x+64)(x-60) = 0$ Either (x-60=0) or (x+64=0) or both=0

$x = 60$ 60 mph is the original speed.

$x = 64$ This is the solution since the time cannot be negative. Check your answer

$$\frac{480}{60} - \frac{1}{2} = \frac{480}{64}$$

$$8 - \frac{1}{2} = 7\frac{1}{2}$$

$$7\frac{1}{2} = 7\frac{1}{2}$$

Cost per Unit

The unit rate for purchasing an item is its price divided by the number of pounds/ounces, etc. in the item. The item with the lower unit rate is the lower price.

Example: Find the item with the best unit price:

$1.79 for 10 ounces
$1.89 for 12 ounces
$5.49 for 32 ounces

$\frac{1.79}{10} = 0.179$ per ounce $\frac{1.89}{12} = 0.1575$ per ounce $\frac{5.49}{32} = 0.172$ [SA3] per ounce

$1.89 for 12 ounces is the best price.

Skill 5.4 Interpret scale drawings to solve real-world problems.

When reading an instrument, students should first determine the interval of scale on the instrument. To achieve the greatest accuracy, they should read the scale to the nearest measurement mark. .

If you are using a scale with a needle that has a mirrored plate behind it, view the scale so that the needle's reflection is hidden behind the needle itself. Do not look at it from an angle. In order to read a balance scale accurately, place the scale on a level surface and make sure that the hand points precisely at 0. Place objects on the plate gently and take them away gently. Face the dial straight on to read the graduation accurately. Students should read from the large graduation to smaller graduation. If the dial hand points between two graduations, they should choose the number that is closest to the hand.

When reading inches on a ruler, the student needs to understand that each inch is divided into halves by the longest mark in the middle; into fourths by the next longest marks; into eighths by the next; and into sixteenths by the shortest. When the measurement falls between two inch marks, they can give the whole number of inches, count the additional fractional marks, and give the answer as the number and fraction of inches. Remind students that the convention is always to express a fraction by its lowest possible denominator.

If students are using the metric system on a ruler, have them focus on the marks between the whole numbers (centimeters). Point out that each centimeter is broken into tenths, with the mark in the middle being longer to indicate a halfway mark. Students should learn to measure things accurately to the nearest tenth of a centimeter, then the nearest hundredth, and finally the nearest thousandth. Measurements using the metric system should always be written using the decimal system, for ex., 3.756 centimeters.

When reading a thermometer, hold it vertically at eye level. Students should check the scale of the thermometer to make certain they read it as many significant digits as possible. Thermometers with heavy or extended lines that are marked 10, 20, 30 ... should be read to the nearest 0.1 degree. Thermometers with fine lines every two degrees may be read to the nearest 0.5 degree.

In order to get an accurate reading in a liquid measuring cup, set the cup on a level surface and read it at eye level. Read the measurement at the bottom of the concave arc at the liquid's surface (the meniscus line). When measuring dry ingredients, dip the appropriate size measuring cup into the ingredient and sweep away the excess across the top with a straight-edged object.

Protractors measure angles in degrees. To measure accurately, find the center hole on the straight edge of the protractor and place it over the vertex of the angle you wish to measure. Line up the zero on the straight edge with one of the sides of the angle. Find the point where the second side of the angle intersects the curved edge of the protractor and read the number that is written at the point of intersection.

When reading an instrument such as a rain gauge, it is again important to read at eye level and at the base of the meniscus. The measuring tube is divided, marked, and labeled in tenths and hundredths. The greatest number of decimal places you will have is two.

Skill 5.5 Relate concepts of measurement, similarity, congruence, and proportionality in a real-world context.

Congruent figures have the same size and shape. If one is placed above the other, it will fit exactly. Congruent lines have the same length. Congruent angles have equal measures. The symbol for congruent is $\cong$.

Polygons (pentagons) *ABCDE* and *VWXYZ* are congruent. They are exactly the same size and shape.

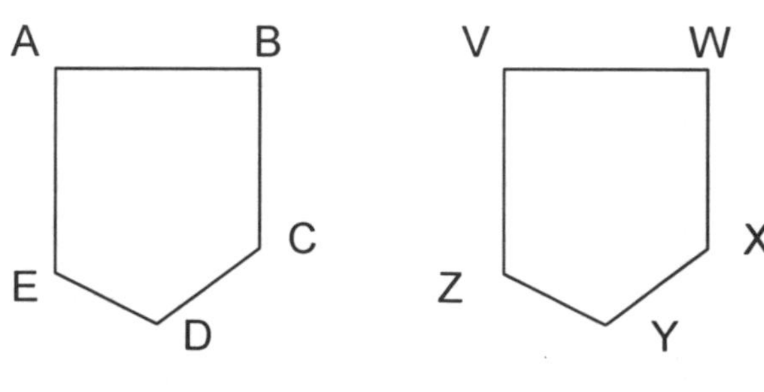

ABCDE $\cong$ *VWXYZ*

Corresponding parts are those congruent angles and congruent sides, that is:

corresponding angles	corresponding sides
$\angle A \leftrightarrow \angle V$	$AB \leftrightarrow VW$
$\angle B \leftrightarrow \angle W$	$BC \leftrightarrow WX$
$\angle C \leftrightarrow \angle X$	$CD \leftrightarrow XY$
$\angle D \leftrightarrow \angle Y$	$DE \leftrightarrow YZ$
$\angle E \leftrightarrow \angle Z$	$AE \leftrightarrow VZ$

Example: Given two similar quadrilaterals. Find the lengths of sides *x*, *y*, and *z*.

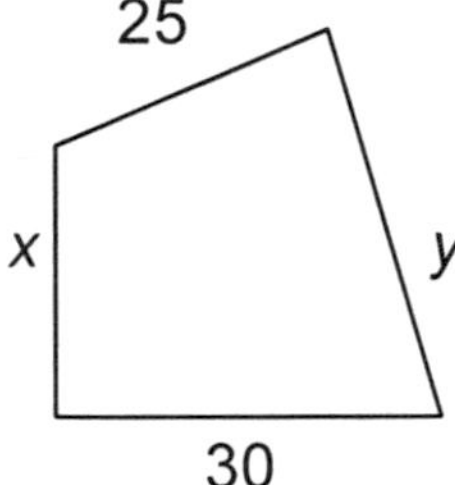

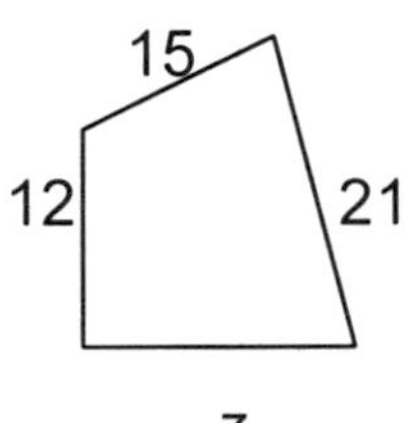

Since corresponding sides are proportional:

= so the scale is

$\frac{12}{x} = \frac{3}{5}$	$\frac{21}{y} = \frac{3}{5}$	$\frac{z}{30} = \frac{3}{5}$
$3x = 60$	$3y = 105$	$5z = 90$
$x = 20$	$y = 35$	$z = 18$

Similarity

Two figures that have the same shape are **similar**. Polygons are similar if and only if corresponding angles are congruent and corresponding sides are in proportion. Corresponding parts of similar polygons are proportional.

Example: Given the rectangles below, compare the area and perimeter.

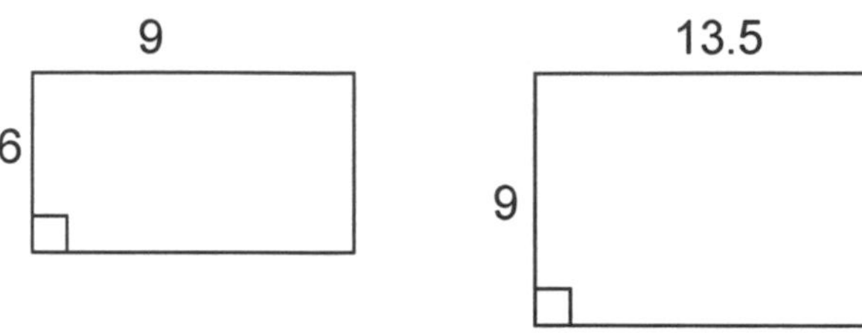

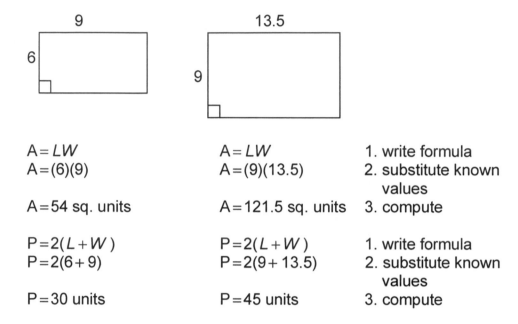

$A = LW$	$A = LW$	1. write formula
$A = (6)(9)$	$A = (9)(13.5)$	2. substitute known values
$A = 54$ sq. units	$A = 121.5$ sq. units	3. compute
$P = 2(L + W)$	$P = 2(L + W)$	1. write formula
$P = 2(6 + 9)$	$P = 2(9 + 13.5)$	2. substitute known values
$P = 30$ units	$P = 45$ units	3. compute

Notice that the areas relate to each other in the following manner:

Ratio of sides $9/13.5 = 2/3$

Multiply the first area by the square of the reciprocal $(3/2)^2$ to get the second area.

$$54 \times (3/2)^2 = 121.5$$

The perimeters relate to each other in the following manner:

Ratio of sides $9/13.5 = 2/3$

Multiply the perimeter of the first by the reciprocal of the ratio to get the perimeter of the second.

$$30 \times 3/2 = 45$$

Example: Tommy draws and cuts out 2 triangles for a school project. One of them has sides of 3, 6, and 9 inches. The other triangle has sides of 2, 4, and 6. Is there a relationship between the two triangles?

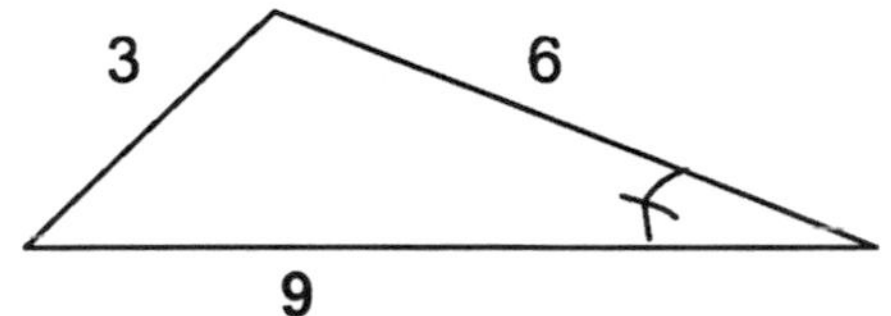

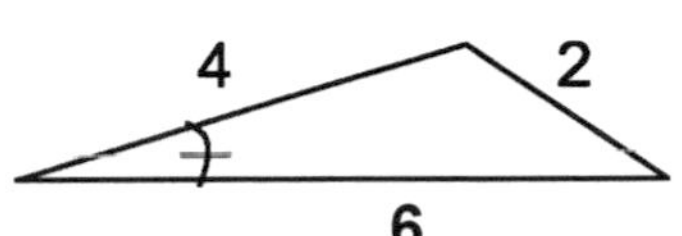

Take the proportion of the corresponding sides.

$\frac{2}{3}$ $\qquad$ $\frac{4}{6} = \frac{2}{3}$ $\qquad$ $\frac{6}{9} = \frac{2}{3}$

The smaller triangle is 2/3 the size of the large triangle.

Sample Test: Mathematics

1) Mr. Brown feeds his cat premium cat food which costs $40 per month. Approximately how much will it cost to feed her for one year? (Easy Rigorous)(Skill 1.1)

A) $500

B) $400

C) $80

D) $4800

2) Which is the better deal? (Easy Rigorous)(Skill 1.1)

A) 4 for $16.34

B) 2 for $8.45

C) 3 for $12.13

D) 1 for $4.89

3) If a horse will probably win three races out of ten, what are the odds that he will win? (Easy Rigorous)(Skill 1.1)

A) 3:10

B) 7:10

C) 3:7

D) 7:3

4) 2^{-3} is equivalent to(Moderate Rigorous)(Skill 1.2)

A) .8

B) -.8

C) 125

D) .125

5) A sofa sells for $520. If the retailer makes a 30% profit, what was the wholesale price? (Easy Rigorous)(Skill 1.2)

A) $400

B) $676

C) $490

D) $364

6) Which are the prime factors of 36? (Moderate Rigorous)(Skill 1.3)

A) 2,2,2,7

B) 2,2,3,3,3

C) 2,2,2,3,3

D) 2,2,2,2,3,3

7) Given W = whole numbers
N = natural numbers
Z = Integers
R = rational numbers
I = irrational numbers

Which of the following is not true? (Moderate Rigorous)(Skill 1.4)

A) $R \subset I$

B) $W \subset Z$

C) $Z \subset R$

D) $N \subset W$

8) Which of the following is an irrational number? (Easy Rigorous)(Skill 1.4)

A) .362626262...

B) $4\frac{1}{3}$

C) $\sqrt{5}$

D) $-\sqrt{16}$

9) Find the GCF of $2^2 \cdot 3^2 \cdot 5$ and $2^2 \cdot 3 \cdot 7$. (Rigorous)(Skill 1.6)

A) $2^5 \cdot 3^3 \cdot 5 \cdot 7$

B) $2 \cdot 3 \cdot 5 \cdot 7$

C) $2^2 \cdot 3$

D) $2^3 \cdot 3^2 \cdot 5 \cdot 7$

10) Given even numbers x and y, which could be the LCM of x and y? (Rigorous)(Skill 1.6)

A) $\frac{xy}{2}$

B) 2xy

C) 4xy

D) xy

11) If three cups of concentrate are needed to make 2 gallons of fruit punch, how many cups are needed to make 5 gallons?(Rigorous)(Skill 1.7)

A) 6 cups

B) 7 cups

C) 7.5 cups

D) 10 cups

12) Corporate salaries are listed for several employees. Which would be the best measure of central tendency? (Moderate Rigorous)(Skill 2.1)

\$24,000	\$24,000	\$26,000
\$28,000	\$30,000	\$120,000

A) mean

B) median

C) mode

D) no difference

13) Find the median of the following set of data(Easy Rigorous)(Skill 2.1)

14 3 7 6 11 20

A) 9

B) 8.5

C) 7

D) 11

14) Which statement is true about George's budget? (Easy Rigorous)(Skill 2.2)

A) George spends the greatest portion of his income on food.

B) George spends twice as much on utilities as he does on his mortgage.

C) George spends twice as much on utilities as he does on food.

D) George spends the same amount on food and utilities as he does on mortgage.

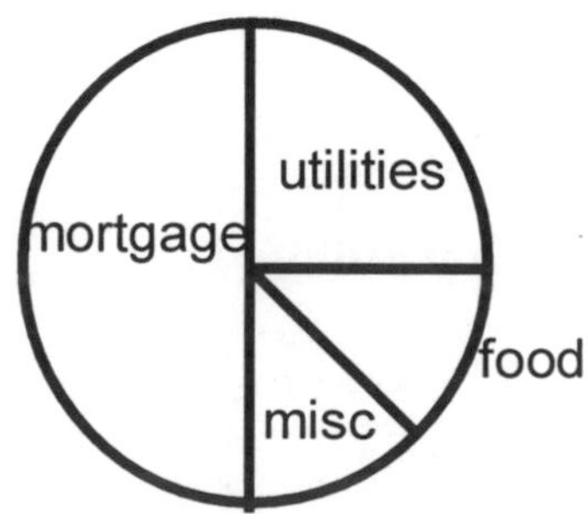

15) Given a spinner with the numbers one through eight, what is the probability that you will spin an even number or a number greater than four? (Moderate Rigorous)(Skill 2.3)

A) 1/4

B) 1/2

C) ¾

D) 1

16) Given a drawer with 5 black socks, 3 blue socks, and 2 red socks, what is the probability that you will draw two black socks in two draws in a dark room? (Moderate Rigorous)(Skill 2.4)

A) 2/9

B) 1/4

C) 17/18

D) 1/18

17) A sack of candy has 3 peppermints, 2 butterscotch drops and 3 cinnamon drops. One candy is drawn and replaced, then another candy is drawn; what is the probability that both will be butterscotch? (Moderate Rigorous)(Skill 2.4)

A) 1/2

B) 1/28

C) 1/4

D) 1/16

18) Which set illustrates a function?(Moderate Rigorous)(Figure 3.1)

A) { (0,1) (0,2) (0,3) (0,4) }

B) { (3,9) (-3,9) (4,16) (-4,16)}

C) { (1,2) (2,3) (3,4) (1,4) }

D) { (2,4) (3,6) (4,8) (4,16) }

19) Solve for x:
$3x + 5 \geq 8 + 7x$
(Rigorous)(Skill 3.3)

A) $x \geq -\frac{3}{4}$

B) $x \leq -\frac{3}{4}$

C) $x \geq \frac{3}{4}$

D) $x \leq \frac{3}{4}$

20) Solve for x:
$|2x + 3| > 4$
(Rigorous)(Skill 3.3)

A) $-\frac{7}{2} > x > \frac{1}{2}$

B) $-\frac{1}{2} > x > \frac{7}{2}$

C) $x < \frac{7}{2}$ or $x < -\frac{1}{2}$

D) $x < -\frac{7}{2}$ or $x > \frac{1}{2}$

21) $3x + 2y = 12$
$12x + 8y = 15$
(Rigorous)(Skill 3.3)

A) all real numbers

B) $x = 4$, $y = 4$

C) $x = 2$, $y = -1$

D) $\varnothing$

22) $x = 3y + 7$
$7x + 5y = 23$ (Rigorous)(Skill 3.3)

A) (-1,4)

B) (4, -1)

C) $(\frac{-29}{7}, \frac{-26}{7})$

D) (10, 1)

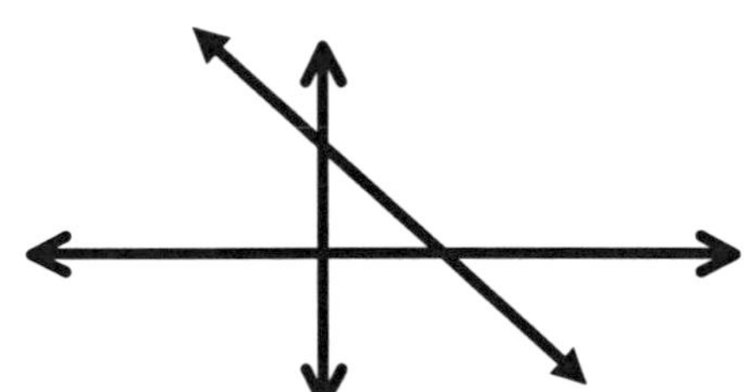

23) Three less than four times a number is five times the sum of that number and 6. Which equation could be used to solve this problem?(Moderate Rigorous)(Skill3.3)

A) $3 - 4n = 5(n + 6)$

B) $3 - 4n + 5n = 6$

C) $4n - 3 = 5n + 6$

D) $4n - 3 = 5(n + 6)$

24) Give the domain for the function over the set of real numbers: (Rigorous)(Skill 3.3)
$y = \dfrac{3x + 2}{2x - 3}$

A) all real numbers

B) all real numbers, $x \neq 0$

C) all real numbers, $x \neq -2$ or 3

D) all real numbers, $x \neq \dfrac{\pm\sqrt{6}}{2}$

25) Which equation is represented by the above graph? (Rigorous)(Skill 3.4)

A) x - y = 3

B) x - y = -3

C) x + y = 3

D) x + y = -3

26) Graph the solution: $|x| + 7 < 13$ (Moderate Rigorous)(Skill 3.4)

A) 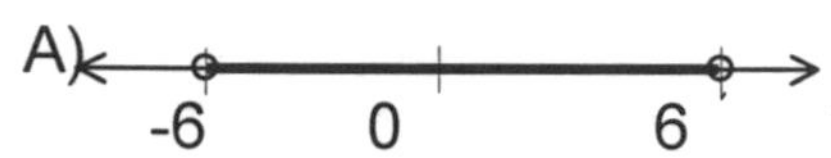

B) 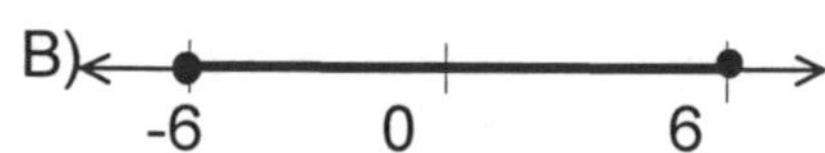

C) 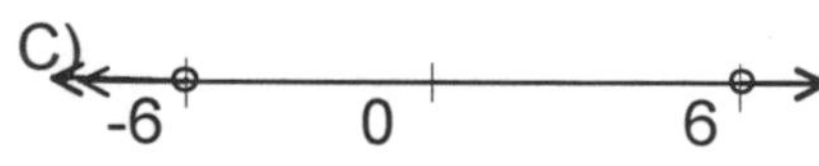

D) 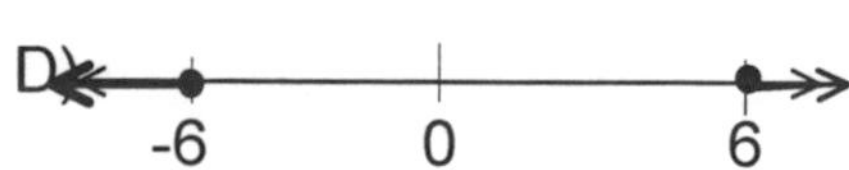

27) The fee is $42 for 5 hours work. What is the fee for 16 hours work: (Moderate Rigorous)(Skill 3.5)

A) $136.30

B) $153.70

C) $122.46

D) $134.40

28) Find the distance between (3,7) and (-3,4). (Rigorous)(Skill 3.7)

A) 9

B) 45

C) $3\sqrt{5}$

D) $5\sqrt{3}$

29) Find the midpoint of (2,5) and (7,-4). (Moderate Rigorous)(Skill 3.7)

A) (9,-1)

B) (5,9)

C) (9/2 , -1/2)

D) (9/2, 1/2)

30) Given segment AC with B as its midpoint find the coordinates of C if A = (5,7) and B = (3, 6.5). (Rigorous)(Skill 3.7)

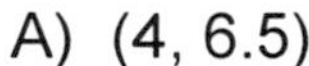

A) (4, 6.5)

B) (1, 6)

C) (2, 0.5)

D) (16, 1)

31)

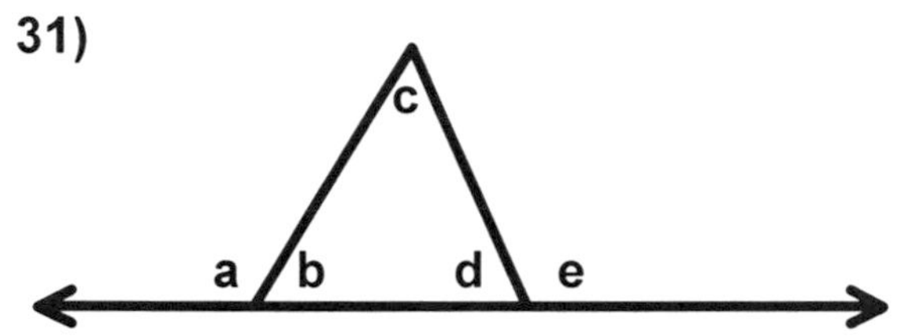

Which of the following statements is true about the number of degrees in each angle? (Easy Rigorous)(Skill 4.4)

A) a + b + c = 180°

B) a = e

C) b + c = e

D) c + d = e

32)

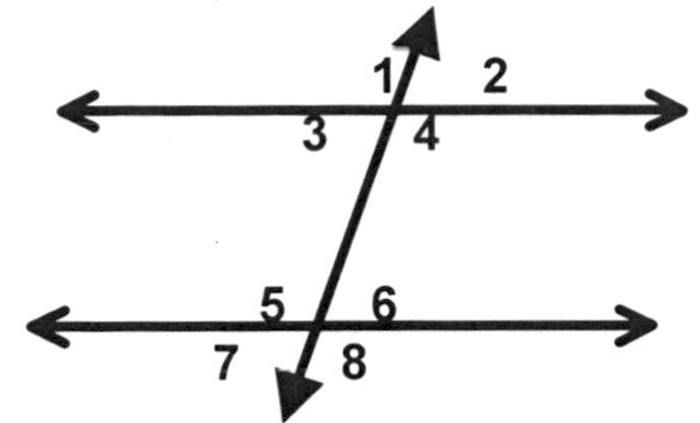

Given $l_1 \parallel l_2$ which of the following is true? (Moderate Rigorous)(Skill 4.4)

A) ∠1 and ∠8 are congruent and alternate interior angles

B) ∠2 and ∠3 are congruent and corresponding angles

C) ∠3 and ∠4 are adjacent and supplementary angles

D) ∠3 and ∠5 are adjacent and supplementary angles

33)

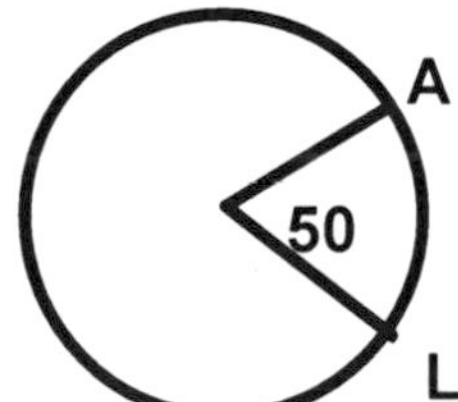

What is the measure of major arc AL ? (Moderate Rigorous)(Skill 4.5)

A) 50°

B) 25°

C) 100°

D) 310°

34)

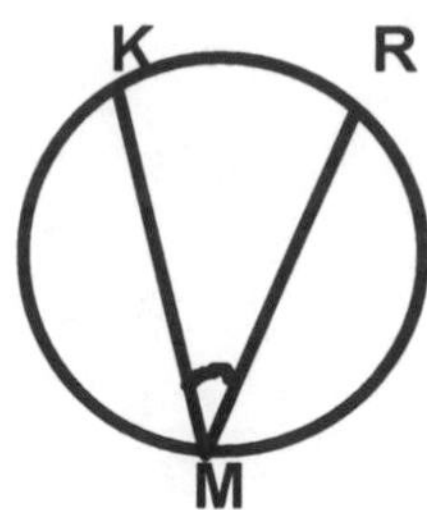

If arc KR = 70° what is the measure of ∠M? (Moderate Rigorous)(Skill 4.5)

A) 290°

B) 35°

C) 140°

D) 110°

35)

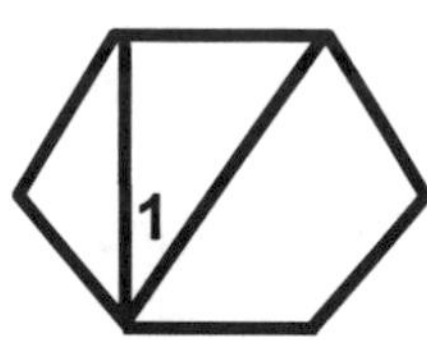

Given the regular hexagon above, determine the measure of angle ∠1. (Rigorous)(Skill 4.5)

A) 30°

B) 60°

C) 120°

D) 45°

36) **3 km is equivalent to (Easy Rigorous)(Skill 5.1)**

A) 300 cm

B) 300 m

C) 3000 cm

D) 3000 m

37) **4 square yards is equivalent To (Moderate Rigorous)(Skill 5.1)**

A) 12 square feet

B) 48 square feet

C) 36 square feet

D) 108 square feet

38) **Determine the volume of a sphere to the nearest cm if the surface area is 113 cm^2. (Rigorous)(Skill 5.2)**

A) 113 cm^3

B) 339 cm^3

C) 37.7 cm^3

D) 226 cm3

39) If a circle has an area of 25 cm2, what is its circumference to the nearest tenth of a centimeter? (Rigorous)(Skill 5.2)

A) 78.5 cm

B) 17.7 cm

C) 8.9 cm

D) 15.7 cm

40) Find the area of the figure below. (Moderate Rigorous)(Skill 5.2)

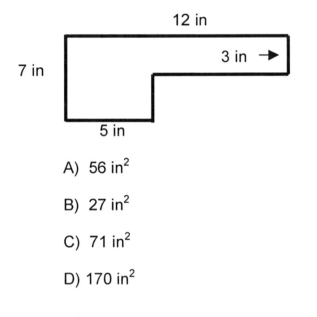

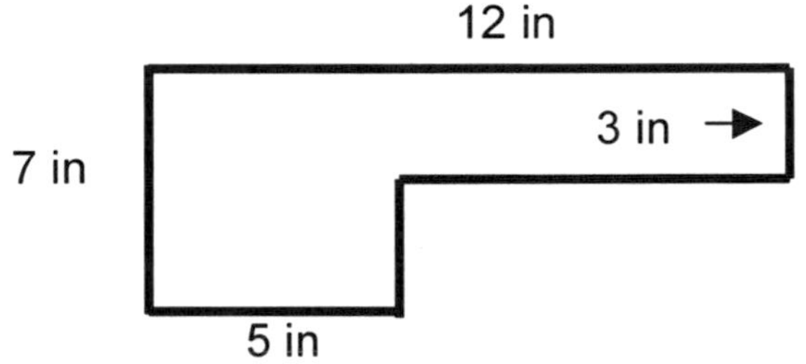

A) 56 in^2

B) 27 in^2

C) 71 in^2

D) 170 in^2

41) Given altitude AK with measurements as indicated, determine the length of AK. (Rigorous)(Skill 5.2)

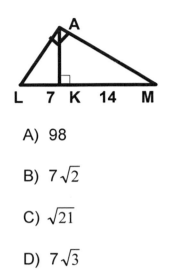

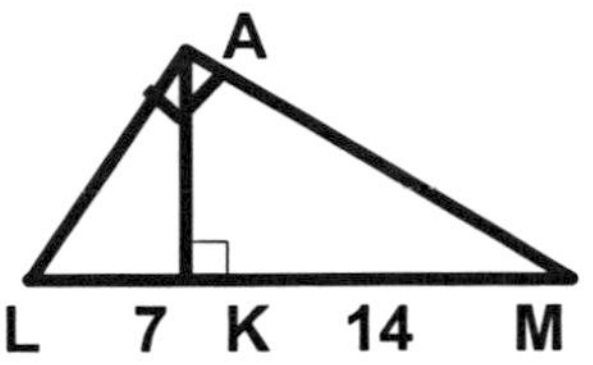

A) 98

B) $7\sqrt{2}$

C) $\sqrt{21}$

D) $7\sqrt{3}$

42) Given similar polygons with corresponding sides of lengths 9 and 15, find the perimeter of the smaller polygon if the perimeter of the larger polygon is 150 units. (Moderate Rigorous)(Skill 5.2)

A) 54

B) 135

C) 90

D) 126

43) Find the area of the shaded region given square ABCD with side AB=10m and circle E. (Rigorous)(Skill 5.2)

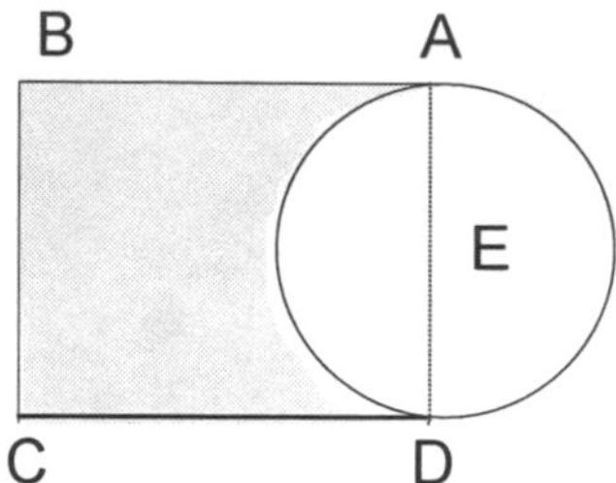

A) 178.5 m^2

B) 139.25 m^2

C) 71 m^2

D) 60.75 m^2

44) A boat travels 30 miles upstream in three hours. It makes the return trip in one and a half hours. What is the speed of the boat in still water? (Rigorous)(Skill 5.3)

A) 10 mph

B) 15 mph

C) 20 mph

D) 30 mph

45) Given similar polygons with corresponding sides 6 and 8, what is the area of the smaller if the area of the larger is 64? (Easy Rigorous)(Skill 5.3)

A) 48

B) 36

C) 144

D) 78

46) If perimeters are in a ratio of x:y, the sides are in a ratio of (Moderate Rigorous)(Skill 5.3)

A) $x : y$

B) $x^2 : y^2$

C) $2x : y$

D) $1/2\ x : y$

47) If the radius of a right circular cylinder is doubled, how does its volume change? (Rigorous)(Skill 5.3)

A) no change

B) also is doubled

C) four times the original

D) pi times the original

48) If the base of a regular square pyramid is tripled, how does its volume change? (Rigorous)(Skill 5.3)

A) double the original

B) triple the original

C) nine times the original

D) no change

49)

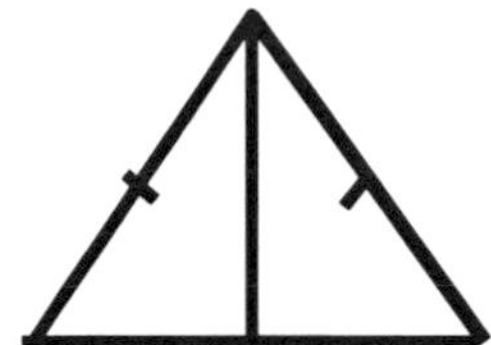

What method could be used to prove the above triangles congruent? (Moderate Rigorous)(Skill 5.5)

A) SSS

B) SAS

C) AAS

D) SSA

50)

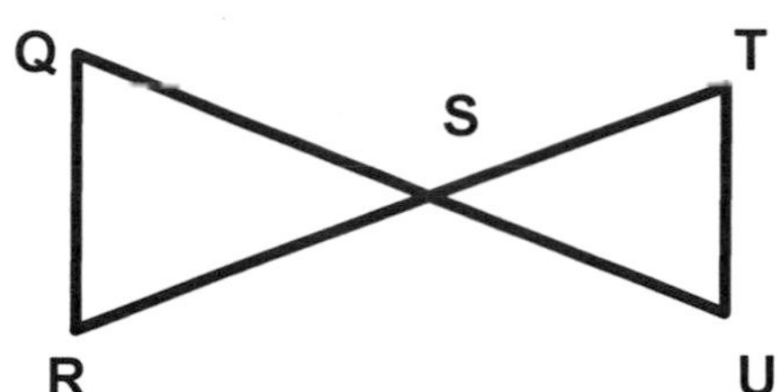

Given QS ≅ TS and RS ≅US, prove ΔQRS ≅ ΔTUS. (Rigorous)(Skill 5.5)

I) QS ≅ TS	1) Given
2) RS ≅ US	2) Given
3) ∠TSU ≅ ∠QSR	3) ?
4) ΔTSU ≅ ΔQSR	4) SAS

Give the reason which justifies step 3.

A) Congruent parts of congruent triangles are congruent

B) Reflexive axiom of equality

C) Alternate interior angle Theorem

D) Vertical angle theorem

Answer Key: Mathematics

1.	A	14.	C	27.	D	40.	A
2.	C	15.	C	28.	C	41.	B
3.	C	16.	A	29.	D	42.	C
4.	D	17.	D	30.	B	43.	D
5.	A	18.	B	31.	C	44.	B
6.	B	19.	B	32.	C	45.	B
7.	C	20.	D	33.	C	46.	A
8.	C	21.	D	34.	C	47.	C
9.	C	22.	B	35.	A	48.	B
10.	A	23.	D	36.	D	49.	B
11.	C	24.	D	37.	C	50.	D
12.	B	25.	C	38.	A		
13.	A	26.	A	39.	B		

Rigor Table: Mathematics

Easy Rigorous (20%)	Moderate Rigorous (40%)	Rigorous (40%)
1,2,3,5,8,13,14,31,36,45	4,6,7,12,15,16,17,23,26,27,29, 32,33,34,37,40,42,46,49	9,10,11,19,20,21,22,24,25, 28,30,35,38,39,41,43,44,47,48,50

Rationale with Sample Questions: Mathematics

1) Mr. Brown feeds his cat premium cat food which costs $40 per month. Approximately how much will it cost to feed her for one year? (Easy Rigorous)(Skill 1.1)

A) $500

B) $400

C) $80

D) $4800

Answer:

A) $500

12(40) = 480 which is closest to $500.

2) Which is the better deal? (Easy Rigorous)(Skill 1.1)

A) 4 for $16.34

B) 2 for $8.45

C) 3 for $12.13

D) 1 for $4.89

Answer:

A) 3 for $12.13

After dividing each number into the dollar amount, D comes to a unit price of $4.04, which is the best deal.

3) If a horse will probably win three races out of ten, what are the odds that he will win? (Easy Rigorous)(Skill 1.1)

A) 3:10

B) 7:10

C) 3:7

D) 7:3

Answer:

C) 3:7

The odds are that he will win 3 and lose 7.

4) 2^{-3} is equivalent to (Moderate Rigorous)(Skill 1.2)

A) .8

B) -.8

C) 125

D) .125

Answer:

D) .125

Express as the fraction 1/8, then convert to a decimal.

5) A sofa sells for $520. If the retailer makes a 30% profit, what was the wholesale price? (Easy Rigorous)(Skill 1.2)

A) $400

B) $676

C) $490

D) $364

Answer:

A) $400

Let x be the wholesale price, then $x + .30x = 520$, $1.30x = 520$. divide both sides by 1.30.

6) Which are the prime factors of 36? (Moderate Rigorous)(Skill 1.3)

A) 2,2,2,7

B) 2,2,3,3

C) 2,2,2,3

D) 2,2,2,3,3

Answer:

B) 2,2,3,3

Prime factors are the factors within a number that are worked down to prime numbers. $36=4\text{x}9=2\text{x}2\text{x}3\text{x}3$

7) Given W = whole numbers
N = natural numbers
Z = integers
R = rational numbers
I = irrational numbers

Which of the following is not true? (Moderate Rigorous)(Skill 1.4)

A) $R \subset I$

B) $W \subset Z$

C) $Z \subset R$

D) $N \subset W$

Answer:

C) $Z \subset R$

The rational numbers are not a subset of the irrational numbers. All of the other statements are true.

8) Which of the following is an irrational number?(Easy Rigorous)(Skill 1.4)

A) .362626262...

B) $4\frac{1}{3}$

C) $\sqrt{5}$

D) $-\sqrt{16}$

Answer:

C) $\sqrt{5}$

5 is an irrational number. A and B can both be expressed as fractions. D can be simplified to -4, an integer and rational number.

9.) Find the GCF of $2^2 \cdot 3^2 \cdot 5$ and $2^2 \cdot 3 \cdot 7$. (Rigorous)(Skill 1.6)

A) $2^5 \cdot 3^3 \cdot 5 \cdot 7$

B) $2 \cdot 3 \cdot 5 \cdot 7$

C) $2^2 \cdot 3$

D) $2^3 \cdot 3^2 \cdot 5 \cdot 7$

Answer:

C) $2^2 \cdot 3$

Choose the number of each prime factor that are in common.

10.) Given even numbers x and y, which could be the LCM of x and y? (Rigorous)(Skill 1.6)

A. A) $\frac{xy}{2}$

B. 2xy

C. 4xy

D. xy

Answer:

A. $\frac{xy}{2}$

Although choices B, C and D are common multiples, when both numbers are even, the product can be divided by two to obtain the least common multiple.

11) If three cups of concentrate are needed to make 2 gallons of fruit punch, how many cups are needed to make 5 gallons? (Rigorous)(Skill 1.7)

A) 6 cups

B) 7 cups

C) 7.5 cups

D) 10 cups

Answer:

C) 7.5 cups

Set up the proportion 3/2 = x/5, cross multiply to obtain 15=2x, then divide both sides by 2.

12) Corporate salaries are listed for several employees. Which would be the best measure of central tendency? (Moderate Rigorous)(Skill 2.1)

$24,000 $24,000 $26,000 $28,000 $30,000 $120,000

A) mean

B) median

C) mode

D) no difference

Answer:

B) median

The median provides the best measure of central tendency in this case where the mode is the lowest number and the mean would be disproportionately skewed by the outlier $120,000.

13) Find the median of the following set of data: (Easy Rigorous)(Skill 2.1)

14 3 7 6 11 20

A) 9

B) 8.5

C) 7

D) 11

Answer:

A) 9

Place the numbers is ascending order: 3 6 7 11 14 20. Find the average of the middle two numbers (7+11)12 =9.

14) Which statement is true about George's budget? (Easy Rigorous)(Skill 2.2)

A) George spends the greatest portion of his income on food.

B) George spends twice as much on utilities as he does on his mortgage.

C) George spends twice as much on utilities as he does on food.

D) George spends the same amount on food and utilities as he does on mortgage.

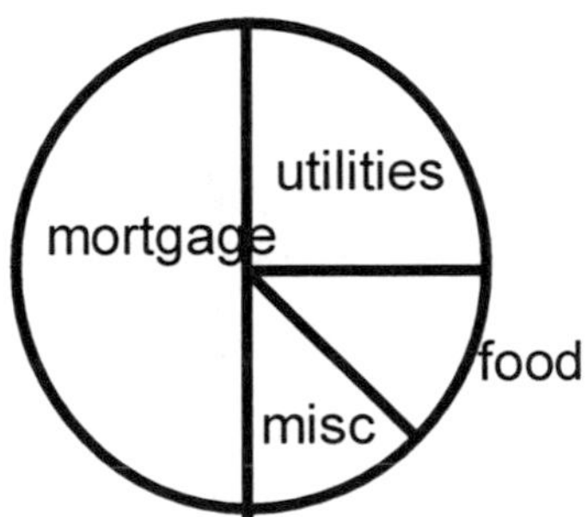

Answer:

C) George spends twice as much on utilities as he does on food.

15) Given a spinner with the numbers one through eight, what is the probability that you will spin an even number or a number greater than four? (Moderate Rigorous)(Skill 2.3)

A) 1/4

B) 1/2

C) ¾

D) 1

Answer:

C) ¾

There are 8 favorable outcomes: 2,4,5,6,7,8 and 8 possibilities. Reduce 6/8 to 3/4.

16) Given a drawer with 5 black socks, 3 blue socks, and 2 red socks, what is the probability that you will draw two black socks in two draws in a dark room? (Moderate Rigorous)(Skill 2.4)

A) 2/9

B) 1/4

C) 17/18

D) 1/18

Answer:

A) 2/9

In this example of conditional probability, the probability of drawing a black sock on the first draw is 5/10. It is implied in the problem that there is no replacement, therefore the probability of obtaining a black sock in the second draw is 4/9. Multiply the two probabilities and reduce to lowest terms.

17) A sack of candy has 3 peppermints, 2 butterscotch drops and 3 cinnamon drops. One candy is drawn and replaced, then another candy is drawn; what is the probability that both will be butterscotch? (Moderate Rigorous)(Skill 2.4)

A) 1/2

B) 1/28

C) 1/4

D) 1/16

Answer:

D) 1/16

With replacement, the probability of obtaining a butterscotch on the first draw is 2/8 and the probability of drawing a butterscotch on the second draw is also 2/8. Multiply and reduce to lowest terms.

18) Which set illustrates a function? (Moderate Rigorous)(Figure 3.1)

A) { (0,1) (0,2) (0,3) (0,4) }

B) { (3,9) (-3,9) (4,16) (-4,16)}

C) { (1,2) (2,3) (3,4) (1,4) }

D) { (2,4) (3,6) (4,8) (4,16) }

Answer:

B) { (3,9) (-3,9) (4,16) (-4,16)}

Each number in the domain can only be matched with one number in the range. A is not a function because 0 is mapped to 4 different numbers in the range. In C, 1 is mapped to two different numbers. In D, 4 is also mapped to two different numbers.

19) Solve for x: $3x + 5 \geq 8 + 7x$ (Rigorous)(Skill 3.3)

A) $x \geq -\frac{3}{4}$

B) $x \leq -\frac{3}{4}$

C) $x \geq \frac{3}{4}$

D) $x \leq \frac{3}{4}$

Answer:

B) $x \leq -\frac{3}{4}$

Using additive equality, $-3 \geq 4x$. Divide both sides by 4 to obtain $-3/4 \geq x$. Carefully determine which answer choice is equivalent.

20) Solve for x: $|2x + 3| > 4$ (Rigorous)(Skill 3.3)

A) $-\frac{7}{2} > x > \frac{1}{2}$

B) $-\frac{1}{2} > x > \frac{7}{2}$

C) $x < \frac{7}{2}$ or $x < -\frac{1}{2}$

D) $x < -\frac{7}{2}$ or $x > \frac{1}{2}$

Answer:

D) $x < -\frac{7}{2}$ or $x > \frac{1}{2}$

The quantity within the absolute value symbols must be either > 4 or < -4. Solve the two inequalities $2x + 3 > 4$ or $2x + 3 < -4$.

21) $3x + 2y = 12$
$12x + 8y = 15$ (Rigorous)(Skill 3.3)

A) all real numbers

B) $x = 4$, $y = 4$

C) $x = 2$, $y = -1$

D) $\varnothing$

Answer:

D) $\varnothing$

Multiplying the top equation by -4 and adding results in the equation $0 = -33$. Since this is a false statement, the correct choice is the null set.

22) $x = 3y + 7$
$7x + 5y = 23$ (Rigorous)(Skill 3.3)

A) (-1,4)

B) (4, -1)

C) $(\frac{-29}{7}, \frac{-26}{7})$

D) (10, 1)

Answer:

B) (4, -1)

Substituting x in the second equation results in $7(3y + 7) + 5y = 23$. Solve by distributing and grouping like terms: $26y+49 = 23$, $26y = -26$, $y = -1$ Substitute y into the first equation to obtain x.

23) Three less than four times a number is five times the sum of that number and 6. Which equation could be used to solve this problem? (Moderate Rigorous)(Skill3.3)

A) 3 - 4n = 5(n + 6)

B) 3 - 4n + 5n = 6

C) 4n - 3 = 5n + 6

D) 4n - 3 = 5(n + 6)

Answer:

D) 4n – 3 = 5(n + 6)

Be sure to enclose the sum of the number and 6 in parentheses.

24) Give the domain for the function over the set of real numbers: (Rigorous)(Skill 3.3)

$$y = \frac{3x + 2}{2x - 3}$$

A) all real numbers

B) all real numbers, $x \neq 0$

C) all real numbers, $x \neq$ -2 or 3

D) all real numbers, $x \neq \frac{\pm\sqrt{6}}{2}$

Answer:

D) all real numbers, $x \neq \frac{\pm\sqrt{6}}{2}$

Solve the denominator for 0. These values will be excluded from the domain.

$$2x^2 - 3 = 0$$
$$2x^2 = 3$$
$$x^2 = 3/2$$
$$x = \sqrt{\tfrac{3}{2}} = \sqrt{\tfrac{3}{2}} \bullet \sqrt{\tfrac{2}{2}} = \tfrac{\pm\sqrt{6}}{2}$$

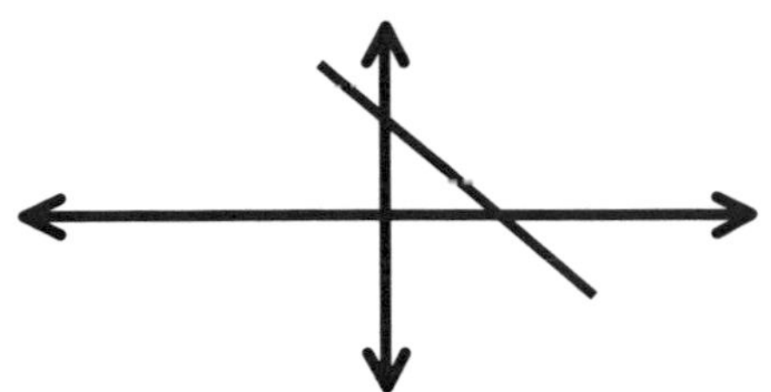

25) Which equation is represented by the above graph? (Rigorous)(Skill 3.4)

A) x - y = 3

B) x - y = -3

C) x + y = 3

D) x + y = -3

Answer:

C) x + y = 3

By looking at the graph, we can determine the slope to be -1 and the y-intercept to be 3. Write the slope intercept form of the line as y = -1x + 3. Add x to both sides to obtain x + y = 3, the equation in standard form.

26) Graph the solution: 13 (Moderate Rigorous)(Skill 3.4)

$|x| + 7 < 13$

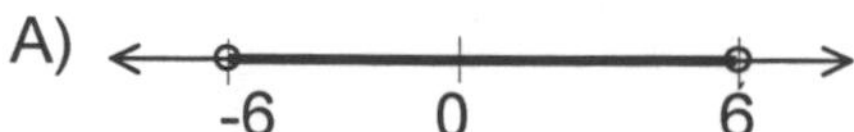

B) -6 0 6

C) -6 0 6

D) -6 0 6

Answer:

A) -6 0 6

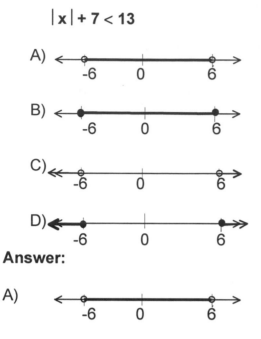

Solve by adding -7 to each side of the inequality. Since the absolute value of x is less than 6, x must be between -6 and 6. The end points are not included so the circles on the graph are hollow.

27) The fee is $42 for 5 hours work. What is the fee for 16 hours work: (Moderate Rigorous)(Skill 3.5)

A) $136.30

B) $153.70

C) $122.46

D) $134.40

Answer:

D) $134.40

The unit price is $8.40 per hour which multiplied by 16 equals $134.40.

28) Find the distance between (3,7) and (-3,4). (Rigorous)(Skill 3.7)

A) 9

B) 45

C) $3\sqrt{5}$

D) $5\sqrt{3}$

Answer:

C) $3\sqrt{5}$

Using the distance formula

$$\sqrt{[3-(-3)]^2 + (7-4)^2}$$
$$= \sqrt{36+9}$$
$$= 3\sqrt{5}$$

29) Find the midpoint of (2,5) and (7,-4). (Moderate Rigorous)(Skill 3.7)

A) (9,-1)

B) (5,9)

C) (9/2 , -1/2)

D) (9/2, 1/2)

Answer:

D) (9/2, 1/2)

Using the midpoint formula

x = (2 + 7)/2 y = (5 + -4)/2

30) Given segment AC with B as its midpoint find the coordinates of C if A = (5,7) and B = (3, 6.5). (Rigorous)(Skill 3.7)

A) (4, 6.5)

B) (1, 6)

C) (2, 0.5)

D) (16, 1)

Answer:

B) (1, 6)

31)

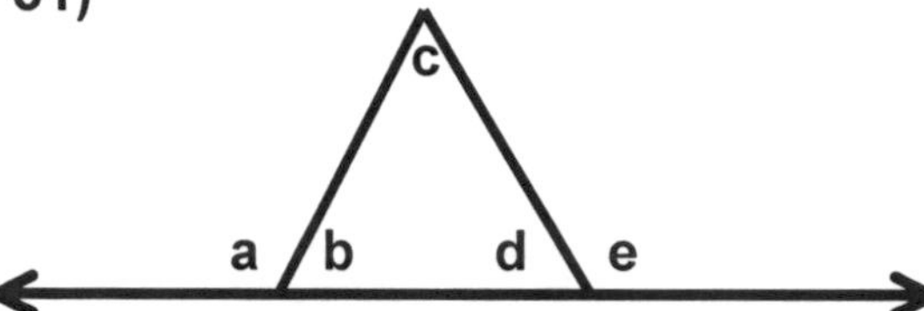

Which of the following statements is true about the number of degrees in each angle? (Easy Rigorous)(Skill 4.4)

A) $a + b + c = 180^\circ$

B) $a = e$

C) $b + c = e$

D) $c + d = e$

Answer:

C) $b + c = e$

In any triangle, an exterior angle is equal to the sum of the remote interior angles.

32)

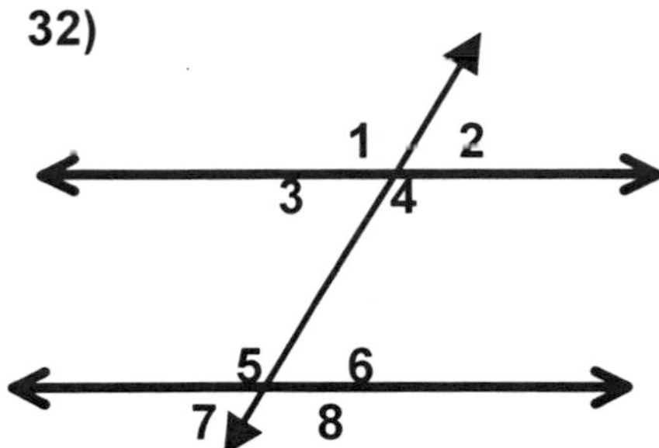

Given $l_1 \parallel l_2$ which of the following is true? (Moderate Rigorous)(Skill 4.4)

A) $\angle 1$ and $\angle 8$ are congruent and alternate interior angles

B) $\angle 2$ and $\angle 3$ are congruent and corresponding angles

C) $\angle 3$ and $\angle 4$ are adjacent and supplementary angles

D) $\angle 3$ and $\angle 5$ are adjacent and supplementary angles

Answer:

C) $\angle 3$ and $\angle 4$ are adjacent and supplementary angles

The angles in A are exterior. In B, the angles are vertical. The angles in D are consecutive, not adjacent.

33)

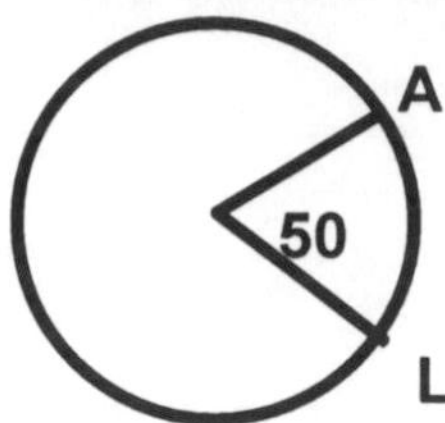

What is the measure of major arc AL? (Moderate Rigorous)(Skill 4.5)

A) 50°

B) 25°

C) 100°

D) 310°

Answer:

C) 100°

An inscribed angle is equal to one half the measure of the intercepted arc.

34)

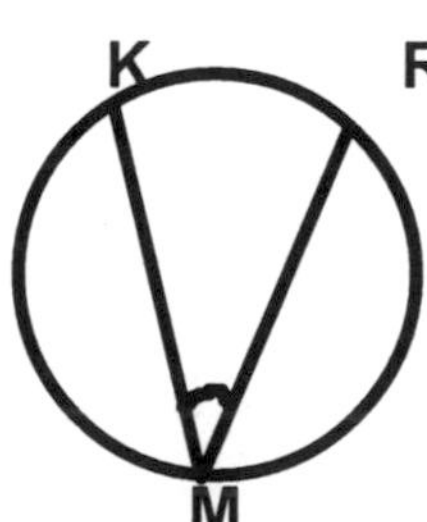

If arc KR = 70° what is the measure of ∠M? (Moderate Rigorous)(Skill 4.5)

A) 290°

B) 35°

C) 140°

D) 110°

Answer:

B) 140°

An inscribed angle is equal to one half the measure of the intercepted arc.

35) 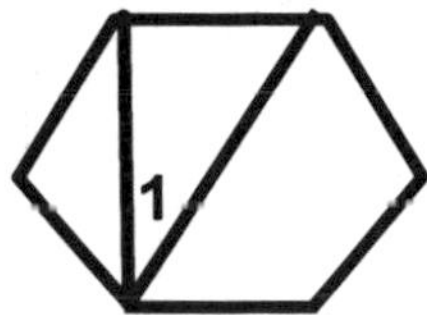

Given the regular hexagon above, determine the measure of angle ∠1. (Rigorous)(Skill 4.5)

A) 30°

B) 60°

C) 120°

D) 45°

Answer:

A) 30°

Each interior angle of the hexagon measures 120°. The isosceles triangle on the left has angles which measure 120, 30, and 30. By alternate interior angle theorem, ∠1 is also 30.

36) 3 km is equivalent to (Easy Rigorous)(Skill 5.1)

A) 300 cm

B) 300 m

C) 3000 cm

D) 3000 m

Answer:

D) 3000 m

To change kilometers to meters, move the decimal 3 places to the right.

37) 4 square yards is equivalent to:
(Moderate Rigorous)(Skill 5.1)

A) 12 square feet

B) 48 square feet

C) 36 square feet

D) 108 square feet

Answer:

C) 36 square feet

There are 9 square feet in a square yard.

38) Determine the volume of a sphere to the nearest cm if the surface area is 113 cm^2. (Rigorous)(Skill 5.2)

A) 113 cm^3

B) 339 cm^3

C) 37.7 cm^3

D) 226 cm3

Answer:

A) 113 cm^3

Solve for the radius of the sphere using $A = 4\Pi r^2$. The radius is 3. Then, find the volume using $4/3\ \Pi r^3$. Only when the radius is 3 are the volume and surface area equivalent.

39) If a circle has an area of 25 cm2, what is its circumference to the nearest tenth of a centimeter? (Rigorous)(Skill 5.2)

A) 78.5 cm

B) 17.7 cm

C) 8.9 cm

D) 15.7 cm

Answer:

B) 17.7 cm

Find the radius by solving $\Pi r^2 = 25$. Then substitute r=2.82 into $C = 2\Pi r$ to obtain the circumference.

40) Find the area of the figure below. (Rigorous)(Skill 5.2)

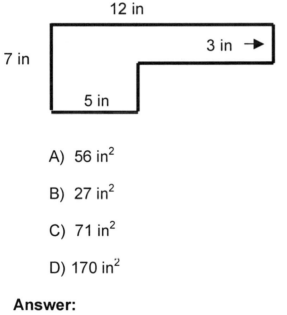

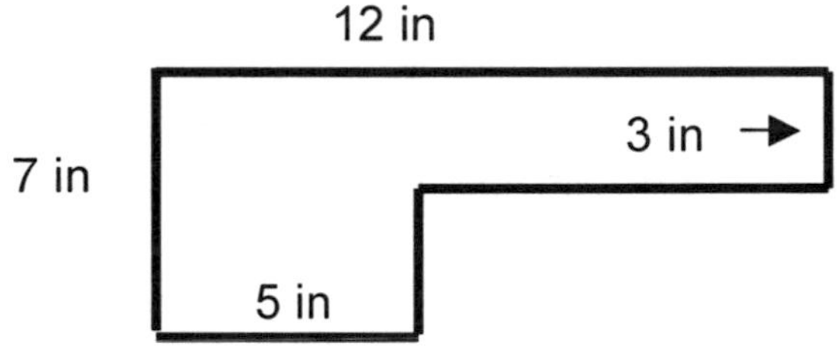

A) 56 in^2

B) 27 in^2

C) 71 in^2

D) 170 in^2

Answer:

A) 56 in^2

Divide the figure into two rectangles with a horizontal line. The area of the top rectangle is 36 in, and the bottom is 20 in.

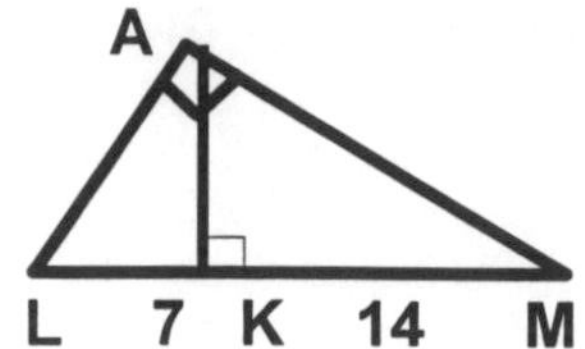

41) Given altitude AK with measurements as indicated, determine the length of AK. (Rigorous)(Skill 5.2)

A) 98

B) $7\sqrt{2}$

C) $\sqrt{21}$

D) $7\sqrt{3}$

Answer:

B) $7\sqrt{2}$

The attitude from the right angle to the hypotenuse of any right triangle is the geometric mean of the two segments which are formed. Multiply 7 x 14 and take the square root.

42) Given similar polygons with corresponding sides of lengths 9 and 15, find the perimeter of the smaller polygon if the perimeter of the larger polygon is 150 units. (Moderate Rigorous)(Skill 5.2)

A) 54

B) 135

C) 90

D) 126

Answer:

C) 90

The perimeters of similar polygons are directly proportional to the lengths of their sides, therefore 9/15 = x/150. Cross-multiply to obtain 1350 = 15x, then divide by 15 to obtain the perimeter of the smaller polygon.

43) Find the area of the shaded region given square ABCD with side AB=10m and circle E. (Rigorous) (Skill 5.2)

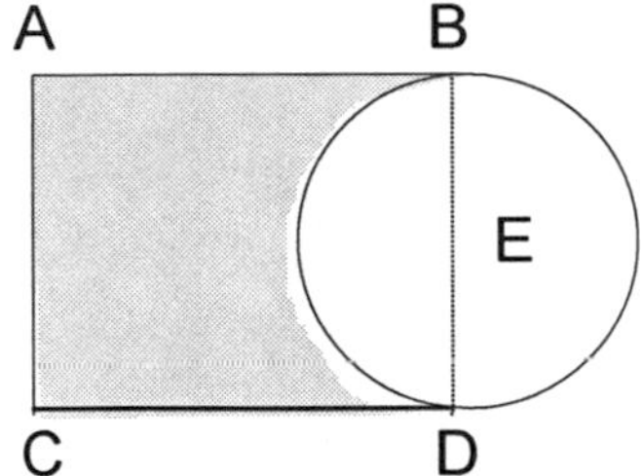

A) 178.5 m^2

B) 139.25 m^2

C) 71 m^2

D) 60.75 m^2

Answer:

D) 60.75 m^2

Find the area of the square $10^2 = 100$, then subtract 1/2 the area of the circle. The area of the circle is $\Pi r^2 = (3.14)(5)(5)=78.5$. Therefore the area of the shaded region is 100 - 39.25 - 60.75.

44) A boat travels 30 miles upstream in three hours. It makes the return trip in one and a half hours. What is the speed of the boat in still water? ? (Rigorous)(Skill 5.3)

A) 10 mph

B) 15 mph

C) 20 mph

D) 30 mph

Answer:

B) 15 mph

Let x = the speed of the boat in still water and c = the speed of the current.

	rate	time	distance
upstream	x - c	3	30
downstream	x + c	1.5	30

Solve the system:

$$3x - 3c = 30$$
$$1.5x + 1.5c = 30$$

45) Given similar polygons with corresponding sides 6 and 8, what is the area of the smaller if the area of the larger is 64? (Easy Rigorous)(Skill 5.3)

A) 48

B) 36

C) 144

D) 78

Answer:

B) 36

In similar polygons, the areas are proportional to the squares of the sides.

36/64 = x/64

46) In similar polygons, if the perimeters are in a ratio of x:y, the sides are in a ratio of: (Moderate Rigorous)(Skill 5.3)

A) x : y

B) x^2: y^2

C) 2x : y

D) 1/2 x : y

Answer:

A) x : y

The sides are in the same ratio.

47) If the radius of a right circular cylinder is doubled, how does its volume change? (Rigorous)(Skill 5.3)

A) no change

B) also is doubled

C) four times the original

D) pi times the original

Answer:

C) four times the original

If the radius of a right circular cylinder is doubled, the volume is multiplied by four because in he formula, the radius is squared, therefore the new volume is 2 x 2 or four times the original.

48) If the base of a regular square pyramid is tripled, how does its volume change? (Rigorous)(Skill 5.3

A) double the original

B) triple the original

C) nine times the original

D) no change

Answer:

B) triple the original

Using the general formula for a pyramid V = 1/3 bh, since the base is tripled and is not squared or cubed in the formula, the volume is also tripled.

49)

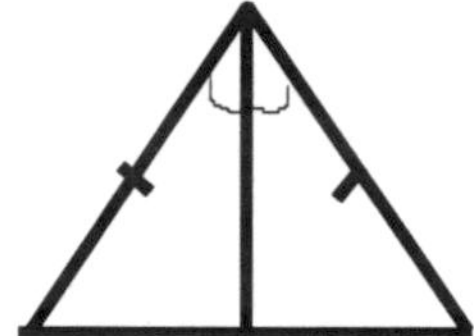

What method could be used to prove the above triangles congruent? (Moderate Rigorous)(Skill 5.5)

A) SSS

B) SAS

C) AAS

D) SSA

Answer:

B) SAS

Use SAS with the last side being the vertical line common to both triangles.

50)

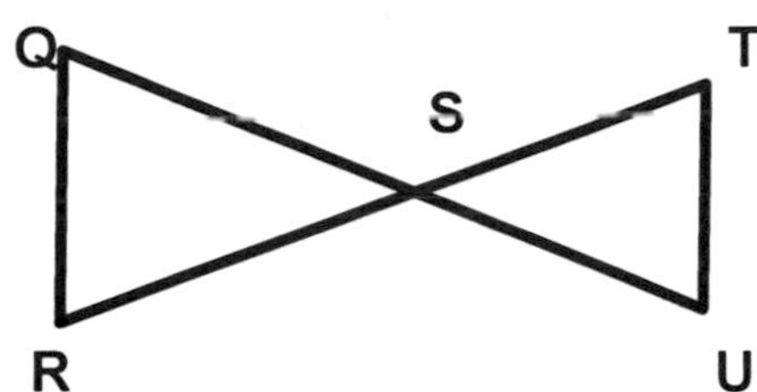

Given QS ≅ TS and RS ≅US, prove ΔQRS ≅ ΔTUS. (Rigorous)(Skill 5.5)

l) QS ≅ TS	1) Given
2) RS ≅ US	2) Given
3) ∠TSU ≅ ∠QSR	3) ?
4) ΔTSU ≅ ΔQSR	4) SAS

Give the reason which justifies step 3.

A) Congruent parts of congruent triangles are congruent

B) Reflexive axiom of equality

C) Alternate interior angle theorem

D) Vertical angle theorem

Answer:

D) Vertical angle theorem

Angles formed by intersecting lines are called vertical angles and are congruent.

DOMAIN II. GENERAL SCIENCE

COMPETENCY 6.0 KNOWLEDGE OF THE NATURE OF SCIENCE

Skill 6.1 Apply knowledge of science skills to real-world situations.

Science may be defined as a body of knowledge that is systematically derived from study, observations, and experimentation. In science, a scientist strives to **observe** a specimen or process, **infer** what may be happening, and **experiment** to test his **prediction**. The goal of this is to identify and establish principles and theories that may be applied to solve problems. Pseudoscience, on the other hand, is a belief that is not warranted. There is no scientific methodology or application. Some of the more classic examples of pseudoscience include witchcraft, alien encounters, or any topics that are explained by hearsay.

Science uses the **metric system** as it is accepted worldwide and allows easier comparison among experiments done by scientists around the world. Learn the following basic units and prefixes:

meter - measure of length
liter - measure of volume
gram - measure of mass

deca(meter, liter, gram) = 10X the base unit	**deci** = 1/10 the base unit
hecto(meter, liter, gram)= 100X the base unit	**centi** = 1/100 the base unit
kilo(meter, liter, gram) = 1000X the base unit	**milli** = 1/1000 the base unit

Graphing is an important skill to visually display collected data for analysis. The two types of graphs most commonly used are the **line graph** and the **bar graph** (histogram). Line graphs are set up to show two variables represented by one point on the graph. The X axis is the horizontal axis and represents the dependent variable. Dependent variables are those that would be present independently of the experiment. A common example of a dependent variable is time. Time proceeds regardless of the experiment. The Y axis is the vertical axis and represents the independent variable. Independent variables are manipulated by the experiment, such as the amount of light or the height of a plant.

Graphs should be calibrated at equal intervals. If one space represents one day, the next space may not represent ten days. A "best fit" line is drawn to join the points and may not include all the points in the data. Axes must always be labeled for the graph to be meaningful. A good title will describe both the dependent and the independent variable. Bar graphs are set up similarly in regards to axes, but points are not plotted. Instead, the dependent variable is set up as a bar where the X axis intersects with the Y axis. Each bar is a separate item of data and is not joined by a continuous line.

Graphing utilizes numbers to demonstrate patterns. The patterns offer a visual representation, making it easier to draw conclusions. Graphing is an excellent way of **communicating** experimental results. It lends a visual explanation, allowing others to decipher critical data. Patterns that might otherwise be missed also emerge when data points are graphed.

Classifying is the grouping of items according to their similarities. It is important for students to realize relationships and similarities as well as differences to reach a reasonable conclusion in a lab experience.

Skill 6.2 Apply knowledge of the science processes to real-world situations.

The **scientific method** is the basic process behind science. It involves several steps beginning with hypothesis formulation and working through to the conclusion.

Posing a question
Although many discoveries happen by chance, the standard thought process of a scientist begins with forming a question to research. The more limited the question, the easier it is to set up an experiment to answer it.

Form a hypothesis
Once the question is formulated, take an educated guess about the answer to the problem or question. This "best guess" is your hypothesis.

Doing the test
To make a test fair, data from an experiment must have a **variable** or condition that can be changed such as temperature or mass. A good test will try to manipulate as few variables as possible so as to see which variable is responsible for the result. This requires a second example called a **control**. A control is an extra setup in which all the conditions are the same except for the variable being tested (this would be considered normal conditions).

Observe and record the data
Reporting of the data should state specifics of how the measurements were calculated. A graduated cylinder needs to be read with proper procedures. As beginning students, technique must be part of the instructional process so as to give validity to the data.

Drawing a conclusion
After recording data, you compare your data with that of other groups. A conclusion is the judgment derived from the data results.

Skill 6.3 Apply knowledge of designing and performing investigations and using indirect evidence, models, and technology to real-world situations.

Normally, knowledge is integrated in the form of a lab report. A report has many sections. It should include a specific **title** and tell exactly what is being studied. The **abstract** is a summary of the report written at the beginning of the paper. The **purpose** should always be defined and will state the problem. The purpose should include the **hypothesis** (educated guess) of what is expected from the outcome of the experiment. The entire experiment should relate to this problem. It is important to describe exactly what was done to prove or disprove a hypothesis. A **control** is necessary to prove that the results occurred from the changed conditions and would not have happened normally. Only one variable should be manipulated at a time. **Observations** and **results** of the experiment should be recorded including all results from data. Drawings, graphs, and illustrations should be included to support information. Observations are objective, whereas analysis and interpretation is subjective. A **conclusion** should explain why the results of the experiment either proved or disproved the hypothesis.

A **scientific theory** is an explanation of a set of related observations based on a proven hypothesis. A **scientific law** usually lasts longer than a scientific theory and has more experimental data to support it.

Laboratory Techniques and Technology

Chromatography uses the principles of capillary action to separate substances such as plant pigments. Molecules of a larger size will move slower up the paper, whereas smaller molecules will move more quickly producing lines of pigments.

Spectrophotometry uses percent light absorbance to measure a color change, thus giving qualitative data a quantitative value.

Centrifugation involves spinning substances at a high speed. The more dense part of a solution will settle to the bottom of the test tube, while the lighter material will stay on top. Centrifugation is used to separate blood into blood cells and plasma, with the heavier blood cells settling to the bottom.

Electrophoresis uses electrical charges of molecules to separate them according to their size. The molecules, such as DNA or proteins, are pulled through a gel toward either the positive end of the gel box (if the material has a negative charge) or the negative end of the gel box (if the material has a positive charge).

Satellites have improved our ability to communicate and transmit radio and television signals. Navigational abilities have been greatly improved through the use of satellite signals. Sonar uses sound waves to locate objects and is especially useful underwater. The sound waves bounce off the object and are used to assist in location. Seismographs record vibrations in the Earth and allow us to measure earthquake activity.

Computer technology and graphing calculators have greatly improved the collection and interpretation of scientific data. Molecular findings have been enhanced through the use of computer images. Technology has revolutionized access to data via the internet and shared databases. Computer engineering advances have produced such products as MRIs and CT scans in medicine. Laser technology has numerous applications with refining precision. The manipulation of data is enhanced by sophisticated software capabilities. These high-tech computer systems are able to model three-dimensional atomic structures, discover complex patterns, and much more.

The use of **models** is important in science. We can create physical models (the solar system or human body you might use in your classroom) to aid in learning. We also use models to scale down or enlarge things of extreme size, for example the DNA helix that you may also be utilizing in your classroom.

Skill 6.4 Identify procedures for the appropriate and safe use, care, handling, storage, and disposal of chemicals, equipment, organisms, and other laboratory materials.

Dissections - Animals which are not obtained from recognized sources should not be used. Decaying animals or those of unknown origin may harbor pathogens and/or parasites. Specimens should be rinsed before handling. Latex gloves are desirable. If gloves are not available, students with sores or scratches should be excused from the activity. Formaldehyde is a carcinogen and should be avoided or disposed of according to district regulations. Students objecting to dissections for moral reasons should be given an alternative assignment.

Live specimens - No dissections may be performed on living mammalian vertebrates or birds. Lower-order life and invertebrates may be used. Biological experiments may be done with all animals except mammalian vertebrates or birds. No physiological harm may result to the animal. All animals housed and cared for in the school must be handled in a safe and humane manner. Animals are not to remain on school premises during extended vacations unless adequate care is provided. Many state laws stipulate that any instructor who intentionally refuses to comply with the laws may be suspended or dismissed.

Microbiology - Pathogenic organisms must never be used for experimentation. Students should adhere to the following rules at all times when working with microorganisms to avoid accidental contamination:

1. Treat all microorganisms as if they were pathogenic.
2. Maintain sterile conditions at all times.

If you are taking a national level exam, you should check the Department of Education for your state's safety procedures. You will want to know what your state expects of you not only for the test but also for performance in the classroom and for the welfare of your students.

Bunsen burners - Hot plates should be used whenever possible to avoid the risk of burns or fire. If Bunsen burners are used, the following precautions should be followed:

1. Know the location of fire extinguishers and safety blankets and train students in their use. Long hair and long sleeves should be secured and out of the way.
2. Turn the gas all the way on and make a spark with the striker. The preferred method to light burners is to use strikers rather than matches.
3. Adjust the air valve at the bottom of the Bunsen burner until the flame shows an inner cone.
4. Adjust the flow of gas to the desired flame height by using the adjustment valve.
5. Do not touch the barrel of the burner (it is hot).

Graduated Cylinder - These are used for precise measurements. They should always be placed on a flat surface. The surface of the liquid will form a meniscus (lens-shaped curve). The measurement is read at the bottom of this curve.

Balance - Electronic balances are easier to use, but they are more expensive. An electronic balance should always be used on a flat surface and tarred (returned to zero) before measuring. Substances should always be placed on a piece of paper to avoid spills and/or damage to the instrument. Triple beam balances must be used on a level surface. There are screws located at the bottom of the balance to make any adjustments. Start with the largest counterweight first and proceed toward the last notch that does not tip the balance. Do the same with the next largest, etc. until the pointer remains at zero. The total mass is the total of all the readings on the beams. Again, use paper under the substance to protect the equipment.

Buret – A buret is used to dispense precisely measured volumes of liquid. A stopcock is used to control the volume of liquid being dispensed at a time.

Light microscopes are commonly used in laboratory experiments. Several procedures should be followed to properly care for this equipment:

- Clean all lenses with lens paper only.
- Carry microscopes with two hands; one on the arm and one on the base.
- Always begin focusing on low power, then switch to higher power.
- Store microscopes with the low power objective down.
- Always use a coverslip when viewing wet mount slides.
- Bring the objective down to its lowest position then focus by moving up to avoid breaking the slide or scratching the lens.

Wet mount slides are made by placing a drop of water on the specimen and then putting a coverslip on top of the drop of water. Dropping the coverslip at a forty-five degree angle will help to avoid air bubbles. Total magnification is determined by multiplying the ocular number (usually 10X) and the objective number (usually 10X on low and 40X on high).

All laboratory solutions should be prepared as directed in the lab manual. Care should be taken to avoid contamination. All glassware should be rinsed thoroughly with distilled water before using and cleaned well after use. Safety goggles should be worn while working with glassware in case of an accident. All solutions should be made with distilled water as tap water contains dissolved particles that may affect the results of an experiment. Chemical storage should be located in a secured, dry area. Chemicals should be stored in accordance with reactability. Acids are to be locked in a separate area. Used solutions should be disposed of according to local disposal procedures. Any questions regarding safe disposal or chemical safety may be directed to the local fire department.

COMPETENCY 7.0 KNOWLEDGE OF LIVING THINGS AND THER ENVIRONMENT

Skill 7.1 Distinguish relationships between structure and function (i.e., reproduction, maintenance, growth, and regulation) in organelles, cells, and organisms.

The organization of living systems builds by levels from small to increasingly more large and complex. All aspects, whether it is a cell or an ecosystem, have the same requirements to sustain life. Life is organized from simple to complex in the following way:

> **Organelles** make up **cells,** which make up **tissues,** which make up **organs**. Groups of organs make up **organ systems**. Organ systems work together to provide life for the **organism.**

Several characteristics have been described to identify living versus non-living substances.

1. **Living things are made of cells**; they grow, are capable of reproduction, and respond to stimuli.
2. **Living things must adapt to environmental changes or perish**.
3. **Living things carry on metabolic processes**. They use and make energy.

<u>**Parts of a Eukaryotic Cell**</u>

1. Nucleus - The brain of the cell. The nucleus contains:

> **Chromosomes -** DNA, RNA, and proteins tightly coiled to conserve space while providing a large surface area.
>
> **Chromatin** - loose structure of chromosomes. Chromosomes are called chromatin when the cell is not dividing.
>
> **Nucleoli** - where ribosomes are made. These are seen as dark spots in the nucleus.
>
> **Nuclear membrane** - contains pores which let RNA out of the nucleus. The nuclear membrane is continuous with the endoplasmic reticulum which allows the membrane to expand or shrink if needed.

2. **Ribosomes** - the site of protein synthesis. Ribosomes may be free floating in the cytoplasm or attached to the endoplasmic reticulum. There may be up to a half a million ribosomes in a cell depending on how much protein is made by the cell.

3. **Endoplasmic Reticulum** - these are folded and provide a large surface area. They are the "roadway" of the cell and allow for transport of materials. The lumen of the endoplasmic reticulum helps to keep materials out of the cytoplasm and headed in the right direction. The endoplasmic reticulum is capable of building new membrane material. There are two types:

> **Smooth Endoplasmic Reticulum** - contain no ribosomes on their surface.
>
> **Rough Endoplasmic Reticulum** - contain ribosomes on their surface. This form of ER is abundant in cells that make many proteins, like in the pancreas, which produces many digestive enzymes.

4. **Golgi Complex or Golgi Apparatus** - this structure is stacked to increase surface area. The Golgi Complex functions to sort, modify, and package molecules that are made in other parts of the cell. These molecules are either sent out of the cell or to other organelles within the cell.

5. **Lysosomes** - found mainly in animal cells. These contain digestive enzymes that break down food, substances not needed, viruses, damaged cell components, and eventually the cell itself. It is believed that lysosomes are responsible for the aging process.

6. **Mitochondria** - large organelles that make ATP to supply energy to the cell. Muscle cells have many mitochondria because they use a great deal of energy. The folds inside the mitochondria are called cristae. They provide a large surface where the reactions of cellular respiration occur. Mitochondria have their own DNA and are capable of reproducing themselves if a greater demand is made for additional energy. Mitochondria are found only in animal cells.

7. **Plastids** - found in photosynthetic organisms only. They are similar to the mitochondria due to their double membrane structure. They also have their own DNA and can reproduce if increased capture of sunlight becomes necessary. There are several types of plastids:

> **Chloroplasts** – green and function in photosynthesis. They are capable of trapping sunlight.
> **Chromoplasts** - make and store yellow and orange pigments; they provide color to leaves, flowers, and fruits.
> **Amyloplasts** - store starch and are used as a food reserve. They are abundant in roots like potatoes.

8. Cell Wall - found in plant cells only, it is composed of cellulose and fibers. It is thick enough for support and protection, yet porous enough to allow water and dissolved substances to enter. Cell walls are cemented to each other.

9. Vacuoles - hold stored food and pigments. Vacuoles are very large in plants. This is allows them to fill with water in order to provide turgor pressure. Lack of turgor pressure causes a plant to wilt.

10. Cytoskeleton - composed of protein filaments attached to the plasma membrane and organelles. They provide a framework for the cell and aid in cell movement. They constantly change shape and move about. Three types of fibers make up the cytoskeleton:

> **Microtubules** - largest of the three; makes up cilia and flagella for locomotion. Flagella grow from a basal body. Some examples are sperm cells and tracheal cilia. Centrioles are also composed of microtubules. They form the spindle fibers that pull the cell apart into two cells during cell division. Centrioles are not found in the cells of higher plants.
>
> **Intermediate Filaments** - they are smaller than microtubules but larger than microfilaments. They help the cell to keep its shape.
>
> **Microfilaments** - smallest of the three, they are made of actin and small amounts of myosin (like in muscle cells). They function in cell movement such as cytoplasmic streaming, endocytosis, and ameboid movement. This structure pinches the two cells apart after cell division, forming two cells.

The structure of the cell is often related to the cell's function. Root hair cells differ from flower stamens or leaf epidermal cells. They all have different functions.

Animal cells – the nucleus as a round body inside the cell. It controls the cell's activities. The nuclear membrane contains threadlike structures called chromosomes. The genes are units that control cell activities found in the nucleus. The cytoplasm has many structures in it. Vacuoles contain the food for the cell. Other vacuoles contain waste materials. Animal cells differ from plant cells because animal cells have cell membranes.

Plant cells – have cell walls. A cell wall differs from a cell membrane. The cell membrane is very thin and is a part of the cell. The cell wall is thick and is a nonliving part of the cell. Chloroplasts, bundles of chlorophyll, are found here.

Single cells – a single celled organism is called a **protist.** When you look under a microscope, the animal-like protists are called **protozoans.** They do not have chloroplasts. They are usually classified by the way they move for food. Amoebas engulf other protists by flowing around and over them. The paramecium has a hair-like structure like a tiny oar that allows it to move back and forth searching for food. The euglena is an example of a protozoan that moves with a tail-like structure called a flagellum. Plant-like protists have cell walls and float in the ocean.

Bacteria are the simplest protists. A bacterial cell is surrounded by a cell wall, but there is no nucleus inside the cell. Most bacteria do not contain chlorophyll so they do not make their own food. The classification of bacteria is by shape. Cocci are round, bacilli are rod-shaped, and spirilla are spiral-shaped.

Plant Structure

Plant Tissues - specialization of tissues enabled plants to grow larger. Be familiar with the following tissues and their functions.

Xylem - transports water.

Phloem - transports food (glucose).

Cortex - storage of food and water.

Epidermis - protective covering.

Endodermis - controls movement between the cortex and the cell interior.

Pericycle - meristematic tissue that can divide when necessary.

Pith - storage in stems.

Sclerenchyma and collenchyma - support in stems.

Stomata - openings on the underside of leaves. They let carbon dioxide in and water out (transpiration).

Guard cells - control the size of the stomata. If the plant has to conserve water, the stomata will close.

Palisade mesophyll - contain chloroplasts in leaves; site of photosynthesis.

Spongy mesophyll - open spaces in the leaf that allow for circulation of gas.

Seed coat - protective covering on a seed.

Cotyledon - small seed leaf that emerges when the seed germinates.

Endosperm - food supply in the seed.

Apical meristem - this is an area of cell division allowing for growth.

Flowers are the reproductive organs of the plant. Know the following functions and locations:

Pedicel - supports the weight of the flower.

Receptacle - holds the floral organs at the base of the flower.

Sepals - green leaf-like parts that cover the flower prior to blooming.

Petals - contain coloration by pigments whose purpose is to attract insects to assist in pollination.

Anther - male part that produces pollen.

Filament - supports the anther; the filament and anther make up the **stamen**.

Stigma - female part that holds pollen grains that came from the male portion.

Style - tube that leads to the ovary (female).

Ovary - contains the ovules; the stigma, style and ovary make up the **carpel**.

Animal Types

Annelida - the segmented worms. The Annelida have specialized tissue. Their circulatory system is more advanced and is a closed system with blood vessels. The nephridia are their excretory organs. They are hermaphrodidic and each worm fertilizes the other upon mating. They support themselves with a hydrostatic skeleton and have circular and longitudinal muscles for movement.

Mollusca - clams, octopus, soft-bodied animals. These animals have a muscular foot for movement. They breathe through gills and most are able to make a shell for protection from predators. They have an open circulatory system with sinuses bathing the body regions.

Arthropoda - insects, crustaceans, and spiders; this is the largest group of the animal kingdom. Phylum arthropoda accounts for about 85% of all the animal species. Animals in the phylum arthropoda possess an exoskeleton made of chitin. They must molt to grow. Insects, for example, go through four stages of development. They begin as an egg, hatch into a larva, form a pupa, and then emerge as an adult. Arthropods breathe through gills, trachea, or book lungs. Movement varies with members being able to swim, fly, and crawl. There is a division of labor among the appendages (legs, antennae, etc). This is an extremely successful phylum with members occupying diverse habitats.

Echinodermata - sea urchins and starfish; these animals have spiny skin. Their habitat is marine. They have tube feet for locomotion and feeding.

Chordata - all animals with a notocord or a backbone. The classes in this phylum include Agnatha (jawless fish), Chondrichthyes (cartilage fish), Osteichthyes (bony fish), Amphibia (frogs and toads; gills which are replaced by lungs during development), Reptilia (snakes, lizards; the first to lay eggs with a protective covering), Aves (birds; warm-blooded with wings consisting of a particular shape and composition designed for flight), and Mammalia (warm blooded animals with body hair that bear their young alive and possess mammary glands for milk production).

Skill 7.2 Apply the principles of genetics, including mitosis and meiosis, Mendelian genetics, molecular biology, and patterns of inheritance, to genetic problem solving.

Gregor Mendel is recognized as the father of genetics. His work in the late 1800s is the basis of our knowledge of genetics. Although unaware of the presence of DNA or genes, Mendel realized there were factors (now known as genes) that were transferred from parents to their offspring. Mendel worked with pea plants and fertilized the plants himself, keeping track of subsequent generations which led to the Mendelian laws of genetics. Mendel found that two "factors" governed each trait, one factor from each parent. Traits or characteristics came in several forms, known as alleles. For example, the trait of flower color had white alleles and purple alleles. Mendel formed three laws:

Law of dominance - in a pair of alleles, one trait may cover up the allele of the other trait. Example: brown eyes are dominant to blue eyes.

Law of segregation - only one of the two possible alleles from each parent is passed on to the offspring from each parent. (During meiosis, the haploid number insures that half the sex cells get one allele, half get the other).

Law of independent assortment - alleles sort independently of each other. (Many combinations are possible depending on which sperm ends up with which egg. Compare this to the many combinations of hands possible when dealing a deck of cards).

Monohybrid cross - a cross using only one trait.

Dihybrid cross - a cross using two traits. More combinations are possible.

Punnet squares - these are used to show the possible ways that genes combine and indicate probability of the occurrence of a certain genotype or phenotype. One parent's genes are put at the top of the box and the other parent at the side of the box. Genes combine on the square just like numbers that are added in the addition tables we learned in elementary school.

Example: Monohybrid Cross - four possible gene combinations

Example: Dihybrid Cross - sixteen possible gene combinations

Genetic screening is now widely available and extremely useful in the detection of **genetic problems**. Some genetic disorders can be prevented. The parents can be screened for genetic disorders before the child is conceived or in the early stages of pregnancy. Genetic counselors determine the risk of producing offspring that may express a genetic disorder. The counselor reviews the family's pedigree and determines the frequency of a recessive allele. While genetic counseling is helpful for future parents, there is no certainty in the outcome.

There are some genetic disorders that can be discovered in a heterozygous parent. For example, sickle-cell anemia and cystic fibrosis alleles can be discovered in carriers by genetic testing. If the parents are carriers but decide to have children anyway, fetal testing is available during the pregnancy. There are a few techniques available to determine if a developing fetus will have the genetic disorder.

Amniocentesis is a procedure in which a needle is inserted into the uterus to extract some of the amniotic fluid surrounding the fetus. Some disorders can be detected by chemicals in the fluid. Other disorders can be detected by karyotyping cells cultured from the fluid to identify certain chromosomal defects.

A physician removes some of the fetal tissue from the placenta in a technique called **chorionic villus sampling (CVS)**. The cells are then karyotyped as they are in amniocentesis. The advantage of CVS is that the cells can be karyotyped immediately, unlike in amniocentesis which take several weeks to culture.

Unlike amniocentesis and CVS, **ultrasounds** are a non-invasive technique for detecting genetic disorders. Ultrasound can only detect physical abnormalities of the fetus.

Newborn screening is now routinely performed in the United States at birth. Phenylketonuria (PKU) is a recessively inherited disorder that does not allow children to properly break down the amino acid phenylalanine. This amino acid and its by-product accumulate in the blood to toxic levels, resulting in mental retardation. This can be prevented by screening at birth for this defect and providing the child with a special diet.

Some Definitions to Know

Dominant - the stronger of the two traits. If a dominant gene is present, it will be expressed. It is shown by a capital letter.

Recessive - the weaker of the two traits. In order for the recessive gene to be expressed, there must be two recessive genes present. It is shown by a lower case letter.

Homozygous - (purebred) having two of the same genes present; an organism may be homozygous dominant with two dominant genes or homozygous recessive with two recessive genes.

Heterozygous - (hybrid) having one dominant gene and one recessive gene. The dominant gene will be expressed due to the Law of Dominance.

Genotype - the genes the organism has. Genes are represented with letters. *AA*, *Bb*, and *tt* are examples of genotypes.

Phenotype - how the trait is expressed in an organism. Blue eyes, brown hair, and red flowers are examples of phenotypes.

Incomplete dominance - neither gene masks the other; a new phenotype is formed. For example, red flowers and white flowers may have equal strength. A heterozygote (*Rr*) would have pink flowers. If one discovers a surprise third phenotype, incomplete dominance is occurring.

Codominance - genes may form new phenotypes. The ABO blood grouping is an example of co-dominance. A and B are of equal strength and O is recessive. Therefore, type A blood may have the genotypes of AA or AO, type B blood may have the genotypes of BB or BO, type AB blood has the genotype A and B, and type O blood has two recessive O genes.

Linkage - genes that are found on the same chromosome usually appear together unless crossing over has occurred in meiosis. (Example - blue eyes paired with blonde hair)

Lethal alleles - these are usually recessive due to the early death of the offspring. If a 2:1 ratio of alleles is found in offspring, a lethal gene combination is usually the reason. Some examples of lethal alleles include sickle cell anemia, tay-sachs and cystic fibrosis. Usually the coding for an important protein is affected.

Inborn errors of metabolism - these occur when the protein affected is an enzyme. Examples include PKU (phenylketonuria) and albinism.

Polygenic characters - many alleles code for a phenotype. There may be as many as twenty genes that code for skin color. This is why there is such a variety of skin tones. Another example is height. A couple of medium height may have very tall offspring.

Sex-linked traits - the Y chromosome found only in males (XY) carries very little genetic information, whereas the X chromosome found in females (XX) carries very important information. Since men have no second X chromosome to cover up a recessive gene, the recessive trait is expressed more often in men. Women need the recessive gene on both X chromosomes to show the trait. Examples of sex-linked traits include hemophilia and color-blindness.

Sex-influenced traits - traits are influenced by the sex hormones. Male pattern baldness is an example of a sex-influenced trait. Testosterone influences the expression of the gene. Mostly men loose their hair due to this trait.

DNA and DNA Replication

The modern definition of a gene is a unit of genetic information. DNA makes up genes which in turn make up the chromosomes. DNA is wound tightly around proteins in order to conserve space. The DNA/protein combination makes up the chromosome. DNA controls the synthesis of proteins, thereby controlling the total cell activity. DNA is capable of making copies of itself.

Review of DNA structure:

1. Made of nucleotides; a five carbon sugar, phosphate group and nitrogen base (either adenine, guanine, cytosine, or thymine).

2. Consists of a sugar/phosphate backbone which is covalently bonded. The bases are joined down the center of the molecule and are attached by hydrogen bonds that are easily broken during replication.

3. The amount of adenine equals the amount of thymine and the amount of cytosine equals the amount of guanine.

4. The shape is that of a twisted ladder called a double helix. The sugar/phosphates make up the sides of the ladder and the base pairs make up the rungs of the ladder.

DNA Replication

Enzymes control each step of the replication of DNA. The molecule untwists. The hydrogen bonds between the bases break and serve as a pattern for replication. Free nucleotides found inside the nucleus join on to form a new strand. Two new identical pieces of DNA are formed. This is a very accurate process. There is only one mistake for every billion nucleotides added. This is because there are enzymes (polymerases) present that proofread the molecule. In eukaryotes, replication occurs in many places along the DNA at once. The molecule may open up at many places like a broken zipper. In prokaryotic circular plasmids, replication begins at a point on the plasmid and goes in both directions until it meets itself.

Base pairing rules are important in determining a new strand of DNA sequence. For example, say our original strand of DNA had the sequence as follows:

1. A T C G G C A A T A G C This may be called our sense strand as it contains a sequence that makes sense or codes for something. The complementary strand (or other side of the ladder) would follow base pairing rules (A bonds with T and C bonds with G) and would read:

2. T A G C C G T T A T C G When the molecule opens up and nucleotides join on, the base pairing rules create two new identical strands of DNA

1. A T C G G C A A T A G C	and	A T C G G C A A T A G C
T A G C C G T T A T C G		2.T A G C C G T T A T C G

Since it's not a perfect world, mistakes happen. Inheritable changes in DNA are called **mutations**. Mutations may be errors in replication or a spontaneous rearrangement of one or more segments by factors like radioactivity, drugs, or chemicals. The amount of the change is not as critical as where the change is. Mutations may occur on somatic or sex cells. Usually the ones on sex cells are more dangerous since they contain the basis of all information for the developing offspring. Mutations are not always bad. They are the basis of evolution, and if they make a more favorable variation that enhances the organism's survival, then they are beneficial. Mutations may also lead to abnormalities, birth defects, and even death.

There are several types of mutations. Let's suppose a normal sequence was as follows:

Normal - A B C D E F

Duplication - one gene is repeated. A B C C D E F

Inversion - a segment of the sequence is flipped around. A E D C B F

Deletion - a gene is left out. A B C E F

Insertion or Translocation - a segment from another place on the DNA is inserted in the wrong place. A B C R S D E F

Breakage - a piece is lost. A B C (DEF is lost)

Nondisjunction – This occurs during meiosis when chromosomes fail to separate properly. One sex cell may get both genes and another may get none. Depending on the chromosomes involved this may or may not be serious. Offspring end up with either an extra chromosome or are missing one. An example of nondisjunction is Down Syndrome, where three of chromosome #21 are present.

Protein Synthesis

It is necessary for cells to manufacture new proteins for growth and repair of the organism. Protein synthesis is the process that allows the DNA code to be read and carried out of the nucleus into the cytoplasm in the form of RNA. This is where the ribosomes, the sites of protein synthesis, are located. The protein is then assembled according to the instructions on the DNA. There are several types of RNA. Familiarize yourself with where they are found and their function.

Messenger RNA - (mRNA) copies the code from DNA in the nucleus and takes it to the ribosomes in the cytoplasm.

Transfer RNA - (tRNA) free floating in the cytoplasm. Its job is to carry and position amino acids for assembly on the ribosome.

Ribosomal RNA - (rRNA) found in the ribosomes. They make a place for the proteins to be made. rRNA is believed to have many important functions so much research is currently being done in this area.

Along with enzymes and amino acids, the RNA's function is to assist in the building of proteins. There are two stages of protein synthesis:

Transcription - this phase allows for the assembly of mRNA and occurs in the nucleus where the DNA is found. The DNA splits open and the mRNA reads the code and "transcribes" the sequence onto a single strand of mRNA. For example, if the code on the DNA is T A C C T C G T A C G A, the mRNA will make a complementary strand reading: A U G G A G C A U G C U (Remember, that uracil replaces thymine in RNA). Each group of three bases is called a **codon**. The codon will eventually code for a specific amino acid to be carried to the ribosome. "Start" codons begin the building of the protein and "stop" codons end transcription. When the stop codon is reached, the mRNA separates from the DNA and leaves the nucleus for the cytoplasm.

Translation - this is the assembly of the amino acids to build the protein and it occurs in the cytoplasm. The nucleotide sequence is translated to choose the correct amino acid sequence. As the rRNA translates the code at the ribosome, tRNAs that contain an **anticodon** seek out the correct amino acid and bring it back to the ribosome. For example, using the codon sequence from the example above:

the mRNA reads A U G / G A G / C A U / G C U
the anticodons are U A C / C U C / G U A / C G A
the amino acid sequence would be: Methionine (start) - Glu - His - Ala.

*Be sure to note if the table you are given is written according to the codon sequence or the anticodon sequence. It will be specified.

This whole process is accomplished through the assistance of **activating enzymes**. Each of the twenty amino acids has their own enzyme. The enzyme binds the amino acid to the tRNA. When the amino acids get close to each other on the ribosome, they bond together using peptide bonds. The start and stop codons are called nonsense codons. There is one start codon (AUG) and three stop codons. (UAA, UGA, and UAG). Additional mutations will cause the whole code to shift, thereby producing the wrong protein or, at times, no protein at all.

Skill 7.3 Identify the major steps of plant and animal physiological processes.

The purpose of cell division is to provide growth and repair in body (somatic) cells and to replenish or create sex cells for reproduction. There are two forms of cell division. **Mitosis** is the division of somatic cells and **meiosis** is the division of sex cells (eggs and sperm). The table below summarizes the major differences between the two processes.

<u>MITOSIS</u>	<u>MEIOSIS</u>
1. Division of somatic cell	1. Division of sex cells
2. Two cells result from each division	2. Four cells or polar bodies result from each division
3. Chromosome number is identical to parent cells	3. Chromosome number is half the number of parent cells
4. For cell growth and repair	4. Recombinations provide genetic diversity

<u>**Some terms to know:**</u>

Gamete - sex cell or germ cell; eggs and sperm.

Chromatin - loose chromosomes; this state is found when the cell is not dividing.

Chromosome - tightly coiled, visible chromatin; this state is found when the cell is dividing.

Homologues - chromosomes that contain the same information. They are of the same length and contain the same genes.

Diploid - 2n number; diploid chromosomes are a pair of chromosomes (somatic cells).

Haploid - 1n number; haploid chromosomes are a half of a pair (sex cells).

<u>**Mitosis**</u>

The cell cycle is the life cycle of the cell. It is divided into two stages: **Interphase** and the **mitotic division** where the cell is actively dividing. Interphase is divided into three steps: G1 (growth) period where the cell is growing and metabolizing; S period (synthesis) where new DNA and enzymes are being made; and the G2 phase (growth) where new proteins and organelles are being made to prepare for cell division. The mitotic stage consists of the stages of mitosis and the division of the cytoplasm.

The stages of mitosis and their events are as follows. Be sure to know the correct order of steps. An acronym to help you remember is IPMAT.

1. Interphase - chromatin is loose, chromosomes are replicated, cell metabolism is occurring. Interphase is technically not a stage of mitosis.

2. Prophase - once the cell enters prophase, it proceeds through the following steps continuously with no stopping. The chromatin condenses to become visible chromosomes. The nucleolus disappears and the nuclear membrane breaks apart. Mitotic spindles form that will eventually pull the chromosomes apart. They are composed of microtubules. The cytoskeleton breaks down and the spindles are pushed to the poles or opposite ends of the cell by the action of centrioles.

3. Metaphase - kinetechore fibers attach to the chromosomes which causes the chromosomes to line up in the center of the cell (think **m**iddle for **m**etaphase).

4. Anaphase - centromeres split in half and homologous chromosomes separate. The chromosomes are pulled to the poles of the cell with identical sets at either end.

5. Telophase - two nuclei each with a full set of DNA that is identical to the parent cell. The nucleoli become visible and the nuclear membrane reassembles. A cell plate is visible in plant cells, whereas a cleavage furrow is formed in animal cells. The cell is pinched into two cells. Cytokinesis, or division, of the cytoplasm and organelles occurs.

Meiosis

Meiosis contains the same five stages as mitosis, but is repeated in order to reduce the chromosome number by one half. This way, when the sperm and egg join during fertilization, the haploid number is reached. The steps of meiosis are as follows:

Prophase I - replicated chromosomes condense and pair with homologues. This forms a tetrad. Crossing over (the exchange of genetic material between homologues to further increase diversity) occurs during Prophase I.

Metaphase I - homologous sets attach to spindle fibers after lining up in the middle of the cell.

Anaphase I - sister chromatids remain joined and move to the poles of the cell.

Telophase I - two new cells are formed; chromosome number is still diploid.

Prophase II - chromosomes condense.

Metaphase II - spindle fibers form again; sister chromatids line up in center of cell; centromeres divide and sister chromatids separate.

Anaphase II - separated chromosomes move to opposite ends of cell.

Telophase II - four haploid cells form for each original sperm germ cell. One viable egg cell gets all the genetic information and three polar bodies form with no DNA. The nuclear membrane reforms and cytokinesis occurs.

Plant Physiological Processes

Photosynthesis is the process by which plants make carbohydrates from the energy of the sun, carbon dioxide, and water. Oxygen is a waste product. Photosynthesis occurs in the chloroplast where the pigment chlorophyll traps sun energy. It is divided into two major steps:

Light Reactions - Sunlight is trapped, water is split, and oxygen is given off. ATP is made and hydrogens reduce NADP to $NADPH_2$. The light reactions occur in light. The products of the light reactions enter into the dark reactions (Calvin cycle).

Dark Reactions - Carbon dioxide enters during the dark reactions. The dark reactions can occur with or without the presence of light. The energy transferred from $NADPH_2$ and ATP allows for the fixation of carbon into glucose.

Respiration - during times of decreased light, plants break down the products of photosynthesis through cellular respiration. Glucose, with the help of oxygen, breaks down and produces carbon dioxide and water as waste. Approximately fifty percent of the products of photosynthesis are used by the plant for energy.

Transpiration - water travels up the xylem of the plant through the process of transpiration. Water sticks to itself (cohesion) and to the walls of the xylem (adhesion). As it evaporates through the stomata of the leaves, the water is pulled up the column from the roots. Environmental factors such as heat and wind increase the rate of transpiration. High humidity will decrease the rate of transpiration.

Reproduction - Angiosperms are the largest group in the plant kingdom. They are the flowering plants and produce true seeds for reproduction. They arose about 70 million years ago when the dinosaurs were disappearing. The land was drying up and their ability to produce seeds that could remain dormant until conditions became acceptable allowed for their success. When compared to other plants, they also had more advanced vascular tissue and larger leaves for increased photosynthesis. Angiosperms reproduce through a method of **double fertilization,** where an ovum is fertilized by two sperm. One sperm produces the new plant, the other forms the food supply for the developing plant.

Seed dispersal - success of plant reproduction involves the seed moving away from the parent plant to decrease competition for space, water, and minerals. Seeds may be carried by wind (maple trees), water (palm trees), carried by animals (burrs), or ingested by animals and released in their feces in another area.

Animal Physiological Processes

Animal respiration takes in oxygen and gives off waste gases. For instance, a fish uses its gills to extract oxygen from the water. Bubbles are evidence that waste gasses are expelled. Respiration without oxygen is called anaerobic respiration. Anaerobic respiration in animal cells is also called lactic acid fermentation. The end product is lactic acid.

Animal reproduction can be asexual or sexual. Geese lay eggs. Animals such as bear, deer, and rabbits are born alive. Some animals reproduce frequently while others do not. Some animals only produce one baby yet others produce many (this is known as clutch size).

Animal digestion – some animals only eat meat (carnivores) while others only eat plants (herbivores). Many animals eat both (omnivores). Nature has created animals with structural adaptations so they may obtain food through sharp teeth or long facial structures. Digestion's purpose is to break down carbohydrates, fats, and proteins. Many organs are needed to digest food. The process begins with the mouth. Certain animals, such as birds, have beaks to puncture wood or allow for large fish to be consumed. The tooth structure of a beaver is designed to cut down trees. Tigers are known for their sharp teeth used to rip hides from their prey. Enzymes are catalysts that help speed up chemical reactions by lowering effective activation energy. Enzyme rate is affected by temperature, pH, and the amount of substrate present. Saliva is an enzyme that changes starches into sugars.

Animal circulation – The blood temperature of all mammals stays constant regardless of the outside temperature. This is called warm-blooded, while cold-blooded animals' (amphibians) circulation will vary with the temperature.

Skill 7.4 Differentiate structures and functions of organs and organ systems of living things.

Skeletal System - The skeletal system functions in support. Vertebrates have an endoskeleton with muscles attached to bones. Skeletal proportions are controlled by area to volume relationships. Body size and shape is limited due to the forces of gravity. Surface area is increased to improve efficiency in all organ systems. In a human, the **axial skeleton** consists of the bones of the skull and vertebrae. The **appendicular skeleton** consists of the bones of the legs, arms, tail, and shoulder girdle. Bone is a connective tissue. Parts of the bone include compact bone which gives strength, spongy bone which contains red marrow to make blood cells, yellow marrow in the center of long bones to store fat cells, and the periosteum which is the protective covering on the outside of the bone.

A **joint** is defined as a place where two bones meet. Joints enable movement. **Ligaments** attach bone to bone. **Tendons** attach bones to muscles.

Muscular System - Its function is for movement. There are three types of muscle tissue. Skeletal muscle is voluntary. These muscles are attached to bones. Smooth muscle is involuntary. It is found in organs and enable functions such as digestion and respiration. Cardiac muscle is a specialized type of smooth muscle. Muscles can only contract; therefore they work in antagonistic pairs to allow back and forward movement. Muscle fibers are made of groups of myofibrils that are made of groups of sarcomeres. Actin and myosin are proteins that make up the sarcomere.

Physiology of muscle contraction - A nerve impulse strikes a muscle fiber. This causes calcium ions to flood the sarcomere. Calcium ions allow ATP to expend energy. The myosin fibers creep along the actin, causing the muscle to contract. Once the nerve impulse has passed, calcium is pumped out and the contraction ends.

Nervous System - The neuron is the basic unit of the nervous system. It consists of an axon which carries impulses away from the cell body; the dendrite which carries impulses toward the cell body; and the cell body which contains the nucleus. Synapses are spaces between neurons. Chemicals called neurotransmitters are found close to the synapse. The myelin sheath, composed of Schwann cells, covers the neurons and provides insulation.

Physiology of the nerve impulse - Nerve action depends on depolarization and an imbalance of electrical charges across the neuron. A polarized nerve has a positive charge outside the neuron. A depolarized nerve has a negative charge outside the neuron. Neurotransmitters turn off the sodium pump which results in depolarization of the membrane. This wave of depolarization (as it moves from neuron to neuron) carries an electrical impulse. This is actually a wave of opening and closing gates that allows for the flow of ions across the synapse. Nerves have an action potential.

There is a threshold of the level of chemicals that must be met or exceeded in order for muscles to respond. This is called the "all or none" response.

The **reflex arc** is the simplest nerve response. The brain is bypassed. When a stimulus (like touching a hot stove) occurs, sensors in the hand send the message directly to the spinal cord. This stimulates motor neurons that contract the muscles to move the hand.

Voluntary nerve responses involve the brain. Receptor cells send the message to sensory neurons that lead to association neurons. The message is taken to the brain. Motor neurons are stimulated and the message is transmitted to effector cells that cause the end effect.

Organization of the Nervous System - The somatic nervous system is controlled consciously. It consists of the central nervous system (brain and spinal cord) and the peripheral nervous system (nerves that extend from the spinal cord to the muscles). The autonomic nervous system is unconsciously controlled by the hypothalamus of the brain. Smooth muscles, the heart and digestion are some processes controlled by the autonomic nervous system. The sympathetic nervous system works opposite of the parasympathetic nervous system. For example, if the sympathetic nervous system stimulates an action, the parasympathetic nervous system would end that action.

Neurotransmitters - these are chemicals released by exocytosis. Some neurotransmitters stimulate, while others inhibit, action.

Acetylcholine - the most common neurotransmitter; it controls muscle contraction and heartbeat. The enzyme acetylcholinesterase breaks it down to end the transmission.

Epinephrine - responsible for the "fight or flight" reaction. It causes an increase in heart rate and blood flow to prepare the body for action. It is also called adrenaline.

Endorphins and enkephalins - these are natural pain killers and are released during serious injury and childbirth.

Digestive System - The function of the digestive system is to break down food and absorb it into the blood stream where it can be delivered to all cells of the body for use in cellular respiration. As animals evolved, digestive systems changed from simple absorption to a system with a separate mouth and anus, capable of allowing the animal to become independent of a host.

The teeth and saliva begin digestion by breaking food down into smaller pieces and lubricating it so it can be swallowed. The lips, cheeks, and tongue form a bolus (ball) of food. It is carried down the pharynx and esophagus by the process of peristalsis (wave like contractions) and enters the stomach through the cardiac sphincter that closes to keep food from going back up. In the stomach, pepsinogen and hydrochloric acid form pepsin, the enzyme that breaks down proteins. The food is broken down further by this chemical action and is turned into chyme.

The pyloric sphincter muscle opens to allow the food to enter the small intestine. Most nutrient absorption occurs in the small intestine. Its large surface area, accomplished by its length and protrusions called villi and microvilli, allow for a great absorptive surface. Upon arrival into the small intestine, chyme is neutralized to allow the enzymes found there to function. Any food left after the trip through the small intestine enters the large intestine. The large intestine functions to reabsorb water and produce vitamin K. The feces, or remaining waste, is passed out through the anus.

Accessory organs - although not part of the digestive tract, these organs function in the production of necessary enzymes and bile. The pancreas makes many enzymes to break down food in the small intestine. The liver makes bile that breaks down and emulsifies fatty acids.

Respiratory System - This system functions in the gas exchange of oxygen (needed) and carbon dioxide (waste). It delivers oxygen to the bloodstream and picks up carbon dioxide for release out of the body. Simple animals diffuse gases from and to their environment. Gills allow aquatic animals to exchange gases in a fluid medium by removing dissolved oxygen from the water. Lungs maintain a fluid environment for gas exchange in terrestrial animals. In humans, air enters the mouth and nose where it is warmed, moistened, and filtered of dust and particles. Cilia in the trachea trap unwanted material in mucus, which can be expelled. The trachea splits into two bronchial tubes and the bronchial tubes divide into smaller and smaller bronchioles in the lungs. The internal surface of the lung is composed of alveoli which are thin-walled air sacs. These allow for a large surface area for gas exchange. The alveoli are lined with capillaries. Oxygen diffuses into the bloodstream and carbon dioxide diffuses out to be exhaled. The oxygenated blood is carried to the heart and delivered to all parts of the body. The thoracic cavity holds the lungs. The diaphragm, a muscle below the lungs, is an adaptation that makes inhalation possible. As the volume of the thoracic cavity increases, the diaphragm muscle flattens out and inhalation occurs. When the diaphragm relaxes, exhalation occurs.

Circulatory System - The function of the circulatory system is to carry oxygenated blood and nutrients to all cells of the body and return carbon dioxide waste to be expelled from the lungs. Be familiar with the parts of the heart and the path blood takes from the heart to the lungs, through the body and back to the heart. Deoxygenated blood enters the heart through the inferior and superior vena cava. The first chamber it encounters is the right atrium. It goes through the tricuspid valve to the right ventricle, on to the pulmonary arteries, and then to the lungs where it is oxygenated. It returns to the heart through the pulmonary vein into the left atrium. It travels through the bicuspid valve to the left ventricle where it is pumped to all parts of the body through the aorta.

Sinoatrial node (SA node) - the pacemaker of the heart. Located on the right atrium, it is responsible for contraction of the right and left atrium.

Atrioventricular node (AV node) - located on the left ventricle, it is responsible for contraction of the ventricles.

Blood vessels include:

Arteries - lead away from the heart. All arteries carry oxygenated blood except the pulmonary artery going to the lungs. Arteries are under high pressure.

Arterioles - arteries branch off to form these smaller passages.

Capillaries - arterioles branch off to form tiny capillaries that reach every cell. Blood moves slowest here due to the small size; only one red blood cell may pass at a time to allow for diffusion of gases into and out of cells. Nutrients are also absorbed by the cells from the capillaries.

Venules - capillaries combine to form larger venules. The vessels are now carrying waste products from the cells.

Veins - venules combine to form larger veins, leading back to the heart. Veins and venules have thinner walls than arteries because they are not under as much pressure. Veins contain valves to prevent the backward flow of blood due to gravity.

Components of the blood include:

Plasma – 60% of the blood is plasma. It contains salts called electrolytes, nutrients, and waste. It is the liquid part of blood.

Erythrocytes - also called red blood cells; they contain hemoglobin which carries oxygen molecules.

Leukocytes - also called white blood cells. White blood cells are larger than red cells. They are phagocytic and can engulf invaders. White blood cells are not confined to the blood vessels and can enter the interstitial fluid between cells.

Platelets - assist in blood clotting. Platelets are made in the bone marrow.

Blood clotting - the neurotransmitter that initiates blood vessel constriction following an injury is called serotonin. A material called prothrombin is converted to thrombin with the help of thromboplastin. The thrombin is then used to convert fibrinogen to fibrin which traps red blood cells to form a scab and stop blood flow.

Lymphatic System (Immune System)

Nonspecific defense mechanisms – They do not target specific pathogens but are a whole body response. Results of nonspecific mechanisms are seen as symptoms of an infection. These mechanisms include the skin, mucous membranes, and cells of the blood and lymph (ie: white blood cells, macrophages). Fever is a result of an increase in white blood cells. Pyrogens are released by white blood cells which then set the body's thermostat to a higher temperature. This inhibits the growth of microorganisms. It also increases metabolism to increase phagocytosis and body repair.

Specific defense mechanisms - They recognize foreign material and respond by destroying the invader. These mechanisms are specific in purpose and diverse in type. They are able to recognize individual pathogens. They are able to differentiate between foreign material and self. Memory of the invaders provides immunity upon further exposure.

Antigen - any foreign particle that invades the body.

Antibody - manufactured by the body, they recognize and latch onto antigens, hopefully destroying them.

Immunity - this is the body's ability to recognize and destroy an antigen before it causes harm. Active immunity develops after recovery from an infectious disease (chicken pox) or after a vaccination (mumps, measles, rubella). Passive immunity may be passed from one individual to another. It is not permanent. A good example is the immunities passed from mother to nursing child.

Excretory System

The function of the excretory system is to rid the body of nitrogenous wastes in the form of urea. The functional units of excretion are the nephrons which make up the kidneys. Antidiuretic hormone (ADH), which is made in the hypothalamus and stored in the pituitary, is released when differences in osmotic balance occur. This will cause more water to be reabsorbed. As the blood becomes more dilute, ADH release ceases.

The Bowman's capsule contains the glomerulus, a tightly packed group of capillaries. The glomerulus is under high pressure. Waste and fluids leak out due to pressure. Filtration is not selective in this area. Selective secretion by active and passive transport occur in the proximal convoluted tubule. Unwanted molecules are secreted into the filtrate. Selective secretion also occurs in the loop of Henle. Salt is actively pumped out of the tube and much water is lost due to the hyperosmosity of the inner part (medulla) of the kidney. As the fluid enters the distal convoluted tubule, more water is reabsorbed. Urine forms in the collecting duct that leads to the ureter then to the bladder where it is stored. Urine is passed from the bladder through the urethra. The amount of water reabsorbed back into the body is dependent upon how much water or fluids an individual has consumed. Urine can be very dilute or very concentrated if dehydration is present.

Endocrine System

The function of the endocrine system is to manufacture proteins called hormones. Hormones are released into the bloodstream and are carried to a target tissue where they stimulate an action. Hormones may build up over time to cause their effect (for example, as in puberty or the menstrual cycle).

Hormone activation - Hormones are specific and fit receptors on the target tissue cell surface. The receptor activates an enzyme that converts ATP to cyclic AMP. Cyclic AMP (cAMP) is a second messenger from the cell membrane to the nucleus. The genes found in the nucleus turn on or off to cause a specific response.

There are two classes of hormones. **Steroid hormones** come from cholesterol. Steroid hormones cause sexual characteristics and mating behavior. Hormones include estrogen and progesterone in females and testosterone in males.

Peptide hormones are made in the pituitary, adrenal glands (kidneys), and the pancreas. They include the following:

Follicle stimulating hormone (FSH) - production of sperm or egg cells

Luteinizing hormone (LH) - functions in ovulation

Luteotropic hormone (LTH) - assists in production of progesterone

Growth hormone (GH) - stimulates growth

Antidiuretic hormone (ADH) - assists in retention of water

Oxytocin - stimulates labor contractions at birth and let-down of milk

Melatonin - regulates circadian rhythms and seasonal changes

Epinephrine (adrenaline) - causes fight or flight reaction of the nervous system

Thyroxin - increases metabolic rate

Calcitonin - removes calcium from the blood

Insulin - decreases glucose level in blood

Glucagon - increases glucose level in blood

Hormones work on a feedback system. The increase or decrease in one hormone may cause the increase or decrease in another. Release of hormones causes a specific response.

Reproductive System

Sexual reproduction greatly increases diversity due to the many combinations possible through meiosis and fertilization. Gametogenesis is the production of the sperm and egg cells. Spermatogenesis begins at puberty in the male. One spermatozoa produces four sperm. The sperm mature in the seminiferous tubules located in the testes. Oogenesis, the production of egg cells, is usually complete by the birth of a female. Egg cells are not released until menstruation begins at puberty. Meiosis forms one ovum with all the cytoplasm and three polar bodies that are reabsorbed by the body. The ovum are stored in the ovaries and released each month from puberty to menopause.

Path of the sperm - sperm are stored in the seminiferous tubules in the testes where they mature. Mature sperm are found in the epididymis located on top of the testes. After ejaculation, the sperm travels up the vas deferens where they mix with semen made in the prostate and seminal vesicles and travel out the urethra.

Path of the egg - eggs are stored in the ovaries. Ovulation releases the egg into the fallopian tubes that are ciliated to move the egg along. Fertilization normally occurs in the fallopian tube. If pregnancy does not occur, the egg passes through the uterus and is expelled through the vagina during menstruation. Levels of progesterone and estrogen stimulate menstruation. In the event of pregnancy, hormonal levels are affected by the implantation of a fertilized egg, so menstruation does not occur.

Pregnancy - if fertilization occurs, the zygote implants about two to three days later in the uterus. Implantation promotes secretion of human chorionic gonadotropin (HCG). This is what is detected in pregnancy tests. The HCG keeps the level of progesterone elevated to maintain the uterine lining in order to feed the developing embryo until the umbilical cord forms. Labor is initiated by oxytocin, which causes labor contractions and dilation of the cervix. Prolactin and oxytocin cause the production of milk.

Skill 7.5 Identify reliable sources of health information and concepts and behaviors related to health promotion and disease prevention.

Good nutrition is paramount in maintaining health for growth and development. A balanced diet includes foods from the major food groups of carbohydrates, proteins, lipids, fruits and vegetables, and sufficient quantities of vitamins and minerals.

Body pollutants, such as tobacco, drugs, and alcohol, interfere with the absorption of nutrients and also may interfere with physical and mental development. They may also damage developing organs, leading to lifelong diseases such as emphysema or asthma.

Exercise is important to maintain a healthy heart and lungs, as well as circulatory and muscular systems. It also helps to alleviate stress which is known to be harmful to a person, both mentally and physically. It is widely recommended that physical activity be conducted at least three times per week for a duration of at least 30 minutes per session. Heart rate during exercise should reach 65-85% of your maximum heart rate (calculate this by determining your pulse for a length of 15 seconds once you have been exercising for ten minutes, then multiply that pulse by four, this is your maximum heart rate).

Reliable sources of health information include, but are not limited to, accredited medical institutions and organizations. For example, if you wanted to find out how to have a healthy heart, a reliable place to acquire information would be the American Heart Association. A great way to assure your own health is to attend regular check-ups with a trusted physician. S/he is also a valuable source of health information.

Skill 7.6 Identify patterns of animal behavior

Animal Behavior is responsible for courtship leading to mating, communication between species, territoriality, aggression between animals, and dominance within a group. Behaviors may include body posture, mating calls, display of feathers/fur, coloration, or baring of teeth and claws.

Innate behavior - behaviors that are inborn or instinctual. An environmental stimulus such as the length of day or temperature results in a behavior. Hibernation among some animals is an innate behavior.

Learned behavior - behavior that is modified due to past experience is called learned behavior.

Territorial behavior - A territory is an area considered by an animal to be in its possession. An organism which defends that area against intrusion is said to be territorial. Common displays of territorial behavior include scratching, hissing, baring of teeth, and charging. An animal that marks his area with his scent (urine) is also practicing territorial behavior.

Social behavior - behavior occurring between animals in a group setting. For example, when one sees monkeys preening each other, that is social behavior. Being part of an established group or pack, hunting together, and resting together are social behaviors. Additional social behaviors include mating rituals. Examples of mating rituals are plumage exhibitions and vocalizations.

Communicative behavior - any behavior that sends a message to another animal. Sometimes this is aggressive (stay away), sometimes this is courtship (seeking attention), and sometimes it is a vocal call (many animal groups send out long reaching calls of fear).

Skill 7.7 Identify current issues and effective methods of conservation of natural resources.

A **renewable resource** is one that is replaced naturally. Living renewable resources are plants and animals. Plants are renewable because they grow and reproduce. Sometimes renewal of the resource doesn't keep up with the demand. Such is the case with trees. Since the housing industry uses lumber for frames and homebuilding, they are often cut down faster than new trees can grow. Now there are specific tree farms and special methods that allow trees to grow faster.

A second renewable resource is animals. They renew by the process of reproduction. Some wild animals need the protection of a wildlife refuge. As the population of humans increases, resources are used faster. Cattle are used for their hides and for food. Some animals, like deer, are killed for sport. Each state has an environmental protection agency with divisions of forest management and wildlife management.

Non-living renewable resources would be water, air, and soil. Water is renewed in a natural cycle called the water cycle. Air is a mixture of gases. Oxygen is given off by plants and taken in by animals that in turn expel the carbon dioxide that the plants need. Soil is another renewable resource. Fertile soil is rich in minerals. When plants grow they remove the minerals and make the soil less fertile. Chemical treatments are one way of renewing the soil composition. It is also accomplished naturally when the plants decay back into the soil. The plant material is used to make compost to mix with the soil.

Nonrenewable resources are not easily replaced in a timely fashion. Minerals are nonrenewable resources. Quartz, mica, salt, and sulfur are some examples. Mining depletes these resources so society may benefit. Glass is made from quartz, electronic equipment from mica, and salt, which has many uses, some more examples of how we use minerals. Sulfur is used in medicine, fertilizers, paper, and matches. Metals are among the most widely used nonrenewable resource. Metals must be separated from the ore. Iron is our most important ore. Gold, silver, and copper are often found in a more pure form called native metals.

Water storage

Precipitation that soaks into the ground through small pores or openings becomes **groundwater**. Gravity causes groundwater to move through interconnected porous rock formations from higher to lower elevations. The upper surface of the zone saturated with groundwater is the water table. A swamp is an area where the water table is at the surface. Sometimes the land dips below the water table and these areas fill with water forming lakes, ponds, or streams. Groundwater that flows out from underground onto the surface is called a spring.

Permeable rocks filled with water are called **aquifers**. When a layer of permeable rock is trapped between two layers of impermeable rock, an aquifer is formed. Groundwater fills the porous spaces in the permeable rock. Layers of limestone are common aquifers.

Groundwater provides drinking water for 53% of the population in the United States and is collected in **reservoirs.** Much groundwater is clean enough to drink without any type of treatment because impurities in the water are filtered out by the rocks and soil through which it flows. However, many groundwater sources are becoming contaminated. Septic tanks, broken pipes, agriculture fertilizers, garbage dumps, rainwater runoff, and leaking underground tanks all pollute groundwater. Toxic chemicals from farmland mix with groundwater. Removal of large volumes of groundwater can cause collapse of soil and rock underground, causing the ground to sink. Along shorelines, excessive depletion of underground water supplies allows the intrusion of salt water into the fresh water field. The groundwater supply becomes undrinkable.

Pollutants are impurities in air and water that may be harmful to life. Spills from barges carrying large quantities of oil pollute beaches and harm all marine life.

All acids contain hydrogen. Acidic substances from factories and car exhausts dissolve in rain forming **acid rain.** Acid rain forms predominantly from pollutant oxides in the air (usually nitrogen-based NO_x or sulfur-based SO_x) which become hydrated into their acids (nitric or sulfuric acid). When the rain falls onto stone, the acids can react with metallic compounds, gradually wearing the stone away.

Radioactivity is the breaking down of atomic nuclei by releasing particles or electromagnetic radiation. Radioactive nuclei give off radiation in the form of streams of particles or energy. Alpha particles are positively charged particles consisting of two protons and two neutrons. It is the slowest form of radiation. It can be stopped by a piece of paper. Beta particles are electrons. It is produced when a neutron in the nucleus breaks up into a proton and an electron. The proton remains inside the nucleus, increasing its atomic number by one. But the electron is given off. They can be stopped by aluminum. Gamma rays are electromagnetic waves with extremely short wavelengths. They have no mass. They have no charge so they are not deflected by an electric field. Gamma rays travel at the speed of light. It takes a thick block of lead to stop them. Uranium is a source of radiation and therefore is radioactive. Marie Curie discovered new elements called radium and polonium that actually give off more radiation than uranium.

The major concern with radioactivity is in the case of a nuclear disaster. Medical misuse is also a threat. Radioactivity ionizes the air it travels through. It is strong enough to kill cancer cells or dangerous enough to cause illness or even death. Gamma rays can penetrate the body and damage cells. Protective clothing is needed when working with gamma rays. Electricity from nuclear energy uses uranium 235. The devastation of the Russian nuclear power plant disaster has evacuated entire regions as the damage to the land and food source will last for hundreds of years.

Skill 7.8 Identify the results of interactions of biotic and abiotic factors in the environment.

- **Biotic factors** - living things in an ecosystem such as plants, animals, bacteria, fungi, etc. If one population in a community increases, it affects the ability of another population to succeed by limiting the available amount of food, water, shelter, and space.
- **Abiotic factors** - non-living aspects of an ecosystem such as soil quality, rainfall, and temperature. Changes in climate and soil can cause effects at the beginning of the food chain, thus limiting or accelerating the growth of populations.
- **Succession** - when one population replaces another. This occurs due to a change in habitat, change in population size, or a large event such as a forest fire or landslide. While many individuals are lost, nature periodically makes room for the growth of new communities.

Definitions of feeding relationships:

Parasitism - two species that occupy a similar place; the parasite benefits from the relationship, the host is harmed.

Commensalism - two species that occupy a similar place; neither species is harmed nor benefits from the relationship.

Mutualism (symbiosis) - two species that occupy a similar place; both species benefit from the relationship.

Competition - two species that occupy the same habitat or eat the same food are said to be in competition with each other.

Predation - animals that eat other animals are called predators. The animals they feed on are called the prey. Population growth depends upon competition for food, water, shelter, and space. The amount of predators determines the amount of prey, which in turn affects the number of predators.

Carrying Capacity - this is the total amount of life a habitat can support. Once the habitat runs out of food, water, shelter, or space, the carrying capacity decreases and then stabilizes.

Ecological Problems - nonrenewable resources are fragile and must be conserved for use in the future. Man's impact and knowledge of conservation will control the future.

Biological magnification - chemicals and pesticides accumulate along the food chain. Tertiary consumers have more accumulated toxins than animals at the bottom of the food chain.

Simplification of the food web - Three major crops feed the world (rice, corn, and wheat). The planting of these foods wipes out habitats and pushes animals residing there into other habitats causing overpopulation or extinction.

Fuel sources - strip mining and the overuse of oil reserves have depleted these resources. At the current rate of consumption, conservation or alternate fuel sources will guarantee our future fuel sources.

Global warming - rainforest depletion and the use of fossil fuels and aerosols have caused an increase in carbon dioxide production. This leads to a decrease in the amount of oxygen that is directly proportional to the amount of ozone. As the ozone layer depletes, more heat enters our atmosphere and is trapped. This causes an overall warming effect that may eventually melt polar ice caps, causing a rise in water levels and changes in climate which will affect weather systems world-wide.

Endangered species - construction of homes to house people in our overpopulated world has caused the destruction of habitat for other animals leading to their extinction.

Overpopulation - the human race is still growing at an exponential rate. Carrying capacity has not been met due to our ability to use technology to produce more food and housing. Space and water cannot be manufactured and eventually our non-renewable resources will reach a crisis state. Our overuse affects every living thing on this planet.

Skill 7.9 Identify the major characteristics of world biomes and communities and the interrelationships of the organisms within them.

Ecology is the study of organisms, where they live, and their interactions with the environment. A **population** is a group of the same species in a specific area. A **community** is a group of populations residing in the same area. Communities that are ecologically similar in regards to temperature, rainfall, and the species that live there are called **biomes**. Specific biomes include:

Marine - covers 75% of Earth. This biome is organized by the depth of the water. The intertidal zone is from the tide line to the edge of the water. The littoral zone is from the water's edge to the open sea. It includes coral reef habitats and is the most densely populated area of the marine biome. The open sea zone is divided into the epipelagic zone and the pelagic zone. The epipelagic zone receives more sunlight and has a larger number of species. The ocean floor is called the benthic zone and is populated with bottom feeders.

Tropical Rain Forest - temperature is constant (25 degrees C) and rainfall exceeds 200 cm. per year. Located around the area of the equator, the rain forest has abundant, diverse species of plants and animals.

Savanna - temperatures range from 0-25 degrees C depending on the location. Rainfall is from 90 to 150 cm per year. Plants include shrubs and grasses. The savanna is a transitional biome between the rain forest and the desert.

Desert - temperatures range from 10-38 degrees C. Rainfall is under 25 cm per year. Plant species include xerophytes and succulents. Lizards, snakes, and small mammals are common animals.

Temperate Deciduous Forest - temperature ranges from -24 to 38 degrees C. Rainfall is between 65 and 150 cm per year. Deciduous trees are common, as well as deer, bear and squirrels.

Taiga - temperatures range from -24 to 22 degrees C. Rainfall is between 35 and 40 cm per year. Taiga is located very north and very south of the equator, getting close to the poles. Plant life includes conifers and plants that can withstand harsh winters. Animals include weasels, mink, and moose.

Tundra - temperatures range from -28 to 15 degrees C. Rainfall is limited, ranging from 10 to 15 cm per year. The tundra is located even further north and south than the taiga. Common plants include lichens and mosses. Animals include polar bears and musk ox.

Polar or Permafrost - temperature ranges from -40 to 0 degrees C. It rarely gets above freezing. Rainfall is below 10 cm per year. Most water is bound up as ice. Life is limited.

COMPETENCY 8.0 KNOWLEDGE OF THE FORCES OF EARTH AND SPACE

Skill 8.1 Identify the characteristics of geologic structures and the mechanisms by which they were formed.

Data obtained from many sources led scientists to develop the theory of plate tectonics. This theory is the most current model that explains not only the movement of the continents, but also the changes in Earth's crust caused by internal forces.

Plates are rigid blocks of Earth's crust and upper mantle. These solid blocks make up the lithosphere. The Earth's lithosphere is broken into nine large sections and several small ones. These moving slabs are called plates. The major plates are named after the continents they are "transporting."

The plates float on and move with a layer of hot, plastic-like rock in the upper mantle. Geologists believe that the heat currents circulating within the mantle cause this plastic zone of rock to slowly flow, carrying along the overlying crustal plates.

Movement of these crustal plates creates areas where the plates diverge as well as areas where the plates converge. A major area of divergence is located in the Mid-Atlantic. Currents of hot mantle rock rise and separate at this point of divergence creating new oceanic crust at the rate of 2 to 10 centimeters per year. Convergence is when the oceanic crust collides with either another oceanic plate or a continental plate. The oceanic crust sinks forming an enormous trench and generating volcanic activity. Convergence also includes continent to continent plate collisions. When two plates slide past one another, a transform fault is created.

These movements produce many major features of Earth's surface, such as mountain ranges, volcanoes, and earthquake zones. Most of these features are located at plate boundaries where the plates interact by spreading apart, pressing together, or sliding past each other. These movements are very slow, averaging only a few centimeters each year.

Boundaries form between spreading plates where the crust is forced apart in a process called rifting. Rifting generally occurs at mid-ocean ridges. Rifting can also take place within a continent, splitting the continent into smaller landmasses that drift away from each other, thereby forming an ocean basin between them. The Red Sea is a product of rifting. As the seafloor spreading takes place, new material is added to the inner edges of the separating plates. In this way, the plates grow larger, and the ocean basin widens. This is the process that broke up the super continent Pangaea and created the Atlantic Ocean.

Boundaries between plates that are colliding are zones of intense crustal activity. When a plate of ocean crust collides with a plate of continental crust, the more dense oceanic plate slides under the lighter continental plate and plunges into the mantle. This process is called **subduction**, and the site where it takes place is called a subduction zone. A subduction zone is usually seen on the sea-floor as a deep depression called a trench.

The crustal movement that is identified by plates sliding sideways past each other produces a plate boundary characterized by major faults that are capable of unleashing powerful earthquakes. The San Andreas Fault forms such a boundary between the Pacific Plate and the North American Plate.

Orogeny is the term given to natural mountain building.

A mountain is terrain that has been raised high above the surrounding landscape by volcanic action or some form of tectonic plate collisions. The plate collisions could be intercontinental or ocean floor collisions with a continental crust (subduction). The physical composition of mountains would include igneous, metamorphic, or sedimentary rocks; some may have rock layers that are tilted or distorted by plate collision forces.

There are many different types of mountains. The physical attributes of a mountain range depend upon the angle at which plate movement thrust layers of rock to the surface. Many mountains (Adirondacks, Southern Rockies) were formed along high angle faults.

Folded mountains (Alps, Himalayas) are produced by the folding of rock layers during their formation. The Himalayas are the highest mountains in the world and contain Mount Everest, which rises almost 9 km above sea level. The Himalayas were formed when India collided with Asia. The movement that created this collision is still in process at the rate of a few centimeters per year.

Fault-block mountains (Utah, Arizona, and New Mexico) are created when plate movement produces tension forces instead of compression forces. The area under tension produces normal faults and rock along these faults is displaced upward.

Dome mountains are formed as magma tries to push up through the crust but fails to break the surface. Dome mountains resemble a huge blister on the Earth's surface.

Upwarped mountains (Black Hills of South Dakota) are created in association with a broad arching of the crust. They can also be formed by rock thrust upward along high angle faults.

Faults are categorized on the basis of the relative movement between the blocks on both sides of the fault plane. The movement can be horizontal, vertical, or oblique.

A dip-slip fault occurs when the movement of the plates is vertical and opposite. The displacement is in the direction of the inclination, or dip, of the fault. Dip-slip faults are classified as normal faults when the rock above the fault plane moves down relative to the rock below.

Reverse faults are created when the rock above the fault plane moves up relative to the rock below. Reverse faults having a very low angle to the horizontal are also referred to as thrust faults.

Faults in which the dominant displacement is horizontal movement along the trend or strike (length) of the fault are called **strike-slip faults**. When a large strike-slip fault is associated with plate boundaries it is called a **transform fault**. The San Andreas Fault in California is a well-known transform fault.

Faults that have both vertical and horizontal movement are called **oblique-slip faults.**

Volcanism is the term given to the movement of magma through the crust and its emergence as lava onto Earth's surface. Volcanic mountains are built up by successive deposits of volcanic materials.

An active volcano is one that is presently erupting or building to an eruption. A dormant volcano is one that is between eruptions but still shows signs of internal activity that might lead to an eruption in the future. An extinct volcano is said to be no longer capable of erupting. Most of the world's active volcanoes are found along the rim of the Pacific Ocean which is also a major earthquake zone. This curving belt of active faults and volcanoes is often called the Ring of Fire.
The world's best known volcanic mountains include: Mount Etna in Italy and Mount Kilimanjaro in Africa. The Hawaiian Islands are actually the tops of a chain of volcanic mountains that rise from the ocean floor.

There are three types of volcanic mountains: shield volcanoes, cinder cones, and composite volcanoes.

Shield Volcanoes are associated with quiet eruptions. Lava emerges from the vent or opening in the crater and flows freely out over Earth's surface until it cools and hardens into a layer of igneous rock. A repeated lava flow builds this type of volcano into the largest volcanic mountain. Mauna Loa, found in Hawaii, is the largest volcano on Earth.

Cinder Cone Volcanoes are associated with explosive eruptions as lava is hurled high into the air in a spray of droplets of various sizes. These droplets cool and harden into cinders and particles of ash before falling to the ground. The ash and cinder pile up around the vent to form a steep, cone-shaped hill called the cinder cone. Cinder cone volcanoes are relatively small but may form quite rapidly.

Composite Volcanoes are described as being built by both lava flows and layers of ash and cinders. Mount Fuji in Japan, Mount St. Helens in Washington, USA, and Mount Vesuvius in Italy are all famous composite volcanoes.

When lava cools, **igneous rock** is formed. This formation can occur either above ground or below ground.

Intrusive rock includes any igneous rock that was formed below Earth's surface. Batholiths are the largest structures of intrusive type rock and are composed of near granite materials; they are at the core of the Sierra Nevada Mountains.

Extrusive rock includes any igneous rock that was formed at Earth's surface.

Dikes are old lava tubes formed when magma entered a vertical fracture and hardened. Sometimes magma squeezes between two rock layers and hardens into a thin horizontal sheet called a **sill**. A **laccolith** is formed in much the same way as a sill, but the magma that creates a laccolith is very thick and does not flow easily. It pools and forces the overlying strata up, creating an obvious surface dome.

A **caldera** is normally formed by the collapse of the top of a volcano. This collapse can be caused by a massive explosion that destroys the cone and empties most, if not all, of the magma chamber below the volcano. The cone collapses into the empty magma chamber forming a caldera.

An inactive volcano may have magma solidified in its pipe. This structure, called a volcanic neck, is resistant to erosion and may be the only visible evidence of the past presence of an active volcano today.

Glaciation

A continental glacier covered a large part of North America during the most recent ice age. Evidence of this glacial coverage remains as abrasive grooves; large boulders from northern environments dropped in southerly locations; glacial troughs created by the rounding out of steep valleys by glacial scouring; and the remains of glacial sources called cirques that were created by frost wedging the rock at the bottom of the glacier. Remains of plants and animals found in warm climates that have been discovered in the moraines and wash plains help to support the theory of periods of warmth during the past ice ages.

The Ice Age began about 2 -3 million years ago. This age saw the advancement and retreat of glacial ice over millions of years. Theories relating to the origin of glacial activity include plate tectonics where it can be demonstrated that some continental masses, now in temperate climates, were at one time blanketed by ice and snow. Another theory involves changes in Earth's orbit around the sun, changes in the angle of Earth's axis, and the wobbling of Earth's axis. Support for the validity of this theory has come from deep ocean research that indicates a correlation between climatic sensitive micro-organisms and the changes in Earth's orbital status.

About 12,000 years ago, a vast sheet of ice covered a large part of the northern United States. This huge, frozen mass had moved southward from the northern regions of Canada as several large bodies of slow-moving ice (glaciers). A time period during which glaciers advance over a large portion of a continent is called an ice age. A glacier is a large mass of ice that moves or flows over the land in response to gravity. Glaciers form among high mountains and in other cold regions.

There are two main types of glaciers: valley glaciers and continental glaciers. Erosion by valley glaciers is characteristic of U-shaped erosion. They produce sharp peaked mountains such as the Matterhorn in Switzerland. Erosion by continental glaciers often rides over mountains in their paths leaving smoothed, rounded mountains and ridges.

Skill 8.2 Identify how fossils are formed, the methods for determining geologic age, and how this information is used to interpret the past.

A fossil is the remains or trace of an ancient organism that has been preserved naturally in the Earth's crust. Sedimentary rocks usually are rich sources of fossil remains. Those fossils found in layers of sediment were embedded in the slowly forming sedimentary rock strata. The oldest fossils known are the traces of 3.5 billion year old bacteria found in sedimentary rocks. Few fossils are found in metamorphic rock and virtually none are found in igneous rocks. The magma is so hot that any organism trapped in the magma is destroyed.

The fossil remains of a woolly mammoth embedded in ice were found by a group of Russian explorers. However, the best-preserved animal remains have been discovered in natural tar pits. When an animal accidentally fell into the tar, it became trapped, sinking to the bottom. Preserved bones of the saber-toothed cat have been found in tar pits.

Prehistoric insects have been found trapped in ancient amber or fossil resin that was excreted by some extinct species of pine trees. Fossil molds are the hollow spaces in a rock previously occupied by bones or shells. A fossil cast is a fossil mold that fills with sediments or minerals that later hardens forming a cast. Fossil tracks are the imprints in hardened mud left behind by birds or animals.

Geologic time periods

The biological history of Earth is partitioned into four major eras that are further divided into major periods. The latter periods are refined into groupings called epochs.

Earth's history extends over more than 4 billion years and is reckoned in terms of a scale. Paleontologists who study the history of Earth have divided this huge period of time into four large time units called eons. Eons are divided into smaller units of time called eras. An era refers to a time interval in which particular plants and animals were dominant or present in great abundance. The end of an era is most often characterized by (1) a general uplifting of the crust; (2) the extinction of the dominant plants or animals; and (3) the appearance of new life-forms.

Each era is divided into several smaller divisions of time called periods. Some periods are divided into smaller time units called epochs.

Methods of geologic dating

Estimates of Earth's age have been made possible with the discovery of **radioactivity** and the invention of instruments that can measure the amount of radioactivity in rocks. The use of radioactivity to make accurate determinations of Earth's age is called **absolute dating**. This process depends upon comparing the amount of radioactive material in a rock with the amount that has decayed into another element. Studying the radiation given off by atoms of radioactive elements is the most accurate method of measuring the Earth's age. These atoms are unstable and are continuously breaking down or undergoing decay. The radioactive element that decays is called the parent element. The new element that results from the radioactive decay of the parent element is called the daughter element.

The time required for one half of a given amount of a radioactive element to decay is called the half-life of that element or compound. Geologists commonly use **carbon dating** to calculate the age of a fossil substance.

Infer the history of an area using geologic evidence

The determination of the age of rocks by cataloging their composition has been outmoded since the middle 1800s. Today a sequential history can be determined by the fossil content (principle of fossil succession) of a rock system as well as its superposition within a range of systems. This classification process was termed stratigraphy and permitted the construction of a geologic column in which rock systems are arranged in their correct chronological order.

Principles of catastrophism and uniformitarianism

Uniformitarianism is a fundamental concept in modern geology. It simply states that the physical, chemical, and biological laws that operated in the geologic past operate in the same way today. The forces and processes that we observe presently shaping our planet have been at work for a very long time. This idea is commonly stated as "the present is the key to the past."

Catastrophism is the concept that the earth was shaped by catastrophic events of a short-term nature.

Skill 8.3 Analyze data to interpret and forecast weather.

Every day every one of us is affected by weather. It may be in the form of a typical thunderstorm, bringing moist air and cumulonimbus clouds, or a severe storm with pounding winds that can cause either hurricanes or tornados (twisters). These are common terms, as well blizzards or ice storms that we can all identify with.

The daily newscast relates terms such as dew point, relative humidity, and barometric pressure. Suddenly, all too common terms become clouded with terms more frequently used by a meteorologist (someone who forecasts weather).

Dew point is the air temperature at which water vapor begins to condense.

Relative humidity is measured by two kinds of weather instruments, the **psychrometer** and the hair **gygrometer.** Relative humidity simply indicates the amount of moisture in the air. Relative humidity is defined as a ration of existing amounts of water vapor and moisture in the air when compared to the maximum amount of moisture that the air can hold at the same given pressure and temperature. Relative humidity is stated as a percentage. For example, the relative humidity can be 100%.

For example, if you were to analyze relative humidity from data, an example might be: If a parcel of air is saturated (meaning it now holds all the moisture it can hold at a given temperature), then the relative humidity is 100%.

Weather instruments that forecast weather include the aneroid barometer and the mercury barometer that measure **air pressure.** The air exerts varying pressures on a metal diaphragm that will then read air pressure. The mercury barometer operates when atmospheric pressure pushes on a pool of mercury in a glass tube. The higher the pressure, the higher up the tube mercury will rise.

Lesson plans for teachers to analyze data and predict weather can be found at:

http://www.srh.weather.gov/srh/jetstream/synoptic/ll_analyze.htm

Analyzing Weather Maps

Once you can read a station plot, you can begin to perform map analyses. Meteorologists use the station plots to draw lines of constant pressure (isobars), temperature (isotherms), and dew point (isodrosotherms) to achieve an understanding of the current state of the atmosphere. This knowledge ultimately leads to better weather forecasts and warnings.

Decoding these plots is easier than it may seem. The values are located in a form similar to a tic-tac-toe pattern.

In the upper left, the temperature is plotted in Fahrenheit. In this example, the temperature is 77°F.

Along the center, the cloud types are indicated. The top symbol is the high-level cloud type followed by the mid-level cloud type. The lowest symbol represents low-level cloud over a number which tells the height of the base of that cloud (in hundreds of feet). In this example, the high level cloud is cirrus, the mid-level cloud is altocumulus and the low-level cloud is a cumulonimbus with a base height of 2000 feet.

At the upper right is the atmospheric pressure reduced to mean sea level in millibars (mb) to the nearest tenth with the leading 9 or 10 omitted. In this case the pressure would be 999.8 mb. If the pressure was plotted as 024 it would be 1002.4 mb. When trying to determine whether to add a 9 or 10, use the number that will give you a value closest to 1000 mb.

On the second row, the far left number is the visibility in miles. In this example, the visibility is 5 miles.

Next to the visibility is the present weather symbol. There 95 symbols which represent the weather that is either presently occurring or has ended within the previous hour. In this example, a light rain shower was occurring at the time of the observation.

The circle symbol in the center represents the amount of total cloud cover reported in eighths. This cloud cover includes all low, middle, and high level clouds. In this example, 7/8th of the sky was covered with clouds.

This number and symbol tell how much the pressure has changed (in tenths of millibars) in the past three hours and the trend in the change of the pressure during that same period. In this example, the pressure was steady then fell (lowered) becoming 0.3 millibars LOWER than it was three hours ago.

These lines indicate wind direction and speed rounded to the nearest five knots. The longest line, extending from the sky cover plot, points in the direction that the wind is blowing **from**. Thus, in this case, the wind is blowing **from** the southwest. The shorter lines, called barbs, indicate the wind speed in knots (kt). The speed of the wind is calculated by the barbs. Each long barb represents 10 kt with short barbs representing 5 kt. In this example, the station plot contains two long barbs so the wind speed is 20 kt, or about 24 mph.

The 71 at the lower left is the dewpoint temperature. The dewpoint temperature is the temperature the air would have to cool to become saturated, or in other words reach a relative humidity of 100%.

The lower right area is reserved for the past weather, which is the most significant weather that has occurred within the past six hours excluding the most recent hour.

Analyze a Map on Your Own

The following are a few sources of current weather maps. Sometimes a site may be down or experiencing data losses. In such a case, try another site listed. This is not meant to be an exhaustive list. These are provided for your convenience.

- NCAR, pick your regional plot: http://www.rap.ucar.edu/weather/surface/
- UNISYS: http://weather.unisys.com/surface/sfc_map.html
- College of DuPage: http://weather.cod.edu/analysis/analysis.sfcplots.html
- NOAA http://www.nws.noaa.gov/
- Ohio State University: http://asp1.sbs.ohio-state.edu/ (Click on "Current Weather" and choose your map)

Weather Map Symbols

Surface Station Model

Temp (F) Weather Dewpoint (F)	45 045 29	Pressure (mb) Sky Cover Wind (kts)	**Data at Surface Station** Temp 45 °F, dewpoint 29 °F, overcast, wind **from** SE at 15 knots, weather light rain, pressure 1004.5 mb

Upper Air Station Model

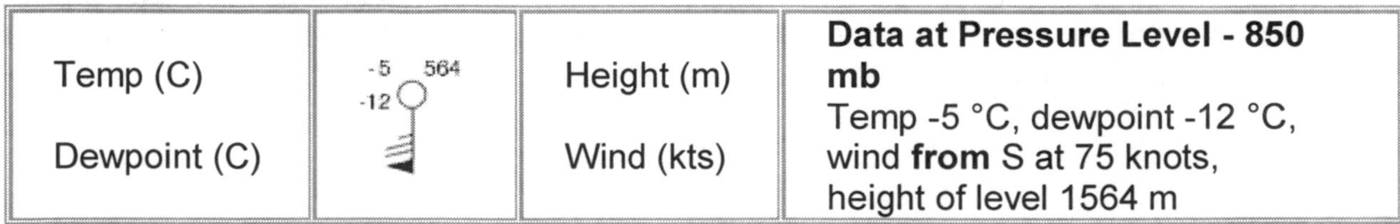

Temp (C) Dewpoint (C)	-5 564 -12	Height (m) Wind (kts)	**Data at Pressure Level - 850 mb** Temp -5 °C, dewpoint -12 °C, wind **from** S at 75 knots, height of level 1564 m

Forecast Station Model

Temp (F) Weather Dewpoint (F)	78 70 64	PoP (%) Sky Cover Wind (kts)	**Forecast at Valid Time** Temp 78 °F, dewpoint 64 °F, scattered clouds, wind **from** E at 10 knots, probability of precipitation 70% with rain showers

Map Symbols

Sky Cover	Wind
clear	Calm
1/8	1-2 knots (1-2 mph)
scattered	3-7 knots (3-8 mph)
3/8	8-12 knots (9-14 mph)
4/8	13-17 knots (15-20 mph)
5/8	18-22 knots (21-25 mph)
broken	23-27 knots (26-31 mph)
7/8	48-52 knots (55-60 mph)
overcast	73-77 knots (84-89 mph)
obscured	103-107 knots (119-123 mph)
missing	Shaft in direction wind is coming **from**

Skill 8.4 Analyze the chemical, physical, and geological characteristics of the ocean.

Currents and tides

World weather patterns are greatly influenced by ocean surface currents in the upper layer of the ocean. These currents continuously move along the ocean surface in specific directions. Ocean currents that flow deep below the surface are called sub-surface currents. These currents are influenced by such factors as the location of landmasses in the current's path and the Earth's rotation.

Surface currents are caused by winds and are classified by temperature. Cold currents originate in the polar regions and flow through surrounding water that is measurably warmer. Those currents with a higher temperature than the surrounding water are called warm currents and can be found near the equator. These currents follow swirling routes around the ocean basins and the equator. The Gulf Stream and the California Current are the two main surface currents that flow along the coastlines of the United States. The Gulf Stream is a warm current in the Atlantic Ocean that carries warm water from the equator to the northern parts of the Atlantic Ocean. Benjamin Franklin studied and named the Gulf Stream. The California Current is a cold current that originates in the Arctic regions and flows southward along the west coast of the United States.

Differences in water density also create ocean currents. Water found near the bottom of oceans is the coldest and the densest. Water tends to flow from a denser area to a less dense area. Currents that flow because of a difference in the density of the ocean water are called density currents. Water with a higher salinity is denser than water with a lower salinity. Water that has salinity different from the surrounding water may form a density current.

Waves

The movement of ocean water is caused by the wind, the sun's heat energy, the Earth's rotation, the moon's gravitational pull on earth, and underwater earthquakes. Most ocean waves are caused by the impact of winds. Wind blowing over the surface of the ocean transfers energy (friction) to the water and causes waves to form. Waves are also formed by seismic activity on the ocean floor. A wave formed by an earthquake is called a seismic sea wave. These powerful waves can be very destructive with wave heights increasing to 30 m or more near the shore. The crest of a wave is its highest point. The trough of a wave is its lowest point. The distance from wave top to wave top is the wavelength. The wave period is the time between the passings of two successive waves.

The ocean floor has many of the same features that are found on land. The sea floor has higher mountains, extensive plains, and deeper canyons than are present on land. Oceanographers have named different parts of the ocean floor according to their structure. The major parts of the ocean floor are as follows:

The **continental shelf** is the sloping part of the continent that is covered with water extending from the shoreline to the continental slope.

The **continental slope** is the steeply sloping area that connects the continental shelf and the deep-ocean floor.

The **continental rise** is the gently sloping surface at the base of the continental slope.

The **abyssal plains** are the flat, level parts of the ocean floor.

A **seamount** is an undersea volcano peak that is at least 1000 m above the ocean floor.

Guyot is a submerged flat-topped seamount.

Mid-ocean **ridges** are continuous undersea mountain chains that are found mostly in the middle portions of the oceans.

Ocean **trenches** are long, elongated narrow troughs or depressions formed where ocean floors collide with another section of ocean floor or continent. The deepest trench in the Pacific Ocean is the Marianas Trench which is about 11 km deep.

Shorelines

The shoreline is the boundary where land and sea meet. Shorelines mark the average position of sea level which is the average height of the sea without consideration of tides and waves. Shorelines are classified according to the way they were formed. The three types of shorelines are **submerged**, **emergent**, and **neutral**. When the sea has risen or the land has sunk, a submerged shoreline is created. An emergent shoreline occurs when sea falls or the land rises. A neutral shoreline does not show the features of a submerged or an emergent shoreline. A neutral shoreline is usually observed as a flat and broad beach.

A **stack** is an island of resistant rock left after weaker rock is worn away by waves and currents. Waves approaching the beach at a slight angle create a current of water that flows parallel to the shore. This longshore current carries loose sediment almost like a river of sand. A **spit** is formed when a weak longshore current drops its load of sand as it turns into a bay.

Rip currents are narrow currents that flow seaward at a right angle to the shoreline. These currents are very dangerous to swimmers. Most of the beach sands are composed of grains of resistant material like quartz and orthoclase, but coral or basalt are found in some locations. Many beaches have rock fragments that are too large to be classified as sand.

Ocean Water

Seventy percent of the Earth's surface is covered with saltwater which is termed the hydrosphere. The mass of this saltwater is about 1.4×10^{24} grams. The ocean waters continuously circulate among different parts of the hydrosphere. There are seven major oceans: North Atlantic Ocean, South Atlantic Ocean, North Pacific Ocean, South Pacific Ocean, Indian Ocean, Arctic Ocean, and Antarctic Ocean.

Pure water is a combination of the elements hydrogen and oxygen. These two elements make up about 96.5% of ocean water. The remaining portion is made up of dissolved solids. The concentration of these dissolved solids determines the water's salinity.

Salinity is the number of grams of these dissolved salts in 1,000 grams of sea water. The average salinity of ocean water is about 3.5%. In other words, one kilogram of sea water contains about 35 grams of salt. Sodium chloride, or salt ($NaCl$), is the most abundant of the dissolved salts. The dissolved salts also include smaller quantities of magnesium chloride, magnesium and calcium sulfates, and traces of several other salt elements. Salinity varies throughout the world oceans; the total salinity of the oceans varies from place to place and also varies with depth. Salinity is low near river mouths where the ocean mixes with fresh water, and salinity is high in areas of high evaporation rates.

The temperature of the ocean water varies with different latitudes and with ocean depths. Ocean water temperature is about constant to depths of 90 meters. The temperature of surface water will drop rapidly from 28°C at the equator to -2°C at the Poles. The freezing point of sea water is lower than the freezing point of pure water. Pure water freezes at 0°C. The dissolved salts in the sea water keep sea water at a freezing point of -2°C. The freezing point of sea water may vary depending on its salinity in a particular location.

The ocean can be divided into three temperature zones. The surface layer consists of relatively warm water and exhibits most of the wave action present. The area where the wind and waves churn and mix the water is called the mixed layer. This is the layer where most living creatures are found due to abundant sunlight and warmth. The second layer is called the thermocline, and it becomes increasingly cold as its depth increases. This change is due to the lack of energy from sunlight. The layer below the thermocline continues to the deep dark, very cold, and semi-barren ocean floor.

Oozes - the name given to the sediment that contains at least 30% plant or animal shell fragments. Ooze contains calcium carbonate. Deposits that form directly from sea water in the place where they are found are called authigenic deposits. Maganese nodules are authigenic deposits found over large areas of the ocean floor.

Causes for the formation of ocean floor features

The surface of the Earth is in constant motion. This motion is the subject of plate tectonics studies. Major plate separation lines lay along the ocean floors. As these plates separate, molten rock rises, continuously forming new ocean crust and creating new and taller mountain ridges under the ocean. The Mid-Atlantic Range, which divides the Atlantic Ocean basin into two nearly equal parts, shows evidence of these deep-ocean floor changes.

Seamounts are formed by underwater volcanoes. Seamounts and volcanic islands are found in long chains on the ocean floor. They are formed when the movement of an oceanic plate positions a plate section over a stationary hot spot located deep in the mantle. Magma rising from the hot spot, punches through the plate, and forms a volcano. The Hawaiian Islands are examples of volcanic island chains.

Magma that rises to produce a curving chain of volcanic islands is called an island arc. An example of an island arc is the Lesser Antilles chain in the Caribbean Sea.

Skill 8.5 Identify the characteristics of rocks, minerals, and soils and the mechanisms by which they were formed.

The three major subdivisions of rocks are sedimentary, metamorphic, and igneous.

Lithification of sedimentary rocks

When fluid sediments are transformed into solid sedimentary rocks, the process is known as **lithification**. One very common process affecting sediments is compaction where the weights of overlying materials compress and compact the deeper sediments. The compaction process leads to cementation. **Cementation** is when sediments are converted to sedimentary rock.

Factors in crystallization of igneous rocks

Igneous rocks can be classified according to their texture, their composition, and the way they were formed.

Molten rock is called magma. When molten rock pours out onto the surface of Earth, it is called lava. As magma cools, the elements and compounds begin to form crystals. The slower the magma cools, the larger the crystals grow. Rocks with large crystals are said to have a coarse-grained texture. Granite is an example of a coarse grained rock. Rocks that cool rapidly before any crystals can form have a glassy texture such as obsidian, also commonly known as volcanic glass.

Metamorphic rocks are formed by high temperatures and great pressures. The process by which the rocks undergo these changes is called metamorphism. The outcome of metamorphic changes include deformation by extreme heat, pressure, compaction, destruction of the original characteristics of the parent rock, bending and folding while in a plastic stage, and the emergence of completely new and different minerals due to chemical reactions with heated water and dissolved minerals.

Metamorphic rocks are classified into two groups: foliated (leaflike) rocks and unfoliated rocks. Foliated rocks consist of compressed, parallel bands of minerals which give the rocks a striped appearance. Examples of such rocks include slate, schist, and gneiss. Unfoliated rocks are not banded and examples of such include quartzite, marble, and anthracite rocks.

Minerals are natural, non-living solids with a definite chemical composition and a crystalline structure. **Ores** are minerals or rock deposits that can be mined for a profit. **Rocks** are earth materials made of one or more minerals. **Rock facies** are groups of rock that differ from comparable rocks (as in composition, age, or fossil content).

Characteristics by which minerals are classified

Minerals must adhere to five criteria. They must (1) be non-living, (2) be formed in nature, (3) be solid in form, (4) their atoms must form a crystalline pattern, and (5) its chemical composition is fixed within narrow limits.

There are over 3000 minerals in Earth's crust. Minerals are classified by composition. The major groups of minerals are silicates, carbonates, oxides, sulfides, sulfates, and halides. The largest group of minerals is the silicates. Silicates are made of silicon, oxygen, and one or more other elements.

Soil types

Soils are composed of particles of sand, clay, various minerals, tiny living organisms, and humus, plus the decayed remains of plants and animals. Soils are divided into three classes according to their texture. These classes are sandy soils, clay soils, and loamy soils.

Sandy soils are gritty, and their particles do not bind together firmly. Sandy soils are porous and water passes through them rapidly. Sandy soils do not hold much water.

Clay soils are smooth and greasy; their particles bind together firmly. Clay soils are moist and usually do not allow water to pass through easily.

Loamy soils feel somewhat like velvet and their particles clump together. Loamy soils are made up of sand, clay, and silt. Loamy soils hold water but some water can pass through.

In addition to three main classes, soils are further grouped into three major types based upon their composition. These groups are pedalfers, pedocals, and laterites.

Pedalfers form in the humid, temperate climate of the eastern United States. Pedalfer soils contain large amounts of iron oxide and aluminum-rich clays, making the soil a brown to reddish brown color. This soil supports forest type vegetation.

Pedocals are found in the western United States where the climate is dry and temperate. These soils are rich in calcium carbonate. This type of soil supports grasslands and brush vegetation.

Laterites are found where the climate is wet and tropical. Large amounts of water flow through this soil. Laterites are red-orange soils rich in iron and aluminum oxides. There is little humus, and this soil is not very fertile.

Skill 8.6 Identify the ways in which earth, air, and water interact.

Erosion is the inclusion and transportation of surface materials by another moveable material, usually water, wind, or ice. The most important cause of erosion is running water. Streams, rivers, and tides are constantly at work removing weathered fragments of bedrock and carrying them away from their original location.

A stream erodes bedrock by the grinding action of the sand, pebbles, and other rock fragments. This grinding against each other is called abrasion. Streams also erode rocks by dissolving or absorbing their minerals. Limestone and marble are readily dissolved by streams.

The breaking down of rocks at or near to the Earth's surface is known as **weathering**. Weathering breaks down these rocks into smaller and smaller pieces. There are two types of weathering: physical weathering and chemical weathering.

Physical weathering is the process by which rocks are broken down into smaller fragments without undergoing any change in chemical composition. Physical weathering is mainly caused by the freezing of water, the expansion of rock, and the activities of plants and animals.

Frost wedging is the cycle of daytime thawing and refreezing at night. This cycle causes large rock masses, especially the rocks exposed on mountain tops, to be broken into smaller pieces.

The peeling away of the outer layers from a rock is called exfoliation. Rounded mountain tops are called exfoliation domes and have been formed in this way.

Chemical weathering is the breaking down of rocks through changes in their chemical composition. An example would be the change of feldspar in granite to clay. Water, oxygen, and carbon dioxide are the main agents of chemical weathering. When water and carbon dioxide combine chemically, they produce a weak acid that breaks down rocks.

Earth's Atmosphere

El Niño refers to a sequence of changes in the ocean and atmospheric circulation across the Pacific Ocean. The water around the equator is unusually hot every two to seven years. Trade winds normally blow east to west across the equatorial latitudes, piling warm water into the western Pacific. A huge mass of heavy thunderstorms usually forms in the area and produces vast currents of rising air that displace heat poleward. This helps create the strong mid-latitude jet streams. The world's climate patterns are disrupted by a change in location of thunderstorm activity.

Air masses moving toward or away from the Earth's surface are called air currents. Air moving parallel to Earth's surface is called **wind**. Weather conditions are generated by winds and air currents carrying large amounts of heat and moisture from one part of the atmosphere to another. Wind speeds are measured by instruments called anemometers.

The wind belts in each hemisphere consist of convection cells that encircle Earth-like belts. There are three major wind belts on Earth: (1) trade winds, (2) prevailing westerlies, and (3) polar easterlies. Wind belt formation depends on the differences in air pressures that develop in the doldrums, the horse latitudes, and the polar regions. The doldrums surround the equator. Within this belt, heated air usually rises straight up into Earth's atmosphere. The horse latitudes are regions of high barometric pressure with calm and light winds, and the polar regions contain cold dense air that sinks to the Earth's surface.

Winds caused by local temperature changes include sea breezes and land breezes. **Sea breezes** are caused by the unequal heating of the land and an adjacent, large body of water. Land heats up faster than water. The movement of cool ocean air toward the land is called a sea breeze. Sea breezes usually begin blowing about mid-morning, ending about sunset. A breeze that blows from the land to the ocean or a large lake is called a **land breeze.**

Monsoons are huge wind systems that cover large geographic areas and that reverse direction seasonally. The monsoons of India and Asia are examples of these seasonal winds. They alternate wet and dry seasons. As denser, cooler air over the ocean moves inland, a steady seasonal wind called a summer or wet monsoon is produced.

Cloud types

Cirrus clouds - White and feathery; high in the sky

Cumulus - thick, white, fluffy

Stratus - layers of clouds cover most of the sky

Nimbus - heavy, dark clouds that represent thunderstorm clouds

Variation on the clouds mentioned above:

Cumulo-nimbus

Strato-nimbus

Types of storms

A **thunderstorm** is a brief, local storm produced by the rapid upward movement of warm, moist air within a cumulo-nimbus cloud. Thunderstorms always produce lightning and thunder and are accompanied by strong wind gusts and heavy rain or hail.

A severe storm with swirling winds that may reach speeds of hundreds of kilometers per hour is called a **tornado**. Such a storm is also referred to as a "twister". The sky is covered by large cumulo-nimbus clouds and violent thunderstorms. A funnel-shaped swirling cloud may extend downward from a cumulo-nimbus cloud and reach the ground. Tornadoes are storms that leave a narrow path of destruction on the ground. A swirling, funnel-shaped cloud that extends downward and touches a body of water is called a **waterspout.**

Hurricanes are storms that develop when warm, moist air carried by trade winds rotate around a low-pressure "eye". A large, rotating, low-pressure system accompanied by heavy precipitation and strong winds is called a tropical cyclone (better known as a hurricane). In the Pacific region, a hurricane is called a typhoon.

Storms that occur only in the winter are known as blizzards or ice storms. A **blizzard** is a storm with strong winds, snow and frigid temperatures. An **ice storm** consists of falling rain that freezes when it strikes the ground, covering everything with a layer of ice.

Hydrologic Cycle

Water that falls to Earth in the form of rain and snow is called **precipitation.** Precipitation is part of a continuous process in which water at the Earth's surface evaporates, condenses into clouds, and returns to Earth. This process is termed the **water cycle**. The water located below the surface is called groundwater.

The impacts of altitude upon climatic conditions are primarily related to temperature and precipitation. As altitude increases, climatic conditions become increasingly drier and colder. Solar radiation becomes more severe as altitude increases, while the effects of convection forces are minimized.

Climatic changes as a function of latitude follow a similar pattern (as a reference, latitude moves either north or south from the equator). The climate becomes colder and drier as the distance from the equator increases. Proximity to land or water masses produces climatic conditions based upon the available moisture. Dry and arid climates prevail where moisture is scarce; lush tropical climates can prevail where moisture is abundant.

Climate, as described above, depends upon the specific combination of conditions making up an area's environment. Man impacts all environments by producing pollutants in earth, air, and water. It follows then, that man is a major player in world climatic conditions.

Sinkholes

Large features formed by dissolved limestone (calcium carbonate) include sinkholes, caves, and caverns. **Sinkholes** are funnel-shaped depressions created by dissolved limestone. Many sinkholes started life as a limestone cavern. Erosion weakens the cavern roof causing it to collapse, forming a sinkhole.

Groundwater usually contains large amounts of dissolved minerals, especially if the water flows through limestone. As groundwater drips through the roof of a cave, gases dissolved in the water can escape into the air. A deposit of calcium carbonate is left behind. Stalactites are icicle-like structures of calcium carbonate that hang from the roofs of caves. Water that falls on a constant spot on the cave floor and evaporates leaving a deposit of calcium carbonate builds a stalagmite.

Skill 8.7 Identify components and pathways of biogeochemical cycles.

Essential elements are recycled through an ecosystem. At times, the element needs to be "fixed" in a useable form. Cycles are dependent on plants, algae, and bacteria to fix nutrients for use by animals.

Water cycle – Two percent of all the available water is fixed and held in ice or the bodies of organisms. Available water includes surface water (lakes, ocean, and rivers) and groundwater (aquifers, wells). 96% of all available water is from groundwater. Water is recycled through the processes of evaporation and precipitation. The water present now is the water that has been here since our atmosphere formed.

Carbon cycle - Ten percent of all available carbon in the air (from carbon dioxide gas) is fixed by photosynthesis. Plants fix carbon in the form of glucose, then animals eat the plants and are able to obtain their source of carbon. When animals release carbon dioxide through respiration, the plants again have a source of carbon to fix.

Nitrogen cycle - Eighty percent of the atmosphere is in the form of nitrogen gas. Nitrogen must be fixed and taken out of the gaseous form to be incorporated into an organism. Only a few genera of bacteria have the correct enzymes to break the triple bond between nitrogen atoms. These bacteria live within the roots of legumes (peas, beans, alfalfa) and add bacteria to the soil so it may be taken up by the plant. Nitrogen is necessary to make amino acids and the nitrogenous bases of DNA.

Phosphorus cycle - Phosphorus exists as a mineral and is not found in the atmosphere. Fungi and plant roots have structures called mycorrhizae that are able to fix insoluble phosphates into useable phosphorus. Urine and decayed matter returns phosphorus to the earth where it can be fixed in the plant. Phosphorus is needed for the backbone of DNA and for the manufacture of ATP.

Skill 8.8 Identify components of Earth's solar system, their individual characteristics, and how they interact

There are eight established planets in our solar system; Mercury, Venus, Earth, Mars, Jupiter, Saturn, Uranus, and Neptune. Pluto was an established planet in our solar system, but as of Summer 2006, its status is being reconsidered. The planets are divided into two groups based on distance from the Sun. The inner planets include: Mercury, Venus, Earth, and Mars. The outer planets include: Jupiter, Saturn, Uranus, and Neptune.

Planets

Mercury is the closest planet to the sun. Its surface has craters and rocks. The atmosphere is composed of hydrogen, helium, and sodium. Mercury was named after the Roman messenger god.

Venus has a slow rotation when compared to Earth. Venus and Uranus rotate in opposite directions from the other planets. This opposite rotation is called retrograde rotation. The surface of Venus is not visible due to the extensive cloud cover. The atmosphere is composed mostly of carbon dioxide. Sulfuric acid droplets in the dense cloud cover give Venus a yellow appearance. Venus has a greater greenhouse effect than observed on Earth. The dense clouds combined with carbon dioxide trap heat. Venus was named after the Roman goddess of love.

Earth is considered a water planet with 70% of its surface covered by water. Gravity holds the masses of water in place. The different temperatures observed on Earth allow for the different states (solid, liquid, gas) of water to exist. The atmosphere is composed mainly of oxygen and nitrogen. Earth is the only planet that is known to support life.

Mars' surface contains numerous craters, active and extinct volcanoes, ridges, and valleys with extremely deep fractures. Iron oxide found in the dusty soil makes the surface seem rust-colored and the skies seem pink in color. The atmosphere is composed of carbon dioxide, nitrogen, argon, oxygen and water vapor. Mars has polar regions with ice caps composed of water. Mars has two satellites. Mars was named after the Roman war god.

Jupiter is the largest planet in the solar system. Jupiter has 16 moons. The atmosphere is composed of hydrogen, helium, methane, and ammonia. There are white-colored bands of clouds indicating rising gas and dark-colored bands of clouds indicating descending gases. The gas movement is caused by heat resulting from the energy of Jupiter's core. Jupiter has a Great Red Spot that is thought to be a hurricane-type cloud. Jupiter has a strong magnetic field.

Saturn is the second largest planet in the solar system. Saturn has rings of ice, rock, and dust particles circling it. Saturn's atmosphere is composed of hydrogen, helium, methane, and ammonia. Saturn has 20 plus satellites. Saturn was named after the Roman god of agriculture.

Uranus is the second planet in the solar system with retrograde revolution. Uranus is a gaseous planet. It has 10 dark rings and 15 satellites. Its atmosphere is composed of hydrogen, helium, and methane. Uranus was named after the Greek god of the heavens.

Neptune is another gaseous planet with an atmosphere consisting of hydrogen, helium, and methane. Neptune has three rings and two satellites. Neptune was named after the Roman sea god because its atmosphere is the same color as the seas.

Pluto was once considered the smallest planet in the solar system; however it's status as a planet is being reconsidered. Pluto's atmosphere probably contains methane, ammonia, and frozen water. Pluto has one satellite. Pluto revolves around the sun every 250 years. Pluto was named after the Roman god of the underworld.

Comets, asteroids, and meteors

Astronomers believe that rocky fragments may have been the remains of the birth of the solar system that never formed into a planet. **Asteroids** are found in the region between Mars and Jupiter.

Comets are masses of frozen gases, cosmic dust, and small rocky particles. Astronomers think that most comets originate in a dense comet cloud beyond Pluto. A comet consists of a nucleus, a coma, and a tail. A comet's tail always points away from the sun. The most famous comet, **Halley's Comet,** is named after Edmond Halley who first discovered it in 240 B.C. It returns to the skies near Earth every 75 to 76 years.

Meteoroids are composed of particles of rock and metal of various sizes. When a meteoroid travels through the Earth's atmosphere, friction causes its surface to heat up and it begins to burn. The burning meteoroid falling through the Earth's atmosphere is called a **meteor** (also known as a "shooting star").

Meteorites are meteors that strike the Earth's surface. A physical example of a meteorite's impact on the Earth's surface can be seen in Arizona. The Barringer Crater is a huge meteor crater. There are many other meteor craters throughout the world.

Skill 8.9 Identify structures in the universe, their characteristics, and scientific theories of their origins.

The **sun** is considered the nearest star to Earth that produces solar energy. By the process of nuclear fusion, hydrogen gas is converted to helium gas. Energy flows out of the core to the surface, and then radiation escapes into space.

Parts of the sun include: (1) **core:** the inner portion of the sun where fusion takes place, (2) **photosphere:** considered the surface of the sun which produces **sunspots** (cool, dark areas that can be seen on its surface), (3) **chromosphere:** hydrogen gas causes this portion to be red in color (also found here are solar flares and solar prominences, gases that shoot outward from the chromosphere), and (4) the **corona**: the transparent area of sun visible only during a total eclipse.

Solar radiation is energy traveling from the sun that radiates into space. **Solar flares** produce excited protons and electrons that shoot outward from the chromosphere at great speeds reaching Earth. These particles disturb radio reception and also affect the magnetic field on Earth.

Knowledge of telescope types

Galileo was the first person to use telescopes to observe the solar system. He invented the first refracting telescope. A **refracting telescope** uses lenses to bend light rays to focus the image.

Sir Isaac Newton invented the **reflecting telescope** which uses mirrors to gather light rays on a curved mirror to produce a small, focused image.

The world's largest telescope is located in Mauna Kea, Hawaii. It uses multiple mirrors to gather light rays.

The **Hubble Space telescope** uses a **single-reflector mirror**. It provides an opportunity for astronomers to observe objects seven times farther away. Even those objects that are 50 times fainter can be viewed better than by any telescope on Earth. There are future plans to make repairs and install new mirrors and other equipment on the Hubble Space telescope.

Refracting and reflecting telescopes are considered **optical telescopes** since they gather visible light and focus it to produce images. A different type of telescope that collects invisible radio waves created by the sun and stars is called a **radio telescope.**

Radio telescopes consist of a reflector or dish with special receivers. The reflector collects radio waves that are created by the sun and stars. Using a radio telescope has many advantages. They can receive signals 24 hours a day, can operate in any kind of weather and dust particles or clouds do not interfere with its performance. The most impressive aspect of the radio telescope is its ability to detect objects from such great distances in space.

The world's largest radio telescope is located in Arecibo, Puerto Rico. It has a collecting dish antenna of more than 300 meters in diameter.

Use spectral analysis to identify or infer features of stars or star systems

The **spectroscope** is a device or an attachment for telescopes that is used to separate white light into a series of different colors by wave lengths. This series of colors of light is called a **spectrum**. A **spectrograph** can photograph a spectrum. Wavelengths of light have distinctive colors. The color red has the longest wavelength and violet has the shortest wavelength. Wavelengths are arranged to form an **electromagnetic spectrum**. They range from very long radio waves to very short gamma rays. Visible light covers a small portion of the electromagnetic spectrum. Spectroscopes observe the spectra, temperatures, pressures, and movement of stars. The movements of stars indicate if they are moving toward or away from Earth. If a star is moving toward Earth, light waves compress and the wavelengths of light seem shorter. This will cause the entire spectrum to move toward the blue or violet end of the spectrum. If a star is moving away from earth, light waves expand and the wavelengths of light seem longer. This will cause the entire spectrum to move toward the red end of the spectrum.

Knowledge of astronomical measurement

The three formulas astronomers use for calculating distances in space are: (1) the **AU or astronomical unit**, (2) **the LY or light year,** and (3) **the parsec**. It is important to remember that these formulas are measurements of distance, not time. The distance between Earth and the sun is about 150×10^{6} km. This distance is known as an astronomical unit or AU. This formula is used to measure distances within the solar system. The distance light travels in one year is a light year (9.5×10^{12} km). Large distances are measured in parsecs. One parsec equals 3.26 light-years. There are approximately 63,000 AU's in one light year or 9.5×10^{12} km/ 150×10^{6} km = 6.3×10^{4} AU.

Other structures in the universe

Astronomers use groups or patterns of stars called **constellations** as reference points to locate other stars in the sky. Familiar constellations include: Ursa Major (also known as the Big Bear) and Ursa Minor (known as the Little Bear). Within Ursa Major, the smaller constellation, The Big Dipper, is found. Within Ursa Minor, the smaller constellation, The Little Dipper, is found.

Different constellations appear as the Earth continues its revolution around the sun with the seasonal changes.

Magnitude stars are 21 of the brightest stars that can be seen from Earth. These are the first stars noticed at night. In the Northern Hemisphere, there are 15 commonly observed first magnitude stars.

A vast collection of stars is defined as a **galaxy**. Galaxies are classified as irregular, elliptical, and spiral. An irregular galaxy has no real structured appearance; most are in their early stages of life. An elliptical galaxy consists of smooth ellipses, contain little dust and gas, and are composed of millions or trillions of stars. Spiral galaxies are disk-shaped and have extending arms that rotate around its dense center. Earth's galaxy is found in the Milky Way, a spiral galaxy.

A **pulsar** is defined as a variable radio source that emits signals in very short, regular bursts; it is believed to be a rotating neutron star.

A **quasar** is defined as an object that photographs like a star but has an extremely large redshift and a variable energy output; it is believed to be the active core of a very distant galaxy.

Black holes are defined as an object that has collapsed to such a degree that light cannot escape from its surface; light is trapped by the intense gravitational field.
Two main hypotheses of the origin of the solar system are: (1) **the tidal hypothesis** and (2) **the condensation hypothesis**.

The tidal hypothesis proposes that the solar system began with a near collision of the sun and a large star. Some astronomers believe that as these two stars passed each other, the great gravitational pull of the large star extracted hot gases out of the sun. The mass from the hot gases started to orbit the sun, which began to cool and then condensed into the nine planets. (Few astronomers support this example).

The condensation hypothesis proposes that the solar system began with rotating clouds of dust and gas. Condensation occurred in the center forming the sun and the smaller parts of the cloud formed the nine planets. Two main theories to explain the origins of the universe include: (1) **The Big Bang Theory** and (2) **The Steady-State Theory.**

The Big Bang Theory has been widely accepted by many astronomers. It states that the universe originated from a magnificent explosion spreading mass, matter, and energy into space. The galaxies formed from this material as it cooled during the next half-billion years.

The Steady-State Theory is the least accepted theory. It states that the universe is continuously being renewed. Galaxies move outward and new galaxies replace the older galaxies. Astronomers have not found any evidence to prove this theory.

The future of the universe is hypothesized with the **Oscillating Universe Hypothesis**. It states that the universe will oscillate or expand and contract. Galaxies will move away from one another and will in time slow down and stop. Then a gradual moving toward each other will again activate the explosion, or Big Bang, theory.

Skill 8.10 Demonstrate knowledge of space travel and exploration and identify examples of their impact on society.

The fundamentals of knowledge of space include: survival (especially for prolonged periods of time), an understanding of how spacecraft get their energy, and how the spacecraft moves through space.

Exploration in space involves the history of space with both unmanned and manned missions.

Knowledge of Space Travel

Life support

The health of the astronauts depends on the quality of food they consume. Long space travels must have packaged food that is lightweight, nutritious, will endure temperature and pressure, and is easily disposable. The water astronauts consume is filtered from their own breath, urine, and portable water brought on board. The purified water astronauts use is cleaner than most systems on Earth.

The atmosphere is composed of roughly 78% nitrogen and 21% oxygen and 1% argon and carbon dioxide. In a spacecraft, you would find liquid oxygen and liquid nitrogen. Cabin pressurization systems regulate the use of oxygen and nitrogen. Fire safety is essential to the life support of the astronauts. Fire does not react the same way in space as it does on Earth. The operating temperatures are maintained by varied means such as covering the space ship with thermal blankets, paints, and specially made products that reduce shrinking as well as expansion.

Energy
There are four major sources of energy a spacecraft will carry. These are batteries, solar panels, RTG's (generators that convert radioisotope waste into electricity- they are heavy and give off radiation), and fuel cells (they convert chemical energy into electricity are regenerative, but they are heavy).

Propulsion
To better understand propulsion technologies, it is essential to lay a foundation in physics. Topics teachers should review include Newton's Law's of motion, rates of change, system of particles, momentum and propulsion, and discussions on impulse and thrust measurements.

Exploration & Missions
Unmanned missions are carried out if they are deemed too dangerous for humans to undertake. **Sputnik** was the first unmanned mission. It was a Russian mission launched on Oct. 4, 1957 during the Cold War. The Americans were driven to compete and ramp up their space program.

Mariner 10 - This American mission was the first to use the gravitational pull of one planet to reach another planet.

Deep Space 1 - This American mission tested twelve advanced technologies to benefit future space travel.

Magellan - The Magellan mission was when the American Magellan took pictures of and collected information on Venus. Magellan was followed by:

Mars Exploration Rover, Mars Pathfinder, and Sputnik I

Sputnik 2 - sent the first life, a dog named Laika, into orbit around Earth.

Voyager 1 / Voyager 2

Manned missions

Throughout history, there have been many manned missions. These missions have included many "firsts" such as first animal, the first man on moon, the first women in space, the first preventable catastrophe, and first fatal catastrophe. As of 2007, the manned missions have been contained to orbiting around the Earth and landing on the moon. With new knowledge of propulsion, it would be possible to reach Mars with a manned mission. Previously, unmanned missions have used land rovers to collect over 17,000 photo images and collect rock and soil samples.

Vostok 1	This Russian mission was the first manned spaceflight in history.
Vostok 6	The Russian Vostok 6 was to continue experiments for joint spaceflights and also observe the effect of space travel on the female body.
Voskhod 1	In this mission, the USSR launched the first space flight with more than one person aboard. This was also the first flight without spacesuits.
Apollo 11	This American mission was the first lunar landing that also brought the first man on the moon.
Apollo 13	This American mission was to gather information and pictures from the moon. There were several problems that resulted in a dangerous explosion, but the astronauts survived.
Apollo-Soyuz	This mission involved a docking of ships between the American Apollo and Russian Soyuz to develop techniques for emergency rescues, as well as to perform some experiments.
Challenger	The American Challenger explosion occurred on the tenth mission of this space shuttle.
Soyuz TM-32	The Russian Soyuz TM-32 was to be kept at the International Space Station as a lifeboat, and the crew that brought it returned to Earth on the Soyuz TM-31.
Shenzhou 5	This was the People's Republic of China's first manned flight. Liwei Yang was the first Chinese man in space.

Dangers of Space
The danger of space travel is well known. The technology failure has caused numerous deaths. But the mission itself has inherent dangers such as crashing into debris which could be fatal. Weightless conditions lead to osteoporosis and the stress of sitting for so long can be mentally taxing.

Radiation
The radiation in space differs from that on Earth in that particles move at such a high speed that their impact causes ionization. This is called ionizing radiation, and it causes all types of damage to human cells. One of the more dangerous results is a mutation in DNA that can lead to cancer. The amount of radiation an astronaut receives depends on orbital inclination, altitude above the Earth, solar cycle, and individual susceptibility.

Researchers are currently searching for ways to lessen radiation damage. Chemoprevention, or the use of chemical agents, drugs, or food supplements to prevent disease, is one option. In a space station, when a radiation storm occurs, astronauts head toward a shelter. However, astronauts in spacecraft are more exposed during radiation storms and damage is more severe.

Impact on Society
What better way to understand the impact on society than to read the letters around the world of people who are commenting on this topic. Typically they are at the doctoral level, but technicality aside, one can understand their sincere nature. Go to the website http://www.spaceandsociety.org/cgi-bin/short-list.pl for more information.

COMPETENCY 9.0 KNOWLEDGE OF MATTER AND ENERGY

Skill 9.1 Identify the physical and chemical properties of matter.

Everything in our world is made up of **matter**, whether it is a rock, a building, an animal, or a person. Matter is defined by its characteristics: it takes up space and has mass.

Mass is a measure of the amount of matter in an object. Two objects of equal mass will balance each other on a simple balance scale no matter where the scale is located. For instance, two rocks with the same amount of mass that are in balance on Earth will also be in balance on the moon. They will feel heavier on Earth than on the moon because of the gravitational pull of the Earth. So, although the two rocks have the same mass, they will have different **weight.** **Weight** is the measure of the Earth's pull of gravity on an object. It can also be defined as the pull of gravity between other bodies. The units of weight measurement commonly used are the pound (English measure) and the kilogram (metric measure).

In addition to mass, matter also has the property of volume. **Volume** is the amount of cubic space that an object occupies. Volume and mass together give a more exact description of the object. Two objects may have the same volume, but different mass, or the same mass but different volumes. For instance, consider two cubes that are each one cubic centimeter, one made from plastic, one from lead. They have the same volume, but the lead cube has more mass. The measure that we use to describe the cubes takes into consideration both the mass and the volume. **Density** is the mass of a substance contained per unit of volume. If the density of an object is less than the density of a liquid, the object will float in the liquid. If the object is denser than the liquid, then the object will sink.

Density is stated in grams per cubic centimeter (g/cm^3) where the gram is the standard unit of mass. To find an object's density, you must measure its mass and its volume. Then divide the mass by the volume ($D = m/V$). To discover an object's density, first use a balance to find its mass. Then calculate its volume. If the object is a regular shape, you can find the volume by multiplying the length, width, and height together. However, if it is an irregular shape, you can find the volume by seeing how much water it displaces. Measure the water in the container before and after the object is submerged. The difference will be the volume of the object.

Specific gravity is the ratio of the density of a substance to the density of water. For instance, the specific density of one liter of turpentine is calculated by comparing its mass (0.81 kg) to the mass of one liter of water (1 kg):

$$\frac{\text{mass of 1 L alcohol}}{\text{mass of 1 L water}} = \frac{0.81\text{ kg}}{1.00\text{ kg}} = 0.81$$

Properties of Matter

Physical properties and chemical properties of matter describe the appearance or behavior of a substance. A **physical property** can be observed without changing the identity of a substance. For instance, you can describe the color, mass, shape, and volume of a book. **Chemical properties** describe the ability of a substance to be changed into new substances. Baking powder goes through a chemical change as it changes into carbon dioxide gas during the baking process.

Matter constantly changes. A **physical change** is a change that does not produce a new substance. The freezing and melting of water is an example of physical change. A **chemical change** (or chemical reaction) is any change of a substance into one or more other substances. Burning materials turn into smoke; a seltzer tablet fizzes into gas bubbles.

Solids, liquids, and gases

The **phase of matter** (solid, liquid, or gas) is identified by its shape and volume. A **solid** has a definite shape and volume. A **liquid** has a definite volume, but no shape. A **gas** has no shape or volume because it will spread out to occupy the entire space of whatever container it is in.

Energy is the ability to cause change in matter. Applying heat to a frozen liquid changes it from solid back to liquid. Continue heating it and it will boil and give off steam, a gas.

Evaporation is the change in phase from liquid to gas. **Condensation** is the change in phase from gas to liquid.

As a substance is heated, the molecules begin moving faster within the container. As the substance becomes a gas and those molecules hit the sides of the container, pressure builds. **Pressure** is the force exerted on each unit of area of a surface. Pressure is measured in a unit called the **Pascal**. One Pascal (pa) is equal to one Newton of force pushing on one square meter of area. Volume, temperature, and pressure of gas are related.

Temperature and pressure: As the temperature of a gas increases, its pressure increases. When you drive a car, the friction between the road and the tire heats up the rubber which heats the air inside the tire. Because the temperature increases, so does the pressure of the air on the inside of the tire.

Temperature and volume: At a constant pressure, an increase in temperature causes an increase in the volume of a gas. If you apply heat to an enclosed container of gas, the pressure inside the bottle will increase as the heat increases. This is called **Charles' Law**.

These relations (pressure and temperature and temperature and volume) are **direct variations**. As one component increases (decreases), the other also increases (decreases). However, pressure and volume vary inversely.

Pressure and volume: At a constant temperature, a decrease in the volume of a gas causes an increase in its pressure. An example of this is a tire pump. The gas pressure inside the pump gets bigger as you press down on the pump handle because you are compressing the gas, or forcing it to exist in a smaller volume. This relationship between pressure and volume is called **Boyle's Law**.

Temperature is not the same as heat

Heat and temperature are different physical quantities. **Heat** is a measure of energy. **Temperature** is the measure of how hot (or cold) a body is with respect to a standard object.

Two concepts are important in the discussion of temperature changes. Objects are in thermal contact if they can affect each other's temperatures. Set a hot cup of coffee on a desk top. The two objects are in thermal contact with each other and will begin affecting each other's temperatures. The coffee will become cooler and the desktop warmer. Eventually, they will have the same temperature. When this happens, they are in **thermal equilibrium.**

We cannot rely on our sense of touch to determine temperature because the heat from a hand may be conducted more efficiently by certain objects, making them feel colder. **Thermometers** are used to measure temperature. A small amount of mercury in a capillary tube will expand when heated. The thermometer and the object whose temperature it is measuring are put in contact long enough for them to reach thermal equilibrium. Then the temperature can be read from the thermometer scale. Three temperature scales are used:

Celsius: The freezing point of water is set at 0 and the steam (boiling) point is 100. The interval between the two is divided into 100 equal parts called degrees Celsius.

Fahrenheit: The freezing point of water is 32 degrees and the boiling point is 212. The interval between is divided into 180 equal parts called degrees Fahrenheit.

Temperature readings can be converted from one to the other as follows.

Fahrenheit to Celsius	**Celsius to Fahrenheit**
C = 5/9 (F - 32)	F = (9/5) C + 32

Kelvin Scale has degrees the same size as the Celsius scale, but the zero point is moved to the triple point of water. Water inside a closed vessel is in thermal equilibrium in all three states (ice, water, and vapor) at 273.15 degrees Kelvin. This temperature is equivalent to .01 degrees Celsius. Because the degrees are the same in the two scales, temperature changes are the same in Celsius and Kelvin.

Temperature readings can be converted from Celsius to Kelvin:

Celsius to Kelvin	**Kelvin to Celsius**
K = C + 273.15	C = K - 273.15

Heat is a measure of energy. If two objects that have different temperatures come into contact with each other, heat flows from the hotter object to the cooler.

Heat capacity of an object is the amount of heat energy that it takes to raise the temperature of the object by one degree.

Heat capacity (C) per unit mass (m) is called **specific heat** (c):

$$c = \frac{C}{m} = \frac{Q / \Delta}{m}$$

There are a number of ways that heat is measured. In each case, the measurement is dependent upon raising the temperature of a specific amount of water by a specific amount. These conversions of heat energy and work are called the **mechanical equivalent of heat**.

The **calorie** is the amount of energy that it takes to raise one gram of water one degree Celsius.

The **kilocalorie** is the amount of energy that it takes to raise one kilogram of water by one degree Celsius. Food calories are kilocalories.
In the International System of Units **(SI),** the calorie is equal to 4.184 **joules**.

A **British thermal unit (BTU)** = 252 calories = 1.054 kJ

Skill 9.2 Apply knowledge of the periodic table to identify the characteristics of atoms, the chemical and physical combinations of atoms, and associated representations.

Elements, compounds, and mixtures

An **element** is a substance that cannot be broken down into other substances. To date, scientists have identified 109 elements: 89 are found in nature and 20 are synthetic.

An **atom** is the smallest particle of the element that retains the properties of that element. All of the atoms of a particular element are the same. The atoms of each element are different from the atoms of other elements.

Elements are assigned an identifying symbol of one or two letters. The symbol for oxygen is O and stands for one atom of oxygen. However, because oxygen atoms in nature are joined together in pairs, the symbol O_2 represents oxygen. This pair of oxygen atoms is a molecule. A **molecule** is the smallest particle of substance that can exist independently and has all of the properties of that substance. A molecule of most elements is made up of one atom. However, oxygen, hydrogen, nitrogen, and chlorine molecules are made of two atoms each.

A **compound** is made of two or more elements that have been chemically combined. Atoms join together when elements are chemically combined. The result is that the elements lose their individual identities when they are joined. The compound that they become has different properties.

We use a formula to show the elements of a chemical compound. A **chemical formula** is a shorthand way of showing what is in a compound by using symbols and subscripts. The letter symbols let us know what elements are involved and the number subscript tells how many atoms of each element are involved. No subscript is used if there is only one atom involved. For example, carbon dioxide is made up of one atom of carbon (C) and two atoms of oxygen (O_2), so the formula would be represented as CO_2.

Substances can combine without a chemical change. A **mixture** is any combination of two or more substances in which the substances keep their own properties. A fruit salad is a mixture. So is an ice cream sundae, although you might not recognize each part if it is stirred together. Colognes and perfumes are other examples. You may not readily recognize the individual elements; however, they can be separated.

Compounds and **mixtures** are similar in that they are made up of two or more substances. However, they have the following opposite characteristics:

Compounds:

1. Made up of one kind of particle
2. Formed during a chemical change
3. Broken down only by chemical changes
4. Properties are different from its parts
5. Has a specific amount of each ingredient.

Mixtures:

1. Made up of two or more particles
2. Not formed by a chemical change
3. Can be separated by physical changes
4. Properties are the same as its parts.
5. Does not have a definite amount of each ingredient.

Common compounds are **acids, bases, salts**, and **oxides,** and are they classified according to their characteristics.

An **acid** contains one element of hydrogen (H). Although it is never wise to taste a substance to identify it, acids have a sour taste. Vinegar and lemon juice are both acids, and acids occur in many foods in a weak state. Strong acids can burn skin and destroy materials. Common acids include:

Sulfuric acid (H_2SO_4)	-	Used in medicines, alcohol, dyes, and car batteries.
Nitric acid (HNO_3)	-	Used in fertilizers, explosives, cleaning materials.
Carbonic acid (H_2CO_3)	-	Used in soft drinks.
Acetic acid ($HC_2H_3O_2$)	-	Used in making plastics, rubber, photographic film, and as a solvent.

Bases have a bitter taste and the stronger ones feel slippery. Like acids, strong bases can be dangerous and should be handled carefully. All bases contain the elements oxygen and hydrogen (OH). Many household cleaning products contain bases. Common bases include:

Sodium hydroxide	NaOH	-	Used in making soap, paper, vegetable oils, and refining petroleum.
Ammonium hydroxide	NH_4OH	-	Making deodorants, bleaching compounds, cleaning compounds.
Potassium hydroxide	KOH	-	Making soaps, drugs, dyes, alkaline batteries, and purifying industrial gases.
Calcium hydroxide	$Ca(OH)_2$	-	Making cement and plaster

An **indicator** is a substance that changes color when it comes in contact with an acid or a base. Litmus paper is an indicator. Blue litmus paper turns red in an acid. Red litmus paper turns blue in a base.

A substance that is neither acid nor base is **neutral**. Neutral substances do not change the color of litmus paper.

Salt is formed when an acid and a base combine chemically. Water is also formed. The process is called **neutralization**. Table salt (NaCl) is an example of this process. Salts are also used in toothpaste, epsom salts, and cream of tartar. Calcium chloride ($CaCl_2$) is used on frozen streets and walkways to melt the ice.

Oxides are compounds that are formed when oxygen combines with another element. Rust is an oxide formed when oxygen combines with iron.

Symbols, formulas, and equations

One or more substances are formed during a **chemical reaction**. Also, energy is released during some chemical reactions. Sometimes the energy release is slow and sometimes it is rapid. In a fireworks display, energy is released very rapidly. However, the chemical reaction that produces tarnish on a silver spoon happens very slowly.

Chemical equilibrium is defined as occurring when the quantities of reactants and products are at a 'steady state' and no longer shifting, but the reaction may still proceed forward and backward. The rate of forward reaction must equal the rate of backward reaction.

In one kind of chemical reaction, two elements combine to form a new substance. We can represent the reaction and the results in a chemical equation. Carbon and oxygen form carbon dioxide. The equation can be written:

C	+	O_2	$\rightarrow$	CO_2
1 atom of carbon	+	2 atoms of oxygen	$\rightarrow$	1 molecule of carbon dioxide

No matter is ever gained or lost during a chemical reaction; therefore the chemical equation must be *balanced.* This means that there must be the same number of atoms on both sides of the equation. Remember that the subscript numbers indicate the number of atoms in the elements. If there is no subscript, assume there is only one atom.

In a second kind of chemical reaction, the molecules of a substance split forming two or more new substances. An electric current can split water molecules into hydrogen and oxygen gas.

$2H_2O$	$\rightarrow$	$2H_2$	+	O_2
2 molecules of water	$\rightarrow$	2 molecules of hydrogen	+	1 molecule of oxygen

The number of molecules is shown by the number in front of an element or compound. If no number appears, assume that it is one molecule.

A third kind of chemical reaction is when elements change places with each other. An example of one element taking the place of another is when iron changes places with copper in the compound copper sulfate:

$CuSo_4$	+	Fe	$\rightarrow$	$FeSO_4$	+	Cu
copper sulfate	+	iron (steel wool)		iron sulfate		copper

Sometimes two sets of elements change places. In this example, an acid and a base are combined:

HCl	+	$NaOH$	$\rightarrow$	$NaCl$	+	H_2O
hydrochloric acid		sodium hydroxide		sodium chloride (table salt)		water

Matter can change, but it cannot be created or destroyed. The sample equations show two things:

1. In a chemical reaction, matter is changed into one or more different kinds of matter.

2. The amount of matter present before and after the chemical reaction is the same.

Many chemical reactions give off energy. Like matter, energy can change form, but it can be neither created nor destroyed during a chemical reaction. This is the **law of conservation of energy.**

The Atom

An **atom** is a nucleus surrounded by a cloud with moving electrons.

The **nucleus** is the center of the atom. It is composed of two particles:

> **Protons** are the positive particles in the nucleus. The mass of a proton is about 2,000 times that of the mass of an electron. The number of protons in the nucleus of an atom is called the **atomic number**. All atoms of the same element have the same atomic number.
>
> **Neutrons** are another type of particle in the nucleus. Neutrons have mass but no charge.

Neutrons were discovered because scientists observed that not all atoms in neon gas have the same mass. They had identified isotopes. **Isotopes** of an element have the same number of protons in the nucleus, but have different masses. Neutrons explain the difference in mass because they have mass but no charge.

The mass of matter is measured against a standard mass such as the gram. Scientists measure the mass of an atom by comparing it to that of a standard atom. The result is relative mass. The **relative mass** of an atom is its mass expressed in terms of the mass of the standard atom. The isotope of the element carbon is the standard atom. It has six (6) neutrons and is called carbon-12.It is assigned a mass of 12 atomic mass units (amu). Therefore, the **atomic mass unit (amu)** is the standard unit for measuring the mass of an atom. It is equal to the mass of a carbon atom.

The **mass number** of an atom is the sum of its protons and neutrons. In any element, there is a mixture of isotopes, some having slightly more or slightly fewer protons and neutrons. The **atomic mass** of an element is an average of the mass numbers of its atoms.

The following table summarizes the terms used to describe atomic nuclei:

Term	Example	Meaning	Characteristic
Atomic Number	# protons (p)	same for all atoms of a given element	Carbon (C) atomic number = 6 (6p)
Mass number	# protons + # neutrons (p + n)	changes for different isotopes of an element	C-12 (6p + 6n) C-13 (6p + 7n)
Atomic mass	average mass of the atoms of the element	usually not a whole number	atomic mass of carbon equals 12.011

Each atom has an equal number of electrons (negative) and protons (positive). Therefore, atoms are neutral. Electrons orbiting the nucleus occupy energy levels that are arranged in order and the electrons tend to occupy the lowest energy level available. A **stable electron arrangement** is an atom that has all of its electrons in the lowest possible energy levels.

Each energy level holds a maximum number of electrons. However, an atom with more than one level does not hold more than eight (8) electrons in its outermost shell.

Level	Name	Max. # of Electrons
First	K shell	2
Second	L shell	8
Third	M shell	18
Fourth	N shell	32

This can help explain why chemical reactions occur. Atoms react with each other when their outer levels are unfilled. When atoms either exchange or share electrons with each other, these energy levels become filled and the atom becomes more stable.

As an electron gains energy, it moves from one energy level to a higher energy level. The electron cannot leave one level until it has enough energy to reach the next level. **Excited electrons** are electrons that have absorbed energy and have moved farther from the nucleus.

Electrons can also lose energy. When they do, they fall to a lower level. However, they can only fall to the lowest level that has room for them. This explains why atoms do not collapse.

Identify groups of elements in the periodic table, given chemical or physical properties

The **periodic table of elements** is an arrangement of the elements in rows and columns so that it is easy to locate elements with similar properties. The elements of the modern periodic table are arranged in numerical order by atomic number.

The **periods** are the rows down the left side of the table. They are called first period, second period, etc. The columns of the periodic table are called **groups** or **families.** Elements in a family have similar properties.

There are three types of elements that are grouped by color: metals, nonmetals, and metalloids.

<u>**Element Key**</u>

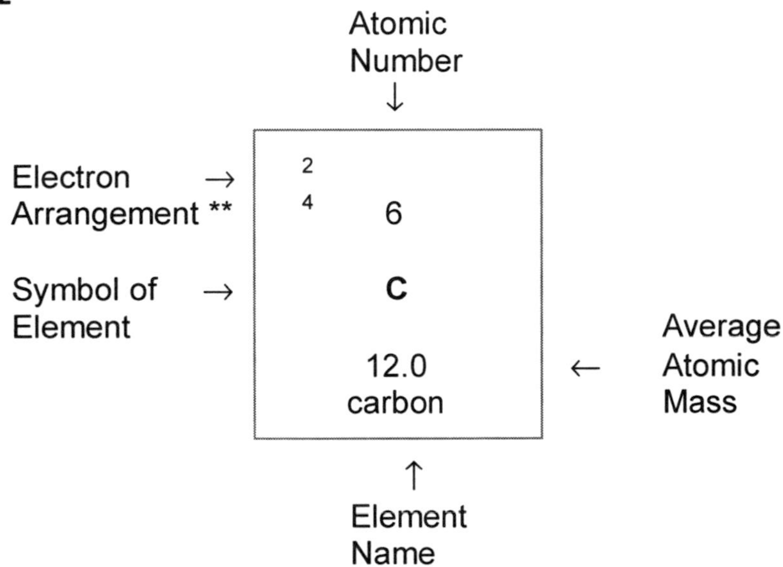

** Number of electrons on each level. Top number represents the innermost level.

The periodic table arranges metals into families with similar properties. The periodic table has its columns marked IA - VIIIA. These are the traditional group numbers. Arabic numbers 1 - 18 are also used as suggested by the Union of Physicists and Chemists. The Arabic numerals will be used in this text.

Metals

With the exception of hydrogen, all elements in Group 1 are **alkali metals**. These metals are shiny, softer, and less dense than other metals. These are the most chemically active.

Group 2 metals are the **alkaline earth metals.** They are harder, denser, have higher melting points, and are chemically active.

The **transition elements** can be found by finding the periods (rows) from 4 to 7 under the groups (columns) 3 - 12. They are metals that do not show a range of properties as you move across the chart. They are hard and have high melting points. Compounds of these elements are colorful, such as silver, gold, and mercury.

Elements can be combined to make metallic objects. An **alloy** is a mixture of two or more elements having properties of metals. The elements do not have to be all metals. For instance, steel is made up of the metal iron and the non-metal carbon.

Nonmetals

Nonmetals are not as easy to recognize as metals because they do not always share physical properties. However, in general the properties of nonmetals are the opposite of metals. They are dull, brittle, and are not good conductors of heat and electricity.

Nonmetals include solids, gases, and one liquid (bromine).

Nonmetals have four to eight electrons in their outermost energy levels and tend to attract electrons. As a result, the outer levels are usually filled with eight electrons. This difference in the number of electrons is what caused the differences between metals and nonmetals. The outstanding chemical property of nonmetals is that they react with metals.

The **halogens** can be found in Group 17. Halogens combine readily with metals to form salts. Table salt, fluoride toothpaste, and bleach all have an element from the halogen family.

The **Noble Gases** got their name from the fact that they did not react chemically with other elements, much like the nobility did not mix with the masses. These gases (found in Group 18) will only combine with other elements under very specific conditions. They are **inert** (inactive).

In recent years, scientists have found this to be only generally true, since chemists have been able to prepare compounds of krypton and xenon.

Metalloids

Metalloids have properties in between metals and nonmetals. They can be found in Groups 13 - 16, but do not occupy the entire group. They are arranged in stair steps across the groups.

Physical Properties:

1. All are solids having the appearance of metals.
2. All are white or gray, but not shiny.
3. They will conduct electricity but not as well as a metal.

Chemical Properties:

1. Have some characteristics of metals and nonmetals.
2. Properties do not follow patterns like metals and nonmetals. Each must be studied individually.

Boron is the first element in Group 13. It is a poor conductor of electricity at low temperatures. However, increase its temperature and it becomes a good conductor. By comparison, metals, which are good conductors, lose their ability as they are heated. It is because of this property that boron is so useful. Boron is a semiconductor. **Semiconductors** are used in electrical devices that have to function at temperatures too high for metals.

Silicon is the second element in Group 14. It is also a semiconductor and is found in great abundance in the Earth's crust. Sand is made of a silicon compound, silicon dioxide. Silicon is also used in the manufacture of glass and cement.

Covalent and ionic bonding

The outermost electrons in the atoms are called **valence electrons.** Because they are the ones involved in the bonding process, they determine the properties of the element.

A **chemical bond** is a force of attraction that holds atoms together. When atoms are bonded chemically, they cease to have their individual properties. For instance, hydrogen and oxygen combine into water and no longer look like hydrogen and oxygen. They look like water.

A **covalent bond** is formed when two atoms share electrons. Recall that atoms whose outer shells are not filled with electrons are unstable. When they are unstable, they readily combine with other unstable atoms. By combining and sharing electrons, they act as a single unit. Covalent bonding happens among nonmetals. Covalent bonds are always polar between two non-identical atoms.

Covalent compounds are compounds whose atoms are joined by covalent bonds. Table sugar, methane, and ammonia are examples of covalent compounds.

An **ionic bond** is a bond formed by the transfer of electrons. It happens when metals and nonmetals bond. Before chlorine and sodium combine, the sodium has one valence electron and chlorine has seven. Neither valence shell is filled, but the chlorine's valence shell is almost full. During the reaction, the sodium gives one valence electron to the chlorine atom. Both atoms then have filled shells and are stable.

Something else has happened during the bonding. Before the bonding, both atoms were neutral. When one electron was transferred, it upset the balance of protons and electrons in each atom. The chlorine atom took on one extra electron and the sodium atom released one atom. The atoms have now become ions. **Ions** are atoms with an unequal number of protons and electrons. To determine whether the ion is positive or negative, compare the number of protons (+charge) to the electrons (-charge). If there are more electrons, the ion will be negative. If there are more protons, the ion will be positive.

Compounds that result from the transfer of metal atoms to nonmetal atoms are called **ionic compounds.** Sodium chloride (table salt), sodium hydroxide (drain cleaner), and potassium chloride (salt substitute) are examples of ionic compounds.

Spontaneous diffusion occurs when random motion leads particles to increase entropy by equalizing concentrations. Particles tend to move into places of lower concentration. For example, sodium will move into a cell if the concentration is greater outside than inside the cell. Spontaneous diffusion keeps cells balanced.

Chemical reactions

There are four kinds of chemical reactions:

In a **composition reaction**, two or more substances combine to form a compound.

$A + B \rightarrow AB$

i.e. silver and sulfur yield silver dioxide

In a **decomposition reaction**, a compound breaks down into two or more simpler substances.

$AB \rightarrow A + B$

i.e. water breaks down into hydrogen and oxygen
In a **single replacement reaction**, a free element replaces an element that is part of a compound.

$A + BX \rightarrow AX + B$

i.e. iron plus copper sulfate yields iron sulfate plus copper

In a **double replacement reaction**, parts of two compounds replace each other. In this case, the compounds seem to switch partners.

$AX + BY \rightarrow AY + BX$

i.e. sodium chloride plus mercury nitrate yields sodium nitrate plus mercury chloride

Skill 9.3 Identify the features and characteristics of different regions of the electromagnetic spectrum.

Nearly all objects in the universe emit, reflect, or transmit some amount of light, although in varying degrees. With this in mind, the electromagnetic spectrum was recorded. The electromagnetic spectrum is measured in frequency (f) in hertz and wavelength (λ) in meters. The frequency times the wavelength of every electromagnetic wave equals the speed of light (3.0×10^9 meters/second). Roughly, the range of wavelengths of the electromagnetic spectrum is:

	f	λ
Radio waves	10^{5} - 10^{-1} hertz	10^{3} -10^{9} meters
Microwaves	10^{-1} - 10^{-3} hertz	10^{9} -10^{11} meters
Infrared radiation	10^{-3} - 10^{-6} hertz	$10^{11.2}$ -$10^{14.3}$ meters
Visible light	$10^{-6.2}$ $10^{-6.9}$ hertz	$10^{14.3}$ -10^{15} meters
Ultraviolet radiation	10^{-7} - 10^{-9} hertz	10^{15} -$10^{17.2}$ meters
X-Rays	10^{-9} - 10^{-11} hertz	$10^{17.2}$ -10^{19} meters
Gamma Rays	10^{-11} - 10^{-15} hertz	10^{19} - $10^{23.25}$ meters

Radio waves are used for transmitting data. Common examples are television, cell phones, and wireless computer networks. Microwaves are used to heat food and deliver Wi-Fi service. Infrared waves are utilized in night vision goggles. We are all familiar with visible light as the human eye is most sensitive to this wavelength range. UV light causes sunburns and would be even more harmful if most of it were not captured in the Earth's ozone layer. X-rays aid us in the medical field, and gamma rays are most useful in the field of astronomy.

Skill 9.4 Apply knowledge of energy forms, energy types, and energy transfer to solve problems.

Energy can be found in either a kinetic or potential state. **Potential energy** is "captured" in an object with the potential waiting to be released. A great example of potential energy is elastic. We all know how much elastic can hurt on contact when its tautness is released. **Kinetic energy** is the energy that an object possesses as a result of its motion. Its definition is: the work needed to accelerate a body from rest to its current velocity. Having gained energy during acceleration, the object maintains this kinetic energy unless its speed is altered. Newton's laws of mechanics describe the calculations for kinetic and potential energy.

object's gravitational potential energy, U_g, is given by

$$U_g = mgh$$

where

m is the mass of the object
g is the acceleration due to gravity (approximately 9.8 m/s^2 at Earth's surface)
h is the height to which the object is raised, relative to a given reference level (such as the earth's surface)

$$E_k = \frac{1}{2}mv^2$$

Where E is kinetic energy, m is the mass, and v is the speed of the body.

Energy can also be solar or electrical. The use of **solar energy** has been implemented widely where other power supplies are absent, such as in remote locations and in space. **Solar power** is the technology of obtaining usable energy from the light of the sun. Solar radiation reaches the Earth's upper atmosphere at a rate of 1,366 watts per square meter. Much is reflected or absorbed, but what arrives is maximized at the equator. Harnessing that energy is a logical step considering that we are depleting many of our other resources.

Electrical energy can refer to the energy stored in an electric field, the potential energy of a charged particle in an electric field, or the energy used by electricity. The unit for measuring electrical energy, no matter the context, is always the **joule**.

Heat energy that is transferred into or out of a system is **heat transfer.** The temperature change is positive for a gain in heat energy and negative when heat is removed from the object or system. The formula for heat transfer is $Q = mc\Delta T$ where Q is the amount of heat energy transferred, m is the amount of substance (in kilograms), c is the specific heat of the substance, and ΔT is the change in temperature of the substance. It is important to assume that the objects in thermal contact are isolated and insulated from their surroundings.

If a substance in a closed container loses heat, then another substance in the container must gain heat.

A **calorimeter** uses the transfer of heat from one substance to another to determine the specific heat of the substance.

When an object undergoes a change of phase, it goes from one physical state (solid, liquid, or gas) to another. For instance, water can go from liquid to solid (freezing) or from liquid to gas (boiling). The heat that is required to change from one state to the other is called **latent heat.**

The **heat of fusion** is the amount of heat that it takes to change from a solid to a liquid or the amount of heat released during the change from liquid to solid.

The **heat of vaporization** is the amount of heat that it takes to change from a liquid to a gaseous state.

Heat is transferred in three ways: **conduction, convection, and radiation.**

> **Conduction** occurs when heat travels through the heated solid.
> The transfer rate is the ratio of the amount of heat per amount of time it takes to transfer heat from area of an object to another. For example, if you place an iron pan on a flame, the handle will eventually become hot. How fast the handle gets too hot to handle is a function of the amount of heat and how long it is applied. Because the change in time is in the denominator of the function, the shorter the amount of time it takes to heat the handle, the greater the transfer rate.
>
> **Convection** is heat transported by the movement of a heated substance. Warmed air rising from a heat source, such as a fire or electric heater, is a common example of convection. Convection ovens make use of circulating air to more efficiently cook food.
>
> **Radiation** is heat transfer as the result of electromagnetic waves**.** The sun warms the Earth by emitting radiant energy.

An example of all three methods of heat transfer occurs in the thermos bottle or Dewar flask. The bottle is constructed of double walls of Pyrex glass that have a space in between. Air is evacuated from the space between the walls and the inner wall is silvered. The lack of air between the walls lessens heat loss by convection and conduction. The heat inside is reflected by the silver, cutting down heat transfer by radiation. Hot liquids remain hotter and cold liquids remain colder for longer periods of time.

Magnetism

Magnets have a north pole and a south pole. Like poles repel and opposing poles attract. A **magnetic field** is the space around a magnet where its force will affect objects. The closer you are to a magnet, the stronger the force. As you move away, the force becomes weaker.

Some materials act as magnets and some do not. This is because magnetism is a result of electrons in motion. The most important motion in this case is the spinning of the individual electrons. Electrons spin in pairs in opposite directions in most atoms. Each spinning electron has the magnetic field that it creates canceled out by the electron that is spinning in the opposite direction.

In an atom of iron, there are four unpaired electrons. The magnetic fields of these are not canceled out. Their fields add up to make a tiny magnet. Their fields exert forces on each other setting up small areas in the iron called **magnetic domains** where atomic magnetic fields line up in the same direction. You can make a magnet out of an iron nail by stroking the nail in the same direction repeatedly with a magnet. This causes poles in the atomic magnets in the nail to be attracted to the magnet. The tiny magnetic fields in the nail line up in the direction of the magnet. The magnet causes the domains pointing in its direction to grow in the nail. Eventually, one large domain results and the nail becomes a magnet.

A bar magnet has a north pole and a south pole. If you break the magnet in half, each piece will have a north and south pole.

The Earth has a magnetic field. In a compass, a tiny, lightweight magnet is suspended and will line its south pole up with the North Pole magnet of the Earth.

A magnet can be made out of a coil of wire by connecting the ends of the coil to a battery. When the current goes through the wire, the wire acts in the same way that a magnet does; it is called an **electromagnet**. The poles of the electromagnet will depend upon which way the electric current runs. An electromagnet can be made more powerful in three ways:

1. Make more coils.
2. Put an iron core (nail) inside the coils.
3. Use more battery power.

Telegraphs use electromagnets to work. When a telegraph key is pushed, current flows through a circuit turning on an electromagnet which attracts an iron bar. The iron bar hits a sounding board which responds with a click. Release the key and the electromagnet turns off. Messages can be sent around the world in this way.

Scrap metal can be removed from waste materials by the use of a large electromagnet that is suspended from a crane. When the electromagnet is turned on, the metal in the pile of waste will be attracted to it. All other materials will stay on the ground.

Air conditioners, vacuum cleaners, and washing machines use electric motors. An electric motor uses an electromagnet to change electric energy into mechanical energy.

Fission and Fusion

Chemical reactions involve the breaking and forming of bonds between atoms. Bonds involve only the outer electrons and do not affect the nucleus. When a reaction involves a nucleus, elements are changed into different elements. This is called a **nuclear reaction**.

The binding energy is released when the nuclei of atoms are split apart in a nuclear reaction. This binding energy is called **nuclear energy**.

There are two types of nuclear reactions:

Nuclear fission occurs when the nuclei are split apart. Smaller nuclei are formed and energy is released. The fission of many atoms in a short time period releases a large amount of energy. “Heavy water” is used in a nuclear reactor to slow down neutrons, controlling and moderating the nuclear reactions. Controlling the environment so that energy is released slowly gives us nuclear submarines and nuclear power plants.

Nuclear fusion is the opposite. It occurs when small nuclei combine to form a larger nucleus. It begins with the hydrogen atom, which has the smallest nuclei. During one type of fusion, four hydrogen nuclei are fused at very high pressures and temperatures. They form one helium atom. The sun and stars are examples of fusion. They are made mostly of hydrogen that is constantly fusing. As the hydrogen forms helium, it releases an energy that we see as light. When all of the hydrogen is used, the star will no longer shine. Scientists estimate that the sun has enough hydrogen to keep it glowing for another four billion years.

During a nuclear reaction, elements change into other elements called **radioactive elements**. Uranium is a radioactive element. The element uranium breaks down and changes into the element lead. Most natural radioactive elements breakdown slowly, so energy is released over a long period of time.

Radioactive particles are used in the treatment of cancer because they can kill cancer cells. However, if they are powerful enough, they can also cause death.

People working around such substances must protect themselves with the correct clothing, equipment, and procedures.

Skill 9.5 Apply laws of force, motion, and energy to solve problems.

SEE also Skill 9.4

The relationship between heat, forms of energy, and work (mechanical, electrical, etc.) are the **Laws of Thermodynamics.** These laws deal strictly with systems in thermal equilibrium and not those within the process of rapid change or in a state of transition. Systems that are nearly always in a state of equilibrium are called **reversible systems.**

The first law of thermodynamics is a restatement of conservation of energy. The change in heat energy supplied to a system (Q) is equal to the sum of the change in the internal energy (U) and the change in the work done by the system against internal forces. $\Delta Q = \Delta U + \Delta W$

The second law of thermodynamics is stated in two parts:

1. No machine is 100% efficient. It is impossible to construct a machine that only absorbs heat from a heat source and performs an equal amount of work because some heat will always be lost to the environment.
2. Heat cannot spontaneously pass from a colder to a hotter object. An ice cube sitting on a hot sidewalk will melt into a little puddle, but it will never spontaneously cool and form the same ice cube. Certain events have a preferred direction called the **arrow of time.**

Entropy is the measure of how much energy or heat is available for work. Work occurs only when heat is transferred from hot to cooler objects. Once this is done, no more work can be extracted. The energy is still being conserved, but is not available for work as long as the objects are the same temperature. Theory has it that, eventually, all things in the universe will reach the same temperature. If this happens, energy will no longer be usable.

Forces

Dynamics is the study of the relationship between motion and the forces affecting motion. **Force** causes motion.

Mass and weight are not the same quantities. An object's **mass** gives it a reluctance to change its current state of motion. It is also the measure of an object's resistance to acceleration. The force that the Earth's gravity exerts on an object with a specific mass is called the object's weight on Earth. Weight is a force that is measured in Newtons. Weight (W) equals mass multiplied by acceleration due to gravity or **W = mg**.

To illustrate the difference between mass and weight, picture two rocks of equal mass on a balance scale. If the scale is balanced in one place, it will be balanced everywhere, regardless of the gravitational field. However, the weight of the stones would vary on a spring scale, depending upon the gravitational field. In other words, the stones would be balanced both on Earth and on the moon. However, the weight of the stones would be greater on Earth than on the moon.

Newton's laws of motion

Newton's first law of motion is also called the law of inertia. It states that an object at rest will remain at rest and an object in motion will remain in motion at a constant velocity unless acted upon by an external force.

Newton's second law of motion states that if a net force acts on an object, it will cause the acceleration of the object. The relationship between force and motion is Force equals mass times acceleration **($F = ma$).**

Newton's third law states that for every action there is an equal and opposite reaction. Therefore, if an object exerts a force on another object, that second object exerts an equal and opposite force on the first.

Surfaces that touch each other have a certain resistance to motion. This resistance is **friction.**

1. The materials that make up the surfaces will determine the magnitude of the frictional force.
2. The frictional force is independent of the area of contact between the two surfaces.
3. The direction of the frictional force is opposite to the direction of motion.
4. The frictional force is proportional to the normal force between the two surfaces in contact.

Static friction describes the force of friction of two surfaces that are in contact but do not have any motion relative to each other (i.e., a block sitting on an inclined plane). **Kinetic friction** describes the force of friction of two surfaces in contact with each other when there is relative motion between the surfaces.

Push and pull – Pushing a volleyball or pulling a bowstring applies muscular force when the muscles expand and contract. Elastic force is when any object returns to its original shape (for example, when a bow is released).

Rubbing – Friction opposes the motion of one surface past another. Friction is common when slowing down a car or sledding down a hill.

Pull of gravity is a force of attraction between two objects. Gravity questions can be raised not only on Earth but also between planets and black hole discussions.

Forces on objects at rest – The formula F= m/a is shorthand for force equals mass over acceleration. An object will not move unless the force is strong enough to move the mass. Also, there can be opposing forces holding the object in place. For instance, a boat may want to be forced by the currents to drift away, but an equal and opposite force is a rope holding it to a dock.

Forces on a moving object - Overcoming inertia is the tendency of any object to oppose a change in motion. An object at rest tends to stay at rest. An object that is moving tends to keep moving.

Inertia and circular motion – When an object moves in a circular path, a force must be directed toward the center of the circle in order to keep the motion going. This constraining force is called **centripetal force**. Gravity is the centripetal force that keeps a satellite circling the Earth. The centripetal force is provided by the high banking of the curved road and by friction between the wheels and the road. This inward force that keeps an object moving in a circle is called centripetal force.

Simple machines include the following:

1. Inclined plane
2. Lever
3. Wheel and axle
4. Pulley

Compound machines are two or more simple machines working together. A wheelbarrow is an example of a complex machine. It uses a lever and a wheel and axle. Machines of all types ease workload by changing the size or direction of an applied force. The amount of effort saved when using simple or complex machines is called mechanical advantage or MA.

Work is done on an object when an applied force moves through a distance.

Power is the work done divided by the amount of time that it took to do it. (Power = Work / time)

Skill 9.6 Apply knowledge of currents, circuits, conductors, insulators, and resistors to everyday situations

An **electric circuit** is a path along which electrons flow. A simple circuit can be created with a dry cell, wire, a bell, or a light bulb. When all are connected, the electrons flow from the negative terminal, through the wire to the device, and back to the positive terminal of the dry cell. If there are no breaks in the circuit, the device will work. The circuit is closed. Any break in the flow will create an open circuit and cause the device to shut off.

The device (bell, bulb) is an example of a **load**. A load is a device that uses energy. Suppose that you also add a buzzer so that the bell rings when you press the buzzer button. The buzzer is acting as a **switch**. A switch is a device that opens or closes a circuit. Pressing the buzzer makes the connection complete and the bell rings. When the buzzer is not engaged, the circuit is open and the bell is silent.

A **series circuit** is one where the electrons have only one path along which they can move. When one load in a series circuit goes out, the circuit is open. An example of this is a set of Christmas tree lights that is missing a bulb. If one bulb is missing, none of the bulbs will work.

A **parallel circuit** is one where the electrons have more than one path to move along. If a load goes out in a parallel circuit, the other load will still work because the electrons can still find a way to continue moving along the path.

When an electron goes through a load, it does work and therefore loses some of its energy. The measure of how much energy is lost is called the **potential difference**. The potential difference between two points is the work needed to move a charge from one point to another.

Potential difference is measured in a unit called the volt. **Voltage** is potential difference. The higher the voltage, the more energy the electrons have. This energy is measured by a device called a voltmeter. To use a voltmeter, place it in a circuit parallel with the load you are measuring.

Current is the number of electrons per second that flow past a point in a circuit. Current is measured with a device called an ammeter. To use an ammeter, put it in series with the load you are measuring.

As electrons flow through a wire, they lose potential energy. Some is changed into heat energy because of resistance. **Resistance** is the ability of the material to oppose the flow of electrons through it. All substances have some resistance, even if they are a good conductor such as copper. This resistance is measured in units called **ohms**. A thin wire will have more resistance than a thick one because it will have less room for electrons to travel. In a thicker wire, there will be more possible paths for the electrons to flow. Resistance also depends upon the length of the wire. The longer the wire, the more resistance it will have. Potential difference, resistance, and current form a relationship know as **Ohm's Law**. Current **(I)** is measured in amperes and is equal to potential difference **(V)** divided by resistance **(R)**.

$$I = V / R$$

If you have a wire with resistance of 5 ohms and a potential difference of 75 volts, you can calculate the current by:

I = 75 volts / 5 ohms
I = 15 amperes

A current of 10 or more amperes will cause a wire to get hot. Twenty-two (22) amperes is about the maximum for a house circuit. Anything above 25 amperes can start a fire.

Electricity can be used to change the chemical composition of a material. For instance, when electricity is passed through water, it breaks the water down into hydrogen gas and oxygen gas.

Circuit breakers in a home monitor the electric current. If there is an overload, the circuit breaker will create an open circuit, stopping the flow of electricity.

Electricity

Electrostatics is the study of stationary electric charges. A plastic rod that is rubbed with fur or a glass rod that is rubbed with silk will become electrically charged and will attract small pieces of paper. The charge on the plastic rod rubbed with fur is negative, and the charge on glass rod rubbed with silk is positive.

Electrically charged objects share these characteristics:

1. Like charges repel one another.
2. Opposite charges attract each other.
3. Charge is conserved. A neutral object has no net change. If the plastic rod and fur are initially neutral when the rod becomes charged by the fur, a negative charge is transferred from the fur to the rod. The net negative charge on the rod is equal to the net positive charge on the fur.

Materials through which electric charges can easily flow are called conductors. On the other hand, an **insulator** is a material through which electric charges do not move easily, if at all. A simple device used to indicate the existence of a positive or negative charge is called an **electroscope**. An electroscope is made up of a conducting knob and attached to it are very lightweight conducting leaves usually made of foil (gold or aluminum). When a charged object touches the knob, the leaves push away from each other because like charges repel. It is not possible to tell whether if the charge is positive or negative.

Charging by induction

Touch the knob with a finger while a charged rod is nearby. The electrons will be repulsed and flow out of the electroscope through the hand. If the hand is removed while the charged rod remains close, the electroscope will retain the charge.

When an object is rubbed with a charged rod, the object will take on the same charge as the rod. However, charging by induction gives the object the opposite charge as that of the charged rod.

Grounding charge

Charge can be removed from an object by connecting it to the Earth through a conductor. The removal of static electricity by conduction is called **grounding**.

Skill 9.7 Identify properties and behaviors of sound and light waves

Sound

Sound waves are produced by a vibrating body. The vibrating object moves forward and compresses the air in front of it. It then reverses direction so that the pressure on the air is lessened and expansion of the air molecules occurs. One compression and expansion creates one longitudinal wave. Sound can be transmitted through any gas, liquid, or solid. However, it cannot be transmitted through a vacuum because there are no particles present to vibrate and bump into their adjacent particles to transmit the wave.

The vibrating air molecules move back and forth parallel to the direction of motion of the wave as they pass the energy from adjacent air molecules (closer to the source) to air molecules farther away from the source.

The **pitch** of a sound depends on the **frequency** that the ear receives. High-pitched sound waves have high frequencies. High notes are produced by an object that is vibrating at a greater number of times per second than one that produces a low note.

The **intensity** of a sound is the amount of energy that crosses a unit of area in a given unit of time. The loudness of the sound is subjective and depends upon the effect on the human ear. Two tones of the same intensity but of different pitches may appear to have different loudness. The intensity level of sound is measured in decibels. Normal conversation is about 60 decibels. A power saw is about 110 decibels.

The **amplitude** of a sound wave determines its loudness. Loud sound waves have large amplitudes. The larger the sound wave, the more energy is needed to create the wave.

An oscilloscope is useful in studying waves because it gives a picture of the wave that shows the crest and trough of the wave. **Interference** is the interaction of two or more waves that meet. If the waves interfere constructively, the crest of each one meets the crests of the others. They combine into a crest with greater amplitude. As a result, you hear a louder sound. If the waves interfere destructively, then the crest of one meets the trough of another. They produce a wave with lower amplitude that produces a softer sound.

If you have two tuning forks that produce different pitches, then one will produce sounds of a slightly higher frequency. When you strike the two forks simultaneously, you may hear beats. **Beats** are a series of loud and soft sounds. This is because when the waves meet, the crests combine at some points and produce loud sounds. At other points, they nearly cancel each other out and produce soft sounds.

When a piano tuner tunes a piano, he only uses one tuning fork, even though there are many strings on the piano. He adjusts to first string to be the same as that of the tuning fork. Then he listens to the beats that occur when both the tuned and untuned strings are struck. He adjusts the untuned string until he can hear the correct number of beats per second. This process of striking the untuned and tuned strings together and timing the beats is repeated until all the piano strings are tuned.

Pleasant sounds have a regular wave pattern that is repeated over and over. Sounds that do not happen with regularity are unpleasant and are called **noise**.

Change in experienced frequency due to relative motion of the source of the sound is called the **Doppler Effect.** When a siren approaches, the pitch is high. When it passes, the pitch drops. As a moving sound source approaches a listener, the sound waves are closer together, causing an increase in frequency in the sound that is heard. As the source passes the listener, the waves spread out and the sound experienced by the listener is lower.

Light

Shadows illustrate one of the basic properties of light. Light travels in a straight line. If you put your hand between a light source and a wall, you will interrupt the light and produce a shadow.

When light hits a surface, it is **reflected.** The angle of the incoming light (angle of incidence) is the same as the angle of the reflected light (angle of reflection). It is this reflected light that allows you to see objects. You see the objects when the reflected light reaches your eyes.

Different surfaces reflect light differently. Rough surfaces scatter light in many different directions. A smooth surface reflects the light in one direction. If it is smooth and shiny (like a mirror) you see your image in the surface.

When light enters a different medium, it bends. This bending, or change of speed, is called **refraction**.

Light can be **diffracted**, or bent, around the edges of an object. Diffraction occurs when light goes through a narrow slit. As light passes through it, the light bends slightly around the edges of the slit. You can demonstrate this by pressing your thumb and forefinger together, making a very thin slit between them. Hold them about 8 cm from your eye and look at a distant source of light. The pattern you observe is caused by the diffraction of light.

Light and other electromagnetic radiation can be polarized because the waves are transverse. The distinguishing characteristic of transverse waves is that they are perpendicular to the direction of the motion of the wave. Polarized light has vibrations confined to a single plane that is perpendicular to the direction of motion. Light is polarized by passing it through special filters that block all vibrations except those in a single plane. By blocking out all but one place of vibration, polarized sunglasses cut down on glare.

Light can travel through thin fibers of glass or plastic without escaping the sides. Light on the inside of these fibers is reflected so that it stays inside the fiber until it reaches the other end. Such fiber optics are being used to carry telephone messages. Sound waves are converted to electric signals that are coded into a series of light pulses which move through the optical fiber until they reach the other end. At that time, they are converted back into sound.

The image that you see in a bathroom mirror is a virtual image because it only seems to be where it is. However, a curved mirror can produce a real image. A real image is produced when light passes through the point where the image appears. A real image can be projected onto a screen. Cameras use a convex lens to produce an image on the film. A **convex lens** is thicker in the middle than at the edges. The image size depends upon the focal length (distance from the focus to the lens). The longer the focal length, the larger is the image. A **converging lens** produces a real image whenever the object is far enough from the lens so that the rays of light from the object can hit the lens and be focused into a real image on the other side of the lens.

Eyeglasses can help correct deficiencies of sight by changing where the image is focused on the retina of the eye. If a person is nearsighted, the lens of his eye focuses images in front of the retina. In this case, the corrective lens placed in the eyeglasses will be concave so that the image will reach the retina. In the case of farsightedness, the lens of the eye focuses the image behind the retina. The correction will call for a convex lens to be fitted into the glass frames so that the image is brought forward into sharper focus

Sample Test: General Science

DIRECTIONS: Read each item and select the best response.

1. **What is the scientific method?**
(Average Rigor) (Skill 6.1)

A. It is the process of doing an experiment and writing a laboratory report.
B. It is the process of using open inquiry and repeatable results to establish theories.
C. It is the process of reinforcing scientific principles by confirming results.
D. It is the process of recording data and observations.

2. **Which of the following is not an acceptable way for a student to acknowledge sources in a laboratory report?**
(Rigorous) (Skill 6.1)

A. The student tells his/her teacher what sources s/he used to write the report.
B. The student uses footnotes in the text, with sources cited, but not in correct MLA format.
C. The student uses endnotes in the text, with sources cited, in correct MLA format.
D. The student attaches a separate bibliography, noting each use of sources.

3. **Which of the following data sets is properly represented by a bar graph?**
(Average Rigor) (Skill 6.2)

A. Number of people choosing to buy cars, vs. Color of car bought.
B. Number of people choosing to buy cars, vs. Age of car customer.
C. Number of people choosing to buy cars, vs. Distance from car lot to customer home.
D. Number of people choosing to buy cars, vs. Time since last car purchase.

4. **In an experiment measuring the inhibition effect of different antibiotic discs on bacteria grown in Petri dishes, what are the independent and dependent variables respectively?**
(Rigorous) (Skill 6.3)

A. Number of bacterial colonies and the antibiotic type.
B. Antibiotic type and the distance between antibiotic and the closest colony.
C. Antibiotic type and the number of bacterial colonies.
D. Presence of bacterial colonies and the antibiotic type.

5. **When designing a scientific experiment, a student considers all the factors that may influence the results. The process goal is to ________.**
(Average Rigor) (Skill 6.3)

A. recognize and manipulate independent variables.
B. recognize and record independent variables.
C. recognize and manipulate dependent variables.
D. recognize and record dependent variables.

6. **Who should be notified in the case of a serious chemical spill?**
(Average Rigor) (Skill 6.4)

A. The custodian.
B. The fire department or their municipal authority.
C. The science department chair.
D. The School Board.

7. **Experiments may be done with any of the following animals except _________ .**
(Rigorous) (Skill 6.4)

A. birds.
B. invertebrates.
C. lower order life.
D. frogs.

8. **Which plant tissues contain chloroplasts?**
(Average Rigor) (Skill 7.1)

A. Stomata
B. Palisade mesophyll
C. Spongy Mesophyll
D. Endosperm

9. **Klinefelter Syndrome is a condition in which a person is born with two X chromosomes and one Y chromosome. What process during meiosis would cause this to happen?**
(Rigorous) (Skill 7.2)

A. Inversion
B. Translocation
C. Non-disjunction
D. Arrangement failure

10. **A white flower is crossed with a red flower. Which of the following is a sign of incomplete dominance?**
(Average Rigor) (Skill 7.2)

A. Pink flowers.
B. Red flowers.
C. White flowers.
D. No flowers.

11. **Which of the following is not a necessary characteristic of living things?**
(Average Rigor) (Skill 7.3)

A. Movement.
B. Reduction of local entropy.
C. Ability to cause change in local energy form.
D. Reproduction.

12. **The process of Transpiration requires which of the following?**
1 Xylem
2 Stomata
3 Roots
4 Capillary action
(Rigorous) (Skill 7.3)

A. 1 and 2
B. 2 and 3
C. 1, 2, 3, and 4
D. 1 and 3

13. **What cell organelle contains the cell's stored food?**
(Rigorous) (Skill 7.4)

A. Vacuoles.
B. Golgi Apparatus.
C. Ribosomes.
D. Lysosomes.

14. **Extensive use of antibacterial soap has been found to increase the virulence of certain infections in hospitals. Which of the following might be an explanation for this phenomenon?**
(Average Rigor) (Skill 7.5)

A. Antibacterial soaps do not kill viruses.
B. Antibacterial soaps do not incorporate the same antibiotics used as medicine.
C. Antibacterial soaps kill a lot of bacteria, and only the hardiest ones survive to reproduce.
D. Antibacterial soaps can be very drying to the skin.

15. **Amino acids are carried to the ribosome in protein synthesis by __________ .**
(Average Rigor) (Skill 7.6)

A. transfer RNA (tRNA).
B. messenger RNA (mRNA).
C. ribosomal RNA (rRNA).
D. transformation RNA (trRNA).

16. A carrier of a genetic disorder is heterozygous for a disorder that is recessive in nature. Hemophilia is a sex-linked disorder. This means that: ***(Easy) (Skill 7.6)***

A. Only females can be carriers
B. Only males can be carriers.
C. Both males and females can be carriers.
D. Neither females nor males can be carriers.

17. Which of the following is the most accurate definition of a non-renewable resource? ***(Average Rigor) (Skill 7.7)***

A. A nonrenewable resource is never replaced once used.
B. A nonrenewable resource is replaced on a timescale that is very long relative to human life-spans.
C. A nonrenewable resource is a resource that can only be manufactured by humans.
D. A nonrenewable resource is a species that has already become extinct.

18. What makes up the largest abiotic portion of the Nitrogen Cycle? ***(Average Rigor) (Skill 7.8)***

A. Nitrogen Fixing Bacteria.
B. Nitrates.
C. Decomposers.
D. Atomsphere.

19. Which one of the following biomes makes up the greatest percentage of the biosphere? ***(Rigorous) (Skill 7.9)***

A. Desert
B. Tropical Rain Forest
C. Marine
D. Temperate Deciduous Forest

20. A wrasse (fish) cleans the teeth of other fish by eating away plaque. This is an example of ___________ between the fish. ***(Average Rigor) (Skill 7.9)***

A. parasitism.
B. symbiosis (mutualism).
C. competition.
D. predation.

21. Which of the following is not a type of volcano? ***(Average Rigor) (Skill 8.1)***

A. Shield Volcanoes.
B. Composite Volcanoes.
C. Stratus Volcanoes.
D. Cinder Cone Volcanoes.

22. ____________ are cracks in the plates of the earth's crust, along which the plates move.
(Easy) (Skill 8.1)

A. Faults.
B. Ridges.
C. Earthquakes.
D. Volcanoes.

23. Recently, New Hampshire's famous "Old Man in the Mountain" collapsed. What type of erosion was the principal cause of this?
(Rigorous) (Skill 8.2)

A. Physical weathering
B. Chemical weathering
C. Exfoliation
D. Frost wedging

24. The end of a geologic era is most often characterized by?
(Average Rigor) (Skill 8.2)

A. A general uplifting of the crust.
B. The extinction of the dominant plants and animals
C. The appearance of new life forms.
D. All of the above.

25. A fossils of a dinosaur genus known as Saurolophus have been found in both Western North America, and in Mongolia. What is the most likely explanation for these findings?
(Rigorous) (Skill 8.3)

A. Convergent Evolution
B. This genus of dinosaurs were powerful swimmers that swam across the Beering Strait.
C. At one time all land masses were conected in a land form known as Pangea, and so the dinsaurs could have easly walked from what is now Mongolia to what is now Western North America.
D. Although Asia and North American were separate continents at the time, low sea levels made it possible for the dinosaurs to walk from one continent to the other.

26. Which of the following instruments measures wind speed?
(Easy) (Skill 8.3)

A. A barometer.
B. An anemometer.
C. A thermometer.
D. A weather vane.

27. **Surface ocean currents are caused by which of the following?**
(Rigorous) (Skill 8.4)

A. temperature.
B. density changes in water.
C. wind.
D. tidal forces.

28. **Which of these best decribes the seafloor along the majority of Florida's Atlantic shoreline?**
(Average Rigor) (Skill 8.4)

A. Continental slope
B. Continental rise
C. Continental shelf
D. Seamount

29. **Igneous rocks can be classified according to which of the following?**
(Easy) (Skill 8.5)

A. Texture.
B. Composition.
C. Formation process.
D. All of the above.

30. **Which of these is a true statement about loamy soil?**
(Average Rigor) (Skill 8.5)

A. Loamy soil is gritty and porous.
B. Loamy soil is smooth and a good barrier to water.
C. Loamy soil is hostile to microorganisms.
D. Loamy soil is velvety and clumpy.

31. **Quicksand is created by the Interaction of very fine sand and water. The process that creates quicksand is callled ______________ .**
(Rigorous) (Skill 8.6)

A. Absorption
B. Percolation
C. Leaching
D. Runoff

32. **What is the most accurate description of the Water Cycle?** ***(Rigorous) (Skill 8.7)***

A. Rain comes from clouds, filling the ocean. The water then evaporates and becomes clouds again.
B. Water circulates from rivers into groundwater and back, while water vapor circulates in the atmosphere.
C. Water is conserved except for chemical or nuclear reactions, and any drop of water could circulate through clouds, rain, ground-water, and surface-water.
D. Water flows toward the oceans, where it evaporates and forms clouds, which causes rain, which in turn flow back to the oceans after it falls.

33. **What are the most significant and prevalent elements in the biosphere?** ***(Easy) (Skill 8.7)***

A. Carbon, Hydrogen, Oxygen, Nitrogen, Phosphorus.
B. Carbon, Hydrogen, Sodium, Iron, Calcium.
C. Carbon, Oxygen, Sulfur, Manganese, Iron.
D. Carbon, Hydrogen, Oxygen, Nickel, Sodium, Nitrogen.

34. **Which of the following is the best definition for 'meteorite'?** ***(Easy) (Skill 8.8)***

A. A meteorite is a mineral composed of mica and feldspar.
B. A meteorite is material from outer space, that has struck the earth's surface.
C. A meteorite is an element that has properties of both metals and nonmetals.
D. A meteorite is a very small unit of length measurement.

35. **The phases of the moon are the result of its _______ in relation to the sun.** ***(Average Rigor) (Skill 8.8)***

A. revolution
B. rotation
C. position
D. inclination

36. What is the main difference between the 'condensation hypothesis' and the 'tidal hypothesis' for the origin of the solar system?
(Rigorous) (Skill 8.9)

A. The tidal hypothesis can be tested, but the condensation hypothesis cannot.
B. The tidal hypothesis proposes a near collision of two stars pulling on each other, but the condensation hypothesis proposes condensation of rotating clouds of dust and gas.
C. The tidal hypothesis explains how tides began on planets such as Earth, but the condensation hypothesis explains how water vapor became liquid on Earth.
D. The tidal hypothesis is based on Aristotelian physics, but the condensation hypothesis is based on Newtonian mechanics.

37. A telescope that collects light by using a concave mirror and can produce small images is called a __________.
(Average Rigor) (Skill 8.10)

A. radioactive telescope
B. reflecting telescope
C. refracting telescope
D. optical telescope

38. A seltzer tablet changing into bubbles is an example of:
(Rigorous) (Skill 9.1)

A. A physical change.
B. A chemical change.
C. Conversion.
D. Diffusion.

39. Vinegar is an example of a __________.
(Easy) (Skill 9.1)

A. strong acid.
B. strong base.
C. weak acid.
D. weak base.

40. Which of the following will not change in a chemical reaction?
(Average Rigor) (Skill 9.2)

A. Number of moles of products.
B. Atomic number of one of the reactants.
C. Mass (in grams) of one of the reactants.
D. Rate of reaction.

41. Carbon bonds with hydrogen by __________.
(Rigorous) (Skill 9.2)

A. ionic bonding.
B. non-polar covalent bonding.
C. polar covalent bonding.
D. strong nuclear force.

42. The electromagnetic radiation with the longest wave length is/are ____________.
(Easy) (Skill 9.3)

A. radio waves.
B. red light.
C. X-rays.
D. ultraviolet light.

43. Hoover Dam is perhaps the most famous hydroeletric dam in North America. Which on of the follwing best describes how Hydroelectric dams generate their power?
(Rigorous) (Skill 9.3)

A Gravity imparts kinetic energy onto the falling water, which acts as a mechnical force turning the generator tubines. The turbines contain a coil of wire, and as the turbine spins it spins the coil of wire. This generates an electrical current in the wire that is then sent out to the power grid.
B. Gravity imparts kinetic energy onto the falling water, which acts as a mechnical force turning the generator tubines. When the turbines spin they spin a series of electromagnets inside a coil of copper wire. This generates an electrical current in the wire that is then sent out to the power grid.
C. Gravity imparts potential energy onto the falling water, which acts as a mechnical force turning the generator tubines. When the turbines spin they spin a series of electromagnets inside a coil of copper wire. This generates an electrical current in the wire that is then sent out to the power grid.
D. Gravity imparts kinetic energy onto the falling water, which acts as a mechnical force turning the generator tubines. When the turbines spin they spin a series of permanment magnets inside a coil of copper wire. This generates an electrical current in the wire that is then sent out to the power grid.

44. All of the following measure energy except for ___________
(Average Rigor) (Skill 9.4)

A. joules.
B. calories.
C. watts.
D. ergs.

45. Which of the following is not true about phase change in matter?
(Rigorous) (Skill 9.4)

A. Solid water and liquid ice can coexist at water's freezing point.
B. At 7 degrees Celsius, water is always in liquid phase.
C. Matter changes phase when enough energy is gained or lost.
D. Different phases of matter are characterized by differences in molecular motion.

46. All of the following are considered Newton's Laws except for:
(Easy) (Skill 9.5)

A. An object in motion will continue in motion unless acted upon by an outside force.
B. For every action force, there is an equal and opposite reaction force."
C. Nature abhors a vacuum.
D. Mass can be considered the ratio of force to acceleration.

47. As in all processess, Plant growth must deal with the Law of Conservation of Mass and Energy. Most people recongize the Sun as the source of a plant's energy however what is the primary source of the introduction of mass?
(Rigorous) (Skill 9.5)

A. Water absorbed through the roots.
B. Nutrient's and minerals absorbed through the roots.
C. Carbon absorbed through the roots.
D. Carbon absorbed through the stomata.

48. A 10 ohm resistor and a 50 ohm resistor are connected in parallel. If the current in the 10 ohm resistor is 5 amperes, the current (in amperes) running through the 50 ohm resistor is
(Rigorous) (Skill 9.6)

A. 1
B. 50
C. 25
D. 60

49. A converging lens produces a real image ________________.
(Rigorous) (Skill 9.7)

A. always.
B. never.
C. when the object is within one focal length of the lens.
D. when the object is further than one focal length from the lens.

50. Sound can be transmitted in all of the following except __________ .
(Easy) (Skill 9.7)

A. air.
B. water.
C. A diamond.
D. a vacuum.

Answer Key: General Science

1.	B	11.	A	21.	C	31.	B	41.	C
2.	A	12.	C	22.	A	32.	C	42.	A
3.	A	13.	A	23.	D	33.	A	43.	B
4.	B	14.	C	24.	D	34.	B	44.	C
5.	A	15.	A	25.	D	35.	C	45.	B
6.	B	16.	A	26.	B	36.	B	46.	C
7.	A	17.	B	27.	C	37.	B	47.	D
8.	B	18.	D	28.	C	38.	B	48.	A
9.	C	19.	C	29.	D	39.	C	49.	D
10.	A	20.	B	30.	D	40.	B	50.	D

Rigor Table: General Science

	Easy %20	Average Rigor %40	Rigorous %40
Question #	16, 22, 26, 29, 33, 34, 39, 42, 46, 50	1, 3, 5, 6, 8, 10, 11, 14, 15, 17, 18, 20, 21, 24, 28, 30, 35, 37, 40, 44	2, 4, 7, 9, 12, 13, 19, 23, 25, 27, 31, 32, 36, 38, 41, 43, 45, 47, 48, 49

Rationales with Sample Questions: General Science

1. **What is the scientific method?**
   (Average Rigor) (Skill 6.1)

   A. It is the process of doing an experiment and writing a laboratory report.
   B. It is the process of using open inquiry and repeatable results to establish theories.
   C. It is the process of reinforcing scientific principles by confirming results.
   D. It is the process of recording data and observations.

Answer: B. It is the process of using open inquiry and repeatable results to establish theories.

Scientific research often includes elements from answers (A), (C), and (D), but the basic underlying principle of the scientific method is that people ask questions and do repeatable experiments to answer those questions and develop informed theories of why and how things happen. Therefore, the best answer is (B).

2. **Which of the following is not an acceptable way for a student to acknowledge sources in a laboratory report?**
   (Rigorous) (Skill 6.1)

   A. The student tells his/her teacher what sources s/he used to write the report.
   B. The student uses footnotes in the text, with sources cited, but not in correct MLA format.
   C. The student uses endnotes in the text, with sources cited, in correct MLA format.
   D. The student attaches a separate bibliography, noting each use of sources.

Answer: A. The student tells his/her teacher what sources s/he used to write the report.

It may seem obvious, but students are often unaware that scientists need to cite all sources used. For the young adolescent, it is not always necessary to use official MLA format (though this should be taught at some point).
Students may properly cite references in many ways, but these references must be in writing, with the original assignment. Therefore, the answer is (A).

3. **Which of the following data sets is properly represented by a bar graph?**
(Average Rigor) (Skill 6.2)

A. Number of people choosing to buy cars, vs. Color of car bought.
B. Number of people choosing to buy cars, vs. Age of car customer.
C. Number of people choosing to buy cars, vs. Distance from car lot to customer home.
D. Number of people choosing to buy cars, vs. Time since last car purchase.

Answer: A. Number of people choosing to buy cars, vs. Color of car bought.

A bar graph should be used only for data sets in which the independent variable is non-continuous (discrete), e.g. gender, color, etc. Any continuous independent variable (age, distance, time, etc.) should yield a scatter-plot when the dependent variable is plotted. Therefore, the answer must be (A).

4. In an experiment measuring the inhibition effect of different antibiotic discs on bacteria grown in Petri dishes, what are the independent and dependent variables respectively?
(Rigorous) (Skill 6.3)

A. Number of bacterial colonies and the antibiotic type.
B. Antibiotic type and the distance between antibiotic and the closest colony.
C. Antibiotic type and the number of bacterial colonies.
D. Presence of bacterial colonies and the antibiotic type.

Answer: B. Antibiotic type and the distance between antibiotic and the closest colony.

To answer this question, recall that the independent variable in an experiment is the entity that is changed by the scientist, in order to observe the effects the dependent variable. In this experiment, antibiotic used is purposely changed so it is the independent variable. Answers A and D list antibiotic type as the dependent variable and thus cannot be the answer, leaving answers B and C as the only two viable choices. The best answer is B, because it measures at what concentration of the antibiotic the bacteria are able to grow at, (as you move from the source of the antibiotic the concentration decreases). Answer C is not as effective because it could be interpreted that that a plate that shows a large number of colonies a greater distance from the antibiotic is a less effective antibiotic than a plate a smaller number of colonies in close proximity to the antibiotic disc, which is reverse of the actually result.

5. **When designing a scientific experiment, a student considers all the factors that may influence the results. The process goal is to ________.**
(Average Rigor) (Skill 6.3)

A. recognize and manipulate independent variables.
B. recognize and record independent variables.
C. recognize and manipulate dependent variables.
D. recognize and record dependent variables.

Answer: A. Recognize and manipulate independent variables.

When a student designs a scientific experiment, s/he must decide what to measure, and what independent variables will play a role in the experiment. S/he must determine how to manipulate these independent variables to refine his/her procedure and to prepare for meaningful observations. Although s/he will eventually record dependent variables (D), this does not take place during the experimental design phase. Although the student will likely recognize and record the independent variables (B), this is not the process goal, but a helpful step in manipulating the variables. It is unlikely that the student will manipulate dependent variables directly in his/her experiment (C), or the data would be suspect. Thus, the answer is (A).

6. **Who should be notified in the case of a serious chemical spill?**
(Average Rigor) (Skill 6.4)

A. The custodian.
B. The fire department or their municipal authority.
C. The science department chair.
D. The School Board.

Answer: B. The fire department or other municipal authority.

Although the custodian may help to clean up laboratory messes, and the science department chair should be involved in discussions of ways to avoid spills, a serious chemical spill may require action by the fire department or other trained emergency personnel. It is best to be safe by notifying them in case of a serious chemical accident. Therefore, the best answer is (B).

7. Experiments may be done with any of the following animals except ________.
(Rigorous) (Skill 6.4)

A. birds.
B. invertebrates.
C. lower order life.
D. frogs.

Answer: A. Birds.

No dissections may be performed on living mammalian vertebrates or birds. Lower order life and invertebrates may be used. Biological experiments may be done with all animals except mammalian vertebrates or birds. Therefore the answer is (A).

8. Which plant tissues contain chloroplasts?
(Average Rigor) (Skill 7.1)

A. Stomata
B. Palisade mesophyll
C. Spongy Mesophyll
D. Endosperm

Answer: B. Palisade mesophyll

Palisade mesophyll is one part of the leaf, in this case the part where chloroplasts exist and photosynthesis occurs. The Spongy Mesophyll is the other part of the leaf, where gas exchange occurs. The Stomata is the part of the leaf that is the opening for air to enter and exit the leaf. The Endosperm is the food source in the seed.

9. Klinefelter Syndrome is a condition in which a person is born with two X chromosomes and one Y chromosome. What process during meiosis would cause this to happen?
(Rigorous) (Skill 7.2)

A. Inversion
B. Translocation
C. Non-disjunction
D. Arrangement failure

Answer: C. Non-disjunction

Non-disjunction describes the process by which chromosomes (or chromatids) fail to separate, and one cell (in this case gamette) recieves both copies and the other cell receives none. Inversion is a process where a gene reverses itself wit in the chromosome. Translocation can lead to some gentic disorders, because a portion of one chromosome is swapped with a portion of another chromosome. As a term arrangement failure might be a good description for a number of genetic processes (including non-disjunction) but does not have a specifc meaning itself.

10. A white flower is crossed with a red flower. Which of the following is a sign of incomplete dominance?
(Average Rigor) (Skill 7.2)

A. Pink flowers.
B. Red flowers.
C. White flowers.
D. No flowers.

Answer: A. Pink flowers.

Incomplete dominance means that neither the red nor the white gene is strong enough to suppress the other. Therefore both are expressed, leading in this case to the formation of pink flowers. Therefore, the answer is (A).

11. Which of the following is not a necessary characteristic of living things?
(Average Rigor) (Skill 7.3)

A. Movement.
B. Reduction of local entropy.
C. Ability to cause change in local energy form.
D. Reproduction.

Answer: A. Movement.

There are many definitions of "life," but in all cases, a living organism reduces local entropy, changes chemical energy into other forms, and reproduces. Not all living things move, however, so the correct answer is (A).

12. The process of Transpiration requires which of the following?
1 Xylem
2 Stomata
3 Roots
4 Capillary action
(Rigorous) (Skill 7.3)

A. 1 and 2
B. 2 and 3
C. 1, 2, 3, and 4
D. 1 and 3

Answer: C. 1, 2, 3, and 4

Transpiration requires all four items to function successfully. The roots are required as the source of the water, and the Xylem is required as the tube to carry the water. The stomata allows for evaporation which creates a pressure difference between the top of the Xylem and the bottom (much the same as when you suck on a straw). Capillary action is the process by which water's cohesive nature allows it to travel up the Xylem. Capillary action is also what causes water to travel up paper when an edge is dipped into a dish of water.

13. What cell organelle contains the cell's stored food?
(Rigorous) (Skill 7.4)

A. Vacuoles.
B. Golgi Apparatus.
C. Ribosomes.
D. Lysosomes.

Answer: A. Vacuoles.

In a cell, the sub-parts are called organelles. Of these, the vacuoles hold stored food (and water and pigments). The Golgi Apparatus sorts molecules from other parts of the cell; the ribosomes are sites of protein synthesis; the lysosomes contain digestive enzymes. This is consistent only with answer (A).

14. Extensive use of antibacterial soap has been found to increase the virulence of certain infections in hospitals. Which of the following might be an explanation for this phenomenon?
(Average Rigor) (Skill 7.5)

A. Antibacterial soaps do not kill viruses.
B. Antibacterial soaps do not incorporate the same antibiotics used as medicine.
C. Antibacterial soaps kill a lot of bacteria, and only the hardiest ones survive to reproduce.
D. Antibacterial soaps can be very drying to the skin.

Answer: C. Antibacterial soaps kill a lot of bacteria, and only the hardiest ones survive to reproduce.

All of the answer choices in this question are true statements, but the question specifically asks for a cause of increased disease virulence in hospitals. This phenomenon is due to natural selection. The bacteria that can survive contact with antibacterial soap are the strongest ones, and without other bacteria competing for resources, they have more opportunity to lourish. This problem has led to several antibiotic-resistant bacterial diseases in hospitals nation-wide. Therefore, the answer is (C). However, note that answers (A) and (D) may be additional problems with over-reliance on antibacterial products.

15. Amino acids are carried to the ribosome in protein synthesis by __________.
(Average Rigor) (Skill 7.6)

A. transfer RNA (tRNA).
B. messenger RNA (mRNA).
C. ribosomal RNA (rRNA).
D. transformation RNA (trRNA).

Answer: A. Transfer RNA (tRNA).

The job of tRNA is to carry and position amino acids to/on the ribosomes. mRNA copies DNA code and brings it to the ribosomes; rRNA is in the ribosome itself. There is no such thing as trRNA. Thus, the answer is (A).

16. A carrier of a genetic disorder is heterozygous for a disorder that is recessive in nature. Hemophilia is a sex-linked disorder. This means that:
(Easy) (Skill 7.6)

A. Only females can be carriers
B. Only males can be carriers.
C. Both males and females can be carriers.
D. Neither females nor males can be carriers.

Answer: A. Only females can be carriers

Since Hemophilia is a sex-linked disorder the gene only appears on the X chromosome, with no counterpart on the Y chromosome. Since males are XY they cannot be heterozygous for the trait, what ever is on the single X chromosome will be expressed. Females being XX can be heterozygous. Answer (C) would describe a genetic disorder that is recessive and expressed on one of the somatic chromosomes (not sex-linked). Answer (D) would describe a genetic disorder that is dominant and expressed on any of the chromosomes. An example of answer (C) is sickle cell anemia. An example of answer (D) is Achondroplasia (the most common type of short-limbed dwarfism), in fact for this condition people that are Homozygous dominant for the gene that creates the disorde rusually have severe health problems if they live past infancy, so almost all individuals with this disorder are carriers.

17. Which of the following is the most accurate definition of a non-renewable resource?
(Average Rigor) (Skill 7.7)

A. A nonrenewable resource is never replaced once used.
B. A nonrenewable resource is replaced on a timescale that is very long relative to human life-spans.
C. A nonrenewable resource is a resource that can only be manufactured by humans.
D. A nonrenewable resource is a species that has already become extinct.

Answer: B. A nonrenewable resource is replaced on a timescale that is very long relative to human life-spans.

Renewable resources are those that are renewed, or replaced, in time for humans to use more of them. Examples include fast-growing plants, animals, or oxygen gas. (Note that while sunlight is often considered a renewable resource, it is actually a nonrenewable but extremely abundant resource.) Nonrenewable resources are those that renew themselves only on very long timescales, usually geologic timescales. Examples include minerals, metals, or fossil fuels. Therefore, the correct answer is (B).

18. What makes up the largest abiotic portion of the Nitrogen Cycle?
(Average Rigor) (Skill 7.8)

A. Nitrogen Fixing Bacteria.
B. Nitrates.
C. Decomposers.
D. Atomsphere.

Answer: D. Atomsphere.

Since answers (A) and (C) are both examples of living organisms they are biotic components of the nitrogen cycle. Nitrates are one type of nitrogen compond, (making it abiotic) that can be found in soil and in living organisms, however it makes up a small portion of the avaible nitrogen. The atmosphere being 78% Nitrogen gas (an abiotic component) makes up the largest source available to the Nitrogen Cycle.

19. Which one of the following biomes makes up the greatest percentage of the biosphere?
(Rigorous) (Skill 7.9)

A. Desert
B. Tropical Rain Forest
C. Marine
D. Temperate Deciduous Forest

Answer: C. Marine

All land biomes, which includes answers (A), (B), and (D) make up approximately 25% of the earths surface, leaving the other 75% to the marine biome. Additionally the marine biome can range in depth from the air above the water, to several miles in depth. THis combined make answer (C) the correct answer.

20. A wrasse (fish) cleans the teeth of other fish by eating away plaque. This is an example of ____________ between the fish.
(Average Rigor) (Skill 7.9)

A. parasitism.
B. symbiosis (mutualism).
C. competition.
D. predation.

Answer: B. Symbiosis (mutualism).

When both species benefit from their interaction in their habitat, this is called 'symbiosis', or 'mutualism'. In this example, the wrasse benefits from having a source of food, and the other fish benefit by having healthier teeth. Note that 'parasitism' is when one species benefits at the expense of the other, 'competition' is when two species compete with one another for the same habitat or food, and 'predation' is when one species feeds on another. Therefore, the answer is (B).

21. Which of the following is not a type of volcano?
(Average Rigor) (Skill 8.1)

A. Shield Volcanoes.
B. Composite Volcanoes.
C. Stratus Volcanoes.
D. Cinder Cone Volcanoes.

Answer: C. Stratus Volcanoes

There are three types of volcanoes. Shield volcanoes (A) are associated with non-violent eruptions and repeated lava flow over time. Composite volcanoes (B) are built from both lava flow and layers of ash and cinders. Cinder cone volcanoes (D) are associated with violent eruptions, such that lava is thrown into the air and becomes ash or cinder before falling and accumulating. 'Stratus' (C) is a type of cloud, not volcano, so it is the correct answer to this question.

22. ____________ are cracks in the plates of the earth's crust, along which the plates move.
(Easy) (Skill 8.1)

A. Faults.
B. Ridges.
C. Earthquakes.
D. Volcanoes.

Answer: A. Faults.

Faults are cracks in the earth's crust, and when the earth moves, an earthquake results. Faults may lead to mismatched edges of ground, forming ridges, and ground shape may also be determined by volcanoes. The answer to this question must therefore be (A).

23. Recently, New Hampshire's famous "Old Man in the Mountain" collapsed. What type of erosion was the principal cause of this? *(Rigorous) (Skill 8.2)*

A. Physical weathering
B. Chemical weathering
C. Exfoliation
D. Frost wedging

Answer: D. Frost wedging

The granite that the "old Man in the Mountain" was composed of tends to be fairly resislent to the first three types of erosion, however the natural cracks in the cliff face gave plently of places for frost to form and thus widen the cracks. Eventually the widening cracks became to large for the weight of the face to continue to be supported, at which point it collapsed. Even manmade attempts to prevent the collapse, which included cables and spikes, were unable to prevent the natural end result of erosion.

24. The end of a geologic era is most often characterized by? *(Average Rigor) (Skill 8.2)*

A. A general uplifting of the crust.
B. The extinction of the dominant plants and animals
C. The appearance of new life forms.
D. All of the above.

Answer: D. All of the above.

Any of these things can be used to characterize the end of a geologic era, and often a combination of factors are applied to determining the end of an era.

25. A fossils of a dinosaur genus known as Saurolophus have been found in both Western North America, and in Mongolia. What is the most likely explanation for these findings?
(Rigorous) (Skill 8.3)

A. Convergent Evolution
B. This genus of dinosaurs were powerful swimmers that swam across the Beering Strait.
C. At one time all land masses were conected in a land form known as Pangea, and so the dinsaurs could have easly walked from what is now Mongolia to what is now Western North America.
D. Although Asia and North American were separate continents at the time, low sea levels made it possible for the dinosaurs to walk from one continent to the other.

Answer: D. Although Asia and North American were separate continents at the time, low sea levels made it possible for the dinosaurs to walk from one continent to the other.

Convergent evolution can explain how different species have developed similar traits but in this case the fossil record indicates too many similarites, and thus the Saurolophus are a single genus of dinosaurs. (an interesting example of convergent evolution, is that one of the few species other than humans to have distinct fingerprints are Koalas). Saurolophus was a land based herbivore with no evidence of strong swimming abilities. As for Pangea, this particular land mass occured roughly 180 million years before the Saurolophus was alive, so it is an unlikely candidate for how evidence of the genus ended up on two continents.

This leaves the ability to walk from Asia to North America, and this was accomplished by means of the Bering Land Bridge (where the Bering Strait is now). The Bering Land bridge exsisted because the level of the water in the oceans was lowered by Water being stored in large glaciers This lowering of ocean level was enough to expose what is now the ocean floor between Alaska and Siberia.

26. Which of the following instruments measures wind speed?
(Easy) (Skill 8.3)

A. A barometer.
B. An anemometer.
C. A thermometer.
D. A weather vane.

Answer: B. Anemometer.

An anemometer is a device to measure wind speed, while a barometer measures pressure, a thermometer measures temperature, and a weather vane indicates wind direction. This is consistent only with answer (B).

27. Surface ocean currents are caused by which of the following?

(Rigorous) (Skill 8.4)

A. temperature.
B. density changes in water.
C. wind.
D. tidal forces.

Answer: C. Wind

A current is a large mass of continuously moving oceanic water. Surface ocean currents are mainly wind-driven and occur in all of the world's oceans (example: the Gulf Stream). This is in contrast to deep ocean currents which are driven by changes in density. Surface ocean currents are classified by temperature. Tidal forces cause changes in ocean level however they do not effect surface currents.

28. Which of these best decribes the seafloor along the majority of Florida's Atlantic shoreline?
(Average Rigor) (Skill 8.4)

A. Continental slope
B. Continental rise
C. Continental shelf
D. Seamount

Answer: C. Continental shelf

Usually off the coast of a continent the progression is, the continental shelf, the continental slope, and then the continental rise. A seamount is a term used to describe any volcano that rises at least a kilometer above the seafloor.

29. Igneous rocks can be classified according to which of the following?
(Easy) (Skill 8.5)

A. Texture.
B. Composition.
C. Formation process.
D. All of the above.

Answer: D. All of the above.

Igneous rocks, which form from the crystallization of molten lava, are classified according to many of their characteristics, including texture, composition, and how they were formed. Therefore, the answer is (D).

30. Which of these is a true statement about loamy soil?
(Average Rigor) (Skill 8.5)

A. Loamy soil is gritty and porous.
B. Loamy soil is smooth and a good barrier to water.
C. Loamy soil is hostile to microorganisms.
D. Loamy soil is velvety and clumpy.

Answer: D. Loamy soil is velvety and clumpy.

The three classes of soil by texture are: Sandy (gritty and porous), Clay (smooth, greasy, and most impervious to water), and Loamy (velvety, clumpy, and able to hold water and let water flow through). In addition, loamy soils are often the most fertile soils. Therefore, the answer must be (D).

31. Quicksand is created by the Interaction of very fine sand and water. The process that creates quicksand is callled _____________ .
(Rigorous) (Skill 8.6)

A. Absorption
B. Percolation
C. Leaching
D. Runoff

Answer: B. Percolation

Quicksand is created when ground water is forced up through sandy soil creating a semiliquid state. Percolation refers to this movement of water through the sand. If Absorption had been the answer then beach sand, rather than being good for making sand castles, would take out an untold number of tourists daily. Leaching is the absorption of soluble compounds from the ground. Leaching is the principle method of groundwater contamination. Runoff is as simple as it sounds, the water that flows over the ground before reaching some form of surface water.

32. What is the most accurate description of the Water Cycle?
(Rigorous) (Skill 8.7)

A. Rain comes from clouds, filling the ocean. The water then evaporates and becomes clouds again.
B. Water circulates from rivers into groundwater and back, while water vapor circulates in the atmosphere.
C. Water is conserved except for chemical or nuclear reactions, and any drop of water could circulate through clouds, rain, ground-water, and surface-water.
D. Water flows toward the oceans, where it evaporates and forms clouds, which causes rain, which in turn flow back to the oceans after it falls.

Answer: C. Water is conserved except for chemical or nuclear reactions, and any drop of water could circulate through clouds, rain, ground-water, and surface-water.

All natural chemical cycles, including the Water Cycle, depend on the principle of Conservation of Mass. (For water, unlike for elements such as Nitrogen, chemical reactions may cause sources or sinks of water molecules.) Any drop of water may circulate through the hydrologic system, ending up in a cloud, as rain, or as surface- or ground-water. Although answers (A), (B) and (D) describe parts of the water cycle, the most comprehensive and correct answer is (C).

33. What are the most significant and prevalent elements in the biosphere?
(Easy) (Skill 8.7)

A. Carbon, Hydrogen, Oxygen, Nitrogen, Phosphorus.
B. Carbon, Hydrogen, Sodium, Iron, Calcium.
C. Carbon, Oxygen, Sulfur, Manganese, Iron.
D. Carbon, Hydrogen, Oxygen, Nickel, Sodium, Nitrogen.

Answer: A. Carbon, Hydrogen, Oxygen, Nitrogen, Phosphorus.

Organic matter (and life as we know it) is based on Carbon atoms, bonded to Hydrogen and Oxygen. Nitrogen and Phosphorus are the next most significant elements, followed by Sulfur and then trace nutrients such as Iron, Sodium, Calcium, and others. Therefore, the answer is (A). If you know that the formula for any carbohydrate contains Carbon, Hydrogen, and Oxygen, that will help you narrow the choices to (A) and (D) in any case.

34. **Which of the following is the best definition for 'meteorite'?**
(Easy) (Skill 8.8)

A. A meteorite is a mineral composed of mica and feldspar.
B. A meteorite is material from outer space, that has struck the earth's surface.
C. A meteorite is an element that has properties of both metals and nonmetals.
D. A meteorite is a very small unit of length measurement.

Answer: B. A meteorite is material from outer space, that has struck the earth's surface.

Meteoroids are pieces of matter in space, composed of particles of rock and metal. If a meteoroid travels through the earth's atmosphere, friction causes burning and a "shooting star"—i.e. a meteor. If the meteor strikes the earth's surface, it is known as a meteorite. Note that although the suffix –ite often means a mineral, answer (A) is incorrect. Answer (C) refers to a 'metalloid' rather than a 'meteorite', and answer (D) is simply a misleading pun on 'meter'. Therefore, the answer is (B)

35. **The phases of the moon are the result of its _______ in relation to the sun.**
(Average Rigor) (Skill 8.8)

A. revolution
B. rotation
C. position
D. inclination

Answer: C. Position

The moon is visible in varying amounts during its orbit around the earth. One half of the moon's surface is always illuminated by the Sun (appears bright), but the amount observed can vary from full moon to none

36. What is the main difference between the 'condensation hypothesis' and the 'tidal hypothesis' for the origin of the solar system? *(Rigorous) (Skill 8.9)*

A. The tidal hypothesis can be tested, but the condensation hypothesis cannot.
B. The tidal hypothesis proposes a near collision of two stars pulling on each other, but the condensation hypothesis proposes condensation of rotating clouds of dust and gas.
C. The tidal hypothesis explains how tides began on planets such as Earth, but the condensation hypothesis explains how water vapor became liquid on Earth.
D. The tidal hypothesis is based on Aristotelian physics, but the condensation hypothesis is based on Newtonian mechanics.

Answer: B. The tidal hypothesis proposes a near collision of two stars pulling on each other, but the condensation hypothesis proposes condensation of rotating clouds of dust and gas.

Most scientists believe the 'condensation hypothesis,' i.e. that the solar system began when rotating clouds of dust and gas condensed into the sun and planets. A minority opinion is the 'tidal hypothesis,' i.e. that the sun almost collided with a large star. The large star's gravitational field would have then pulled gases out of the sun; these gases are thought to have begun to orbit the sun and condense into planets. Because both of these hypotheses deal with ancient, unrepeatable events, neither can be tested, eliminating answer (A). Note that both 'tidal'and 'condensation' have additional meanings in physics, but those are not relevant here, eliminating answer (C). Both hypotheses are based on best guesses using modern physics, eliminating answer (D). Therefore, the answer is (B).

37. A telescope that collects light by using a concave mirror and can produce small images is called a ___________.
(Average Rigor) (Skill 8.10)

A. radioactive telescope
B. reflecting telescope
C. refracting telescope
D. optical telescope

Answer: B. reflecting telescope

Reflecting telescopes are commonly used in laboratory settings. Images are produced via the reflection of waves off of a concave mirror. The larger the image produced the more likely it is to be imperfect. Refracting telscopes use lenses to bend light to focus the image. The term optical telescope can be used to describe both reflecting and refracting telescopes.

38. A seltzer tablet changing into bubbles is an example of:
(Rigorous) (Skill 9.1)

A. A physical change.
B. A chemical change.
C. Conversion.
D. Diffusion.

Answer: B. A chemical change.

A physical change is a change that does not produce a new substance. Conversion is usually used when discussing phase changes of matter, Diffusion occurs in aspects of a mixture when the concentration is equalized. A seltzer tablet changing into bubbles produces a new substance- gas-which is a characteristic of chemical changes.

39. Vinegar is an example of a _________ .
(Easy) (Skill 9.1)

A. strong acid.
B. strong base.
C. weak acid.
D. weak base.

Answer: C. Weak acid.

The main ingredient in vinegar is acetic acid, a weak acid. Vinegar is a useful acid in science classes, because it makes a frothy reaction with bases such as baking soda (e.g. in the quintessential volcano model). Vinegar is not a strong acid, such as hydrochloric acid, because it does not dissociate as fully or cause as much corrosion. It is not a base. Therefore, the answer is (C).

40. Which of the following will not change in a chemical reaction?
(Average Rigor) (Skill 9.2)

A. Number of moles of products.
B. Atomic number of one of the reactants.
C. Mass (in grams) of one of the reactants.
D. Rate of reaction.

Answer: B. Atomic number of one of the reactants.

Atomic number, i.e. the number of protons in a given element, is constant unless involved in a nuclear reaction. Meanwhile, the amounts (measured in moles (A) or in grams(C)) of reactants and products change over the course of a chemical reaction, and the rate of a chemical reaction (D) may change due to internal or external processes. Therefore, the answer is (B).

41. Carbon bonds with hydrogen by __________ .
(Rigorous) (Skill 9.2)

A. ionic bonding.
B. non-polar covalent bonding.
C. polar covalent bonding.
D. strong nuclear force.

Answer: C. Polar covalent bonding.

Each carbon atom contains four valence electrons, while each hydrogen atom contains one valence electron. A carbon atom can bond with one or more hydrogen atoms, such that two electrons are shared in each bond. This is covalent bonding, because the electrons are shared. (In ionic bonding, atoms must gain or lose electrons to form ions. The ions are then electrically attracted in oppositely-charged pairs.) Covalent bonds are always polar when between two non-identical atoms, so this bond must be polar. ("Polar" means that the electrons are shared unequally, forming a pair of partial charges, i.e. poles.) In any case, the strong nuclear force is not relevant to this problem. The answer to this question is therefore (C).

42. The electromagnetic radiation with the longest wave length is/are ____________.
(Easy) (Skill 9.3)

A. radio waves.
B. red light.
C. X-rays.
D. ultraviolet light.

Answer: A. Radio waves.

As one can see on a diagram of the electromagnetic spectrum, radio waves have longer wave lengths (and smaller frequencies) than visible light, which in turn has longer wave lengths than ultraviolet or X-ray radiation. If you did not remember this sequence, you might recall that wave length is inversely proportional to frequency, and that radio waves are considered much less harmful (less energetic, i.e. lower frequency) than ultraviolet or X-ray radiation. The correct answer is therefore (A).

43. Hoover Dam is perhaps the most famous hydroeletric dam in North America. Which on of the follwing best describes how Hydroelectric dams generate their power?
(Rigorous) (Skill 9.3)

A. Gravity imparts kinetic energy onto the falling water, which acts as a mechnical force turning the generator tubines. The turbines contain a coil of wire, and as the turbine spins it spins the coil of wire. This generates an electrical current in the wire that is then sent out to the power grid.
B. Gravity imparts kinetic energy onto the falling water, which acts as a mechnical force turning the generator tubines. When the turbines spin they spin a series of electromagnets inside a coil of copper wire. This generates an electrical current in the wire that is then sent out to the power grid.
C. Gravity imparts potential energy onto the falling water, which acts as a mechnical force turning the generator tubines. When the turbines spin they spin a series of electromagnets inside a coil of copper wire. This generates an electrical current in the wire that is then sent out to the power grid.
D. Gravity imparts kinetic energy onto the falling water, which acts as a mechnical force turning the generator tubines. When the turbines spin they spin a series of permanment magnets inside a coil of copper wire. This generates an electrical current in the wire that is then sent out to the power grid.

Answer: B. Gravity imparts kinetic energy onto the falling water, which acts as a mechnical force turning the generator tubines. When the turbines spin they spin a series of electromagnets inside a coil of copper wire. This generates an electrical current in the wire that is then sent out to the power grid.

Most electric generators work in a process that reverses the process that is used in electric motors. In a motor an electomagnetic spins in response to the electric current traveling through the coils around it thus creating the mechnical force that drives the motor. A generator just needs a source of mechnical energy to reverse the process and create an electric current.

44. All of the following measure energy except for __________
(Average Rigor) (Skill 9.4)

A. joules.
B. calories.
C. watts.
D. ergs.

Answer: C. Watts.

Energy units must be dimensionally equivalent to (force)x(length), which equals (mass)x(length squared)/(time squared). Joules, Calories, and Ergs are all metric measures of energy. Joules are the SI units of energy, while Calories are used to allow water to have a Specific Heat of one unit. Ergs are used in the 'cgs' (centimeter-gram-second) system, for smaller quantities. Watts, however, are units of power, i.e. Joules per Second. Therefore, the answer is (C).

45. Which of the following is not true about phase change in matter?
(Rigorous) (Skill 9.4)

A. Solid water and liquid ice can coexist at water's freezing point.
B. At 7 degrees Celsius, water is always in liquid phase.
C. Matter changes phase when enough energy is gained or lost.
D. Different phases of matter are characterized by differences in molecular motion.

Answer: B. At 7 degrees Celsius, water is always in liquid phase.

According to the molecular theory of matter, molecular motion determines the 'phase' of the matter, and the energy in the matter determines the speed of molecular motion. Solids have vibrating molecules that are in fixed relative positions; liquids have faster molecular motion than their solid forms, and the molecules may move more freely but must still be in contact with one another; gases have even more energy and more molecular motion. (Other phases, such as plasma, are yet more energetic.) At the 'freezing point' or 'boiling point' of a substance, both relevant phases may be present. For instance, water at zero degrees Celsius may be composed of some liquid and some solid, or all liquid, or all solid. Pressure changes, in addition to temperature changes, can cause phase changes. For example, nitrogen can be liquefied under high pressure, even though its boiling temperature is very low. Therefore, the correct answer must be (B). Water may be a liquid at that temperature, but it may also be a solid, depending on ambient pressure.

46. All of the following are considered Newton's Laws except for:
(Easy) (Skill 9.5)

A. An object in motion will continue in motion unless acted upon by an outside force.
B. For every action force, there is an equal and opposite reaction force."
C. Nature abhors a vacuum.
D. Mass can be considered the ratio of force to acceleration.

Answer: C. Nature abhors a vacuum.

Newton's Laws include his law of inertia (an object in motion (or at rest) will stay in motion (or at rest) until acted upon by an outside force) (A), his law that (Force)=(Mass)(Acceleration) (D), and his equal and opposite reaction force law (B). Therefore, the answer to this question is (C), because "Nature abhors a vacuum" is not one of these.

47. As in all processess, Plant growth must deal with the Law of Conservation of Mass and Energy. Most people recongize the Sun as the source of a plant's energy however what is the primary source of the introduction of mass?
(Rigorous) (Skill 9.5)

A. Water absorbed through the roots.
B. Nutrient's and minerals absorbed through the roots.
C. Carbon absorbed through the roots.
D. Carbon absorbed through the stomata.

Answer: D. Carbon absorbed through the stomata.

Although water, nutrients, and minerals are absorbed through the roots by a plant, they do not make up the bulk of the added mass when a plant grows. Most of the added mass during plant growth is in the form of organic compounds, meaning the plant neds a large source of carbon to grow. Carbon Dioxide taken in by the plant when it opens it's stomata is usually turned into glucose by photosynthesis. This glucose can then be either metabolized for energy or altered to form the other organic compounds the plant requires.

48. A 10 ohm resistor and a 50 ohm resistor are connected in parallel. If the current in the 10 ohm resistor is 5 amperes, the current (in amperes) running through the 50 ohm resistor is
(Rigorous) (Skill 9.6)

A. 1
B. 50
C. 25
D. 60

Answer: A. 1

To answer this question, use Ohm's Law, which relates voltage to current and resistance: V = IR where V is voltage; I is current; R is resistance.We also use the fact that in a parallel circuit, the voltage is the same across the branches.Because we are given that in one branch, the current is 5 amperes and the resistance is 10 ohms, we deduce that the voltage in this circuit is their product, 50 volts (from V = IR). We then use V = IR again, this time to find I in the second branch. Because V is 50 volts, and R is 50 ohm, we calculate that I has to be 1 ampere. This is consistent only with answer (A).

49. A converging lens produces a real image _______________.
(Rigorous) (Skill 9.7)

A. always.
B. never.
C. when the object is within one focal length of the lens.
D. when the object is further than one focal length from the lens.

Answer: D. When the object is further than one focal length from the lens.

A converging lens produces a real image whenever the object is far enough from the lens (outside one focal length) so that the rays of light from the object can hit the lens and be focused into a real image on the other side of the lens. When the object is closer than one focal length from the lens, rays of light do not converge on the other side; they diverge. This means that only a virtual image can be formed, i.e. the theoretical place where those diverging rays would have converged if they had originated behind the object. Thus, the correct answer is (D).

50. Sound can be transmitted in all of the following except __________ .
(Easy) (Skill 9.7)

A. air.
B. water.
C. A diamond.
D. a vacuum.

Answer: D. A vacuum.

Sound, a longitudinal wave, is transmitted by vibrations of molecules. Therefore, it can be transmitted through any gas, liquid, or solid. However, it cannot be transmitted through a vacuum, because there are no particles present to vibrate and bump into their adjacent particles to transmit the waves. This is consistent only with answer (D). (It is interesting also to note that sound is actually faster in solids and liquids than in air.)

DOMAIN III. SOCIAL SCIENCE

COMPETENCY 10.0 KNOWLEDGE OF HISTORY

Skill 10.1 Identify major themes and historical events that are related by cause and effect.

The **Age of Exploration** actually had its beginnings centuries before exploration actually took place. The rise and spread of Islam in the seventh century and its subsequent control over the holy city of Jerusalem led to the European holy wars, or **Crusades**, to free Jerusalem and the Holy Land from this control. Even though the Crusades were not a success, those who survived and returned to their homes and countries in Western Europe brought back with them new products such as silks, spices, perfumes, and new and different foods. These were luxuries that were unheard of that gave new meaning to colorless, drab, and dull lives.

Also coming into importance at this time was the era of knighthood and its code of chivalry as well as the tremendous influence of the Church (Roman Catholic). Until the period of the Renaissance, the Church was the only place where people could be educated. The *Bible* and other books were hand-copied by monks in the monasteries. Cathedrals were built and were decorated with art depicting religious subjects.

New ideas, new inventions, and new methods also went to Western Europe with the returning Crusaders, and from these new influences was the intellectual stimulation which led to the period known as the Renaissance. The revival of interest in classical Greek art, architecture, literature, science, astronomy, medicine, increased trade between Europe and Asia, and the invention of the printing press helped to push the spread of knowledge and the start of exploration.

For many centuries, various mapmakers made many maps and charts which in turn stimulated curiosity and the seeking of more knowledge. At the same time, the Chinese were using the magnetic compass in their ships. Pacific islanders were going from island to island covering thousands of miles in open canoes while navigating by sun and stars. Arab traders were sailing all over the Indian Ocean in their dhows.

The trade routes between Europe and Asia were slow, difficult, dangerous, and very expensive. Between sea voyages on the Indian Ocean and Mediterranean Sea and the camel caravans in central Asia and the Arabian Desert, the trade was controlled by the Italian merchants in Genoa and Venice. It would take months to years for the exotic luxuries of Asia to reach the markets of Western

Europe. A faster, cheaper way had to be found. A way had to be found which would bypass traditional routes and end the control of the Italian merchants.

The importance of the Age of Exploration was not just the discovery and colonization of the New World, but better maps and charts, newer, more accurate navigational instruments, increased knowledge, and great wealth. There were new and different foods and items unknown in Europe and a new hemisphere as a refuge from poverty, persecution, and a place to start a new and better life.

With the increase in trade and travel, cities sprang up and began to grow. Craft workers in the cities developed their skills to a high degree, eventually organizing guilds to protect the quality of the work and to regulate the buying and selling of their products. City governments centered on strong town councils developed and flourished. Active in city government and the town councils were the wealthy businessmen who made up the growing middle class.

The rise of Christianity in early modern Europe was due as much to the iron hand of feudalism as it was to the Church itself. Feudalism, more than any other element, helped the Church get its grip on Europe. That grip, some would argue, has yet to be relinquished.

Like the caste system in India, feudalism kept people under strict control according to their social class. If you were a peasant, you had been born that way and you would stay that way for your entire life. The rich and powerful were also the highest class in society, and the friends of the rich and powerful were the clergy.

The Church, through its warnings of death and damnation without salvation, had rigid control of the belief systems of most of the people throughout Europe. In this way, the Church was able to assume more than just traditional religious roles in people's lives. Clergy were respected and trusted members of society, and people consulted them on secular matters as well as religious ones.

Christianity unified Europe in a way that governments never could. With the Pope at the head of the religion, the peoples of Europe could correctly be called Christendom because they all had the same beliefs, the same worries, and the same tasks to perform in order to achieve the salvation that they so desperately sought. The Church capitalized on this power which increased throughout the Middle Ages until it met a stalwart from Germany named Martin Luther (1483 – 1546), the leader of the Protestant Reformation.

The period from the 1700s to the 1800s was characterized in Western countries by opposing political ideas of democracy and nationalism. This resulted in strong nationalistic feelings and people of common cultures asserting their belief in the right to have a part in their government.

The **American Revolution** resulted in the successful efforts of the English colonists in America to win their freedom from Great Britain. After more than one hundred years of mostly self-government, the colonists resented the increased British meddling and control. They declared their freedom, won the Revolutionary War with aid from France, and formed a new independent nation.

The **French Revolution** was the revolt of the middle and lower classes against the gross political and economic excesses of the rulers and the supporting nobility. It ended with the establishment of the First Republic which was the first in a series of French Republics. Conditions leading to revolt included extreme taxation, inflation, lack of food, and the total disregard for the impossible, degrading, and unacceptable condition of the people on the part of the rulers, nobility, and the Church.

The American Revolution and the French Revolution were similar, yet different, as they liberated their people from unwanted government interference and installed a different kind of government. They both fought for the liberty of the common people, and both were built on writings and ideas that embraced such an outcome. Both revolutions proved that people could expect more from their government and that such rights as self-determination were worth fighting—and dying—for.

However, several important differences need to be emphasized. The British colonists were striking back against unwanted taxation and other sorts of "government interference". The French people were starving and, in many cases, destitute and were striking back against an autocratic regime that cared more for high fashion and courtly love than bread. The American Revolution involved a long campaign of often bloody battles, skirmishes, and stalemates. The French Revolution was bloody to a degree, but it was mainly an overthrow of society and its outdated traditions.

The American Revolution resulted in a representative government, which marketed itself as a beacon of democracy for the rest of the world. The French Revolution resulted in a consulship, a generalship, and then an emperor — probably not what the perpetrators of the Revolution had in mind when they first struck back at the king and queen.

Still, both revolutions are looked back on as turning points in history; as times when the governed stood up to the governors and said, "Enough."

The **Reformation** period consisted of two phases: the **Protestant Revolution** and the **Catholic Reformation**. The Protestant Revolution came about because of religious, political, and economic reasons. The religious reasons stemmed from abuses in the Catholic Church including fraudulent clergy with their scandalous immoral lifestyles; the sale of religious offices, indulgences, and dispensations; different theologies within the Church; and frauds involving sacred relics.

During the eighteenth and especially the nineteenth centuries, **nationalism** emerged as a powerful force in Europe and elsewhere in the world. Strictly speaking, nationalism was a belief in one's own nation, or country's people. More so than in previous centuries, the people of the European nations began to think in terms of a nation of people who had similar beliefs, concerns, and needs. This was partly a reaction to a growing discontent with the autocratic governments of the day and also just a general realization that there was more to life than the individual. People could feel a part of something like their nation, making themselves more than just an insignificant soul struggling to survive.

Nationalism precipitated several changes in government, most notably in France. It also brought large groups of people together, as with the unifications of Germany and Italy. What it didn't do, however, was provide sufficient outlets for this sudden rise in national fervor.

An additional reason for **European imperialism** was the harsh, urgent demand for the raw materials needed to fuel and feed the great Industrial Revolution. Europe in the nineteenth century was a crowded place. Populations were growing but resources were not. Resources were not available in the huge quantities so desperately needed which necessitated (and rationalized) the partitioning of the continent of Africa and parts of Asia. In turn, these colonial areas would purchase the finished manufactured goods. The peoples of many European countries were also agitating for rights as never before. To address these concerns, European powers began to look elsewhere for relief. In the 1700s and 1800s, European powers and peoples began looking to Africa and Asia in order to find colonies for rich sources of goods, trade, and cheap labor.

One of the main places for European imperialist expansion was Africa. Britain, France, Germany, and Belgium took over countries in Africa and claimed them as their own. The resources (including people) were then shipped back to the mainland and claimed as colonial gains. The Europeans made a big deal about "civilizing the savages," reasoning that their technological superiority gave them the right to rule and "educate" the peoples of Africa.

Southeast Asia was another area of European expansion at this time, mainly by France. So, too, was India which was colonized by Great Britain. These two nations combined with Spain to occupy countries in Latin America. Spain also seized the rich lands of the Philippines.

This colonial expansion would come back to haunt the European imperialists in a very big way as colonial skirmishes spilled over into alliance that dragged the European powers into World War I. Some of these colonial battles were still being fought as late as the start of World War I.

In Europe, Italy and Germany each were totally united into one nation from many smaller states. There were revolutions in Austria and Hungary, the Franco-Prussian War, the dividing of Africa among the strong European nations, interference and intervention of Western nations in Asia, and the breakup of Turkish dominance in the Balkans.

On the African continent, France, Great Britain, Italy, Portugal, Spain, Germany, and Belgium controlled the entire continent except Liberia and Ethiopia. In Asia and the Pacific Islands, only China, Japan, and present-day Thailand (Siam) kept their independence. The others were controlled by the strong European nations.

In the United States, **territorial expansion** occurred in the expansion westward under the banner of **"Manifest Destiny".** In addition, the U.S. was involved in the War with Mexico, the Spanish-American War, and support of the Latin American colonies of Spain in their revolt for independence. In Latin America, the Spanish colonies were successful in their fight for independence and self-government.

The time from 1830 to 1914 is characterized by the extraordinary growth and spread of patriotic pride in a nation along with intense, widespread imperialism. Loyalty to one's nation included national pride; extension and maintenance of sovereign political boundaries; unification of smaller states with common language, history, and culture into a more powerful nation; and smaller national groups who, as part of a larger multi-cultural empire, wished to separate into smaller, political, cultural nations.

Skill 10.2 Evaluate examples of primary source documents to show historical perspective

Primary sources include the following kinds of materials:

Documents that reflect the immediate, everyday concerns of people: memoranda, bills, deeds, charters, newspaper reports, pamphlets, graffiti, popular writings, journals or diaries, records of decision-making bodies, letters, receipts, snapshots, etc.

Narrative accounts of events, ideas, trends, etc. written with intention by someone contemporary with the events described.

Statistical data, although statistics may be misleading.

Literature and nonverbal materials, novels, stories, poetry and essays from the period, as well as coins, archaeological artifacts, and art produced during the period are also primary resources. Guidelines for the use of primary resources:

1. Be certain that you understand how language was used at the time of writing and that you understand the context in which it was produced.
2. Do not read history blindly; be certain that you understand both explicit and implicit references in the material.
3. Read the entire text you are reviewing; do not simply extract a few sentences to read.
4. Although anthologies of materials may help you identify primary source materials, the full original text should be consulted.

Secondary sources include the following kinds of materials:

- Books written on the basis of primary materials about the period of time
- Books written on the basis of primary materials about persons who played a major role in the events under consideration
- Books and articles written on the basis of primary materials about the culture, the social norms, the language, and the values of the period
- Quotations from primary sources
- Statistical data on the period
- The conclusions and inferences of other historians
- Multiple interpretations of the ethos of the time

Guidelines for the use of secondary sources:

- Do not rely upon only a single secondary source.
- Check facts and interpretations against primary sources whenever possible.
- Do not accept the conclusions of other historians uncritically.
- Place greatest reliance on secondary sources created by the best and most respected scholars.
- Do not use the inferences of other scholars as if they were facts.
- Ensure that you recognize any bias the writer brings to his/her interpretation of history.
- Understand the primary point of the book as a basis for evaluating the value of the material presented in it and how it pertains to your questions.

Skill 10.3 Identify the cultural contributions and technological developments of Eastern and Western civilizations.

Ancient Civilizations

The earliest known civilizations developed in the Tigris-Euphrates valley of Mesopotamia (modern Iraq) and the Nile valley of Egypt between 4000 BCE and 3000 BCE. Because these civilizations arose in river valleys, they are known as **fluvial civilizations.** Geography and the physical environment played a critical role in the rise and the survival of both of these civilizations. The Fertile Crescent was bounded on the west by the Mediterranean, on the south by the Arabian Desert, on the north by the Taurus Mountains, and on the east by the Zagros Mountains.

First, the rivers provided a source of water that would sustain life, including animal life. The hunters of the society had ample access to a variety of animals initially for hunting to provide food, but also to provide hides, bones, antlers, etc. from which clothing, tools and art could be made. Second, the proximity to water provided a natural attraction to animals which could then be herded and husbanded to provide a stable supply of food and animal products. Third, the rivers of these regions overflowed their banks each year, leaving behind a deposit of very rich soil. As these early people began to experiment with growing crops rather than gathering food, the soil was fertile and water was readily available to produce sizeable harvests. In time, the people developed systems of irrigation that channeled water to the crops without significant human effort on a continuing basis.

The designation **"Fertile Crescent"** was applied by the famous historian and Egyptologist James Breasted to the part of the Near East that extended from the Persian Gulf to the Sinai Peninsula. It included Mesopotamia, Syria, and Palestine. This region was marked by almost constant invasions and migrations. These invaders and migrants seemed to have destroyed the culture and civilization that existed.

The first empire in history was probably in **Mesopotamia**, and it was probably that of the Akkadians, led by Sargon, conqueror of Sumeria. Sargon didn't last long as an emperor, however. He was succeeded as the master of Mesopotamia by a host of famous names, including the Amorite leader, Hammurabi. Another of the famous leaders of the Middle Eastern peoples was Nebuchadnezzar, leader of the Chaldeans. We know this name better for two famous episodes in world history: the building of the Hanging Gardens of Babylon and the Babylonian Captivity, the capture of and transport of the ancient Israelites. Other rulers of the Fertile Crescent include the warrior-tribes the Hittites and the Assyrians, both powerful and successful in their day. But the Middle East empire-building phase didn't really build up until Darius the Great came onto the scene.

Darius was the man who built a collection of cities and satraps into the Persian Empire, one of the largest empires the world had ever seen. It stretched from Egypt, which it conquered eventually, to the boundaries of India. Millions of people owed their lives and their allegiances to Darius and to his successors. The head of the Persian Empire was the most powerful man in the world. He was also the head of the various religions that dotted his large empire with various locations believing in local gods and spirits representing aspects of Nature. This was not a new idea since it had been done in Mesopotamian empires before and especially well in Egypt.

As big as the Persian Empire was, the Persians always wanted more. They grew covetous of the growing Greek civilization which was looking to expand in all directions, especially to the east to areas claimed by the Persians. A series of disagreements escalated into a series of battles and then a full-blown war which the Greeks refer to as the Persian Wars. This struggle had in it some of the most famous battles in the world, including Marathon (which the Greeks won despite being vastly outnumbered), Thermopylae (in which a valiant group of Spartans held off thousands of Persian warriors for several days), Salamis (a naval battle that the Greeks won despite being outgunned and outnumbered), and Plataea (in which the Greeks prevailed by finally outnumbering the Persians). These victories convinced the Persians not to attempt another invasion of Greece, but it didn't mean the end of the Empire.

Greece

The classical civilization of Greece reached the highest levels in man's achievements based on the foundations already laid by such ancient groups as the Egyptians, Phoenicians, Minoans, and Mycenaeans. Among the more important contributions of Greece were: (1) the Greek alphabet derived from the Phoenician letters which formed the basis for the Roman and our present-day alphabets, (2) extensive trading and colonization resulting in the spread of the Greek civilization, (3) the love of sports with emphasis on a sound body, leading to the tradition of the Olympic games, (4) the rise of independent, strong city-states, (5) the complete contrast between independent, freedom-loving Athens with its practice of pure democracy (direct, personal, active participation in government by qualified citizens) and rigid, totalitarian, militaristic Sparta, (6) important accomplishments in drama, epic and lyric poetry, fables, and myths which were centered around the gods and goddesses, science, astronomy, medicine, mathematics, philosophy, art, architecture, and the writing about and recording of historical events, (7) the conquests of Alexander the Great which spread Greek ideas to the areas he conquered and brought ideas from Asia back to the Greek world, and above all (8) the value of ideas, wisdom, curiosity, and the desire to learn as much about the world as was possible.

That end came at the hands of **Alexander the Great**, a Macedonian general, who conquered both Greece and Persia, and eventually Egypt, Phoenician cities, and part of India, creating a new empire that was staggering in its geography and impact. This empire resulted in cultural exchange more than any other. This was known as **Hellenization**, and it brought the Greek enlightened way of life to the peoples of the East while also bringing the exotic goods and customs of the East to Greece. Until this time, the peoples of East and West exchanged goods and customs in small ways, but they were overall suspicious of their enemies. Alexander changed all that, bringing both sides together under one banner and beginning an exchange of ideas, beliefs, and goods that would capture the imagination of rulers for years after his untimely death.

Rome

Rome was the next and most successful of the ancient empires, building itself from one town that borrowed from its Etruscan neighbors into a worldwide empire stretching from the Scotland to the shores of the Middle East. Building on the principles of Hellenization, Rome imported and exported goods and customs, melding the production capabilities and the belief systems of all it conquered into a heterogeneous, yet distinctly, Roman civilization. Like no other empire before it, Rome conquered and absorbed its conquests. Trade, religion, science, and political structure—all these things were incorporated into the Roman Empire, with all of the benefits that assimilation brought being passed on to the Empire's citizens.

Although the ancient civilization of Rome lasted approximately 1,000 years including the periods of republic and empire, its lasting influence on Europe and its history was for a much longer period. There was a very sharp contrast between the curious, imaginative, inquisitive Greeks and the practical, simple, down-to-earth, no-nonsense Romans, who spread and preserved the ideas of ancient Greece and other culture groups. The contributions and accomplishments of the Romans are numerous, but their greatest included language, engineering, building, law, government, roads, trade, and the "**Pax Romana**". Pax Romana was the long period of peace enabling free travel and trade, which spread people, cultures, goods, and ideas over a vast area of the known world. In the end, though, Rome grew too big to manage and its enemies were too many to turn back. The sprawling nature of the Empire made it too big in the end to protect, and the heterogeneity dissolved into chaos and violence.

The official end of the **Roman Empire** came when Germanic tribes took over and controlled most of Europe. The five major tribes were the Visigoths, Ostrogoths, Vandals, Saxons, and the Franks. In later years, the Franks successfully stopped the invasion of southern Europe by Muslims by defeating them under the leadership of Charles Martel at the Battle of Tours in 732 AD. Thirty-six years later, in 768 AD, the grandson of Charles Martel became King of the Franks and is known throughout history as Charlemagne. Charlemagne was a man of war, but he was unique in his respect for and encouragement of learning. He made great efforts to rule fairly and ensure just treatment for his people.

Asia

The East had its share of empires as well, especially in **China**. From an early age, China had emperors who were in charge of vast territories and vast numbers of people. The Chinese, especially, were good at exporting their goods and customs, especially along the famous Silk Road. Exotic spices flowed along this road to the Middle East and to Rome. The Chinese empire steadily expanded, rivaling even Rome in breadth and accomplishments by the time of the famous Han Dynasty. When Rome fell, China lived on.

The Middle East

The Middle East is defined by its name and its geographic position. It is in the middle of the globe, a position that enables it to exert tremendous influence on not only the trade that passes through its realm of influence but also the political relations between its countries and those of different parts of the world.

From the beginnings of civilization, the Middle East has been a destination—for attackers, for adventure-seekers, for those starving for food and for those seeking a progressively more technologically advanced series of other resources from iron to oil. Now, as then, the countries of the Middle East play an important role in the economics of the world.

Religious conflict is prominent in Israel, as Israelis and Palestinians continue a centuries-old fight over religion and geography. This conflict goes back to the seventh century at the beginnings of Islam. Muslims claimed Jerusalem, the capital of the ancient civilization of Israel, as a holy city, in the same way that Jews and Christians did. Muslims seized control of Palestine and Jerusalem and held it for a great many years, prompting Christian armies from Europe to muster for the Crusades in a series of attempts to "regain the Holy Land." For hundreds of years after Christendom's failure, these lands were ruled by Muslim leaders and armies. In recent centuries, Palestine was made a British colony and then was eliminated in favor of the modern state of Israel. Since that last event, in 1948, the conflict has escalated to varying degrees.

The **Byzantine Empire**, which the Eastern Empire became, was closer to the Middle East and so inherited the traditions of Mesopotamia and Persia. This was in stark contrast to the Western Empire, which inherited the traditions of Greece and Carthage. Byzantium was known for its exquisite artwork (including the famous church Hagia Sophia), something for which the West was never known. Perhaps the most wide-ranging success of the Byzantine Empire was in the area of trade. Uniquely situated at the gateway to both West and East, Byzantium could control trade going in both directions. Indeed, the Eastern Empire was much more centralized and rigid in its enforcement of its policies than the feudal West.

Before this time, Arabians played only an occasional role in history. Arabia was a vast desert of rock and sand except on the coastal areas along the Red Sea. It was populated by nomadic wanderers called **Bedouins**, who lived in scattered tribes near oases where they watered their herds. Tribal leaders engaged in frequent war with one another.

The family or tribe was the social and political unit. Under the authority of the head of the family, there was cruelty, infanticide, and suppression of women. Their religion was a crude and superstitious paganism and idolatry. Although there was regular contact with Christians and Jews through trading interactions, the idea of monotheism was foreign. What vague unity there was within the religion was based upon common veneration of certain sanctuaries. The most important of these was a small square temple called **the Kaaba** (cube) located in the town of **Mecca**. Arabs came from all parts of the country in annual pilgrimages to Mecca during the sacred months when warfare was prohibited. For this reason, Mecca was considered the center of Arab religion.

A few years after the death of the Emperor Justinian, **Mohammed** was born (570 CE) in a small Arabian town near the Red Sea. In about 610, Mohammed came to some prominence. He called his new religion **Islam** (submission to the will of God) and his followers were called **Moslems** – those who had surrendered themselves. His first converts were members of his family and his friends. As the new faith began to grow, it remained a secret society. But when they began to make their faith public, they met with opposition and persecution from the pagan Arabians who feared the new religion and the possible loss of the profitable trade with the pilgrims who came to the Kaaba every year.

Islam slowly gained ground, and the persecutions became more severe around Mecca. In 622, Mohammed and his close followers fled the city and found refuge in **Medina** to the north. His flight is called the **Hegira**. This event marks the beginning of the Moslem calendar. Mohammed took advantage of the ongoing feuds between Jews and Arabs in the city and became the rulers of Medina, making it the capital of a rapidly growing state.

In the years that followed, Islam changed significantly. It became a fighting religion and Mohammed became a political leader. The group survived by raiding caravans on the road to Mecca and plundering nearby Jewish tribes. This was a victorious religion that promised plunder and profit in this world and the blessings of paradise after death. It attracted many converts from the Bedouin tribes. By 630, Mohammed was strong enough to conquer Mecca and make it the religious center of Islam toward which all Moslems turned to pray. Medina remained the political capital.

Mohammed left behind a collection of divine revelations (**surahs**) he believed were delivered by the angel Gabriel. These were collected and published in a book called the ***Koran***, the holy scripture of Islam. The revelations were never dated or kept in any kind of chronological order. After the prophet's death, they were organized by length (in diminishing order). The *Koran* contains Mohammed's teachings on moral and theological questions, his legislation on political matters, and his comments on current events.

These Moslem Arabians immediately launched an amazing series of conquests which, in time, extended the empire from the Indus to Spain. It has often been said that these conquests were motivated by religious fanaticism and the determination to force Islam upon the infidel. In fact, however, the motives were economic and political.

Reading and writing in Arabic, the study of the *Koran*, arithmetic, and other elementary subjects were taught to children in schools attached to the mosques. In larger and wealthier cities, the mosques offered more advanced education in literature, logic, philosophy, law, algebra, astronomy, medicine, science, theology, and the traditions of Islam. Books were produced for the large reading public. The wealthy collected private libraries, and public libraries arose in large cities.

The most popular subjects were theology and law, but the more important field of study was philosophy. The works of the Greek and Hellenistic philosophers were translated into Arabic and interpreted with commentaries. These were later passed on to the Western Christian societies and schools in the twelfth and thirteenth centuries. The basis of Moslem philosophy was Aristotelian and Neo-platonic ideas which were essentially transmitted without creative modification.

The Moslems were also interested in natural science. They translated the works on Galen and Hippocrates into Arabic and added the results of their own experience in medicine. Avicenna was regarded in Western Europe as one of the great masters of medicine. They also adopted the work of the Greeks in the other sciences and modified and supplemented them with their own discoveries. Much of their work in chemistry was focused on alchemy (the attempt to transmute base metals into gold). The **Muslim** culture outdistanced the Western world in the field of medicine primarily because the people weren't constrained by the sort of superstitious fervor that had so embraced the West at this time. The Muslim doctor **Al-Razi** was one of the most well-known physicians in the world and was the author of a medical encyclopedia and a handbook for smallpox and measles.

Adopting the heritage of Greek mathematics, the Moslems also borrowed a system of numerals from India. This laid the foundation for modern arithmetic, geometry, trigonometry, and algebra.

Moslem art and architecture tended to be mostly uniform in style allowing for some regional modification. They borrowed from Byzantine, Persian, and other sources. The floor plans of the mosques were generally based on Mohammed's house at Medina. The notable unique elements were the tall minarets from which the faithful were called to prayer. Interior decoration was the style now called arabesque. Mohammed had banned paintings or other images of living creatures. These continued to be absent from mosques although they occasionally appeared in book illustrations and secular contexts. But their skilled craftsmen produced the finest art in jewelry, ceramics, carpets, and carved ivory.

The system of **feudalism** became a dominant feature of the economic and social system in Europe. It was a system of loyalty and protection. The strong protected the weak that returned the service with farm labor, military service, and loyalty. Life was lived out on a vast estate, called a "manor" which was owned by a nobleman and his family. It was a complete village supporting a few hundred people, mostly peasants. Improved tools and farming methods made life more bearable although most never left the manor or traveled from their village during their lifetime.

Europe

Feudalism was the organization of people based on the ownership of land by a **lord** or other **noble** who allows individuals known as peasants or **serfs** to farm the land and to keep a portion of it. The lord or noble, in return for the serfs' loyalty, offers them his protection. In practical effect, the serf is considered owned by his lord with little or no rights at all. The lord's sole obligation to the serfs is to protect them so they could continue to work for him (most, though not all, lords were men). This system would last for many centuries. In Russia, it would last until the 1860s.

The end of the feudal manorial system was sealed by the outbreak and spread of the infamous **Black Death**, which killed over one-third of the total population of Europe. Those who survived and were skilled in any job or occupation were in demand and many serfs or peasants found freedom and, for that time, a decidedly improved standard of living. Strong nation-states became powerful, and people developed a renewed interest in life and learning.

Japan

From its beginnings, Japan morphed into an imperial form of government, with the divine emperor being able to do no wrong and, therefore, serving for life. **Kyoto**, the capital, became one of the largest and most powerful cities in the world. The nobles were lords of great lands and were called **daimyos**. They were of the highest social class and had working for them people of lower social classes, including the lowly peasants who had few privileges other than being allowed to work for the great men that the daimyos told everyone they were. The daimyos had **shogun** warriors serving them and they answered only to the daimyo. The shogun code of honor was an exemplification of the overall Japanese belief that every man was a soldier and a gentleman. The contradiction was that the emerging social classes and the needs of women didn't seem to get noticed much.

Feudalism developed in Japan later than it did in Europe and lasted longer as well. Japan dodged one huge historical bullet when a huge Mongol invasion was driven away by the famed **kamikaze**, or "divine wind," in the 12th century. Japan was thus free to continue to develop itself as it saw fit and to refrain from interacting with the West. This isolation lasted until the nineteenth century.

Skill 10.4 Identify significant historical individuals, events, and ideas that have influenced Eastern and Western civilizations.

Ancient Civilizations

Ancient civilizations were those cultures which developed to a greater degree and were considered advanced. These included the following with their major accomplishments.

The culture of **Mesopotamia** was definitely autocratic in nature. The various civilizations that criss-crossed the Fertile Crescent were very much top-heavy, with a single ruler at the head of the government and, in many cases, also the head of the religion. The people followed his strict instructions or faced the often dire and often life-threatening consequences.

The civilizations of the Sumerians, Amorites, Hittites, Assyrians, Chaldeans, and Persians controlled various areas of the land called Mesopotamia. With few exceptions, tyrants and military leaders controlled the vast majority of aspects of society including trade, religions, and the laws. Each Sumerian city-state (and there were a few) had its own god with the city-state's leader doubling as the high priest of worship of that local god. Subsequent cultures had a handful of gods as well, although they had more of a national worship structure with high priests centered in the capital city as advisers to the tyrant.

Trade was very important to these civilizations, since they had access to some, but not all, of the things that they needed to survive. Some trading agreements led to occupation, as was the case with the Sumerians who didn't bother to build walls to protect their wealth of knowledge. Egypt and the Phoenician cities were powerful and regular trading partners of the various Mesopotamian cultures.

Legacies handed down to us from these people include:

- The first use of writing, the wheel, and banking (Sumeria)
- The first written set of laws (Code of Hammurabi)
- The first epic story (*Gilgamesh*)
- The first library dedicated to preserving knowledge (instituted by the Assyrian leader Ashurbanipal)
- The Hanging Gardens of Babylon (built by the Chaldean Nebuchadnezzar)

The ancient civilization of the **Sumerians** invented the wheel, developed irrigation through use of canals, dikes, and devices for raising water, devised the system of cuneiform writing, learned to divide time, and built large boats for trade. The Babylonians devised the famous **Code of Hammurabi**, a code of laws.

Egypt made numerous significant contributions including construction of the great pyramids, development of hieroglyphic writing, preservation of bodies after death, and the making paper from papyrus. There were also contributions to developments in arithmetic and geometry, the invention of the method of counting in groups of 1-10 (the decimal system), completion of a solar calendar, and laying the foundation for science and astronomy.

Egyptian sources document the earliest historical record of **Kush,** one of the African civilizations to develop in the Nile River Valley. They describe a region upstream from the first cataract of the Nile as "wretched". This civilization was characterized by a settled way of life in fortified mud-brick villages. They subsisted on hunting and fishing, herding cattle, and gathering grain. Skeletal remains suggest that the people were a blend of Negroid and Mediterranean peoples. This civilization appears to be the second oldest in Africa (after Egypt).

In government, the king ruled through a law of custom that was interpreted by priests. The king was elected from the royal family with descent determined through the mother's line (as in Egypt). In an unparalleled innovation, the Kushites were ruled by a series of female monarchs. The Kushite religion was polytheistic, including all of the primary Egyptian gods. There were, however, regional gods which were the principal gods in their regions. Derived from other African cultures, there was also a lion warrior god. This civilization was vital through the last half of the first millennium BC, but it suffered about 300 years of gradual decline until it was eventually conquered by the Nuba people.

The ancient **Assyrians** were a warlike and aggressive people due to a highly organized military and used horse drawn chariots.

The **Hebrews**, also known as the ancient Israelites, instituted monotheism (the worship of one God, Yahweh) and combined the 66 books of the Hebrew and Christian Greek scriptures into the *Bible* we have today.

The **Minoans** had a system of writing which used symbols to represent syllables in words. They built palaces with multiple levels containing many rooms, water and sewage systems with flush toilets, bathtubs, hot and cold running water, and bright paintings on the walls.

The **Mycenaeans** changed the Minoan writing system to aid their own language and used symbols to represent syllables.

The **Phoenicians** were sea traders well known for their manufacturing skills in glass and metals and the development of their famous purple dye. They became so very proficient in the skill of navigation that they were able to sail by the stars at night. Further, they devised an alphabet using symbols to represent single sounds, which was an improved extension of the Egyptian principle and writing system.

For the accomplishments of **Greece**, please review Skill 10.3.
The conquests of **Alexander the Great** spread Greek ideas to the areas he conquered and brought many ideas from Asia to the Greek world. Above all, the value of ideas, wisdom, curiosity, and the desire to learn as much about the world as possible satisfied Alexander's thirst for knowledge.

For information on the accomplishments of **Rome**, please review Skill 10.3.

India

In India, the caste system was developed, the principle of zero in mathematics was discovered, and the major religion of Hinduism was founded. Hinduism was a continuing influence along with the rise of Buddhism. Industry and commerce developed along with extensive trading with the Near East. Outstanding advances in the fields of science and medicine were made and they were one of the first to be active in navigation and maritime enterprises during this time.

Hinduism began with people called Aryans around 1500 BC and spread into India. The Aryans blended their culture with the culture of the Dravidians, natives they had conquered. Today it has many sects, promotes worship of hundreds of gods and goddesses, and maintains the belief of reincarnation. Though forbidden today by law, a prominent feature of Hinduism in the past was a rigid adherence to and practice of the infamous caste system.

Asia & Japan

China is considered by some historians to be the oldest, uninterrupted civilization in the world and was already in existence at the same time as the ancient civilizations founded in **Egypt**, **Mesopotamia**, and the **Indus Valley**. The Chinese studied nature and weather; stressed the importance of education, family, and a strong central government; followed the religions of Buddhism, Confucianism, and Taoism; and invented such things as gunpowder, paper, printing, and the magnetic compass.

China practiced crop rotation and terrace farming, increased the importance of the silk industry, and developed caravan routes across Central Asia for extensive trade. In addition, they increased proficiency in rice cultivation and developed a written language based on drawings or pictographs with no alphabet symbolizing sounds as each word or character had a form different from all others.

Ancient China was a land in constant turmoil. Tribes warred with one another almost from the start, and the **Great Wall of China** resulted from a consolidation of walls built to keep out invaders. The Great Wall was built at the direction of China's emperor, and the idea of an emperor or very strong "government of one" was the rule of law until the twentieth century. Chinese people became very proficient at producing beautiful artworks and exporting them, along with silk, to the rest of the world along the Silk Road.

The story of **China** during this time is one of dynasties controlling various parts of what is now China and Tibet. The **Tang Dynasty** was one of the most long-lasting and the most proficient, inventing the idea of civil service and the practice of block printing. Next was the Sung Dynasty which produced some of the world's greatest paintings and porcelain pottery, but it failed to unify China in a meaningful way. This would prove instrumental in the takeover of China by the Mongols, led by Genghis Khan and his most famous grandson, Kublai.

Genghis Khan was known as a conqueror, and Kublai was known as the one who could unite. They both extended the borders of their empire, and at its height, the Mongol Empire was the largest the world has ever seen. It encompassed all of China, Russia, Persia, and central Asia. Following the Mongols were the Ming and Manchu Dynasties, both of which focused on isolation. As a result, China at the end of the eighteenth century knew very little of the outside world and vice versa. Ming artists created beautiful porcelain pottery, but not much of it saw its way into the outside world until much later. The Manchus were known for their focus on farming and road building, two practices that were instituted in greater numbers in order to try to keep up with the expanding population. Confucianism, Taoism, and ancestor worship—the staples of Chinese society for hundreds of years—continued to flourish during all this time.

The civilization in **Japan** appeared during this time having borrowed much of their culture from China. It was the last of these classical civilizations to develop. Although they used, accepted, and copied Chinese art, law, architecture, dress, and writing, the Japanese refined these into their own unique way of life, including incorporating the religion of Buddhism into their culture. Early Japanese society focused on the emperor and on the farm, in that order. The Sea of Japan protected Japan from more than one Chinese invasion, including the famous Mongol one that was blown back by the "divine wind". The power of the emperor declined as it was usurped by the era of the daimyo and his loyal soldiers, the **samurai**.

Japan flourished economically and culturally during many of these years, and their policy of isolation kept the rest of the world from knowing such things. Buddhism and local religions were joined by Christianity in the sixteenth century, but it wasn't until the mid-nineteenth century that Japan rejoined the world community.

Buddhism: developed in India from the teachings of Prince Gautama and spread to most of Asia. Its beliefs opposed the worship of numerous deities, the Hindu caste system, and the supernatural. Worshippers must be free of attachment to all things worldly and devote themselves to finding release from life's suffering.

Confucianism: a Chinese religion based on the teachings of the Chinese philosopher Confucius. There is no clergy, no organization, and no belief in a deity or in life after death. It emphasizes political and moral ideas with respect for authority and ancestors. Rulers were expected to govern according to high moral standards.

Taoism: a native Chinese religion with worship of more deities than almost any other religion. It teaches all followers to make the effort to achieve the two goals of happiness and immortality. Practices and ceremonies include meditation, prayer, magic, reciting scriptures, special diets, breath control, beliefs in witchcraft, fortune telling, astrology, and communicating with the spirits of the dead.

Shinto: the native religion of Japan developed from native folk beliefs of worshipping spirits and demons in animals, trees, and mountains. According to its mythology, deities created Japan and its people which resulted in worshipping the emperor as a god. Shinto was strongly influenced by Buddhism and Confucianism but never had strong doctrines on salvation or life after death.

Middle East

The ancient **Persians** developed an alphabet, contributed the religions/philosophies of **Zoroastrianism**, **Mithraism**, and **Gnosticism**, and allowed conquered peoples to retain their own customs, laws, and religions.

The ancient **Israelites** created a powerful legacy of political and philosophical traditions, much of which survives to this day. In law and religion, especially, we can draw a more or less straight line from then to now.

Israel was not the first ancient civilization to have a series of laws for its people to follow. However, thanks to the staggering popularity of the **Ten Commandments**, we think of the Israelites in this way. This simple set of laws, some of which are not laws at all but societal instructions, maintains to this day a central role in societies the world over. Such commandments as the ones that prohibit stealing and killing were revolutionary in their day because they applied to everyone, not just the disadvantaged. In many ancient cultures, the rich and powerful were above the law because they could buy their way out of trouble and because it wasn't always clear what the laws were. Echoing the Code of Hammurabi and preceding Rome's Twelve Tables, the Ten Commandments provided a written record of laws, so all knew what was prohibited.

The civilization of Israel is also known as the first to assume a worship of just one god. The Christian communities built on this tradition, and both faiths exist and are expanding today, especially in western countries. Rather than a series of gods, each of which was in charge of a different aspect of nature or society, the ancient Israelites and Christians believed in just one god, called Yahweh or God, depending on which religion you consider. This divine being was the "one, true god," This worship of just one god resulted in the believers feeling they themselves were able to talk (or, more properly, pray) directly to their god, whereas the peoples of Mesopotamia and Egypt thought the gods were distant and unapproachable.

Africa

The civilizations in Africa south of the Sahara were developing the refining and use of iron, especially for farm implements and later for weapons. Trading took place over land by using camels and important seaports. The Arab influence was extremely important, as was their later contact with Indians, Christian Nubians, and Persians. In fact, their trading activities were probably the most important factor in the spread of and assimilation of different ideas and stimulation of cultural growth.

African civilizations during these centuries were few and far between. Most of northern coastal Africa had been conquered by Moslem armies. The preponderance of deserts and other inhospitable lands restricted African settlements to a few select areas. The city of Zimbabwe became a trading center in south-central Africa in the 5th century but didn't last long. More successful was Ghana, a Muslim-influenced kingdom that arose in the 9th century and lasted for nearly 300 years. Ghanaians had large farming areas and also raised cattle and elephants. They traded with people from Europe and the Middle East. Eventually overrunning Ghana was **Mali**, whose trade center, Timbuktu, survived its own empire's demise and blossomed into one of the world's caravan destinations.

Iron, tin, and leather came out of Mali with a vengeance. The Songhai civilization was relatively successful in maintaining the success of their predecessors.

Religion in all of these places was definitely Muslim, and even after extended contact with other cultures, technological advancements were few and far between.

Europe

The word "**Renaissance**" literally means "rebirth": it signaled the rekindling of interest in the glory of ancient classical Greek and Roman civilizations. It was the period in human history marking the beginning of many ideas and innovations leading to our modern age. The Renaissance began in Italy with many of its ideas starting in Florence, controlled by the infamous Medici family. Education, especially for some of the merchants, required reading, writing, math, the study of law, and the writings of classical Greek and Roman writers.

Most famous are the Renaissance artists, first and foremost Leonardo, Michelangelo, and Raphael, but also Titian, Donatello, and Rembrandt. All of these men pioneered a new method of painting and sculpture—that of portraying real events and real people as they really looked, not as the artists imagined them to be. One need look no further than Michelangelo's *David* to illustrate this.

Literature was a focus as well during the Renaissance. Humanists Petrarch, Boccaccio, Erasmus, and Sir Thomas More advanced the idea of being interested in life here on Earth and the opportunities it can bring, rather than constantly focusing on heaven and its rewards. The monumental works of Shakespeare, Dante, and Cervantes found their origins in these ideas, as well as the ideas that drove the painters and sculptors. All of these works, of course, owe much of their existence to the invention of the printing press, which occurred during the Renaissance.

The Renaissance changed music as well. No longer just a religious experience, music could be fun and composed for its own sake, to be enjoyed in fuller and more humanistic ways than in the Middle Ages. Musicians worked for themselves, rather than for the churches, as before, and so could command good money for their work and increase their prestige.

The **Scientific Revolution** and the **Enlightenment** were two of the most important movements in the history of civilization, resulting in a new sense of self-examination and a wider view of the world than ever before. The Scientific Revolution was, above all, a shift in focus from **belief to evidence**. Scientists and philosophers wanted to see the proof, not just believe what other people told them.

A Polish astronomer, **Nicolaus Copernicus**, began the Scientific Revolution. He condensed a lifetime of observations into a book that was published about the time of his death. In this book, Copernicus argued that the Sun, not the Earth, was the center of a solar system and that other planets revolved around the Sun. This flew in the face of established church-mandated doctrines. The Church still wielded tremendous power at this time, including the power to banish people or sentence them to prison or even death.

The Danish astronomer **Tycho Brahe** was the first to catalog his observations of the night sky. Building on Brahe's data, German scientist Johannes Kepler instituted his theory of planetary movement embodied in his famous *Laws of Planetary Movement*. Using Brahe's data, Kepler also confirmed Copernicus's observations and argument that the Earth revolved around the Sun.

The most famous defender of this idea was **Galileo Galilei**, an Italian scientist who conducted many famous experiments in the pursuit of science. He is most well-known, however, for his defense of the heliocentric (sun-centered) idea. He wrote a book comparing the two theories, but most readers could tell easily that he favored the new one. He was convinced of this mainly because of what he had seen with his own eyes. He had used the relatively new invention of the telescope to see four moons of Jupiter. His ideas were not at all favored with the Church which continued to assert its authority in this and many other matters. The Church was still powerful enough at this time, especially in Italy, to order Galileo to be placed under house arrest. Galileo died under house arrest, but his ideas didn't die with him.

An English scientist named **Isaac Newton**, who became perhaps the most famous scientist of all, continued this work. He is known as the discoverer of gravity and a pioneering voice in the study of optics (light), calculus, and physics. More than any other scientist, Newton argued for and proved the idea of a mechanistic view of the world: You can see how the world works and prove how the world works through observation; if you can see these things with your own eyes, they must be so. Up to this time, people believed what other people told them. Newton, following in the footsteps of Copernicus and Galileo, changed all that.

This naturally led to the **Enlightenment**, a period of intense self-study that focused on ethics and logic. More so than at any time before, scientists and philosophers questioned cherished truths, widely-held beliefs, and their own sanity in an attempt to discover why the world worked as it did. "I think, therefore I am," was one of the famous sayings of that or any day. It was uttered by Rene Descartes, a French scientist-philosopher whose dedication to logic and the rigid rules of observation were a blueprint for the thinkers who came after him.

One of the giants of the era was England's **David Hume**. As a pioneer of the doctrine of empiricism requiring proof before accepting any concept or idea, Hume was also a prime believer in the value of skepticism. In other words, he was naturally suspicious of things that other people told him to be true and constantly set out to discover the truth for himself. These two related ideas influenced a great many thinkers after Hume, and his many writings continue to inspire philosophers to this day.

Immanuel Kant of Germany is the Enlightenment thinker who might be the most famous. He was both a philosopher and a scientist, and he took a definite scientific view of the world. He wrote the movement's most famous essay, "Answering the Question: What Is Enlightenment?" and he answered his famous question with the motto "Dare to Know." For Kant, the human being was a rational being capable of creative thought and intense self-evaluation. He encouraged all to examine themselves and the world around them. Kant believed that the source of morality lay not in the nature of the grace of God but in the human soul itself. He believed that man believed in God for practical, not religious or mystical, reasons.

Also prevalent during the Enlightenment was the idea of the "**social contract**." This was the belief that government existed because people wanted it to; that the people had an agreement with the government that they would submit to it as long as it protected them and didn't encroach on their basic human rights. The Frenchman Jean-Jacques Rousseau popularized this idea which was also adopted by England's John Locke and America's Thomas Jefferson. **John Locke** was one of the most influential political writers of the 17th century who put great emphasis on human rights and the belief that when governments violate those rights, people should rebel. He wrote the book *Two Treatises of Government* in 1690 which had tremendous influence on political thought in the American colonies and helped shape the U.S. Constitution and Declaration of Independence.

The Americas

The people who lived in the Americas before Columbus arrived had a thriving, connected society. The civilizations in North America tended to spread out more and were in occasional conflict; however, they managed to maintain their sovereignty for the most part. Native Americans in North America had a spiritual and personal relationship with the various spirits of nature and a keen appreciation of the ways of woodworking and metalworking. Various tribes dotted the landscape of what is now the U.S. They struggled against one another for control of resources such as food and water, but they had no concept of ownership of land since they believed that they were living on the land with the permission of the spirits. The North Americans mastered the art of growing many crops and, to their credit, were willing to share that knowledge with the various Europeans who arrived later.

The South American civilizations, however, tended to migrate into empires with the strongest city or tribe assuming control of the lives and resources of the rest of the nearby peoples. The most well-known empires of South America were the **Aztec, Inca, and Maya**. Each of these empires had a central capital where the emperor who controlled all aspects of the lives of his subjects, lived. The empires traded with other peoples, and if the relations soured, the results were usually absorption of the trading partners into the empire. These empires, especially the Aztecs, had access to large numbers of metals and jewels, and they created weapons and artwork that continue to impress historians today. The Inca Empire stretched across a vast period of territory down the western coast of South America and was connected by a series of roads. A series of messengers ran along these roads, carrying news and instructions from the capital, Cusco. The Incas, however, did not have the wheel. The Mayas are most well-known for their famous pyramids and calendars, as well as their language, which still stumps archaeologists.

Russia

Until the early years of the twentieth century Russia was ruled by a succession of czars. The czars ruled as autocrats or, sometimes, despots. Society was essentially feudalistic and was structured in three levels. The top level was held by the czar. The second level was composed of the rich nobles who held government positions and owned vast tracts of land. The third level of the society was composed of the remaining people who lived in poverty as peasants or serfs. There was discontent among the peasants. There were several unsuccessful attempts to revolt during the nineteenth century, but they were quickly suppressed. The revolutions of 1905 and 1917, however, were quite different.

<u>The causes of the 1905 Revolution were</u>

- Discontent with the social structure
- Discontent with the living conditions of the peasants
- Discontent with working conditions despite industrialization
- The general discontent was aggravated by the Russo-Japanese War (1904-1905) with inflation, rising prices, etc.
- Many of the fighting troops were killed in battles lost to Japan because of poor leadership, lack of training, and inferior weaponry
- Czar Nicholas II refused to end the war despite setbacks
- In January 1905, Port Arthur fell

A trade union leader, **Father Gapon**, organized a protest to demand an end to the war, industrial reform, more civil liberties, and a constituent assembly. More than 150,000 peasants joined a demonstration outside the czar's winter palace. Before the demonstrators even spoke, the palace guard opened fire on the crowd. This destroyed the people's trust in the czar. Illegal trade unions and political parties formed and organized strikes to gain power. The strikes eventually brought the Russian economy to a halt. This led Czar Nicholas II to sign the October Manifesto which created a constitutional monarchy, extended some civil rights, and gave the parliament limited legislative power. In a very short period of time, the czar disbanded the parliament and violated the promised civil liberties. This violation contributed to the foment of the 1917 Revolution.

The causes of the 1917 Revolution were:

- The violation of the October Manifesto
- Defeats on the battlefields during WW I caused discontent, loss of life, and a popular desire to withdraw from the war
- The czar continued to appoint unqualified people to government posts and handled the situation with general incompetence
- The czar also listened to his wife's (Alexandra) advice. She was strongly influenced by Rasputin. This caused increased discontent among all levels of the social structure.
- WW I had caused another surge in prices and scarcity of many items. Most of the peasants could not afford to buy bread.

Workers in Petrograd went on strike in 1917 over the need for food. The czar again ordered troops to suppress the strike. This time, however, the troops sided with the workers. The revolution then took a unique direction. The parliament created a provisional government to rule the country. The military and the workers also created their own governments called soviets which were popularly elected local councils. The parliament was composed of nobles who soon lost control of the country when they failed to comply with the wishes of the populace. The result was chaos.

The most significant differences between the 1905 and 1917 revolutions were the formation of political parties, their use of propaganda, and the support of the military and some of the nobles in 1917.

World War I ■ 1914 to 1918

In Europe, war broke out in 1914 and ended in 1918. Over the course of the war, it eventually involved nearly 30 nations. One of the major causes of the war was the tremendous surge of nationalism during the 1800s and early 1900s. People of the same nationality or ethnic group sharing a common history, language, or culture began uniting or demanding the right of unification. This was especially true in the empires of Eastern Europe, such as Russian Ottoman and Austrian-Hungarian Empires. The beliefs of these peoples in loyalty to common political, social, and economic goals were becoming stronger and more intense and were considered to be before any loyalty to the controlling nation or empire. Other causes included the increasing strength of military capabilities, massive colonization for raw materials needed for industrialization and manufacturing, and military and diplomatic alliances. The initial spark, which started the conflagration, was the assassination of Austrian Archduke Francis Ferdinand and his wife in Sarajevo.

To secure the huge sums of money needed to finance the war, the government sold “Liberty Bonds” to the people. Nearly $25 billion worth of bonds were sold in four separate issues. After the war “Victory Bonds” were sold. The first Liberty loan was issued at 3.5%, the second at 4%, the remaining ones at 4.25%. A strong appeal was made to the people to buy bonds. The total response meant that more than 1/5 of the inhabitants of the U.S. bought bonds. For the first time in their lives, millions of people had begun saving money.

Under the administration of Theodore Roosevelt, the U.S. armed forces were strengthened. Roosevelt's foreign policy was summed up in the slogan of "Speak softly and carry a big stick" to back up the efforts in diplomacy with a strong military. During the years before the outbreak of World War I, evidence of U.S. emergence as a world power could be seen in a number of actions. President Roosevelt forced Italy, Germany, and Great Britain to remove their blockade of Venezuela by involing the Monroe Doctrine which required non-involvement of Europe in the affairs of the Western Hemisphere. Roosevelt also gained the rights to construct the Panama Canal by threatening force; assumed the finances of the Dominican Republic to stabilize it and prevent any intervention by Europeans; and in 1916 under President Woodrow Wilson, U.S. troops were sent to the Dominican Republic to keep order.

The war effort required massive production of weapons, ammunition, radios, and other equipment of war and the support of war. During wartime, work hours were shortened, wages were increased, and working conditions improved. But when the war ended and business and industrial owners and managers attempted a return to pre-war conditions, the workers revolted. These conditions contributed to the Red Scare and the establishment of new labor laws.

World War I saw the introduction of such warfare as use of tanks, airplanes, machine guns, submarines, poison gas, and flame throwers. Fighting on the western front was characterized by a series of trenches that were used throughout the war until 1918. When the war began in 1914, President Woodrow Wilson declared that the U.S. was neutral and most Americans were opposed to any involvement anyway. U.S. involvement in the war did not occur until 1916 when Wilson was reelected to a second term based on the slogan proclaiming his efforts at keeping America out of the war. For a few months after, he put forth most of his efforts to stopping the war, but German submarines began unlimited warfare against American merchant shipping.

The United States war effort for WW I included over four million people who served in the military in some capacity, with over two million serving overseas. The cost of the war up to April 30, 1919 was over 22.5 billion dollars. Nearly 50,000 Americans were killed in battle and an additional 221,000 were wounded. On the home front, people energetically supported the war effort in every way necessary. The menace of German submarines was causing the loss of ships faster than new ships could be built. At the beginning of the war, the U.S. had little overseas shipping. Scores of shipyards were quickly constructed to build both wooden and steel ships. At the end of the war the United States had more than 2,000 ships.

World War I ended November 11, 1918 with the signing of the Treaty of Versailles. Economically, the war cost a total of $337 billion. It also increased inflation and huge war debts, and caused a loss of markets, goods, jobs, and factories.

Herbert Hoover had chaired the Belgian Relief Commission previously. He was named "food commissioner," later called the U.S. Food Administration Board. His function was to manage conservation and distribution of the food supply to ensure that there was adequate food to supply every American both at home and overseas, as well as providing additional food to people who were suffering in Europe.

Pre-war empires lost tremendous amounts of territories as well as the wealth of natural resources in them. New, independent nations were formed and some predominately ethnic areas came under control of nations of different cultural backgrounds. Some national boundary changes overlapped and created tensions and hard feelings as well as political and economic confusion. The wishes and desires of every national or cultural group could not possibly be realized and satisfied, resulting in disappointments for both those who were victorious and those who were defeated. Germany received harsher terms than expected from the treaty which weakened its post-war government and, along with the world-wide depression of the 1930s, set the stage for the rise of Adolf Hitler and his Nationalist Socialist Party and World War II.

World War II 1939 to 1945

Ironically, **the Treaty of Paris,** the peace treaty ending World War I, ultimately led to the Second World War. Countries that fought in the first war were either dissatisfied over the "spoils" of war, or were punished so harshly that resentment continued building to an eruption twenty years later. In addition:

The **economic problems** of both winners and losers of the first war were never resolved and the worldwide Great Depression of the 1930s dealt the final blow to any immediate rapid recovery. Democratic governments in Europe were severely strained and weakened which in turn gave strength and encouragement to those political movements that were extreme and made promises to end the economic chaos in their countries.

Nationalism, which was a major cause of World War I, grew even stronger and seemed to feed the feelings of discontent, which became increasingly rampant.

Because of **unstable economic** conditions and political unrest, harsh dictatorships arose in several of the countries, especially where there was no history of experience in democratic government.

Countries such as Germany, Japan, and Italy began to **aggressively expand their borders** and acquire additional territory.

In all, 59 nations became embroiled in World War II, which began September 1, 1939 and ended September 2, 1945. These dates include both the European and Pacific Theaters of war. The horrible tragic results of this second global conflagration were more deaths and more destruction than in any other armed conflict. It completely uprooted and displaced millions of people. The end of the war brought renewed power struggles, especially in Europe and China, with many Eastern European nations as well as China coming under complete control and domination of the Communists, supported and backed by the Soviet Union. With the development of and two-time deployment of an atomic bomb against two Japanese cities, the world found itself in the nuclear age. The peace settlement established the United Nations Organization, which is still an important operating organization today.

Internment of people of Japanese ancestry. From the turn of the twentieth century, there was tension between Caucasians and Japanese in California. A series of laws had been passed discouraging Japanese immigration and prohibiting land ownership by Japanese. The Alien Registration Act of 1940 (the Smith Act) required the fingerprinting and registration of all aliens over the age of 14. Aliens were also required to report any change of address within 5 days. Almost 5 million aliens registered under the provisions of this act. The Japanese attack on Pearl Harbor (December 7, 1941) raised suspicion that Japan was planning a full-scale attack on the West Coast. Many believed that American citizenship did not necessarily imply loyalty and some authorities feared sabotage of both civilian and military facilities within the country. By February 1942, Presidential Executive Orders had authorized the arrest of all aliens suspected of subversive activities and the creation of exclusion zones where people could be isolated from the remainder of the population and kept where they could not damage national infrastructure. These War Relocation Camps were used to isolate about 120,000 Japanese and Japanese Americans (62% were citizens) during World War II.

Allied response to the Holocaust. International organizations received sharp criticism during WW II for their failure to act to save the European Jews. The Allied Powers, in particular, were accused of gross negligence. Many organizations and individuals did not believe reports of the abuse and mass genocide that was occurring in Europe. Many nations did not want to accept Jewish refugees. The International Red Cross was one of the organizations that discounted reports of atrocities. One particular point of criticism was the failure of the Allied Powers to bomb the death camp at Auschwitz-Birkenau or the railroad tracks leading there. Military leaders argued that their planes did not have the range to reach the camp; they argued that they could not provide sufficiently precise targeting to safeguard the inmates. Critics have claimed that even if Allied bombs killed all inmates at Auschwitz at the time, the destruction of the camp would have saved thousands of other Jews. The usual response was that, had the Allies destroyed the camp, the Nazis would have turned to other methods of extermination.

Within the military theater, women and minorities filled a number of new roles. Women served in the military as drivers, nurses, communications operators, clerks, etc. The Flight Nurses corps was created at the beginning of the war. Among the most notable minority groups in the military were:

The Tuskegee Airmen were a group of African American aviators who made a major contribution to the war effort. Although they were not considered eligible for the gold wings of a Navy Pilot until 1948, these men completed standard Army flight classroom instruction and the required flying time. This group of fliers were the first blacks permitted to fly for the military. They flew more than 15,000 missions, destroyed over 1,000 German aircraft earned more than 150 Distinguished Flying Crosses and hundreds of Air Medals.

The 442nd Regimental Combat Team was a unit composed of Japanese Americans who fought in Europe. This unit was the most highly decorated unit of its size and length of service in the history of the U.S. Army. This self-sufficient force served with great distinction in North Africa, Italy, southern France, and Germany. The medals earned by the group include 21 Congressional Medals of Honor, the highest award given. The unit was awarded 9,486 purple hearts (for being wounded in battle). The casualty rate, combining those killed in action, missing in action, and wounded and removed from action, was 93%.

The Navajo Code Talkers have been credited with saving countless lives and accelerating the end of the war. There were over 400 Navajo Indians who served in all six Marine divisions from 1942 to 1945. At the time of WW II, less than 30 non-Navajo people understood the Navajo language. Because it was a very complex language and because it was not a code, it was unbreakable by the Germans or the Japanese. The job of these men was to talk and transmit information on tactics, troop movements, orders and other vital military information. Not only was the enemy unable to understand the language, but also it was far faster than translating messages into Morse Code. It is generally accepted that without the Navajo Code Talkers, Iwo Jima could not have been taken.

The statistics on minority representation in the military during WWII are interesting:

Negroes	1,056,841
Chinese	13,311
Japanese	20,080
Hawaiians	1,320
American Indians	19,567
Filipinos	11,506
Puerto Ricans	51,438

The role of women and minority groups at home overturned many expectations and assumptions. Most able-bodied men of appropriate age were called up for military service. Minorities were generally not drafted. Many critical functions remained to be fulfilled by those who remained at home.

WW II required industrial production to a greater extent than any previous war. Those who remained at home were needed to build the planes, tanks, ships, bombs, torpedoes, etc. The men who remained at home were working, but more labor was desperately needed. In particular, a call went out to women to join the effort and enter the industrial work force. A vast campaign was launched to recruit women to these tasks that combined emotional appeals and patriotism. One of the most famous recruiting campaigns featured "Rosie the Riveter."

By the middle of 1944 more than 19 million women had entered the work force. Women worked building planes and tanks, but they also did more. Some operated large cranes to move heavy equipment; some loaded and fired machine guns and other weapons to ensure that they were in working order; some operated hydraulic presses; some were volunteer fire fighters; some were welders, riveters, drill press operators, and cab drivers. Women worked all manufacturing shifts making everything from clothing to fighter jets. Yet all of the recruitment efforts emphasized that the need for women in industry was temporary. Most women and their families tended "Victory Gardens" to produce food items that were in short supply.

Major developments in aviation, weaponry, communications, and medicine were achieved during the war. The years between WW I and WW II produced significant advancement in aircraft technology, but the pace of aircraft development and production was dramatically increased during WW II. Major developments included flight-based weapon delivery systems, the long-range bomber, the first jet fighter, the first cruise missile, and the first ballistic missile. The cruise and ballistic missiles were not widely used during the war even though they were available, Glider planes were heavily used in WW II because they were silent upon approach. Another significant development was the broad use of paratrooper units. Finally, hospital planes came into use to remove the seriously wounded from the front and transport them to hospitals for treatment.

Weapons and technology in other areas also improved rapidly during the war. These advances were critical in determining the outcome of the war. Radar, electronic computers, nuclear weapons, and new tank designs were used for the first time. More new inventions were registered for patents than ever before. Most of these new ideas were intended either to kill or prevent being killed.

The war began with essentially the same weaponry that had been used in WW I. The aircraft carrier joined the battleship; the Higgins boat, the primary landing craft, was invented; light tanks were developed to meet the needs of a changing battlefield; other armored vehicles were developed. Submarines were also perfected during this period. Numerous other weapons were also developed or invented to meet the needs of battle during WW II. These included the bazooka, the rocket propelled grenade, anti-tank weapons, assault rifles, the tank destroyer, mine-clearing Flail tanks, Flame tanks, submersible tanks, cruise missiles, rocket artillery and air launched rockets, guided weapons, torpedoes, self-guiding weapons and Napalm. The Atomic Bomb was also developed and used for the first time during WW II.

Communism

One of the major political movements in the twentieth century was communism. Invented by a German philosopher, it spread in the Soviet Union and parts of China, North Korea and Vietnam where it survives to this day. Communism was, at its heart, an economic theory, with the famous doctrine of "class struggle" controlling every aspect of life, including what kind of government a people should live under.

Communism has a rigid theology, and a bible (*Das Capital*) that sees Communism emerging as a result of almost cosmic laws. Modern socialism is much closer to the ground. It too sees change in human society and hopes for improvement, but there is no unchanging millennium at the end of the road. Communism is sure that it will achieve the perfect state, and in this certainty, it is willing to use any and all means, however ruthless, to bring it about.

Communist states controlled nearly every aspect of society, including religion and economics. The government owned factories, ports, machines, and ships; this means that the income from goods produced therein went into the state-controlled coffers. This kind of economic theory was in stark contrast to the famous **laissez faire** attitude that occupied much of the western nations during the 1700s, 1800s, and 1900s.

Socialism

This is a fairly recent political phenomenon, though its roots can be traced pretty far back in time in many respects. At the core, both socialism and communism are fundamentally economic philosophies that advocate public, rather than private ownership, especially over the means of production. Yet even here, there are many distinctions. Karl Marx basically concentrated his attention on the industrial worker and on state domination over the means of production.

In practice, this Marxian dogma has largely been followed the most in those countries that profess to be communist. In conjunction with massive programs for the development of heavy industry, this emphasis is on production regardless of the wants or comforts of the individual in the given society. Socialism by contrast, usually occurring where industry has already been developed and has concerned itself more with the welfare of the individual and the fair distribution of whatever wealth is available.

Socialism does not justify brutalities. This distinction in philosophy, of course, makes for an immense conflict in methods. Communism, believing that revolution is inevitable, works toward it by emphasizing class antagonisms. Socialism, while seeking change, insists on the use of democratic procedures within the existing social order of a given society. In it, the upper classes and capitalists are not to be violently overthrown, but they are instead to be won over by logical persuasion.

Fascism

Fascism is the last important historical economic system to arise. It has been called a reaction against the last two ideologies discussed. It can, at times, cooperate with a monarchy if it has to.

In general, fascism is a dictatorial state in which a viable national society has competing interests adjusted to each other by being entirely subordinated to the service of the state. The following features have been characteristic of fascism in its various manifestations: (1) an origin at a time of serious economic disruption and of rapid and bewildering social change, (2) a philosophy that rejects democratic and humanitarian ideals and glorifies the absolute sovereignty of the state, the unity and destiny of the people, and their unquestioning loyalty and obedience to the dictator, (3) an aggressive nationalism which calls for the mobilization and regimentation of every aspect of national life and makes open use of violence and intimidation, (4) the simulation of mass popular support, accomplished by outlawing all but a single political party and by using suppression, censorship, and propaganda, and (5) a program of vigorous action including economic reconstruction, industrialization, pursuit of economic self-sufficiency, territorial expansion, and war which is dramatized as bold, adventurous, and promising a glorious future.

Fascist movements often had socialist origins. For example, in Italy, where fascism first arose in place of socialism, **Benito Mussolini**, sought to impose what he called "corporativism". A fascist "corporate" state would, in theory, run the economy for the benefit of the whole country like a corporation. It would be centrally controlled and managed by the elite who would see that its benefits would go to everyone.

Genocide

The most well-known genocide of the twentieth century is the **Holocaust** of Jews before and during World War II. Much of this took place in Germany, although the practice increased throughout German-occupied countries throughout the war. German authorities capitalized on hundreds of years of distrust of Jewish people and invented what they saw as "the final solution of the Jewish question" or extermination of the Jewish people. Germans in charge of this "final solution" constructed a vast, complicated mechanism of transport systems and concentration camps, where Jews were imprisoned, forced to work, and killed in increasingly large numbers.

This Holocaust was known especially for its efficiency and its extensive record-keeping. Thousands of pages of documents describe in excruciating detail how thorough and determined Nazi authorities were in pursuing their goals. The number of Jews killed during the Holocaust is generally said to be six million. This figure includes people from all over Europe. The Holocaust didn't kill just Jews, however. Gypsies, communists, homosexuals, Jehovah's Witnesses, Catholics, psychiatric patients, and even common criminals were systematically incarcerated and, in many cases, killed for being "enemies of the state". There were more than 40 concentration camps in Nazi-controlled lands during World War II, but not all of them were death camps. However, the most famous ones, including Auschwitz, were.

The Holocaust ended with Germany's defeat in World War II. The liberating troops of the west and east uncovered the concentration camps and all of the killing that the Nazis wrought. Much of the meticulous record-keeping was intact, preserving for the world the horrors that these people had wrought.

The most recent case of genocide took place in the former **Yugoslavia** in very recent times. The country was a melting pot of ethnic peoples, all of whom were struggling for meager resources and living space. The people who had the most power, including control of the government and the army, were the Serbs. They set about systematically eliminating the Bosnian people by following a policy they called "ethnic cleansing". Thousands and thousands of Bosnians and other Serb enemies died. United Nations troops sent to monitor the situation were powerless to stop the killing. Only a determined military buildup and a series of devastating air strikes by the United States and other countries convinced the Serbs to stop. Bosnia is its own country, as is Croatia and Serbia and Montenegro. The leaders of this genocide have been convicted of their crimes, as were the Nazi perpetrators before them.

Post World War II

The world after World War II was a complicated place. The Axis powers were defeated, but the Cold War had sprung up in its place. Many countries struggled to get out of the debt and devastation that their Nazi occupiers had wrought. The American Marshall Plan helped the nations of Western Europe get back on their feet. The Soviet Union helped the eastern European nations return to greatness, with communist governments at the helm. The nations of Asia were rebuilt as well, with communism taking over China and Americanization taking over Japan and Taiwan. The East and West struggled for control in this arena, especially in Korea and Southeast Asia. When communism fell in the USSR and eastern Europe, it remained in China, North Korea, and Vietnam.

In America, President Wilson lost in his efforts to get the U.S. Senate to approve the peace treaty. The Senate at the time was a reflection of American public opinion and its rejection of the treaty was a rejection of Wilson. The approval of the treaty would have made the U.S. a member of the League of Nations, but Americans had just come off a bloody war to ensure that democracy would exist throughout the world. Americans just did not want to accept any responsibility that resulted from its new position of power and were afraid that membership in the League of Nations would embroil the U.S. in future disputes in Europe.

The kind of nationalism that Europe saw in the nineteenth century spilled over into the mid-twentieth century with former colonies of European powers declaring themselves independent all the time, especially in Africa. India, a longtime British protectorate, also achieved independence at this time. With independence, these countries continued to grow. Some of these nations now experience severe overcrowding and dearth of precious resources. Those who can escape do; others have no way to escape.

Skill 10.5 Identify individuals, events, and ideas that have influenced economic, social, and political institutions in the United States

Native American tribes lived throughout what we now call the United States in varying degrees of togetherness. They adopted different customs, pursued different avenues of agriculture and food gathering, and made slightly different weapons. They fought among themselves and with other peoples. Perhaps the most famous of the Native American tribes is the **Algonquians**. We know so much about this tribe because they were one of the first to interact with the newly arrived English settlers in Plymouth and elsewhere. Another group of tribes who lived in the Northeast were the **Iroquois** who were fierce fighters but also forward thinkers. They lived in long houses and wore clothes made of buckskin. They, too, were expert farmers, growing the "Three Sisters" (corn, squash, and beans). Five of the Iroquois tribes formed a Confederacy which was a shared form of government.

Living in the Southeast were the **Seminoles** and **Creeks**, a huge collection of people who lived in chickees (open, bark-covered houses) and wore clothes made from plant fibers. They were expert planters and hunters and were proficient at paddling hand-made dugout canoes. The **Cherokee** also lived in the Southeast. They were one of the most advanced tribes, living in domed houses and wearing deerskin and rabbit fur. They also played a game called lacrosse, which survives to this day in countries around the world.

In the middle of the continent lived the Plains tribes, such as the **Sioux, Cheyenne, Blackfeet, Comanche, and Pawnee**. Famous Plains people include Crazy Horse and Sitting Bull, authors of the Custer Disaster; Sacagawea, leader of the Lewis & Clark expedition; and Chief Joseph, the famous Nez Perce leader.

Dotting the deserts of the Southwest were a handful of tribes, including the famous **Pueblo** who lived in houses that bear their tribe's name, wore clothes made of wool and woven cotton, farmed crops in the middle of desert land, created exquisite pottery and Kachina dolls, and had one of the most complex religions of all the tribes. The Pueblos chose their own chiefs. This was perhaps one of the oldest representative governments in the world.

Another well-known Southwestern tribe was the **Apache** with their famous leader, **Geronimo**. The Apache lived in homes called wickiups which were made of bark, grass, and branches. The **Navajo**, also residents of the Southwest, lived in hogans (round homes built with forked sticks) and wore clothes of rabbit skin.

Living in the Northwest were the **Inuit** who lived in tents made from animal skins or, in some cases, igloos. They wore clothes made of seals or caribou skins. They were excellent fishermen and hunters, and they crafted efficient kayaks and umiaks to take them through waterways. They also crafted harpoons with which to hunt animals. The Inuit are perhaps best known for the great carvings that they left behind. Among these are ivory figures and tall totem poles.

By the 1750s, Spain was no longer the most powerful nation in Europe. The remaining rivalry was between Britain and France. For nearly 25 years, between 1689 and 1748, a series of "armed conflicts" involving these two powers had been taking place. These conflicts had spilled over into North America. The War of the League of Augsburg in Europe, 1689 to 1697, had been King William's War. The War of the Spanish Succession, 1702 to 1713, had been Queen Anne's War. The War of the Austrian Succession, 1740 to 1748, was called King George's War in the colonies. The two nations fought for possession of colonies, especially in Asia and North America, and for control of the seas. However none of these conflicts was decisive.

In 1754, the conflict which determined the most powerful nation began in North America in the Ohio River Valley. It was known in America as **the French and Indian War** (in Europe, it was know as the Seven Years' War since it began there in 1756). In America, both sides had advantages and disadvantages. The British colonies were well established and consolidated in a smaller area. British colonists outnumbered French colonists 23 to 1. Except for a small area in Canada, French settlements were scattered over a much larger area (roughly half of the continent) and were smaller. However, the French settlements were united under one government and were quick to act and cooperate when necessary. In addition, the French had many more Indian allies than the British. The British colonies had separate, individual governments and very seldom cooperated, even when needed. In Europe, at that time, France was the more powerful of the two nations.

In 1763 in Paris, Spain, France, and Britain met to draw up the Treaty of Paris. Great Britain got most of India and all of North America east of the Mississippi River, except for New Orleans. Britain received control of Florida from Spain and Cuba and the islands of the Philippines, which had been taken during the war, were returned to Spain. France lost nearly all of its possessions in America and India, but was allowed to keep four islands: Guadeloupe, Martinique, Haiti on Hispaniola, and Miquelon and St. Pierre. France gave Spain New Orleans and the vast territory of Louisiana west of the Mississippi River. Britain was now the most powerful nation.

The American Colonies

The **New England** colonies consisted of Massachusetts, Rhode Island, Connecticut, and New Hampshire. Life in these colonies was centered on the towns. Farming was done by each family on its own plot of land, but a short summer growing season and limited amount of good soil gave rise to other economic activities such as manufacturing, fishing, shipbuilding, and trade. The vast majority of the settlers shared similar origins, coming from England and Scotland. Towns were carefully planned and laid out the same way. The form of government was the town meeting where all adult males met to make the laws. The legislative body, the General Court, consisted of an upper and lower house.

The **Middle Atlantic** colonies included New York, New Jersey, Pennsylvania, Delaware, and Maryland. New York and New Jersey were at one time the Dutch colony of New Netherland, and Delaware at one time was New Sweden. These five colonies, from their beginnings, were considered "melting pots" with settlers from many different nations and backgrounds. The main economic activity was farming with the settlers scattered over the countryside cultivating rather large farms.

The Indians were not as much of a threat as in New England so they did not have to settle in small farming villages. The soil was very fertile and a milder climate provided a longer growing season. These farms produced a large surplus of food, not only for the colonists themselves but also for sale. This colonial region became known as the "breadbasket" of the New World and the New York and Philadelphia seaports were constantly filled with ships being loaded with meat, flour, and other foodstuffs for the West Indies and England.

The **Southern** colonies included Virginia, North and South Carolina, and Georgia. Virginia was the first permanent successful English colony and Georgia was the last. The year 1619 was a very important year in the history of Virginia and the United States with three very significant events. First, sixty women were sent to Virginia to marry and establish families; second, twenty Africans, the first of thousands, arrived; and third, most importantly, the Virginia colonists were granted the right to self-government and they began by electing their own representatives to the House of Burgesses, their own legislative body.

The settlers in these four colonies came from diverse backgrounds and cultures. Virginia was colonized mostly by people from England while Georgia was started as a haven for debtors from English prisons. Pioneers from Virginia settled in North Carolina while South Carolina welcomed people from England and Scotland, French Protestants, Germans, and emigrants from islands in the West Indies. Products from farms and plantations included rice, tobacco, indigo, cotton, some corn and wheat. Other economic activities included lumber and naval stores (tar, pitch, rosin, and turpentine) from the pine forests and fur trade on the frontier. Cities such as Savannah and Charleston were important seaports and trading centers.

The major economic activity in this region was farming. Here, too, the soil was very fertile and the climate was very mild with an even longer growing season. The large plantations eventually requiring large numbers of slaves were established in the coastal and tidewater areas. Although the wealthy slave-owning planters set the pattern of life in this region, most of the people lived inland away from coastal areas.

Slavery in the English colonies began in 1619 when 20 Africans arrived in the colony of Virginia at Jamestown. From then on, slavery had a foothold, especially in the agricultural South where a large amount of slave labor was needed for the extensive plantations. Free men refused to work for wages on the plantations when land was available for settling on the frontier. Therefore, slave labor was the only recourse left.

Life inland on the frontier had marked differences. All facets of daily living (clothing, food, home, economic and social activities) were all connected to what was needed to sustain life and survive in the wilderness. Everything was produced practically by the settlers. They were self-sufficient and extremely individualistic and independent. There were little, if any, levels of society or class distinctions as they considered themselves to be the equal to all others, regardless of station in life. The roots of equality, independence, individual rights, and freedoms were extremely strong and well developed. People were not judged by their fancy dress, expensive house, eloquent language, or titles following their names.

Causes for the War for Independence

With the end of the French and Indian War (called the The Seven Years' War in Europe), England decided to reassert control over the colonies in America. They particularly needed the revenue from the control of trade to pay for the recent war and to defend the new territory obtained as a result of the war.

English leaders decided to impose a tax that would pay for the military defense of the American lands. The colonists rejected this idea for two reasons: (1) they were undergoing an economic recession, and (2) they believed it unjust to be taxed unless they had representation in Parliament.

England passed a series of laws that provoked fierce opposition. Leaders denounced "taxation without representation" and a boycott was organized against imported English goods. The movement spread to other colonies rapidly.

The situation in the colonies between colonists and British troops became increasingly strained. Despite a skirmish in New York and the "Boston Massacre" in 1770, tensions abated over the next few years.

The Tea Act of 1773 gave the British East India Company a monopoly on sales of tea. The colonists responded with the "Boston Tea Party. England responded with the "Coercive Acts (called the "Intolerable Acts" by the colonists) in 1774. This closed the port of Boston, changed the charter of the Massachusetts colony, and suppressed town meetings. Eleven colonies sent delegates to Philadelphia to attend the First Continental Congress in 1774. The group issued the "Declaration of Rights and Grievances" which vowed allegiance to the king but protested the right of Parliament to tax the colonies. The boycotts resumed at the same time.

Massachusetts mobilized its colonial militia in anticipation of difficulties with England. The British troops attempted to seize their weapons and ammunition. The result was two clashes with "minute men" at Lexington and Concord. The Second Continental Congress met a month later. Many of the delegates

recommended declaring their independence from Britain. The group established an army and commissioned George Washington as its commander.
When the war began, the colonies began to establish state governments. To a significant extent, the government that was defined for the new nation was intentionally weak. The colonies/states feared centralized government. But the lack of continuity between the individual governments was confusing and economically damaging.

The **Declaration of Independence** was the founding document of the United States of America. The Declaration was intended to demonstrate the reasons that the colonies were seeking separation from Great Britain. Conceived by and written for the most part by Thomas Jefferson, it is not only important for what it says, but also for how it says it. The Declaration is in many respects a poetic document. Instead of a simple recitation of the colonists' grievances, it set out clearly the reasons why the colonists were seeking their freedom from Great Britain. They had tried all means to resolve the dispute peacefully. It was the right of a people, when all other methods of addressing their grievances have been tried and failed, to separate themselves from that power that was keeping them from fully expressing their rights to "life, liberty, and the pursuit of happiness".

The **Articles of Confederation** was the first political system under which the newly independent colonies tried to organize themselves. It was drafted in 1776 after the Declaration of Independence and was passed by the Continental Congress on November 15, 1777 where it was ratified by the thirteen states. The newly independent states were unwilling to give too much power to a national government. They were already fighting Great Britain. They did not want to replace one harsh ruler with another. After many debates, the form of the Articles was accepted. Each state agreed to send delegates to the Congress. Each state had one vote in the Congress. The Articles gave Congress the power to declare war, appoint military officers, and coin money. The Congress was also responsible for foreign affairs. The Articles of Confederation limited the powers of Congress by giving the states final authority. Although Congress could pass laws, at least nine of the thirteen states had to approve a law before it went into effect. Congress could not pass any laws regarding taxes. To get money, Congress had to ask each state for it, and no state could be forced to pay.

By 1776, the colonists and their representatives in the Second Continental Congress realized that things were past the point of no return. The Declaration of Independence was drafted and declared on July 4, 1776. George Washington labored against tremendous odds to wage a victorious war. The turning point in the Americans' favor occurred in 1777 with the American victory at **Saratoga**. This victory resulted in the French aligning themselves with the Americans against the British. With the aid of Admiral deGrasse and French warships blocking the entrance to Chesapeake Bay, British General Cornwallis was trapped at Yorktown, Virginia. Cornwallis surrendered in 1781 and the war was over. The Treaty of Paris officially ending the war was signed in 1783.

The Articles of Confederation created early in the war established a loose alliance among the thirteen states. The national government was weak, in part, because it didn't have a strong chief executive to carry out laws passed by the legislature. This weak national government might have worked if the states were able to get along with each other. However, many different disputes arose and there was no way of settling them. Thus, the delegates went to meet again to try to fix the Articles. Instead they ended up scrapping them and created a new Constitution that learned from these earlier mistakes.

The Constitutional Convention in 1787 devised an entirely new form of government and outlined it in the Constitution of the United States. The Constitution was ratified quickly and took effect in 1789. Concerns that had been raised in or by the states regarding civil liberties and states' rights led to the immediate adoption of 12 amendments to the constitution, the first 10 known as the Bill of Rights.

Ratification of the U.S. Constitution was by no means a foregone conclusion. The representative government had powerful enemies, especially those who had seen firsthand the failure of the Articles of Confederation. The strong central government had powerful enemies, including some of the guiding lights of the American Revolution.

Those who wanted to see a strong central government were called **Federalists** because they wanted to see a federal government reign supreme. Among the leaders of the Federalists were Alexander Hamilton and John Jay. These two, along with James Madison, wrote a series of letters to New York newspapers, urging that that state ratify the Constitution. These became known as the **Federalist Papers.**

In the Anti-Federalist camp were Thomas Jefferson and Patrick Henry. These men, and many others like them, were worried that a strong national government would descend into the kind of tyranny that they had just worked so hard to abolish. In the same way that they took their name from their foes, and wrote a series of arguments against the Constitution called the **Anti-Federalist Papers.**

In the end, both sides got most of what they wanted. The Federalists got their strong national government which was held in place by the famous "checks and balances". The Anti-Federalists got the Bill of Rights, the first ten Amendments to the Constitution and a series of laws that protect some of the most basic of human rights. The states that were in doubt for ratification of the Constitution signed on when the Bill of Rights was promised.

After serving as Commander in Chief of the Continental Army, George Washington served as the first president of the United States. By the time Washington retired from office in 1796, the new political parties would come to play an important role in choosing his successor. Each party would put up its own candidates for office. The election of 1796 was the first one in which political parties played a role. A role that, for better or worse, has continued to play in various forms since American history began. By the beginning of the 1800s, the Federalist Party, torn by internal divisions, began suffering a decline.

The election in 1800 named Thomas Jefferson, Alexander Hamilton's bitter rival, as President. After Hamilton was killed in 1804 in a duel with Aaron Burr, the Federalist Party began to collapse. By 1816, after losing a string of important elections (Jefferson was reelected in 1804, and James Madison, a Democratic-Republican was elected in 1808), the Federalist Party ceased to be an effective political force, and soon passed off the national stage.

By the late 1820s, new political parties had grown up. The **Democratic-Republican** Party had been the major party for many years, but there were differences within it about the direction the country was headed in and this caused a split after 1824. Those who favored strong national growth took the name **Whigs** after a similar party in Great Britain and united around then President John Quincy Adams. Many business people in the Northeast as well as some wealthy planters in the South supported the Whig party.

Those who favored slower growth and were more worker and small farmer-oriented went on to form the new Democratic Party. Andrew Jackson became its first leader and was eventually the first Democratic president from it. It is the forerunner of today's present party of the same name.

In the mid-1850s, the slavery issue was beginning to heat up, and in 1854, those opposed to slavery, the Whigs and some northern Democrats opposed to slavery, united to form the **Republican Party**. Before the Civil War, the Democratic Party was more heavily represented in the South and was thus pro-slavery for the most part.

Thus, by the time of the Civil War, the present form of the major political parties had been formed. Though there would sometimes be drastic changes in ideology and platforms over the years, no other political parties would manage to gain enough strength to seriously challenge the "Big Two" parties.

Expansion & Conflict with Mexico

In the United States, territorial expansion occurred in a westward direction under the banner of "**Manifest Destiny,**" the belief in the divinely given right of the nation to expand westward and incorporate more of the continent into the nation. This belief had been expressed, at the end of the Revolutionary War, in the demand that Britain cede all lands east of the Mississippi River to America.

The goal of expanding westward was further confirmed with the Northwest Ordinance (1787) and the Louisiana Purchase (1803). After the U.S. purchased the Louisiana Territory in 1803, Jefferson appointed Captains Meriwether Lewis and William Clark to explore it and to find out exactly what had been bought. The Corps of Discovery went all the way to the Pacific Ocean, returning two years later with maps, journals, and artifacts. This led the way for future explorers to make available more knowledge about the territory and resulted in the Westward Movement and the later belief in the doctrine of Manifest Destiny.

Manifest Destiny was the justification of the Mexican-American war (1846-48) which resulted in the annexation of Texas and California, as well as much of the southwest. Due to the U.S. involvement in the War with Mexico, the Spanish-American War, and support of the Latin American colonies of Spain in their revolt for independence, the Spanish colonies were successful in their fight for independence and self-government.

The U.S. and Britain had shared the Oregon country. By the 1840s, with the increase in the free and slave populations and the demand of the settlers for control and government by the U.S., the conflict had to be resolved. In a treaty, signed in 1846, by both nations, a peaceful resolution occurred with Britain giving up its claims south of the 49th parallel.

In the American southwest, the results were exactly the opposite. Spain had claimed this area since the 1540s, had spread northward from Mexico City, and, in the 1700s, had established missions, forts, villages, towns, and very large ranches. After the purchase of the Louisiana Territory in 1803, Americans began moving into Spanish territory. A few hundred American families in what is now Texas were allowed to live there, but they had to agree to become loyal subjects to Spain. In 1821, Mexico successfully revolted against Spanish rule, won independence, and chose to be more tolerant toward the American settlers and traders.

The Mexican government encouraged and allowed extensive trade and settlement, especially in Texas. Many of the new settlers were southerners and brought with them their slaves. Slavery was outlawed in Mexico and was technically illegal in Texas, although the Mexican government rather looked the other way.

Friction increased between land-hungry Americans and the Mexican government, which controlled these western lands. The clash was not only political but also cultural and economic. The Spanish influence permeated all parts of southwestern life: law, language, architecture, and customs. By this time, the doctrine of Manifest Destiny was in the hearts and on the lips of those seeking new areas of settlement and a new life. Americans were demanding U.S. control of not only the Mexican Territory but also Oregon. Peaceful negotiations with Great Britain secured Oregon, but it took two years of war to gain control of the southwestern U.S.

In addition, the Mexican government owed debts to U.S. citizens whose property was damaged or destroyed during its struggle for independence from Spain. By the time war broke out in 1845, Mexico had not paid its war debts. The government was weak, corrupt, irresponsible, tom by revolutions, and not in decent financial shape. Mexico was also bitter over American expansion into Texas and the 1836 revolution, which had resulted in Texas independence. In the 1844 presidential election, the Democrats pushed for annexation of Texas and Oregon and after winning, they started the procedure to admit Texas to the Union.

When statehood occurred, diplomatic relations between the U.S. and Mexico was ended. President Polk wanted U.S. control of the entire southwest from Texas to the Pacific Ocean. He sent a diplomatic mission with an offer to purchase New Mexico and upper California, but the Mexican government refused to even receive the diplomat. Consequently, in 1846, each nation claimed aggression on the part of the other and war was declared. The treaty signed in 1848 and a subsequent one in 1853 completed the southwestern boundary of the United States, reaching to the Pacific Ocean, as President Polk wished.

The Civil War

At the Constitutional Convention, one of the slavery compromises concerned counting slaves for deciding the number of representatives for the House and the amount of taxes to be paid. Southerners pushed for counting the slaves for representation but not for taxes. The Northerners pushed for the opposite. The resulting compromise, sometimes referred to as the "three-fifths compromise," was that both groups agreed that three-fifths of the slaves would be counted for both taxes and representation.

The other compromise over slavery was part of the disputes over how much regulation the central government would control over commercial activities such as trade with other nations and the slave trade. It was agreed that Congress would regulate commerce with other nations including taxing imports. Southerners were worried about the taxing of slaves coming into the country and the possibility of Congress prohibiting the slave trade altogether. The agreement reached allowed the states to continue importation of slaves for the next 20 years, until 1808, at which time Congress would make the decision as to the future of the slave trade. During the 20-year period, no more than $10 per person could be levied on slaves coming into the country.

An additional provision of this compromise was that with the admission of Missouri, slavery would not be allowed in the rest of the Louisiana Purchase territory north of latitude 36 degrees 30'. This was acceptable to the southern congressmen since it was not profitable to grow cotton on land north of this latitude line anyway.

It was thought that the crisis had been resolved, but in the next year, it was discovered that in its state constitution, the Missouri Territory allowed slavery. Admitting Missouri as a state was the first serious clash between North and South. In 1819, the U.S. consisted of 21 states: 11 free states and 10 slave states. The Missouri Territory allowed slavery, and if admitted, would cause an imbalance in the number of U.S. senators. Alabama had already been admitted as a slave state and that had balanced the Senate with the North and South each having 22 senators.

The first Missouri Compromise resolved the conflict by approving admission of Maine as a free state along with Missouri as a slave state, thus continuing to keep a balance of power in the Senate with the same number of free and slave states. Henry Clay, known as the Great Compromiser, then proposed a second Missouri Compromise which was acceptable to everyone. His proposal stated that the Constitution of the United States guaranteed protections and privileges to citizens of states, and Missouri's proposed constitution could not deny these to any of its citizens. The acceptance in 1820 of this second compromise opened the way for Missouri's statehood--a temporary reprieve only.

These two "slavery" compromises were a necessary concession to have Southern support and approval for the new document and new government. Many Americans felt that the system of slavery would eventually die out in the U.S., but by 1808, cotton was becoming increasingly important in the primarily agricultural South and the institution of slavery had become firmly entrenched in Southern culture. It is also evident that as early as the Constitutional Convention, active anti-slavery feelings and opinions were very strong, leading to extremely active groups and societies.

The doctrine of nullification states that the states have the right to "nullify" – declare invalid – any act of Congress they believed to be unjust or unconstitutional. The nullification crisis of the mid-nineteenth century climaxed over a new tariff on imported manufactured goods that was enacted by the Congress in 1828. While this tariff protected the manufacturing and industrial interests of the North, it placed an additional burden of cost on the South, which was only affected by the tariff as consumers of manufactured goods. The North had become increasingly economically dependent on industry and manufacturing, while the South had become increasingly agricultural. Despite the fact that the tariff was primarily intended to protect northern manufacturing interests in the face of imports from other countries, the effect on the South was to simply raise the prices of needed goods.

The slavery issue was at the root of every problem, crisis, event, decision, and struggle from then on. The next crisis involved the issue concerning Texas. By 1836, Texas was an independent republic with its own constitution. During its fight for independence, Americans were sympathetic to and supportive of the Texans and some recruited volunteers who crossed into Texas to help the struggle. Problems arose when the state petitioned Congress for statehood. Texas wanted to allow slavery, but northerners in Congress opposed admission to the Union because it would disrupt the balance between free and slave states and give southerners in Congress increased influence.

On May 25, 1854, Congress passed the infamous Kansas-Nebraska Act which nullified this provision, created the territories of Kansas and Nebraska, and provided for the people of these two territories to decide for themselves whether or not to permit slavery to exist there. Feelings were so deep and divided that any further attempts to compromise would meet with little, if any, success. Political and social turmoil swirled everywhere. Kansas was called "Bleeding Kansas" because of the extreme violence and bloodshed throughout the territory because two governments existed there, one pro-slavery and the other anti-slavery.

In 1858, Abraham Lincoln and Stephen A. Douglas were running for the office of U.S. Senator from Illinois and participated in a series of debates, which directly affected the outcome of the 1860 presidential election. Douglas, a Democrat, was up for re-election and knew that if he won this race, he had a good chance of becoming president in 1860. Lincoln, a Republican, was not an abolitionist, but he believed that slavery was morally wrong, and he firmly believed in and supported the Republican Party principle that slavery must not be allowed to extend any further.

The slavery issue flared again not to be done away with until the end of the Civil War. It was obvious that newly acquired territory would be divided up into territories and later become states. In addition to the two factions of northerners who advocated prohibition of slavery and of Southerners who favored slavery existing there, a third faction arose supporting the doctrine of "**popular sovereignty**". This doctrine stated that people living in territories and states should be allowed to decide for themselves whether or not slavery should be permitted. In 1849, California applied for admittance to the Union and the furor began. The result was the Compromise of 1850, a series of laws designed as a final solution to the issue. Concessions made to the North included the admission of California as a free state and the abolition of slave trading in Washington, D.C. The laws also provided for the creation of the New Mexico and Utah territories. As a concession to southerners, the residents there would decide whether to permit slavery when these two territories became states. In addition, Congress authorized implementation of stricter measures to capture runaway slaves.

Douglas, on the other hand, originated the doctrine of "popular sovereignty" and was responsible for supporting and guiding through Congress the inflammatory Kansas-Nebraska Act. In the course of the debates, Lincoln challenged Douglas to show that popular sovereignty reconciled with the Dred Scott decision. Either way he answered Lincoln, Douglas would lose crucial support from one group or the other. If he supported the Dred Scott decision, southerners would support him but he would lose Northern support. If he stayed with popular sovereignty, Northern support would be his, but Southern support would be lost. His reply to Lincoln, stating that territorial legislatures could exclude slavery by refusing to pass laws supporting it, gave him enough support and approval to be re-elected to the Senate. But it cost him the Democratic nomination for president in 1860.

Southerners came to the realization that Douglas supported, and was devoted to, popular sovereignty but not necessarily to the expansion of slavery. On the other hand, two years later, Lincoln received the nomination of the Republican Party for president.

The final straw came with the election of Lincoln to the Presidency the next year. Due to a split in the Democratic Party, there were four candidates from four political parties. When economic issues and the issue of slavery came to a head, the North declared slavery illegal. With Lincoln receiving a minority of the popular vote and a majority of electoral votes, the southern states, one by one, voted to secede from the Union as they had promised they would do if Lincoln and the Republicans were victorious. The South acted on the principles of the doctrine of nullification, declared the new laws null, and acted upon their presumed right as states to secede from the union and form their own government. The North saw secession as a violation of the national unity and contract. The die was cast.

It is ironic that South Carolina was the first state to secede from the Union and the first shots of the war were fired on Fort Sumter in Charleston Harbor. Both sides quickly prepared for war. The North had more in its favor: a larger population; superiority in finances and transportation facilities; and manufacturing, agricultural, and natural resources. The North possessed most of the nation's gold, had about 92% of all industries, and almost all known supplies of copper, coal, iron, and various other minerals. Since most of the nation's railroads were in the North and Mid-West, men and supplies could be moved wherever needed and food could be transported from the farms of the Mid-West to workers in the East and soldiers on the battlefields. Trade with nations overseas could go on as usual due to control of the navy and the merchant fleet. The Northern states numbered 24 and included western (California and Oregon) and border states (Maryland, Delaware, Kentucky, Missouri, and West Virginia).

The Southern states numbered 11 and included South Carolina, Georgia, Florida, Alabama, Mississippi, Louisiana, Texas, Virginia, North Carolina, Tennessee, and Arkansas to make up the Confederacy. Although outnumbered in population, the South was completely confident of victory. They knew that all they had to do was fight a defensive war, protecting their own territory until the North, who had to invade and defeat an area almost the size of Western Europe, tired of the struggle and gave up. Another advantage of the South was that a number of its best officers had graduated from the U.S. Military Academy at West Point and had had long years of army experience, some even exercising varying degrees of command in the Indian Wars and the war with Mexico.

Men from the South were conditioned to living outdoors and were more familiar with horses and firearms than many men from northeastern cities. Since cotton was such an important crop, southerners felt that British and French textile mills were so dependent on raw cotton that they would be forced to help the Confederacy in the war.

The South had specific reasons and goals for fighting the war, more so than the North. The major aim of the Confederacy never wavered: to win independence, the right to govern themselves as they wished, and to preserve slavery. The northerners were not as clear in their reasons for conducting war. At the beginning, most believed, along with Lincoln, that preservation of the Union was paramount. Only a few extremely fanatical abolitionists looked on the war as a way to end slavery. However, by war's end, more and more northerners had come to believe that freeing the slaves was just as important as restoring the Union.

Major military and political turning points of the Civil War

The war strategies for both sides were relatively clear and simple. The South planned a defensive war, wearing down the North until it agreed to peace on Southern terms. The only exception was to gain control of Washington, D.C. by going north through the Shenandoah Valley into Maryland and Pennsylvania in order to drive a wedge between the Northeast and Mid-West, therefore interrupting the lines of communication, and ending the war quickly.

The North had three basic strategies:

1) Blockade the Confederate coastline in order to cripple the South
2) Seize control of the Mississippi River and interior railroad lines to split the Confederacy in two
3) Seize the Confederate capital of Richmond, Virginia, driving southward to join up with Union forces coming east from the Mississippi Valley

The South won decisively until the Battle of Gettysburg, July 1 - 3, 1863. Until Gettysburg, Lincoln's commanders, McDowell and McClellan, were less than desirable and Burnside and Hooker were not what was needed. General Lee, on the other hand, had many able officers, Jackson and Stuart, and were depended on heavily by him. Jackson died at Chancellorsville and was replaced by Longstreet. Lee decided to invade the North and depended on J.E.B. Stuart and his cavalry to keep him informed of the location of Union troops and their strengths. Four things worked against Lee at Gettysburg:

1) The Union troops gained the best positions and the best ground first, making it easier to make a stand there
2) Lee's move into Northern territory put him and his army a long way from food and supply lines
3) Lee thought that his Army of Northern Virginia was invincible and could fight and win under any conditions or circumstances
4) Stuart and his men did not arrive at Gettysburg until the end of the second day of fighting and by then, it was too late. He and the men had had to detour around Union soldiers and he was delayed in getting the information Lee needed.

Consequently, Lee made the mistake of failing to listen to Longstreet and following the strategy of regrouping back into Southern territory to the supply lines. Lee felt that regrouping was retreating and almost an admission of defeat. He was convinced the army would be victorious. Longstreet was concerned about the Union troops occupying the best positions and felt that regrouping to a better position would be an advantage. He was also very concerned about the distance from supply lines.

The Civil War took more American lives than any other war in history with the South losing one-third of its soldiers in battle compared to about one-sixth for the North. More than half of the total deaths were caused by disease and the horrendous conditions of field hospitals. Both sections paid a tremendous economic price, but the South suffered more severely from direct damages. Destruction was pervasive with towns, farms, trade, industry, lives, and homes of men, women, and children all destroyed. An entire Southern way of life was lost.

The deep resentment, bitterness, and hatred that remained for generations gradually lessened as the years went by, but legacies of it surface and remain to this day. The South had no voice in the political, social, and cultural affairs of the nation, lessening to a great degree the influence of the more traditional Southern ideals. The Northern Yankee Protestant ideals of hard work, education, and economic freedom became the standard of the United States and helped influence the development of the nation into a modem, industrial power.

The effects of the Civil War were tremendous. It changed the methods of waging war and has been called the first modern war. It introduced weapons and tactics that, when improved upon later, were used extensively in wars of the late 1800s and 1900s. Civil War soldiers were the first to fight in trenches, first to fight under a unified command, and first to wage a defense called "major cordon defense", a strategy of advance on all fronts. They were also the first to use repeating and breech loading weapons. Observation balloons were first used during the war along with submarines, ironclad ships, and mines.

Telegraphy and railroads were put to use first in the Civil War. It was considered a modern war because of the vast destruction and was a "total war", involving the use of all resources of the opposing sides. There was probably no way it could have ended other than in total defeat and unconditional surrender of one side or the other.

By executive proclamation and constitutional amendment, slavery was officially and finally ended, although there remained deep prejudice and racism which still emerges today. Also, the Union was preserved, and the states were finally truly united. Sectionalism, especially in the area of politics, remained strong for another 100 years, but not to the degree and with the violence as existed before 1861.

The victory of the North established that no state has the right to end or leave the Union. Because of unity, the U.S. became a major global power. Lincoln never proposed to punish the South. He was most concerned with restoring the South to the Union in a program that was flexible and practical rather than rigid and unbending. In fact he never really felt that the states had succeeded in leaving the Union, but that they had left the 'family circle" for a short time. His plans consisted of two major steps:

1) All Southerners must swear an oath of allegiance to the Union promising to accept all federal laws and proclamations dealing with slavery in order to receive a full pardon. The only ones excluded from this were men who had resigned from civil and military positions in the federal government to serve in the Confederacy, those who were part of the Confederate government, those in the Confederate army above the rank of lieutenant, and Confederates who were guilty of mistreating prisoners of war and blacks.

2) A state would be able to write a new constitution, elect new officials, and return to the Union fully equal to all other states on certain conditions: a minimum number of persons (at least 10% of those who were qualified voters in their states before secession from the Union who had voted in the 1860 election) must take an oath of allegiance.

Native Americans

By the terms of the Treaty of Paris which ended the Revolutionary War, a large amount of land occupied and claimed by American Indians was ceded to the United States. The British, however, did not inform the native people of the change. The government of the new nation first tried to treat the tribes who had fought with the British as conquered people and claimed their land. This policy was later abandoned because it could not be enforced.

The next phase of the government's policy toward the American Indians was to purchase their land in treaties in order to continue national expansion. This created tension with the states and with settlers.

The Indian Removal Act of 1830 authorized the government to negotiate treaties with Native Americans to provide land west of the Mississippi River in exchange for lands east of the river. This policy resulted in the relocation of more than 100,000 Native Americans. Theoretically, the treaties were expected to result in voluntary relocation of the native people. In fact, however, many of the native chiefs were forced to sign the treaties.

One of the worst examples of "removal" was the Treaty of New Echota. This treaty was signed by a faction of the Cherokees rather than the actual leaders of the tribe. When the leaders attempted to remain on their ancestral lands, the treaty was enforced by President Martin Van Buren. The removal of the Cherokees came to be known as "The Trail of Tears" and resulted in the deaths of more than 4,000 Cherokees, mostly due to disease.

During the nineteenth century, the nation expanded westward. This expansion and settlement of new territory forced the Native Americans to continue moving farther west. The Native Americans were gradually giving up their homelands, their sacred sites, and the burial grounds of their ancestors. Some of the American Indians chose to move west. Many, however, were relocated by force.

Numerous conflicts, often called the "Indian Wars," broke out between the U.S. army and numerous native tribes. Many treaties were signed with the various tribes, but most were broken by the government for a variety of reasons. Two of the most notable battles were the Battle of Little Bighorn in 1876 in which native people defeated General Custer and his forces, and the massacre of Native Americans in 1890 at Wounded Knee. In 1876, the U.S. government ordered all surviving Native Americans to move to reservations. This forced migration of the Native Americans to lands that were deemed marginal, combined with the near-extermination of the buffalo, caused a downturn in prairie culture that relied on the horse for hunting, trading, and traveling.

In the late nineteenth century, the avid reformers of the day instituted a practice of trying to "civilize" Indian children by educating them in Indian Boarding Schools. The children were forbidden to speak their native languages, they were forced to convert to Christianity, and generally forced to give up all aspects of their native culture and identity. There are numerous reports of abuse of the Indian children at these schools.

During World War I, a large number of Native Americans were drafted into military service. Most served heroically. This fact, combined with a growing desire to see the native peoples effectively merged into mainstream society, led to the enactment of The Indian Citizenship Act of 1924 by which Native Americans were granted U.S. citizenship.

Until recent years, the policy of the federal government was to segregate and marginalize Native Americans. Their religion, arts, and culture have been largely ignored until recent years. Safely restricted to reservations in the "Indian territory," various attempts were made to strip them of their inherited culture, just as they were stripped of their ancestral lands. Life on the reservations has been difficult for most Native Americans. The policies of extermination and relocation, as well as the introduction of disease among them, significantly decimated their numbers by the end of the nineteenth century.

Reconstruction

Following the Civil War, the nation was faced with repairing the torn Union and readmitting the Confederate states. Reconstruction refers to this period between 1865 and 1877 when the federal and state governments debated and implemented plans to provide civil rights to freed slaves and to set the terms under which the former Confederate states might once again join the Union.

The economic and social chaos in the South after the war was unbelievable with starvation and disease rampant, especially in the cities. The U.S. Army provided some relief of food and clothing for both white and blacks, but the major responsibility fell to the Freedmen's Bureau. Though the bureau agents helped southern whites, their main responsibility was to the freed slaves. They were to assist the freedmen in becoming self-supporting citizens and protect them from being taken advantage of by others. Northerners looked on it as a real, honest effort to help the South out of the chaos it was in. Most white Southerners charged the bureau with causing racial friction, deliberately encouraging the freedmen to consider former owners as enemies.

Lincoln and Johnson had considered the conflict of Civil War as a "rebellion of individuals," but congressional radicals, such as Charles Sumner in the Senate, considered the southern states as complete, political organizations who were now in the same position as any unorganized territory and should be treated as such. Radical House leader Thaddeus Stevens considered the Confederate States, not as territories, but as conquered provinces, and he felt they should be treated that way. President Johnson refused to work with Congressional moderates and insisted on having his own way. As a result, the radicals gained control of both houses of Congress, and when Johnson opposed their harsh measures, they came within one vote of impeaching him.

Planning for Reconstruction began early in the war in 1861. Abraham Lincoln's Republican Party in Washington favored the extension of voting rights to black men but was divided as to how far to extend the right. Moderates, such as Lincoln, wanted only literate blacks and those who had fought for the Union to be allowed to vote. Radical Republicans wanted to extend the vote to all black men. Conservative Democrats did not want to give black men the vote at all. In the case of former Confederate soldiers, moderates wanted to allow all but former leaders to vote. The radicals wanted to require an oath from all eligible voters that they had never borne arms against the US which would have excluded all former rebels. On the issue of readmission into the Union, moderates favored a much lower standard with the radicals demanding nearly impossible conditions for rebel states to return.

Lincoln's moderate plan for Reconstruction was actually part of his effort to win the war. Lincoln and the moderates felt that if it remained easy for states to return to the Union, and if moderate proposals on black suffrage were made, that Confederate states involved in the hostilities might be swayed to re-join the Union rather than continue fighting. The radical plan was to ensure that Reconstruction did not actually start until after the war was over.

In 1863, Abraham Lincoln was assassinated leaving his Vice President Andrew Johnson to oversee the beginning of the actual implementation of Reconstruction. Johnson struck a moderate pose and was willing to allow former Confederates to keep control of their state governments. These governments quickly enacted Black Codes that denied the vote to blacks and granted them only limited civil rights.

The radical Republicans in Congress responded to the Black Codes by continuing their hard line on allowing former rebel states back into the Union. In addition, they sought to override the Black Codes by granting US citizenship to blacks by passing a civil rights bill. Johnson, supported by Democrats, vetoed the bill, but Congress had the necessary votes to override it, and the bill became law.

In 1866, the radical Republicans won control of Congress and passed the Reconstruction Acts which placed the governments of the southern states under the control of the federal military. With this backing, the Republicans began to implement their radical policies such as granting all black men the vote and denying the vote to former confederate soldiers. Congress had passed the 13th, 14th and 15th Amendments granting citizenship and civil rights to blacks. Ratification of these amendments was a condition of readmission into the Union by the rebel states. The Republicans found support in the South among freedmen (former slaves), white southerners who had not supported the Confederacy (Scalawags), and northerners who had moved to the south (Carpetbaggers).

Federal troops were stationed throughout the South and protected Republicans who took control of southern governments. Bitterly resentful, white southerners fought the new political system by joining a secret society called the Ku Klux Klan. They used violence to keep black Americans from voting and getting equality and was a loose group made up mainly of former Confederate soldiers who opposed the Reconstruction government and espoused a doctrine of white supremacy. KKK members intimidated and sometimes killed their proclaimed enemies. The first KKK was never completely organized, despite having nominal leadership. In 1871, President Grant took action to use federal troops to halt the activities of the KKK and actively prosecuted them in federal court.

However, before being allowed to rejoin the Union, the Confederate states were required to agree to all federal laws. Between 1866 and 1870, all of them had returned to the Union, but northern interest in Reconstruction was fading.

Reconstruction was a limited success. Its goals had been both the reunification of the South with the North and the granting of civil rights to freed slaves. In the eyes of blacks was considered a failure. It can be said that Reconstruction had a limited success as it set up public school systems and expanded legal rights of black Americans; however, white supremacy came to be in control again and its bitter fruitage is still with us today.

Life after Reconstruction

Reconstruction officially ended when the last federal troops left the South in 1877 under President Rutherford B. Hayes. Without this support, the Republican governments were replaced by so-called Redeemer governments. Segregation laws were foreshadowed in the **Black Codes**, strict laws proposed by some southern states during Reconstruction that sought to essentially recreate the conditions of pre-war servitude. Under these codes, blacks were to remain subservient to their white employers and were subject to fines and beatings if they failed to work.

After the Civil War, the Emancipation Proclamation in 1863 and the 13th Amendment in 1865 ended slavery in the United States, but these measures did not erase the centuries of racial prejudices among whites that held blacks to be inferior in intelligence and morality. The rise of the Redeemer governments marked the beginning of the **Jim Crow** laws and official segregation. Blacks were still allowed to vote, but ways were found to make it difficult for them to do so, such as literacy tests and poll taxes.

These prejudices, along with fear of economic competition from newly freed slaves, led to a series of state laws that permitted or required businesses, landlords, school boards, and others to physically segregate blacks and whites in their everyday lives. Jim Crow laws varied from state to state, but the most significant of them required separate school systems and libraries for blacks and whites and separate ticket windows, waiting rooms, and seating areas on trains and, later, other public transportation. Restaurant owners were permitted or sometimes required to provide separate entrances and tables and counters for blacks and whites so that the two races could not see one another while dining. Public parks and playgrounds were constructed for each race. Landlords were not allowed to mix black and white tenants in apartment houses in some states.

The Jim Crow laws were given credibility in 1896 when the Supreme Court handed down its decision in the case *Plessy vs. Ferguson.* In 1890, Louisiana had passed a law requiring separate train cars for blacks and whites. In 1892, Homer Plessey, a man who had a black great grandparent and so was considered legally "black" in that state, challenged this law, by purchasing a ticket in the white section. Upon informing the conductor that he was black, he was told to move to the black car. He refused and was arrested. His case was eventually decided by the Supreme Court.

The Court ruled against Plessy, thereby ensuring that the Jim Crow laws would continue to proliferate and be enforced. The Court held that segregating races was not unconstitutional as long as the facilities for each were identical. This became known as the "separate but equal" principle. In practice, facilities were seldom equal. Black schools were not funded at the same level, for instance. Streets and parks in black neighborhoods were not maintained.

The National Association for the Advancement of Colored People (NAACP) was founded in 1909 to assist African Americans. In the early years, the work of the organization focused on working through the courts to overturn "Jim Crow" statutes that legalized racial discrimination. The group organized voters to oppose Woodrow Wilson's efforts to weave racial segregation into federal government policy. Between WW I and WW II, much energy was devoted to stopping the lynching of blacks throughout the country.

Legal segregation was a part of life for generations of Americans until the separate but equal fallacy was finally challenged in 1954 in another Supreme Court case, *Brown vs. Board of Education.* This case arose when a Topeka, Kansas man attempted to enroll his third-grade daughter in a segregated white elementary school and was refused. In the Court decision, the policy of maintaining separate schools was found to be inherently unequal and unconstitutional.

Some states refused to integrate their schools in spite of the new legal interpretation. In Virginia, the state closed some schools rather than integrate them. In Arkansas, the Governor Orville Faubus mobilized the National Guard to prevent the integration of Little Rock High School. President Eisenhower sent federal troops to enforce the integration.

Opposition to Jim Crow laws became an important part of the civil rights movement led by **Martin Luther King, Jr**. and others and which culminated in the **Civil Rights Act of 1964**. This act ended legal segregation in the United States, however some forms of de facto segregation continued to exist, particularly in the area of housing.

The Industrial Revolution

The Industrial Revolution, which began in Great Britain and spread elsewhere, was the development of power-driven machinery (fueled by coal and steam) leading to the accelerated growth of industry with large factories replacing homes and small workshops as work centers. Before 1800, most manufacturing activities were done in small shops or in homes. However, starting in the early 1800s, factories with modern machines were built making it easier to produce goods faster. The eastern part of the country became a major industrial area although some developed in the West.

At the same time, improvements began to be made in building roads, railroads, canals, and steamboats. The increased ease of travel facilitated the westward movement as well as boosted the economy with faster and cheaper shipment of goods and products, covering larger and larger areas. Some of the innovations include the Erie Canal which connected the interior and Great Lakes with the Hudson River and the coastal port of New York. Many other natural waterways were connected by canals.

Robert Fulton's "**Clermont**," the first commercially successful steamboat, led the way in the fastest way to ship goods, making it the most important way to do so. Later, steam-powered railroads soon became the biggest rival of the steamboat as a means of shipping, eventually being the most important transportation method opening the West. With expansion into the interior of the country, the United States became the leading agricultural nation in the world. The hardy pioneer farmers produced a vast surplus and emphasis went to producing products with a high-sale value.

Implements like the cotton gin and reaper also aided in production. Travel and shipping were greatly assisted in areas not yet touched by railroad or by improved or new roads, such as the National Road in the East and in the West the Oregon and Santa Fe Trails.

The lives of people changed drastically and a largely agricultural society changed to an industrial one. In Western Europe, the period of empire and colonialism began. The industrialized nations seized and claimed parts of Africa and Asia in an effort to control and provide the raw materials needed to feed the industries and machines in the "mother country". Later developments included power based on electricity and internal combustion, replacing coal and steam.

There was a marked degree of industrialization before and during the Civil War, but at the war's end, industry in America was small. After the war, dramatic changes took place. Machines replaced hand labor; extensive nationwide railroad service made possible the wider distribution of goods; invention of new products made available in large quantities; and large amounts of money from bankers and investors for expansion of business operations. A great variety of new products or inventions became available such as: the typewriter, the telephone, barbed wire, the electric light, the phonograph, and the gasoline automobile.

American life was definitely affected by this phenomenal industrial growth. Cities became the centers of this new business activity resulting in mass population movements. This new boom in business resulted in huge fortunes for some Americans and extreme poverty for many others. The discontent this caused resulted in a number of new reform movements. Measures to control the power and size of big business resulted.

The use of machines in industry enabled workers to produce a large quantity of goods much faster than by hand. With the increase in business, hundreds of workers were hired and assigned to perform a certain job in the production process. This was a method of organization called "**division of labor**" and due to increased rate of production, businesses lowered prices for their products, making the products affordable for more people. As a result, sales and businesses were increasingly successful and profitable.

Another innovation of the 1920s was the introduction of **mass production**. This is the production of large amounts of standardized products on production lines. The method became very popular when Henry Ford used mass production to build the Model T Ford. The process facilitates high production rates per worker and thus, created very inexpensive products. The process is, however, capital intensive. It requires expensive machinery in high proportion to the number of workers needed to operate it.

The increase in business and industry was greatly affected by the many rich natural resources that were found throughout the nation. The industrial machines were powered by the abundant water supply. The construction industry, as well as products made from wood, depended heavily on lumber from the forests. Coal and iron ore were needed in abundance for the steel industry which profited from the use of steel in such things as skyscrapers, automobiles, bridges, railroad tracks, and machines. Other minerals such as silver, copper, and petroleum played a large role in industrial growth (especially petroleum from which gasoline was refined as fuel for the increasingly popular automobile).

Between 1870 and 1916, more than 25 million immigrants came into the United States adding to the phenomenal population growth taking place. This tremendous growth aided business and industry in two ways: (1) The number of consumers increased, creating a greater demand for products and thus enlarging the markets for the products, and (2) with increased production and expanding business, more workers were available for newly created jobs. The completion of the nation's transcontinental railroad in 1869 contributed greatly to the nation's economic and industrial growth. Some examples of the benefits of using the railroads included that raw materials were shipped quickly by the mining companies and finished products were sent to all parts of the country. Many wealthy industrialists and railroad owners saw tremendous profits steadily increasing due to this improved method of transportation.

Urbanization brings certain needs in its wake, including: adequate water supply; management of sewage and garbage; the need for public services, such as fire and police, road construction and maintenance; building of bridges to connect parts of cities; and taller buildings. This last led to the invention of steel-framed buildings and of the elevator. In addition, electricity and telephone lines were needed, department stores and supermarkets grew, and the need for additional schools was related to urbanization. With the large migration and low wages came overcrowding, often in old buildings. Slums began to appear. Soon public health issues began to arise.

The "inventive spirit" of the time was a major force propelling the Industrial Revolution forward. This spirit led to improvement in products, development of new production processes and equipment, and even to the creation of entirely new industries. During the last 40 years of the nineteenth century, inventors registered almost 700,000 new patents.

The industrial boom produced several very wealthy and powerful "captains of industry" such as Andrew Carnegie, John D. Rockefeller, Jay Gould, J.P Morgan and Philip Armour. While they were envied and respected for their business acumen and success, they were condemned for exploitation of workers and questionable business practices. Most workers were required to put in long hours in dangerous conditions doing monotonous work for low wages. Most were not able to afford to participate in the new comforts and forms of entertainment that were becoming available. Farmers believed they were also being exploited by the bankers, suppliers, and the railroads. This produced enough instability to fuel several recessions and two severe depressions.

People were exposed to works of literature, art, newspapers, drama, live entertainment, and political rallies. With better communication and travel, more information was desired about previously unknown areas of the country, especially the West. The discovery of gold and other mineral wealth resulted in a literal surge of settlers and even more interest.

Social & Reform Movements

The late 1800s and early 1900s were a period of the efforts of many to make significant reforms and changes in the areas of politics, society, and the economy. During the nineteenth century, there arose a great spirit of reform. This spirit of reform found expression in the effort to protect the rights and opportunities of all. Skilled laborers were organized into a labor union called the American Federation of Labor in an effort to gain better working conditions and wages for its members. The beginning of the labor organization movement in the 1830s – 50s resulted in the establishment of a ten-hour workday in several states.

Farmers joined organizations such as the National Grange and Farmers Alliances. Farmers were producing more food than people could afford to buy. This was the result of (1) new farmlands rapidly sprouting on the plains and prairies, and (2) development and availability of new farm machinery and newer and better methods of farming. They tried selling their surplus abroad, but they faced stiff competition from other nations selling the same farm products. Other problems contributed significantly to their situation. Items they needed for daily life were priced exorbitantly high which meant the had to borrow money to carry on farming activities and this kept them constantly in debt. Higher interest rates, shortage of money, falling farm prices, dealing with the so-called middlemen, and the increasingly high charges by the railroads to haul farm products to large markets all contributed to the desperate need for reform to relieve the plight of American farmers.

Populism is the philosophy that is concerned with the common sense needs of average people. Populism often finds expression as a reaction against perceived oppression of the average people by the wealthy elite in society. Populism is often connected with religious fundamentalism, racism, or nationalism. Populist movements claim to represent the majority of the people and call them to stand up to institutions or practices that seem detrimental to their well being.

Populism flourished in the late nineteenth and early twentieth centuries. Several political parties were formed out of this philosophy, including: the Greenback Party, the Populist Party, the Farmer-Labor Party, the Single Tax movement of Henry George, the Share Our Wealth movement of Huey Long, the Progressive Party, and the Union Party.

There was a need to reduce the levels of poverty and to improve the living conditions of those affected by it. Regulation of big business and ridding government of corruption to make it more responsive to the needs of the people were also on the list of reforms to be accomplished. Until 1890, there was very little success. However from 1890 on, the reformers gained increased public support and were able to achieve some influence in government. Since some of these individuals referred to themselves as "**progressives**".

This fire was fueled by the writings on investigative journalists – the "muckrakers" – who published scathing exposes of political and business wrongdoing and corruption. The result was the rise of a group of politicians and reformers who supported a wide array of populist causes. The period from 1890 to 1917 came to be known as the **Progressive Era**. Although these leaders came from many different backgrounds and were driven by different ideologies, they shared a common fundamental belief that government should be eradicating social ills and promoting the common good and the equality guaranteed by the Constitution.

The reforms initiated by these leaders and the spirit of Progressivism were far-reaching. Politically, many states enacted the initiative and the referendum. The adoption of the recall occurred in many states. Several states enacted legislation that would undermine the power of political machines. On a national level, the two most significant political changes were: (1) the ratification of the 17th Amendment which required that all U.S. Senators be chosen by popular election, and (2) the ratification of the 19th Amendment which granted women the right to vote.

The overriding theme of the life in the eighteenth, nineteenth, and twentieth centuries was progress. Technological advancements brought great and terrible things in all aspects of life. New theories in economics brought great changes in the way the world does business. New theories in government brought about new nations, uprisings, and wars galore. New theories in art changed the landscape of painting forever.

Things changed in the worlds of literature and art as well. The main development in the nineteenth century was **Romanticism**, an emphasis on emotion and the imagination that was a direct reaction to the logic and reason so stressed in preceding times. Famous Romantic authors included John Keats, William Wordsworth, Victor Hugo, and Johann Wolfgang von Goethe. The horrors of the Industrial Revolution gave rise to the very famous realists such as Charles Dickens, Fyodor Dostoevsky, Leo Tolstoy, and Mark Twain who described life as they saw it, for better or for worse (and it was usually worse). Echoing Dickens's dislike of an industrialized world, twentieth century authors stressed individual ction and responsibility. Important authors of the 1900s include James Joyce, T.S. Eliot, John Steinbeck, Ernest Hemingway, William Faulkner, and George Orwell, all of whom to varying degrees expressed distrust at the power of machines and weapons and most of modern society.

The most famous movement of the 1800s, however, was **Impressionism**. The idea was to present an impression of a moment in time - one of life's fleeting moments memorialized on canvas. A list of famous impressionists includes Monet, Degas, van Gogh, Manet, Cezanne, Renoir, and many more. More than any other time in the history of the arts, Impressionism produced famous faces and famous canvases.

The Second Great Awakening was an evangelical Protestant revival that preached personal responsibility for one's actions, both individually and socially. This movement was led by preachers such as Charles Finney who traveled the country preaching the gospel of social responsibility. This point of view was taken up by the "mainline" Protestant denominations (Episcopal, Methodist, Presbyterian, Lutheran, and Congregational). Part of the social reform movement that led to an end to child labor, to better working conditions, and to other changes in social attitudes, arose from this new recognition that the Christian faith should be expressed for the good of society.

Closely allied to the Second Great Awakening was **the temperance movement**. This movement to end the sale and consumption of alcohol arose from religious beliefs, the violence many women and children experienced from heavy drinkers, and from the effect of alcohol consumption on the work force. The Society for the Promotion of Temperance was organized in Boston in 1826.

Other social issues were also addressed. It was during this period that efforts were made to transform the prison system and its emphasis on punishment into a penitentiary system that attempted rehabilitation. It was also during this period that Dorothea Dix led a struggle in the North and the South to establish hospitals for the insane. A group of women emerged in the 1840s that was the beginning of the first women's rights movement in the nation's history. Among the early leaders of the movement were Elizabeth Cady Stanton, Lucretia Mott, and Ernestine Rose. At this time very few states recognized women's rights to vote, own property, sue for divorce, or execute contracts. In 1869, Susan B. Anthony, Ernestine Rose, and Elizabeth Cady Stanton founded the National Woman Suffrage Association.

Utopianism is the dream of or the desire to create the perfect society. However by the nineteenth century, few believed this was possible. One of the major "causes" of utopianism is the desire for moral clarity. The young nation is trying to define itself and to ensure the rights and freedoms of its citizens, and within the context of the second great awakening, it becomes quite easy to see how the reform movements, the religious sentiment, and the gathering national storm would lead to the rise of expressions of desire to create the perfect society.

A new understanding of education led to movements for public education for all children. The public school system became common in the North. Public schools were established in many of the states with more and more children being educated. With more literacy and more participation in literature and the arts, the young nation was developing its own unique culture, becoming less and less influenced by and dependent on that of Europe.

Responding to concern over the environmental effects of the timber, ranching, and mining industries, President Roosevelt set aside 238 million acres of federal lands to protect them from development. Wildlife preserves were established, the national park system was expanded, and the National Conservation Commission was created. The Newlands Reclamation Act also provided federal funding for the construction of irrigation projects and dams in semi-arid areas of the country.

The Wilson Administration carried out additional reforms. The Federal Reserve Act created a national banking system, that provided a stable money supply. The Sherman Act and the Clayton Antitrust Act defined unfair competition, made corporate officers liable for the illegal actions of employees, and exempted labor unions from antitrust lawsuits. The Federal Trade Commission was established to enforce these measures. Finally, the 16th amendment was ratified, establishing an income tax. This measure was designed to relieve the poor of a disproportionate burden in funding the federal government and make the wealthy pay a greater share of the nation's tax burden.

The Anti-Defamation League was created in 1913 to stop discrimination against the Jewish people. Its charter states, "Its ultimate purpose is to secure justice and fair treatment to all citizens alike and to put an end forever to unjust and unfair discrimination against ridicule of any sect or body of citizens. The organization has historically opposed all groups considered anti-Semitic and/or racist. This has included the Ku Klux Klan, the Nazis, and a variety of others.

The U.S. as a World Power & Foreign Policies

When Great Britain finally acknowledged American independence in 1783, the country claimed about 900,000 square miles of territory. The nation had more than quadrupled in size by 1899 due to the purchase of the Louisiana Territory from France and Florida from Spain, the addition of Texas, California and the southwest, the Oregon Country, and the purchase of Alaska from Russia . The American "Empire" was now the fifth largest in the world.

Spain's tyrannical and short-sighted colonial policy led to a revolt on the island of Cuba (1895-98). When the revolution began in Cuba, it aroused the interest and concern of Americans who were aware of what was happening "at their doorstep." When the Spanish attempted to put down the revolt, the women and children of Cuba were treated with great cruelty. They were gathered into camps surrounded by armed guards and given little food. Much of the food that kept them alive came from supplies sent by the U.S. Americans were already concerned over years of anarchy and misrule by the Spanish. When reports of gross atrocities reached America, public sentiment clearly favored the Cuban people. President McKinley had refused to recognize the rebellion, but he had affirmed the possibility of American intervention. Spain resented this attitude of the Americans.

In February 1898, the American battleship *Maine* was blown up in Havana harbor. Although there was no incontrovertible evidence that the Spanish were responsible, popular sentiment accused Spanish agents and war became inevitable. Two months later, Congress declared war on Spain and the U.S. quickly defeated them. The peace treaty gave the U.S. possession of Puerto Rico, the Philippines, Guam and Hawaii, which was annexed during the war.

Until the middle of the nineteenth century, American foreign policy and expansionism was essentially restricted to the North American Continent. America had shown no interest in establishing colonies in other lands. Specifically, the U.S. had stayed out of the rush to claim African territories. The variety of imperialism that found expression under the administrations of McKinley and Theodore Roosevelt was not precisely comparable to the imperialistic goals of European nations. There was a type of idealism in American foreign policy that sought to use military power in territories and other lands only in the interest of human rights and the spread of democratic principles. Much of the concern and involvement in Central and South America, as well as the Caribbean, was to link the two coasts of the nation and to protect the American economy from European encroachment.

Although the idea of a canal in Panama goes back to the early 16th century, work did not begin until 1880 by the French. The effort collapsed and the U.S. completed the task, opening the **Panama Canal** in 1914. Construction was an enormous task of complex engineering. The significance of the canal is that it connects the Gulf of Panama in the Pacific Ocean with the Caribbean Sea and the Atlantic Ocean. It eliminated the need for ships to skirt the southern boundary of South America, effectively reducing the sailing distance from New York to San Francisco by 8,000 miles (over half of the distance). The U.S. helped Panama win independence from Colombia in exchange for control of the Panama Canal Zone. After WW II, control of the canal became an issue of contention between the U.S. and Panama. Negotiations toward a settlement began in 1974, resulting in the Torrijos-Carter Treaties of 1977. Thus began the process of handing the canal over to Panama. On December 31, 1999, control of the canal was handed over to the Panama Canal Authority. Tolls for the use of the canal have ranged from $0.36, when Richard Halliburton swam the canal, to about $226,000.

The **Open Door Policy** refers to maintaining equal commercial and industrial rights for the people of all countries in a particular territory. The Open Door policy generally refers to China, but it has also been used in application to the Congo basin. The policy was first suggested by the U.S., but its basis is the typical nation clause of the treaties made with China after the Opium War (1829-1842). The essential purpose of the policy was to permit equal access to trade for all nations with treaties with China while protecting the integrity of the Chinese empire.

This policy was in effect from about 1900 until the end of WW II. After the war, China was recognized as a sovereign state. There was no longer opportunity for other nations to attempt to carve out regions of influence or control. When the Communist party came to power in China, the policy was rejected. This continued until the late 1970s, when China began to adopt a policy of again encouraging foreign trade.

Big Stick Diplomacy was a term adopted from an African proverb, "speak softly and carry a big stick," to describe President Theodore Roosevelt's policy of the U.S. assuming international police power in the Western Hemisphere. The phrase implied the power to retaliate if necessary. The intention was to safeguard American economic interests in Latin America. The policy led to the expansion of the U.S. Navy and to greater involvement in world affairs. Should any nation in the Western Hemisphere become vulnerable to European control because of political or economic instability, the U.S. had both the right and the obligation to intervene.

Dollar Diplomacy describes U.S. efforts under President Taft to extend its foreign policy goals in Latin America and East Asia via economic power. The designation derives from Taft's claim that U.S. interests in Latin America had changed from "warlike and political" to "peaceful and economic." Taft justified this policy in terms of protecting the Panama Canal. The practice of dollar diplomacy was from time to time anything but peaceful, particularly in Nicaragua. When revolts or revolutions occurred, the U.S. sent troops to resolve the situation. Immediately upon resolution, bankers were sent in to loan money to the new regimes. The policy persisted until the election of Woodrow Wilson to the Presidency in 1913.

Wilson repudiated the dollar diplomacy approach to foreign policy within weeks of his inauguration. Wilson's "moral diplomacy" became the model for American foreign policy to this day and envisioned a federation of democratic nations, believing that democracy and representative government were the foundation stones of world stability. Specifically, he saw Great Britain and the United States as the champions of self-government and the promoters of world peace.

Wilson's beliefs and actions set in motion an American foreign policy that was dedicated to the interests of all humanity rather than merely American national interests. Wilson promoted the power of free trade and international commerce as the key to enlarging the national economy into world markets as a means of acquiring a voice in world events. This approach to foreign policy was based on three elements: (1) maintain a combat-ready military to meet the needs of the nation, (2) promote democracy abroad, and (3) improve the U.S. economy through international trade. Wilson believed that democratic states would be less inclined to threaten U.S. interests.

Post WW I and the 1920s

Marcus Garvey, an English-educated Jamaican, established an organization call the *Universal Negro Improvement and Conservation Association and African Communities League* (usually called the Universal Negro Improvement Association). In 1919, this "Black Moses" claimed followers numbering about two million. He spoke of a "new Negro" who was proud to be black and published a newspaper in which he taught about the "heroes" of the race and the strengths of African culture. He told blacks that they would be respected only when they were economically strong and he created a number of businesses by which he hoped to achieve this goal. He then called blacks to work with him to build an all-black nation in Africa. His belief in racial purity and black separatism was not shared by a number of black leaders. In 1922 he and other members of the organization were jailed for mail fraud. His sentence was commuted and he was deported to Jamaica as an undesirable alien.

The Klan entered a second period beginning in 1915. Using the new film medium, this group tried to spread its message with *The Birth of a Nation* as well as by publishing a number of anti-Semitic newspaper articles. The group became a structured membership organization whose membership did not begin to decline until the Great Depression. Although the KKK began in the South, its membership at its peak extended into the Midwest, the northern states, and even into Canada. Membership during the 1920s reached approximately four million – 20% of the adult white male population in many regions and as high as 40% in some areas. The political influence of the group was significant. They essentially controlled the governments of Tennessee, Indiana, Oklahoma, and Oregon as well as some southern legislatures.

The 1920s were a period of relative prosperity under the leadership of Warren G. Harding and Calvin Coolidge. Harding had promised a return to "normalcy" in the aftermath of World War I and the radical reactions of labor. During most of the decade, the output of industry boomed and the automobile industry put almost 27 million cars on the road. Per capita income rose for almost everyone except farmers.

A huge wave of labor strikes sought a return to war-time working conditions when the work day was shorter, wages were higher, and conditions were better. Many of these labor strikes turned violent. The majority of the population viewed the early strikes as the work of radicals who were labeled "reds" (communists). As the news spread and other strikes occurred, the "**red scare**" swept the country.

Americans feared a Bolshevik-type revolution in America. As a result, people were jailed for expressing views that were considered anarchist, communist, or socialist. In an attempt to control the potential for revolution, civil liberties were ignored and thousands were deported. The Socialist Party also came to be viewed as a group of anarchist radicals. Several state and local governments passed a variety of laws designed to reduce radical speech and activity. Congress considered more than 70 anti-sedition bills, though none was passed. Within a year, the Red Scare had essentially run its course.

Within the context of fear of radicalism, rampant racism, and efforts to repress various groups within the population, it is not surprising that several groups were formed to protect the civil rights and liberties guaranteed to all citizens by the U.S. Constitution. The *American Civil Liberties Union* was formed in 1920. It was originally an outgrowth of the American Union Against Militarism which had opposed American involvement in WW I. It had provided legal advice and assistance for conscientious objectors and those who were being prosecuted under the Espionage Act of 1917 and the Sedition Act of 1918. With the name change, there was attention to additional concerns and activities. The agency began to try to protect immigrants threatened with deportation and citizens threatened with prosecution for communist activities and agendas. They also opposed efforts to repress the Industrial Workers of the World and other labor unions.

The end of World War I and the decade of the 1920s saw tremendous changes in the United States, signifying the beginning of its development into its modern society today. The shift from farm to city life was occurring in tremendous numbers. Social changes and problems were occurring at such a fast pace that it was extremely difficult and perplexing for many Americans to adjust to them. Politically, the 18th Amendment to the Constitution, the so-called Prohibition Amendment, prohibited selling alcoholic beverages throughout the U.S. resulting in problems affecting all aspects of society.

The passage of the 19th Amendment gave to women the right to vote in all elections. The decade of the 1920s also showed a marked change in roles and opportunities for women with more and more of them seeking and finding careers outside the home. They began to think of themselves as the equal of men and not as much as housewives and mothers.

The influence of the automobile, the entertainment industry, and the rejection of the morals and values of pre-World War I life, resulted in the fast-paced "Roaring Twenties". There were significant effects on events leading to the depression-era 1930s and another world war. Many Americans greatly desired the pre-war life and supported political policies and candidates in favor of the return to what was considered normal. It was desirable to end the government's strong role and to adopt a policy of isolating the country from world affairs. This was a result of the war.

Although the British patent for the **radio** was awarded in 1896, it was not until WW I that the equipment and capability of the use of radio was recognized. The first radio program was broadcast on August 31, 1920 and the first entertainment broadcasts began in 1922 from England. One of the first developments in the twentieth century was the use of commercial AM radio stations for aircraft navigation. In addition, radio was used to communicate orders and information between army and navy units on both sides of the war during WW I. Broadcasting became practical in the 1920s. Radio receivers were introduced on a wide scale.

The relative economic boom of the 1920s made it possible for many households to own a radio. The beginning of broadcasting and the proliferation of receivers revolutionized communication. The news was transmitted into every home with a radio. With the beginning of entertainment broadcasting, people were able to remain in their homes for entertainment. Rather than obtaining filtered information, people were able to hear the actual speeches and information that became news. By the time of the Stock Market Crash in 1929, approximately 40% of households had a radio.

Immigration

Immigration has played a crucial role in the growth and settlement of the United States from the beginning. With a large interior territory to fill and ample opportunity, the U.S. encouraged immigration throughout most of the nineteenth century, maintaining an almost completely open policy. Famine in Ireland and Germany in the 1840s resulted in over 3.5 million immigrants from these two countries alone between the years of 1830 and 1860.

Following the Civil War, rapid expansion in rail transportation brought the interior states within easy reach of new immigrants who still came primarily from Western Europe and entered the U.S. on the east coast. As immigration increased, several states adopted individual immigration laws, and in 1875, the U.S. Supreme Court declared immigration a federal matter. Following a huge surge in European immigration in 1880, the United States began to regulate immigration, first by passing a tax to new immigrants, then by instituting literacy requirements and barring those with mental or physical illness. A large influx of Chinese immigration to the western states had resulted in the complete exclusion of immigrants from that country in 1882. In 1891, the Federal Bureau of Immigration was established. Even with these new limits in place, immigration remained relatively open in the U.S. to those from European countries, and it increased steadily until World War I.

With much of Europe left in ruins after WW I, immigration to the U.S. exploded in the years following the war. In 1920 and 1921, some 800,000 new immigrants arrived. Unlike previous immigrants who came mainly from western European countries, the new wave of immigrants was from southern and eastern Europe. The U.S. responded to this sudden shift in the makeup of new immigrants with a quota system, first enacted by Congress in 1921. This system limited immigration in proportion to the ethnic groups that were already settled in the U.S. according to previous census records. This national-origins policy was extended and further defined by Congress in 1924.

This policy remained the official policy of the U.S. for the next 40 years. Occasional challenges to the law from non-white immigrants re-affirmed that the intention of the policy was to limit immigration primarily to white, western Europeans who the government felt were most likely to assimilate into American culture. Strict limitations on Chinese immigration were extended throughout the period and didn't relax until 1940. In 1965, Congress overhauled immigration policy, removing the quotas and replacing them with a preference based system. Now, immigrants reuniting with family members and those with special skills or education were given preference. As a result, immigration from Asian and African countries began to increase. The 40-year legacy of the 1920s immigration restrictions had a direct and dramatic impact on the makeup of modern American society. Had Congress not imposed what amounted to racial limits on new arrivals to the country, the U.S. would perhaps be a larger, more diverse nation today.

The Great Depression and the New Deal

The 1929 Stock Market Crash was the powerful event that is generally interpreted as the beginning of the Great Depression in America. Although the crash of the Stock Market was unexpected, it was not without identifiable causes. The 1920s had been a decade of social and economic growth and hope. But the attitudes and actions of the 1920s regarding wealth, production, and investment created several trends that quietly set the stage for the 1929 disaster.

The other factor contributing to the Great Depression was the economic condition of Europe. The U.S. was lending money to European nations to rebuild. Many of these countries used this money to purchase U.S. food and manufactured goods. But they were not able to pay off their debts. While the U.S. was providing money, food, and goods to Europe, it was not willing to buy European goods. Trade barriers were enacted to maintain a favorable trade balance.

Several other factors are cited by some scholars as contributing to the Great Depression. First, in 1929, the Federal Reserve increased interest rates. Second, some believe that as interest rates rose and the stock market began to decline, people began to hoard money. This was certainly the case after the crash.

In September 1929, stock prices began to slip somewhat, yet people remained optimistic. On Monday, October 21, stock prices began to fall quickly. The volume traded was so high that the tickers were unable to keep up. Investors were frightened, and they started selling very quickly. This caused further collapse. For the next two days, prices stabilized somewhat. On **Black Thursday**, October 24, prices plummeted again. By this time investors had lost confidence. On Friday and Saturday an attempt to stop the crash was made by some leading bankers. But on Monday the 28th, prices began to fall again, declining by 13% in one day. The next day, **Black Tuesday, October 29**, saw 16.4 million shares traded. Stock prices fell so far, that at many times, no one was willing to buy at any price.

Unemployment quickly reached 25% nationwide. People thrown out of their homes created makeshift domiciles of cardboard, scraps of wood, and tents. With unmasked reference to President Hoover, who was quite obviously overwhelmed by the situation, these communities were called "**Hoovervilles**." Families stood in bread lines, rural workers left the plains to search for work in California, and banks failed. More than 100,000 businesses failed between 1929 and 1932. The despair that swept the nation left an indelible scar on all who endured the Depression.

By far the worst natural disaster of the decade came to be known as the **Dust Bowl.** Due to severe and prolonged drought in the Great Plains and previous reliance on inappropriate farming techniques, a series of devastating dust storms occurred in the 1930s that resulted in destruction, economic ruin for many, and dramatic ecological change. Crops were ruined, the land was destroyed, and people either lost or abandoned homes and farms. Fifteen percent of Oklahoma's population left. Because so many of the migrants were from Oklahoma, the migrants came to be called "**Okies**" no matter where they came from. Estimates of the number of people displaced by this disaster range from 300,000 to 2.5 million.

When the stock market crashed, businesses collapsed. Without demand for certain products, other businesses and industries collapsed. This set in motion a domino effect, bringing down the businesses and industries that provided raw materials or components to these industries. Hundreds of thousands became jobless. The jobless often became homeless. Desperation prevailed. Little had been done to assess the toll hunger, inadequate nutrition, and starvation of families and children during this time. Indeed, food was cheap, relatively speaking, but there was little money to buy it.

Hoover's bid for re-election in 1932 failed. The new president, Franklin D. Roosevelt, won the White House on his promise to the American people of a "new deal." Upon assuming the office, Roosevelt and his advisers immediately launched a massive program of innovation and experimentation to try to bring the Depression to an end and get the nation back on track. Congress gave the President unprecedented power to act to save the nation. During the next eight years, the most extensive and broadly-based legislation in the nation's history was enacted. The legislation was intended to accomplish three goals: relief, recovery, and reform.

The first step in the "**New Deal"** was to relieve suffering. This was accomplished through a number of job-creation projects. The second step, the recovery aspect, was to stimulate the economy. The third step was to create social and economic change through innovative legislation.

To provide economic stability and prevent another crash, Congress passed the **Glass-Steagall Act** which separated banking and investing. The Securities and Exchange Commission was created to regulate dangerous speculative practices on Wall Street. The Wagner Act guaranteed a number of rights to workers and unions in an effort to improve worker-employer relations. The **Social Security Act of 1935** established pensions for the aged and unwell as well as a system of unemployment insurance.

Many of the steps taken by the Roosevelt administration have had far-reaching effects. They alleviated the economic disaster of the Great Depression, they enacted controls that would mitigate the risk of another stock market crash, and they provided greater security for workers. The nation's economy, however, did not fully recover until America entered World War II.

The gains and losses or organized labor in the 1930s

There were several major events or actions that are particularly important to the history of organized labor during this decade:

- The Supreme Court upheld the Railway Labor Act, including its prohibition of employer interference or coercion in the choice of bargaining representatives (1930)
- The Davis-Bacon Act provided that employers of contractors and subcontractors on public construction should be paid the prevailing wages (1931)
- The Anti-Injunction Act prohibited Federal injunctions in most labor disputes (1932)
- Wisconsin created the first unemployment insurance act in the country (1932)
- The Wagner-Peyser Act created the United States Employment Service within the Department of Labor (1933)

- Half a million Southern mill workers walked off the job in the Great Uprising of 1934
- The Secretary of Labor called the first National Labor Legislation Conference to get better cooperation between the Federal Government and the States in defining a national labor legislation program (1934)
- The U.S. joined the International Labor Organization (1934)
- The Wagner Act (The National Labor Relations Act) established a legal basis for unions, set collective bargaining as a matter of national policy required by the law, provided for secret ballot elections for choosing unions, and protected union members from employer intimidation and coercion. This law was later amended by the Taft-Hartley Act (1947) and by the Landrum Griffin Act (1959).
- The Guffey Act stabilized the coal industry and improved labor conditions (1935). It was later declared unconstitutional (1936)
- The Social Security Act was approved (1935)
- The Committee for Industrial Organization (CIO) was formed within the AFL to carry unionism to the industrial sector. (1935)
- The United Rubber Workers staged the first sit-down strike (1936)
- The United Auto Workers used the sit-down strike against General Motors (1936)
- The Anti-Strikebreaker Act (the Byrnes Act) made it illegal to transport or aid strikebreakers in interstate or foreign trade (1936)
- The Public Contracts Act (the Walsh-Healey Act) of 1936 established labor standards, including minimum wages, overtime pay, child and convict labor provisions and safety standards on federal contracts
- General Motors recognized the United Auto Workers in 1937
- US Steel recognized the Steel Workers Organizing Committee in 1937
- The Wagner Act was upheld by the Supreme Court (1937)
- During a strike of the Steel Workers Organizing Committee against Republic Steel, police attacked a crowd gathered in support of the strike, killing ten and injuring eighty. This came to be called **The Memorial Day Massacre** (1937).
- The CIO was expelled from the AFL over charges of dual unionism or competition (1937).
- The National Apprenticeship Act established the Bureau of Apprenticeship within the Department of Labor (1937)
- The Merchant Marine Act created a Federal Maritime Labor Board (1938)
- The Fair Labor Standards Act created a $0.25 minimum wage, stipulated time-and-a-half pay for hours over 40 per week
- The CIO becomes the Congress of Industrial Organizations

The significance and ramifications of the decision to drop the atomic bomb

The development of the atomic bomb was probably the most profound military development of the war years. This invention made it possible for a single plane to carry a single bomb that was sufficiently powerful to destroy an entire city. It was believed that possession of the bomb would serve as a deterrent to any nation because it would make aggression against a nation with a bomb a decision for mass suicide. Two nuclear bombs were dropped in 1945 on the cities of Nagasaki and Hiroshima. They caused the immediate deaths of 100,000 to 200,000 people, and far more deaths over time. The decision to drop the atomic bomb was (and still is) controversial. Those who opposed the use of the atom bomb argued that was an unnecessary act of mass killing, particularly of non-combatants. Proponents argued that it ended the war sooner, thus resulting in fewer casualties on both sides. The development and use of nuclear weapons marked the beginning of a new age in warfare that created greater distance from the act of killing and eliminated the ability to minimize the effect of war on non-combatants. The introduction and possession of nuclear weapons by the United States quickly led to the development of similar weapons by other nations and led to the Cold War.

The American isolationist mood was given a shocking and lasting blow in 1941 with the Japanese attack on Pearl Harbor. The nation arose and forcefully entered the international arena as never before. Declaring itself "the arsenal of democracy", it entered the Second World War and emerged not only victorious, but also as the strongest power on the Earth and a permanent and leading place in world affairs.

After 1945, social and economic chaos continued in Western Europe, especially in Germany. Secretary of State George C. Marshall proposed a program known as the European Recovery Program or the Marshall Plan to provide assistance. Although the Soviet Union withdrew from any participation, the U.S. continued the work of assisting Europe in regaining economic stability. In Germany, the situation was critical with the American Army shouldering the staggering burden of relieving the serious problems of the German economy. In February 1948, Britain and the U.S. combined their two zones, with France joining in June.

At the end of the Second World War, the United States perceived its greatest threat to be the expansion of Communism in the world. To that end, it devoted a large share of its foreign policy, diplomacy, and both economic and military might to combating it.

In 1946, Josef Stalin stated publicly that the presence of capitalism and its development of the world's economy made international peace impossible. This resulted in an American diplomat in Moscow named George F. Kennan to propose, as a response to Stalin and as a statement of U.S. foreign policy, the idea and goal of the U.S. to be to contain or limit the extension or expansion of Soviet Communist policies and activities. After Soviet efforts to cause trouble in Iran, Greece, and Turkey, U.S. President Harry Truman stated what is known as the Truman Doctrine which committed the U.S. to a policy of intervention in order to contain or stop the spread of communism throughout the world.

In the aftermath of the Second World War, with the Soviet Union having emerged as the *second* strongest power on Earth, the United States embarked on a policy known as "**Containment.**". This involved what came to be known as the "**Marshall Plan**" and the "**Truman Doctrine**". The Marshall Plan involved the economic aid that was sent to Europe in the aftermath of the Second World War aimed at preventing the spread of communism.

The Truman Doctrine offered military aid to those countries that were in danger of communist upheaval. This led to the era known as the **Cold War** in which the United States took the lead along with the Western European nations against the Soviet Union and the Eastern Bloc countries. It was also at this time that the United States finally gave up on George Washington's' advice against "European entanglements" and joined the **North Atlantic Treaty Organization** or **NATO**. This was formed in 1949 and was comprised of the United States and several Western European nations joined for the purposes of opposing communist aggression.

The Cold War was, more than anything else, an ideological struggle between proponents of democracy and those of communism. The two major players were the United States and the Soviet Union, but other countries were involved as well. It was a “cold” war because no large-scale fighting took place directly between the two big protagonists.

The Soviet Union kept much more of a tight leash on its supporting countries, including all of Eastern Europe, which made up a military organization called the Warsaw Pact. The Western nations responded with a military organization of their own, NATO. Another prime battleground was Asia, where the Soviet Union had allies in China, North Korea, and North Vietnam and the U.S. had allies in Japan, South Korea, Taiwan, and South Vietnam. The Korean War and Vietnam War were major conflicts in which both protagonists played large roles but didn't directly fight each other. The main symbol of the Cold War was the arms race, a continual buildup of missiles, tanks, and other weapons that became ever more technologically advanced and increasingly more deadly. The ultimate weapon, which both sides had in abundance, was the nuclear bomb. Spending on weapons and defensive systems eventually occupied large percentages of the budgets of the U.S. and the USSR, and some historians argue that this high level of spending played a large part in the end of the latter.

The war was a cultural struggle as well. Adults brought up their children to hate "the Americans" or "the Communists." Cold War tensions spilled over into many parts of life in countries around the world. The ways of life in countries on either side of the divide were so different that they served entirely foreign to outside observers.

The Cold War continued to varying degrees from 1947 to 1991, when the Soviet Union collapsed. Other Eastern European countries had seen their communist governments overthrown by this time as well, marking the shredding of the "Iron Curtain."

The **United Nations**, a more successful successor to the League of Nations (which couldn't prevent World War II), began in the waning days of the war. It brought the nations of the world together to discuss their problems, rather than fight about them. Another successful method of keeping the peace since the war has been the atomic bomb. On a more specific note, UNICEF, a worldwide children's fund, has been able to achieve great things in just a few decades of existence. Other peace-based organizations like the Red Cross and Doctors Without Borders have seen their membership and their efficacy rise during this time as well.

In the 1950s, the United States embarked on what was called the "**Eisenhower Doctrine**. This aimed at trying to maintain peace in the Middle East. However, unlike the Truman Doctrine in Europe, it would have little success.

The United States also became involved in a number of world conflicts in the ensuing years. Each had at the core the struggle against communist expansion. Among these were the **Korean War** (1950-1953), the **Vietnam War** (1965-1975), and various continuing entanglements in Central and South America and the Middle East. By the early 1970's under the leadership of then Secretary of State, Henry Kissinger, the United States and its allies embarked on the policy that became known as "**Détente**". This was aimed at the easing of tensions between the United States and its allies and the Soviet Union and its allies.

By the 1980s, the United States embarked on what some saw as a renewal of the Cold War. This owed to the fact that the United States was becoming more involved in trying to prevent communist insurgency in Central America. A massive expansion of its armed forces and the development of space-based weapons systems were undertaken at this time. As this occurred, the Soviet Union, with a failing economic system and a foolhardy adventure in Afghanistan, found itself unable to compete. By 1989, events had come to a head culminating in the breakdown of the Communist Bloc, the virtual end of the monolithic Soviet Union, and the collapse of the communist system by the early 1990's.

Harry S. Truman. Truman became president near the end of WW II. He is credited with some of the most important decisions in history. When Japan refused to surrender, Truman authorized the dropping of atomic bombs on Japanese cities dedicated to war support: Hiroshima and Nagasaki. He took to the Congress a 21-point plan that came to be known as the **Fair Deal**. It included: expansion of Social Security, a full-employment program, public housing and slum clearance, and a permanent Fair Employment Practices Act. The Truman Doctrine provided support for Greece and Turkey when they were threatened by the Soviet Union. The Marshall Plan stimulated amazing economic recovery for Western Europe. Truman participated in the negotiations that resulted in the formation of the North Atlantic Treaty Organization. He and his administration believed it necessary to support South Korea when it was threatened by the communist government of North Korea. But he contained American involvement in Korea so as not to risk conflict with China or Russia.

The first "hot war" in the post-World War II era was the Korean War, begun June 25, 1950 and ending July 27, 1953. Troops from Communist North Korea invaded democratic South Korea in an effort to unite both sections under Communist control. The United Nations organization asked its member nations to furnish troops to help restore peace. Many nations responded and President Truman sent American troops to help the South Koreans. The war dragged on for three years and ended with a truce, not a peace treaty. Korea remains divided to this day.

Causes: Korea was under control of Japan from 1895 to the end of the Second World War in 1945. At war's end, the Soviet and U.S. military troops moved into Korea with the U.S. troops in the southern half and the Soviet troops in the northern half with the 38 degree North Latitude line as the boundary.

Dwight David Eisenhower succeeded Truman. Eisenhower obtained a truce in Korea and worked during his two terms to mitigate the tension of the Cold War. When Stalin died, he was able to negotiate a peace treaty with Russia that neutralized Austria. His domestic policy was a middle road. He continued most of the programs introduced under both the New Deal and the Fair Deal. When desegregation of schools began, he sent troops to Little Rock, Arkansas to enforce desegregation of the schools. He ordered the complete desegregation of the military. During his administration, the Department of Health, Education and Welfare was established and the National Aeronautics and Space Administration was formed.

The General Assembly of the UN in 1947 ordered elections throughout all of Korea to select one government for the entire country. The Soviet Union would not allow the North Koreans to vote, so they set up a Communist government there. The South Koreans set up a democratic government but both claimed the entire country. At times, there were clashes between the troops from 1948 to 1950. After the U.S. removed its remaining troops in 1949 and announced in early 1950 that Korea was not part of its defense line in Asia, the Communists decided to act and invaded the south.

Participants were: North and South Korea, United States of America, Australia, New Zealand, China, Canada. France, Great Britain, Turkey, Belgium, Ethiopia, Colombia, Greece, South Africa, Luxembourg, Thailand, the Netherlands, and the Philippines. It was the first war in which a world organization played a major military role and it presented quite a challenge to the UN, which had only been in existence five years.

The war began June 25, 1950 and ended July 27, 1953. A truce was drawn up and an armistice agreement was signed ending the fighting. A permanent treaty of peace has never been signed and the country remains divided between the Communist North and the Democratic South. It was a very costly and bloody war destroying villages and homes, displacing and killing millions of people.

John F. Kennedy is widely remembered for his Inaugural Address in which the statement was made, "Ask not what your country can do for you – ask what you can do for your country." His campaign pledge was to get America moving again. During his brief presidency, his economic programs created the longest period of continuous expansion in the country since WW II. He wanted the U.S. to again take up the mission as the first country committed to the revolution of human rights. Through the Alliance for Progress and the Peace Corps, the hopes and idealism of the nation reached out to assist developing nations. He was deeply and passionately involved in the cause of equal rights for all Americans and he drafted new civil rights legislation. He also drafted plans for a broad attack on the systemic problems of privation and poverty. He believed the arts were critical to a society and instituted programs to support the arts.

In 1962, during the administration of President John F. Kennedy, Premier Khrushchev and the Soviets decided to install nuclear missiles on Cuba, as a protective measure for Cuba against an American invasion. In October, American U-2 spy planes photographed over Cuba what were identified as missile bases under construction. The decision in the White House was how to handle the situation without starting a war. The only recourse was removal of the missile sites and preventing more being set up. Kennedy announced that the U.S. had set up a "quarantine" of Soviet ships heading to Cuba. It was in reality a blockade but the word itself could not be used publicly as a blockade was actually considered an act of war.

Lyndon B. Johnson assumed the presidency after the assassination of Kennedy. His vision for America was called "A Great Society." He won support in Congress for the largest group of legislative programs in the history of the nation. These included programs Kennedy had been working on at the time of his death, including a new civil rights bill and a tax cut. He defined the "great society" as "a place where the meaning of man's life matches the marvels of man's labor." The legislation enacted during his administration included: an attack on disease, urban renewal, Medicare, aid to education, conservation and beautification, development of economically depressed areas, a war on poverty, voting rights for all, and control of crime and delinquency. Johnson managed an unpopular military action in Vietnam and encouraged the exploration of space. During his administration the Department of Transportation was formed and the first black, Thurgood Marshall, was nominated and confirmed to the Supreme Court.

Richard Nixon inherited racial unrest and the Vietnam War, from which he extracted the American military. His administration is probably best known for improved relations with both China and the USSR. However, the Watergate scandal shocked the country and led to his resignation. His major domestic achievements were: the appointment of conservative justices to the Supreme Court, new anti-crime legislation, a broad environmental program, revenue sharing legislation and the end of the draft.

Probably the highlight of the foreign policy of President Richard Nixon, after the end of the Vietnam War and withdrawal of troops, was his 1972 trip to China. When the Communists gained control of China in 1949, the policy of the U.S. government was refusal to recognize the Communist government. It regarded as the legitimate government of China to be that of Chiang Kai-shek, exiled on the island of Taiwan.

Gerald Ford was the first Vice President selected under the rules of Presidential accession passed in the 25th Amendment. The challenges that faced his administration were a depressed economy, inflation, energy shortages, and the need to champion world peace. Once inflation slowed and recession was the major economic problem, he instituted measures that would stimulate the economy. He tried to reduce the role of the federal government. He reduced business taxes and lessened the controls on business. His international focus was on preventing a major war in the Middle East. He negotiated with Russia limitations on nuclear weapons.

Jimmy Carter strove to make the government "competent and compassionate" in response to the American people and their expectations. The economic situation of the nation was intensely difficult when he took office. Although significant progress was made by his administration in creating jobs and decreasing the budget deficit, inflation and interest rates were nearly at record highs. There were several notable achievements: establishment of a national energy policy to deal with the energy shortage, decontrolling petroleum prices to stimulate production, civil service reform that improved government efficiency, deregulation of the trucking and airline industries, the creation of the Department of Education, negotiated the framework for peace in the Middle East, led in the establishment of diplomatic relations with China and reached a Strategic Arms Limitation Agreement with the Soviet Union. He expanded the national park system, supported the Social Security system, and appointed a record number of women and minorities to government jobs.

In 1983, in Lebanon, 241 American Marines were killed when an Islamic suicide bomber drove an explosive-laden truck into the United States Marines headquarters located at the airport in Beirut. This tragic event came as part of the unrest and violence between the Israelis and the Palestinian Liberation Organization (PLO) forces in southern Lebanon.

Iran's Ayatollah Khomeini's extreme hatred for the U.S. was the result of the 1953 overthrow of Iran's Mossadegh government, sponsored by the CIA. To make matters worse, the CIA proceeded to train the Shah's ruthless secret police force. So when the terminally ill exiled Shah was allowed into the U.S. for medical treatment, a fanatical mob stormed into the American embassy taking the 53 Americans as prisoners, supported and encouraged by Khomeini.

President Carter froze all Iranian assets in the U.S., set up trade restrictions, and approved a risky rescue attempt, which failed. He had appealed to the UN for aid in gaining release for the hostages and to European allies to join the trade embargo on Iran. Khomeini ignored UN requests for releasing the Americans and Europeans refused to support the embargo so as not to risk losing access to Iran's oil. American prestige was damaged and Carter's chances for reelection were doomed. The hostages were released on the day of Ronald Reagan's inauguration as President when Carter released Iranian assets as ransom.

Ronald Reagan introduced an innovative program that came to be known as the Reagan Revolution. The goal of this program was to reduce the reliance of the American people upon government. The Reagan administration restored the hope and enthusiasm of the nation with his many legislative accomplishments including economic growth stimulation, curbing inflation, increasing employment, and strengthening the national defense. He won Congressional support for a complete overhaul of the income tax code in 1986. By the time he left office there was prosperity in peacetime with no depression or recession. His foreign policy was "peace through strength." Reagan nominated Sandra Day O'Connor as the first female justice on the Supreme Court.

George H. W. Bush was committed to "traditional American values" and to making America a "kinder and gentler nation". During the Reagan administration, Bush held responsibility for anti-drug programs and Federal deregulation. When the Cold War ended and the Soviet Union broke apart, he supported the rise of democracy, but took a position of restraint toward the new nations. Bush also dealt with defense of the Panama Canal and Iraq's invasion of Kuwait, which led to the first Gulf War, known as Desert Storm. Although his international affairs record was strong, he was not able to turn around increased violence in the inner cities and a struggling economy.

William Clinton led the nation in a time of greater peace and economic prosperity than has been experienced at any other time in history. His domestic accomplishments include: the lowest inflation in 30 years, the lowest unemployment rate in modern days, the highest home ownership rate in history, lower crime rates in many places, and smaller welfare rolls. He proposed and achieved a balanced budget and achieved a budget surplus.

Civil Rights Movement

The phrase "the civil rights movement" generally refers to the nation-wide effort made by black people and those who supported them to gain equal rights to whites and to eliminate segregation. Discussion of this movement is generally understood in terms of the period of the 1950s and 1960s.

The **key people** in the civil rights movement are:

Rosa Parks -- a black seamstress from Montgomery Alabama who, in 1955, refused to give up her seat on the bus to a white man. This event is generally understood as the spark that lit the fire of the Civil Rights Movement. She has been generally regarded as the "mother of the Civil Rights Movement."

Martin Luther King, Jr.-- the most prominent member of the Civil Rights movement. King promoted nonviolent methods of opposition to segregation. The "Letter from Birmingham Jail" explained the purpose of nonviolent action as a way to make people notice injustice. He led the march on Washington in 1963, at which he delivered the "I Have a Dream" speech. He received the 1968 Nobel Prize for Peace.

James Meredith – the first African American to enroll at the University of Mississippi.

Emmett Till – a teenage boy who was murdered in Mississippi while visiting from Chicago. The crime of which he was accused was "whistling at a white woman in a store." He was beaten and murdered, and his body was dumped in a river. His two white abductors were apprehended and tried. They were acquitted by an all-white jury. After the acquittal, they admitted their guilt, but remained free because of double jeopardy laws.

Ralph Abernathy – a major figure in the Civil Rights Movement who succeeded Martin Luther King, Jr. as head of the Southern Christian Leadership Conference

Malcolm X – a political leader and part of the Civil Rights Movement. He was a prominent Black Muslim.

Stokeley Carmichael – one of the leaders of the Black Power movement that called for independent development of political and social institutions for blacks. Carmichael called for black pride and maintenance of black culture. He was head of the Student Nonviolent Coordinating Committee.

Key events of the Civil Rights Movement include:

Brown vs. Board of Education, 1954

The murder of Emmett Till, 1955

Rosa Parks and the Montgomery Bus Boycott, 1955-56 – After refusing to give up her seat on a bus in Montgomery, Alabama, Parks was arrested, tried, and convicted of disorderly conduct and violating a local ordinance. When word reached the black community a bus boycott was organized to protest the segregation of blacks and whites on public buses. The boycott lasted 381 days, until the ordinance was lifted.

Strategy shift to "direct action" – nonviolent resistance and civil disobedience, 1955 – 1965. This action consisted mostly of bus boycotts, sit-ins, freedom rides.

Formation of the Southern Christian Leadership Conference, 1957. This group, formed by Martin Luther King, Jr., John Duffy, Rev. C. D. Steele, Rev. T. J. Jemison, Rev. Fred Shuttlesworth, Ella Baker, A. Philip Randolph, Bayard Rustin and Stanley Levison. The group provided training and assistance to local efforts to fight segregation. Non-violence was its central doctrine and its major method of fighting segregation and racism.

The Desegregation of Little Rock, 1957. Following up on the decision of the Supreme Court in *Brown vs. Board of Education*, the Arkansas school board voted to integrate the school system. The NAACP chose Arkansas as the place to push integration because it was considered a relatively progressive Southern state. However, the governor called up the National Guard to prevent nine black students from attending Little Rock's Central High School.

Sit-ins – In 1960, students began to stage "sit-ins" at local lunch counters and stores as a means of protesting the refusal of those businesses to desegregate. The first was in Greensboro, NC. This led to a rash of similar campaigns throughout the South. Demonstrators began to protest parks, beaches, theaters, museums, and libraries. When arrested, the protesters made "jail-no-bail" pledges. This called attention to their cause and put the financial burden of providing jail space and food on the cities.

Freedom Rides – Activists traveled by bus throughout the deep South to desegregate bus terminals (required by federal law). These protesters undertook extremely dangerous protests. Many buses were firebombed, attacked by the KKK, and beaten. They were crammed into small, airless jail cells and mistreated in many ways. Key figures in this effort included John Lewis, James Lawson, Diane Nash, Bob Moses, James Bevel, Charles McDew, Bernard Lafayette, Charles Jones, Lonnie King, Julian Bond, Hosea Williams, and Stokeley Carmichael.

The Birmingham Campaign, 1963-64. A campaign was planned to use sit-in, kneel-ins in churches, and a march to the county building to launch a voter registration campaign. The City obtained an injunction forbidding all such protests. The protesters, including Martin Luther King, Jr., believed the injunction was unconstitutional, and defied it. They were arrested. While in jail, King wrote his famous Letter from Birmingham Jail. When the campaign began to falter, the "Children's Crusade" called students to leave school and join the protests. The events became news when more than 600 students were jailed. The next day more students joined the protest. The media was present, and broadcast to the nation, vivid pictures of fire hoses being used to knock down children and dogs attacking some of them. The resulting public outrage led the Kennedy administration to intervene. About a month later, a committee was formed to end hiring discrimination, arrange for the release of jailed protesters, and establish normative communication between blacks and whites. Four months later, the KKK bombed the Sixteenth Street Baptist Church, killing 4 girls.

The March on Washington, 1963. This was a march on Washington for jobs and freedom. It was a combined effort of all major civil rights organizations. The goals of the march were: meaningful civil rights laws, a massive federal works program, full and fair employment, decent housing, the right to vote, and adequate integrated education. It was at this march that Martin Luther King, Jr. made the famous "I Have a Dream" speech.

Mississippi Freedom Summer, 1964. Students were brought from other states to Mississippi to assist local activists in registering voters, teaching in "Freedom schools" and in forming the Mississippi Freedom Democratic Party. Three of the workers disappeared: they were murdered by the KKK. It took six weeks to find their bodies. The national uproar forced President Johnson to send in the FBI. Johnson was able to use public sentiment to effect passage in Congress of the Civil Rights Act of 1964.

Selma to Montgomery marches, 1965. Attempts to obtain voter registration in Selma, Alabama had been largely unsuccessful due to opposition from the city's sheriff. M.L. King came to the city to lead a series of marches. He and over 200 demonstrators were arrested and jailed. Each successive march was met with violent resistance by police. In March, a group of over 600 intended to walk from Selma to Montgomery (54 miles). News media were on hand when, 6 blocks into the march, state and local law enforcement officials attacked the marchers. They were driven back to Selma. National broadcast of the footage provoked a nation-wide response. President Johnson again used public sentiment to achieve passage of the Voting Rights Act of 1965. This law changed the political landscape of the South irrevocably.

Key policies, legislation and court cases included the following:

Brown v. Board of Education, 1954 – the Supreme Court declared that Plessy v. Ferguson was unconstitutional. This was the ruling that had established "Separate but Equal" as the basis for segregation. With this decision, the Court ordered immediate desegregation.

Civil Rights Act of 1964 – bars discrimination in public accommodations, employment and education

Voting Rights Act of 1965 – suspended poll taxes, literacy tests and other voter tests for voter registration.

Since 1941 a number of anti-discrimination laws have been passed by the Congress. These acts have protected the civil rights of several groups of Americans. These laws include:

- Fair Employment Act of 1941
- Civil Rights Act of 1964
- Immigration and Nationality Services Act of 1965
- Voting Rights Act of 1965
- Civil Rights Act of 1968
- Age Discrimination in Employment Act of 1967
- Age Discrimination Act of 1975
- Pregnancy Discrimination Act of 1978
- Americans with Disabilities Act of 1990
- Civil Rights Act of 1991
- Employment Non-Discrimination Act

"Minority rights" encompasses two ideas: the first is the normal individual rights of members of ethnic, racial, class, religious or sexual minorities; the second is collective rights of minority groups. Various civil rights movements have sought to guarantee that the individual rights of persons are not denied on the basis of being part of a minority group. The effects of these movements may be seen in guarantees of minority representation, affirmative action quotas, etc.
The disability rights movement was a successful effort to guarantee access to public buildings and transportation, equal access to education and employment, and equal protection under the law in terms of access to insurance, and other basic rights of American citizens. As a result of these efforts, public buildings and public transportation must be accessible to persons with disabilities. Discrimination in hiring or housing on the basis of disability is also illegal.

A "prisoners' rights" movement has been working for many years to ensure the basic human rights of persons incarcerated for crimes. Immigrant rights movements have provided for employment and housing rights, as well as preventing abuse of immigrants through hate crimes. In some states, immigrant rights movements have led to bi-lingual education and public information access. Another group movement to obtain equal rights is the lesbian, gay, bisexual and transgender social movement. This movement seeks equal housing, freedom from social and employment discrimination, and equal recognition of relationships under the law.

The women's rights movement is concerned with the freedoms of women as differentiated from broader ideas of human rights. These issues are generally different from those that affect men and boys because of biological conditions or social constructs. The rights the movement has sought to protect throughout history include:

- The right to vote
- The right to work
- The right to fair wages
- The right to bodily integrity and autonomy
- The right to own property
- The right to an education
- The right to hold public office
- Marital rights
- Parental rights
- Religious rights
- The right to serve in the military
- The right to enter into legal contracts

Some of the most famous leaders in the women's movement throughout American history are:

- Abigail Adams
- Susan B. Anthony
- Gloria E. Anzaldua
- Betty Friedan
- Olympe de Gouges
- Gloria Steinem
- Harriet Tubman
- Mary Wollstonecraft
- Virginia Woolf
- Germaine Greer

Skill 10.6 Identify individuals, events, and ideas that have influenced economic, social, and political institutions in Florida.

Florida's first human inhabitants were Indians, as shown by the burial mounds found in varying locations around the state. When Europeans eventually arrived, there were about 10,000 Indians belonging to as many as five major tribes. In the south, were the Calusa and the Tequesta; the Ais were found on the Atlantic coast in the central part of the peninsula; the Timucans were in the central and northeast area of the state; and in the northwest part of Florida dwelled the Apalachee.

Written records about life in Florida began with the arrival of the first European, Spanish explorer and adventurer Juan Ponce de León, in 1513, searching for the fabled fountain of youth. Sometime between April 2 and April 8, Ponce de León waded ashore on the northeast coast of Florida, possibly near present-day St. Augustine. He called the area la Florida, in honor of Pascua Florida ("feast of the flowers"), Spain's Easter time celebration. Other Europeans may have reached Florida earlier, but no firm evidence of such achievement has been found.

The Spanish flag flew over Florida for the next 250 years. Other Spanish explorers who spent time in Florida included Panfilo de Narvaez, Hernando de Soto (who became the first European to reach the Mississippi River), and Pedro Menendez de Aviles (who put an end to French attempts to settle in eastern Florida and founded the first permanent European settlement in the present-day United States, St. Augustine).

On another voyage in 1521, Ponce de León landed on the southwestern coast of the peninsula, accompanied by two hundred people, fifty horses, and numerous beasts of burden. His colonization attempt quickly failed because of attacks by native people. However, Ponce de León's activities served to identify Florida as a desirable place for explorers, missionaries, and treasure seekers.

In 1539, Hernando de Soto began another expedition in search of gold and silver on a long trek through Florida and what is now the southeastern United States. For four years, de Soto's expedition wandered, in hopes of finding the fabled wealth of the Indian people. De Soto and his soldiers camped for five months in the area now known as Tallahassee. Although De Soto died near the Mississippi River in 1542, survivors of his expedition eventually reached Mexico.

No great treasure troves awaited the Spanish conquistadores who explored Florida. However, their stories helped inform Europeans about Florida and its relationship to Cuba, Mexico, and Central and South America, from which Spain regularly shipped gold, silver, and other products. Groups of heavily laden Spanish vessels, called plate fleets, usually sailed up the Gulf Stream through the straits that parallel Florida's Keys. Aware of this route, pirates preyed on the fleets.

Hurricanes created additional hazards, sometimes wrecking the ships on the reefs and shoals along Florida's eastern coast.

In 1559, Tristán de Luna y Arellano led another attempt by Europeans to colonize Florida. He established a settlement at Pensacola Bay, but a series of misfortunes caused his efforts to be abandoned after two years.

Spain was not the only European nation that found Florida attractive. In 1562, the French Protestant Jean Ribault explored the area. Two years later, fellow Frenchman René Goulaine de Laudonnière established Fort Caroline at the mouth of the St. Johns River, near present-day Jacksonville.

These French adventurers prompted Spain to accelerate her plans for colonization. Pedro Menéndez de Avilés hastened across the Atlantic, his sights set on removing the French and creating a Spanish settlement. Menéndez arrived in 1565 at a place he called San Augustín (St. Augustine) and established the first permanent European settlement in what is now the United States. He accomplished his goal of expelling the French, attacking and killing all settlers except for non-combatants and Frenchmen who professed belief in the Roman Catholic faith. Menéndez captured Fort Caroline and renamed it San Mateo.

The French response came two years later, when Dominique de Gourgues recaptured San Mateo and made the Spanish soldiers stationed there pay with their lives. However, this incident did not halt the Spanish advance. Their pattern of constructing forts and Roman Catholic missions continued. Spanish missions established among native people soon extended across north Florida and as far north along the Atlantic coast as the area that we now call South Carolina.

The English, also eager to exploit the wealth of the Americas, increasingly came into conflict with Spain's expanding empire. In 1586 the English captain Sir Francis Drake looted and burned the tiny village of St. Augustine. However, Spanish control of Florida was not diminished.

In fact, as late as 1600, Spain's power over what is now the southeastern United States was unquestioned. When English settlers came to America, they established their first colonies well to the North—at Jamestown (in the present state of Virginia) in 1607 and Plymouth (in the present state of Massachusetts) in 1620. English colonists wanted to take advantage of the continent's natural resources and gradually pushed the borders of Spanish power southward into present-day southern Georgia. At the same time, French explorers were moving down the Mississippi River valley and eastward along the Gulf Coast.

The English colonists in the Carolina colonies were particularly hostile toward Spain. Led by Colonel James Moore, the Carolinians and their Creek Indian allies attacked Spanish Florida in 1702 and destroyed the town of St. Augustine. However, they could not capture the fort, named Castillo de San Marcos. Two years later, they destroyed the Spanish missions between Tallahassee and St. Augustine, killing many native people and enslaving many others. The French continued to harass Spanish Florida's western border and captured Pensacola in 1719, twenty-one years after the town had been established.

Spain's adversaries moved even closer when England founded Georgia in 1733, its southernmost continental colony. Georgians attacked Florida in 1740, assaulting the Castillo de San Marcos at St. Augustine for almost a month. While the attack was not successful, it did point out the growing weakness of Spanish Florida.

Britain gained control of Florida in 1763 in exchange for Havana, Cuba, which the British had captured from Spain during the Seven Years' War (1756–63). Spain evacuated Florida after the exchange, leaving the province virtually empty. At that time, St. Augustine was still a garrison community with fewer than five hundred houses, and Pensacola also was a small military town.

The British had ambitious plans for Florida. First, it was split into two parts: East Florida, with its capital at St. Augustine; and West Florida, with its seat at Pensacola. British surveyors mapped much of the landscape and coastline and tried to develop relations with a group of Indian people who were moving into the area from the North. The British called these people of Creek Indian descent **Seminolies or Seminoles**. Britain attempted to attract white settlers by offering land on which to settle and help for those who produced products for export. Given enough time, this plan might have converted Florida into a flourishing colony, but British rule lasted only twenty years.

The two Florida's remained loyal to Great Britain throughout the War for American Independence (1776–83). However, Spain—participating indirectly in the war as an ally of France—captured Pensacola from the British in 1781. In 1784, it regained control of the rest of Florida as part of the peace treaty that ended the American Revolution. The second period of Spanish control lasted until 1821. On one of those military operations, in 1818, General **Andrew Jackson** made a foray into Florida. Jackson's battles with Florida's Indian people later would be called the First Seminole War. When the British evacuated Florida, Spanish colonists as well as settlers from the newly formed United States came pouring in. Many of the new residents were lured by favorable Spanish terms for acquiring property, called land grants. Others who came were escaped slaves, trying to reach a place where their U.S. masters had no authority and effectively could not reach them. Instead of becoming more Spanish, the two Florida's increasingly became more "American."

Finally, after several official and unofficial U.S. military expeditions into the territory, Spain formally ceded Florida to the United States in 1821, according to terms of the Adams-Onís Treaty.

Andrew Jackson returned to Florida in 1821 to establish a new territorial government on behalf of the United States. What the U.S. inherited was a wilderness sparsely dotted with settlements of native Indian people, African Americans, and Spaniards.

As a territory of the United States, Florida was particularly attractive to people from the older Southern plantation areas of Virginia, the Carolinas, and Georgia, who arrived in considerable numbers. After territorial status was granted, the two Florida's were merged into one entity with a new capital city in Tallahassee. Established in 1824, Tallahassee was chosen because it was halfway between the existing governmental centers of St. Augustine and Pensacola.

As Florida's population increased through immigration, so did pressure on the federal government to remove the Indian people from their lands. The Indian population was made up of several groups—primarily, the Creek and the Miccosukee people; and many African American refugees lived with the Indians. Indian removal was popular with white settlers because the native people occupied lands that white people wanted and because their communities often provided a sanctuary for runaway slaves from northern states.

Among Florida's native population, the name of Osceola has remained familiar after more than a century and a half. Osceola was a Seminole war leader who refused to leave his homeland in Florida. Seminoles, already noted for their fighting abilities, won the respect of U.S. soldiers for their bravery, fortitude, and ability to adapt to changing circumstances during the Second Seminole War (1835–42). This war, the most significant of the three conflicts between Indian people and U.S. troops in Florida, began over the question of whether Seminoles should be moved westward across the Mississippi River into what is now Oklahoma.

Under President Andrew Jackson, the U.S. government spent $20 million and the lives of many U.S. soldiers, Indian people, and U.S. citizens to force the removal of the Seminoles. In the end, the outcome was not as the federal government had planned. Some Indians migrated "voluntarily." Some were captured and sent west under military guard; and others escaped into the Everglades, where they made a life for themselves away from contact with whites.

Today, reservations occupied by Florida's Indian people exist at Immokalee, Hollywood, Brighton (near the city of Okeechobee), and along the Big Cypress Swamp. In addition to the Seminole people, Florida also has a separate Miccosukee tribe.

By 1840 white Floridians were concentrating on developing the territory and gaining statehood. The population had reached 54,477 people, with African American slaves making up almost one-half of the population. Steamboat navigation was well established on the Apalachicola and St. Johns Rivers, and railroads were planned.

Florida now was divided informally into three areas: East Florida, from the Atlantic Ocean to the Suwannee River; Middle Florida, between the Suwannee and the Apalachicola Rivers; and West Florida, from the Apalachicola to the Perdido River. The southern area of the territory (south of present-day Gainesville) was sparsely settled by whites. The territory's economy was based on agriculture. Plantations were concentrated in Middle Florida, and their owners established the political tone for all of Florida until after the Civil War.

Florida became the twenty-seventh state in the United States on March 3, 1845. **William D. Moseley** was elected the new state's first governor, and David Levy Yulee, one of Florida's leading proponents for statehood, became a U.S. Senator. By 1850, the population had grown to 87,445, including about 39,000 African American slaves and 1,000 free blacks.

The slavery issue began to dominate the affairs of the new state. Most Florida voters—who were white males, aged twenty-one years or older—did not oppose slavery. However, they were concerned about the growing feeling against it in the North, and during the 1850s they viewed the new anti-slavery Republican Party with suspicion. Shortly after Lincoln's election, a special convention drew up an ordinance that allowed Florida to secede from the Union on January 10, 1861. Within several weeks, Florida joined other southern states to form the Confederate States of America.

During the Civil War, Florida was not ravaged as several other southern states were. Indeed, no decisive battles were fought on Florida soil. While Union forces occupied many coastal towns and forts, the interior of the state remained in Confederate hands.

Florida provided an estimated 15,000 troops and significant amounts of supplies—including salt, beef, pork, and cotton—to the Confederacy, but more than 2,000 Floridians, both African American and white, joined the Union army. Confederate and foreign merchant ships slipped through the Union navy blockade along the coast, bringing in needed supplies from overseas ports. Tallahassee was the only southern capital east of the Mississippi River to avoid capture during the war, spared by southern victories at Olustee (1864) and Natural Bridge (1865). Ultimately, the South was defeated, and federal troops occupied Tallahassee on May 10, 1865.

Before the Civil War, Florida had been well on its way to becoming another of the southern cotton states. Afterward, the lives of many residents changed. The ports of Jacksonville and Pensacola again flourished due to the demand for lumber and forest products to rebuild the nation's cities. Those who had been slaves were declared free. Plantation owners tried to regain prewar levels of production by hiring former slaves to raise and pick cotton. However, such programs did not work well, and much of the land came under cultivation by tenant farmers and sharecroppers, both African American and white.

Beginning in 1868, the federal government instituted a congressional program of "reconstruction" in Florida and the other southern states. During this period, Republican officeholders tried to enact sweeping changes, many of which were aimed at improving conditions for African Americans.

At the time of the 1876 presidential election, federal troops still occupied Florida. The state's Republican government and recently enfranchised African American voters helped to put Rutherford B. Hayes in the White House. However, Democrats gained control of enough state offices to end the years of Republican rule and prompt the removal of federal troops the following year. A series of political battles in the state left African Americans with little voice in their government.

During the final quarter of the nineteenth century, large-scale commercial agriculture in Florida, especially cattle-raising, grew in importance. Industries such as cigar manufacturing took root in the immigrant communities of the state. Large phosphate deposits were discovered, citrus groves were planted and cultivated, swamplands were drained, and **Henry Plant** and **Henry Flagler** built railroad lines opening the state for further growth and development.

Potential investors became interested in enterprises that extracted resources from the water and land. These extractive operations were as widely diverse as sponge harvesting in Tarpon Springs and phosphate mining in the southwestern part of the state. The Florida citrus industry grew rapidly, despite occasional freezes and economic setbacks. The development of industries throughout the state prompted the construction of roads and railroads on a large scale. Jobs created by the state helped develop the natural resources; private industries' construction of paper mills resulted in conservation programs for the state's forests and to help preserve perishable fruits and vegetables, cooling plants were built. To aid farmers, cooperative markets and cooperative farm groups were established.

Beginning in the 1870s, residents from northern states visited Florida as tourists to enjoy the state's natural beauty and mild climate. Steamboat tours on Florida's winding rivers were a popular attraction for these visitors.

The growth of Florida's transportation industry had its origins in 1855, when the state legislature passed the Internal Improvement Act. Like legislation passed by several other states and the federal government, Florida's act offered cheap or free public land to investors, particularly those interested in transportation. The act, and other legislation like it, had its greatest effect in the years between the end of the Civil War and the beginning of World War I. During this period, many railroads were constructed throughout the state by companies owned by Henry Flagler and Henry B. Plant, who also built lavish hotels near their railroad lines. The Internal Improvement Act stimulated the initial efforts to drain the southern portion of the state in order to convert it to farmland.

These development projects had far-reaching effects on the agricultural, manufacturing, and extractive industries of late nineteenth-century Florida. The citrus industry especially benefited, since it was now possible to pick oranges in south Florida; put them on a train heading north; and eat them in Baltimore, Philadelphia, or New York in less than a week.

In 1898, national attention focused on Florida, as the Spanish-American War began. The port city of Tampa served as the primary staging area for U.S. troops bound for the war in Cuba. Many Floridians supported the Cuban peoples' desire to be free of Spanish colonial rule.

By the turn of the century, Florida's population and per capita wealth were increasing rapidly; the potential of the "Sunshine State" appeared endless. By the end of World War I, land developers had descended on this virtual gold mine. With more Americans owning automobiles, it became commonplace to vacation in Florida. Many visitors stayed on, and exotic projects sprang up in southern Florida. Some people moved onto land made from drained swamps. Others bought canal-crossed tracts through what had been dry land. The real estate developments quickly attracted buyers, and land in Florida was sold and resold. Profits and prices for many developers reached inflated levels.

The early 1900s saw the settlement and economic development of south Florida, especially along the East Coast. A severe depression in 1926, the1926 and 1928 hurricanes, and the Great Depression of the 1930s burst the economic bubble.

During World War II, many military bases were constructed as part of the vital defense interests of the state and nation. After the War, prosperity and population grew resulting in tourism becoming the most important industry and it remains so today. Continued agricultural development and industrial expansion also played an important role in the state's economy. Such industries as paper and paper products, chemicals, electronics, and ocean and space exploration gave a tremendous boost to the labor force. From the 1950s to the present day, The Kennedy Space Center at Cape Canaveral has been a space and rocket center with the launching of orbiting satellites, manned space flights and today's space shuttles.

Florida faces serious problems Since many immigrants from places like Cuba and Haiti have entered the state by the thousands since the early 1960s, both legally and illegally. Increasing population growth puts a strain on public and social services and pollution and overbuilding has threatened the environment. Tremendous growth occurred during the 1970s with the opening of Walt Disney World. With other tourist attractions and the resulting need for hotels, restaurants, and a larger airport, Orlando leads Tampa, Miami, Jacksonville, Fort Lauderdale, and West Palm Beach as the fastest growing region of the state. Although the state's economy continues to rely mainly on tourism and the citrus industry, stable growth remains consistent due to the expanding trade, financial, and service industries.

For more information on the subject of Florida's history, consult the following:

http://www.floridahistory.org
http://www.floridamemory.com

Perhaps the most wide-ranging yet personal civil rights case to come about in the last decade is ***Bush* v. *Palm Beach County Canvassing Board***. Presidential candidate George W. Bush sued to invalidate the recount that had begun in the wake of Bush's narrow victory over Al Gore in Florida. Bush claimed, among other things, that his Fifth Amendment due process rights were violated by the various decisions made in the wake of the close vote counts. The result was a decision by the Court to stop all recounting and declare Bush the winner. This was not a classical civil rights case, *per se*, but it was one that argued as such and involved the sort of protection that had been argued under previous Fifth and Fourteenth Amendment cases.

COMPETENCY 11.0 KNOWLEDGE OF GEOGRAPHY

Skill 11.1 Identify the five themes of geography and the specific terms for each theme

Every point on Earth has a specific *location* that is determined by an imaginary grid of lines denoting latitude and longitude. Parallels of latitude measure distances north and south of the line called the Equator. Meridians of longitude measure distances east and west of the line called the Prime Meridian. Geographers use latitude and longitude to pinpoint a place's absolute, or exact, location.

To know the absolute location of a place is only part of the story. It is also important to know how that place is related to other places—in other words, to know that place's relative location. Relative location deals with the interaction that occurs between and among places. It refers to the many ways—by land, by water, even by technology—that places are connected.

All places have characteristics that give them meaning and character and distinguish them from other places on earth. Geographers describe places by their physical and human characteristics. Physical characteristics include such elements as animal life. Human characteristics of the landscape can be noted in architecture, patterns of livelihood, land use and ownership, town planning, and communication and transportation networks. Languages, as well as religious and political ideologies, help shape the character of a place. Studied together, the physical and human characteristics of places provide clues to help students understand the nature of places on the earth.

The environment means different things to different people, depending on their cultural backgrounds and technological resources. In studying human/environment interaction, geographers look at all the effects—positive and negative—that occur when people interact with their surroundings. Sometimes a human act, such as damming a river to prevent flooding or to provide irrigation, requires consideration of the potential consequences. The construction of Hoover Dam on the Colorado River, for example, changed the natural landscape, but it also created a reservoir that helps provide water and electric power for the arid Southwest. Studying the consequences of human/environment interaction helps people plan and manage the environment responsibly.

People interact with other people, places, and things almost every day of their lives. They travel from one place to another; they communicate with each other; and they rely upon products, information, and ideas that come from beyond their immediate environment.

Students should be able to recognize where resources are located, who needs them, and how they are transported over the earth's surface. The theme of movement helps students understand how they themselves are connected with, and dependent upon, other regions, cultures, and people in the world.

A basic unit of geographic study is the region, an area on the earth's surface that is defined by certain unifying characteristics. The unifying characteristics may be physical, human, or cultural. In addition to studying the unifying characteristics of a region, geographers study how a region changes over times. Using the theme of regions, geographers divide the world into manageable units for study.

(From nationalgeographic.com)

Skill 11.2 Interpret and use maps and other graphic representations, tools, and technologies to acquire, process, and report information from a spatial perspective.

We use **illustrations** of various sorts because it is often easier to demonstrate a given idea visually instead of orally. Sometimes it is even easier to do so with an illustration than a description. This is especially true in the areas of education and research because humans are visually stimulated. Among the more common illustrations used are various types of **maps, graphs and charts**.

The major problem of all maps comes about because most maps are flat and the Earth is sphere shaped. In order to put the earth's features onto a map they must be stretched in some way. This stretching is called **distortion.**

Distortion does not mean that maps are wrong it simply means that they are not perfect representations of the Earth or its parts. **Cartographers,** or mapmakers, understand the problems of distortion. They try to design maps so that there is as little distortion as possible in the maps.

The process of putting the features of the Earth onto a flat surface is called **projection**. All maps are really map projections. There are many different types. Each one deals in a different way with the problem of distortion. Map projections are made in a number of ways. Some are done using complicated mathematics. However, the basic ideas behind map projections can be understood by looking at the three most common types:

(1) **Cylindrical Projections** - These are done by taking a cylinder of paper and wrapping it around a globe. A light is used to project the globe's features onto the paper. Distortion is least where the paper touches the globe. For example, suppose that the paper was wrapped so that it touched the globe at the equator, the map from this projection would have just a little distortion near the equator. However, in moving north or south of the equator, the distortion would increase as the distance from the equator increased. The most widely used cylindrical projection is the **Mercator Projection.** Gerardus Mercator, a Flemish mapmaker, first developed it in 1569.

(2) **Conical Projections** - The name for these maps come from the fact that the projection is made onto a cone of paper. The cone is made so that it touches a globe at the base of the cone only. It can also be made so that it cuts through part of the globe in two different places. Again, there is the least distortion where the paper touches the globe. If the cone touches at two different points, there is some distortion at both of them. Conical projections are most often used to map areas in the **middle latitudes**. Maps of the United States are most often conical projections. This is because most of the country lies within these latitudes.

(3) **Flat-Plane Projections** - These are made with a flat piece of paper. It touches the globe at one point only. Areas near this point show little distortion. Flat-plane projections are often used to show the areas of the north and south poles. One such flat projection is called a **Gnomonic Projection**. On this kind of map all meridians appear as straight lines, Gnomonic projections are useful because any straight line drawn between points on it forms a **Great-Circle Route**.

Great-Circle Routes can best be described by thinking of a globe and when using the globe the shortest route between two points on it can be found by simply stretching a string from one point to the other. However, if the string was extended in reality, so that it took into effect the globe's curvature, it would then make a great-circle. A Great-Circle is any circle that cuts a sphere, such as the globe, into two equal parts. Because of distortion, most maps do not show great-circle routes as straight lines, Gnomonic projections, however, do show the shortest distance between the two places as a straight line, because of this they are valuable for navigation. They are called Great-Circle Sailing Maps.

To properly analyze a given map one must be familiar with the various parts and symbols that most modern maps use. For the most part, this is standardized, with different maps using similar parts and symbols, these can include:

The Title - All maps should have a title, just like all books should. The title tells you what information is to be found on the map.

The Legend - Most maps have a legend. A legend tells the reader about the various symbols that are used on that particular map and what the symbols represent, (also called a ***map key***).

The Grid - A grid is a series of lines that are used to find exact places and locations on the map. There are several different kinds of grid systems in use; however, most maps use the longitude and latitude system known as the **Geographic Grid System**.

Directions - Most maps have some directional system to show which way the map is being presented. Often on a map, a small compass will be present, with arrows showing the four basic directions, north, south, east, and west.

The Scale - This is used to show the relationship between units of measurement on the map versus the real world measure on the Earth. Maps are drawn to many different scales. Some maps show a lot of detail for a small area. Others show a greater span of distance, whichever is being used one should always be aware of just what scale is being used. For instance the scale might be something like 1 inch = 10 miles for a small area or for a map showing the whole world it might have a scale in which 1 inch = 1,000 miles. The point is that one must look at the map key in order to see what units of measurements the map is using.

Maps have four main properties. They are (1) the size of the areas shown on the map, (2) the shapes of the areas, (3) consistent scales, and (4) straight line directions. A map can be drawn so that it is correct in one or more of these properties. No map can be correct in all of them.

Equal areas - In an equal area map, the meridians and parallels are drawn so that the areas shown have the same proportions as they do on the Earth. For example, Greenland is about one-eighteenth the size of South America, thus it will be shown as one-eighteenth the size on an equal area map. The **Mercator projection** is an example of a map that does not have equal areas. In it, Greenland appears to be about the same size of South America. This is because the distortion is very bad at the poles and Greenland lies near the North Pole.

Conformality - A second map property is conformality, or correct shapes. There are no maps which can show very large areas of the earth in their exact shapes. Only globes can really do that, however Conformal Maps are as close as possible to true shapes. The United States is often shown by a Lambert Conformal Conic Projection Map.

Consistent Scales - Many maps attempt to use the same scale on all parts of the map. Generally, this is easier when maps show a relatively small part of the earth's surface. For example, a map of Florida might be a Consistent Scale Map. Generally maps showing large areas are not consistent-scale maps. This is so because of distortion. Often such maps will have two scales noted in the key. One scale, for example, might be accurate to measure distances between points along the Equator. Another might be then used to measure distances between the North Pole and the South Pole.

Maps showing physical features often try to show information about the elevation or ***relief*** of the land. ***Elevation*** is the distance above or below the sea level. The elevation is usually shown with colors, for instance, all areas on a map which are at a certain level will be shown in the same color.

Relief Maps - Show the shape of the land surface, flat, rugged, or steep. Relief maps usually give more detail than simply showing the overall elevation of the land's surface. Relief is also sometimes shown with colors, but another way to show relief is by using ***contour lines***. These lines connect all points of a land surface which are the same height surrounding the particular area of land.
Thematic Maps - These are used to show more specific information, often on a single ***theme***, or topic. Thematic maps show the distribution or amount of something over a certain given area. Things such as population density, climate, economic information, cultural, political information, etc.

Information can be gained looking at a map that might take hundreds of words to explain otherwise. Maps reflect the great variety of knowledge covered by political science. To show such a variety of information maps are made in many different ways. Because of this variety, maps must be understood in order to make the best sense of them.

Spatial organization is a description of how things are grouped in a given space. In geographical terms, this can describe people, places, and environments anywhere and everywhere on Earth.

The most basic form of spatial organization for people is where they live. The vast majority of people live near other people, in villages and towns and cities and settlements. These people live near others in order to take advantage of the goods and services that naturally arise from cooperation. These villages and towns and cities and settlements are, to varying degrees, near bodies of water. Water is a staple of survival for every person on the planet and is also a good source of energy for factories and other industries, as well as a form of transportation for people and goods.

Another way to describe where people live is by the **geography** and **topography** around them. The vast majority of people on the planet live in areas that are very hospitable. People do live in inhospitable regions such as the Himalayas and in the Sahara, but the populations in those areas are small compared to the plains of China, India, Europe, and the United States. People naturally want to live where they can find the resources to survive, and world population patterns reflect this.

We can examine the spatial organization of the places where people live. For example, in a city, where are the factories and heavy industry buildings? Are they near airports or train stations? Are they on the edge of town, near major roads? What about housing developments? Are they near these industries, or are they far away? Where are the other industry buildings? Where are the schools and hospitals and parks? What about the police and fire stations? How close are homes to each of these things? Towns and especially cities are routinely organized into neighborhoods, so that each house or home is near to most things that its residents might need on a regular basis. This means that large cities have multiple schools, hospitals, grocery stores, fire stations, etc.

Related to this is the distance between cities, towns, villages, or settlements. In certain parts of the United States and definitely in many countries in Europe, the population settlement patterns achieve megalopolis standards, with no clear boundaries from one town to the next. Other, more sparsely populated areas have towns that are few and far between and have relatively few people in them. Some exceptions to this exist, of course, like oases in the deserts; for the most part, however, population centers tend to be relatively near one another or at least near smaller towns.

Most places in the world are in some manner close to agricultural land as well. Food makes the world go round and some cities are more agriculturally inclined than others. Rare is the city, however, that grows absolutely no crops. The kind of food grown is almost entirely dependent on the kind of land available and the climate surrounding that land. Rice doesn't grow well in the desert, for instance, nor do bananas grow well in snowy lands. Certain crops are easier to transport than others and the ones that aren't are usually grown near ports or other areas of export.

The one thing that changes all of these things, of course, is the airplane. Flight has made possible global commerce and goods exchange on a level never before seen. Foods from all around the world can be kept fresh enough to sell in markets nearly everywhere. The same is true of medicine.

Skill 11.3 Identify the factors that influence the selection of a location for a specific activity.

Ecology is the study of how living organisms interact with the physical aspects of their surroundings or environment, including soil, water, air, and other living things. ***Biogeography*** is the study of how the surface features of the earth – form, movement, and climate – affect living things.

Three levels of environmental understanding are critical:

1. *An ecosystem* is a community of any size consisting of a physical environment and the organisms that live within it.

2. *A biome* is a large area of land with characteristic climate, soil, and mixture of plants and animals. Biomes are made up of groups of ecosystems. Major biomes are: desert, chaparral, savanna, tropical rain forest, temperate grassland, temperate deciduous forest, taiga, and tundra.

3. *A habitat* is the set of surroundings within which members of a species normally live. Elements of the habitat include soil, water, predators, and competitors.

Within habitats interactions between members of the species occur. These interactions occur between members of the same species and between members of different species. Interaction tends to be of three types:

1. *Competition.* Competition occurs between members of the same species or between members of different species for resources required to continue life, to grow, or to reproduce. For example, competition for acorns can occur between squirrels or it can occur between squirrels and woodpeckers. One species can either push out or cause the demise of another species if it is better adapted to obtain the resource. When a new species is introduced into a habitat, the result can be a loss of the native species and/or significant change to the habitat. For example, the introduction of the Asian plant Kudzu into the American South has resulted in the destruction of several species because Kudzu grows and spreads very quickly and smothers everything in its path.

2. *Predation.* Predators are organisms that live by hunting and eating other organisms. The species best suited for hunting other species in the habitat will be the species that survives. Larger species that have better hunting skills reduce the amount of prey available for smaller and/or weaker species. This affects both the amount of available prey and the diversity of species that are able to survive in the habitat.

3. *Symbiosis* is a condition in which two organisms of different species are able to live in the same environment over an extended period of time without harming one another. In some cases one species may benefit without harming the other. In other cases both species benefit.

Different organisms are by nature best suited for existence in particular environments. When an organism is displaced to a different environment or when the environment changes for some reason, its ability to survive is determined by its ability to *adapt* to the new environment. Adaptation can take the form of structural change, physiological change, or behavioral modification.

Biodiversity refers to the variety of species and organisms, as well as the variety of habitats available on the earth. Biodiversity provides the life-support system for the various habitats and species. The greater the degree of biodiversity, the more species and habitats will continue to survive.

When population and migration change, climate changes, or natural disasters disrupt the delicate balance of a habitat or an ecosystem, species either adapt or become extinct.

Natural changes can occur that alter habitats – floods, volcanoes, storms, earthquakes. These changes can affect the species that exist within the habitat, either by causing extinction or by changing the environment in a way that will no longer support the life systems. Climate changes can have similar effects. Inhabiting species, however, can also alter habitats, particularly through migration. Human civilization, population growth, and efforts to control the environment can have many negative effects on various habitats. Humans change their environments to suit their particular needs and interests. This can result in changes that result in the extinction of species or changes to the habitat itself. For example, deforestation damages the stability of mountain surfaces. One particularly devastating example is in the removal of the grasses of the Great Plains for agriculture. Tilling the ground and planting crops left the soil unprotected. Sustained drought dried out the soil into dust. When windstorms occurred, the topsoil was stripped away and blown as far away as the Atlantic Ocean.

By nature, people are essentially social creatures. They generally live in communities or settlements of some kind. Settlements are the centers of culture, political structure, education, and the management of resources. The relative placement of these settlements or communities are shaped by the proximity to natural resources, the movement of raw materials, the production of finished products, the availability of a work force, and the delivery of finished products. The composition of communities will, at least to some extent, be determined by shared values, language, culture, religion, and subsistence.

Settlements begin in areas that offer the natural resources to support life – food and water. With the ability to manage the environment one finds a concentration of populations. With the ability to transport raw materials and finished products, comes mobility. With increasing technology and the rise of industrial centers, comes a migration of the workforce.

Cities are the major hubs of human settlement. Almost half of the population of the world now lives in cities. These percentages are much higher in developed regions. Established cities continue to grow. The fastest growth, however, is occurring in developing areas. In some regions there are "metropolitan areas" made up of urban and sub-urban areas. In some places cities and urban areas have become interconnected into "megalopoli" (e.g., Tokyo-Kawasaki-Yokohama).

The concentrations of populations and the divisions of these areas among various groups that constitute the cities can differ significantly. North American cities are different from European cities in terms of shape, size, population density, and modes of transportation. While in North America, the wealthiest economic groups tend to live outside the cities, the opposite is true in Latin American cities.

There are significant differences among the cities of the world in terms of connectedness to other cities. While European and North American cities tend to be well linked both by transportation and communication connections, there are other places in the world in which communication between the cities of the country may be inferior to communication with the rest of the world.

Rural areas tend to be less densely populated due to the needs of agriculture. More land is needed to produce crops or for animal husbandry than for manufacturing, especially in a city in which the buildings tend to be taller. Rural areas, however, must be connected via communication and transportation in order to provide food and raw materials to urban areas.

Skill 11.4 Interpret statistics that show how places differ in their human and physical characteristics.

Demography is the branch of science of statistics most concerned with the social well being of people. **Demographic tables** may include: (1) Analysis of the population on the basis of age, parentage, physical condition, race, occupation and civil position, giving the actual size and the density of each separate area. (2) Changes in the population as a result of birth, marriage, and death. (3) Statistics on population movements and their effects and their relations to given economic, social and political conditions. (4) Statistics of crime, illegitimacy and suicide. (5) Levels of education and economic and social statistics.

Such information is also similar to that area of science known as **vital statistics** and as such is indispensable in studying social trends and making important legislative, economic, and social decisions. Such demographic information is gathered from census and registrar reports and the like. State laws require vital information to be kept by physicians, attorneys, funeral directors, members of the clergy, and similar professional people. In the United States such demographic information is compiled, kept and published by the Public Health Service of the United States Department of Health, Education, and Welfare.

The most important element of this information is the so-called **rate**, which customarily represents the average of births and deaths for a unit of 1000 population over a given calendar year. These general rates are called **crude rates**, which are then sub-divided into *sex, color, age, occupation, locality, etc.* They are then known as **refined rates**.

In examining **statistics** and the sources of statistical data one must also be aware of the methods of statistical information gathering. For instance, there are many good sources of raw statistical data. Books such as *The Statistical Abstract of the United States,* published by the United States Chamber of Commerce, *The World Fact Book,* published by the Central Intelligence Agency or *The Monthly Labor Review* published by the United States Department of Labor are excellent examples that contain much raw data. Many similar publications are readily available from any library, or from the government itself. However, knowing how that data and information was gathered is at least equally as important as the figures themselves.

By having knowledge of statistical language and methodology, one is able to gauge the usefulness of any given piece of data presented. Therefore we must first understand just what statistics are and what they can and cannot, tell us.

Simply put, statistics is the mathematical science that deals with the collection, organization, presentation, and analysis of various forms of numerical data and with the problems such as interpreting and understanding such data. The raw materials of statistics are sets of numbers obtained from enumerations or measurements collected by various methods of extrapolation, such as census taking, interviews, and observations.

In collecting any such statistical information and data, care and adequate precautions must always be taken in order to assure that the knowledge obtained is complete and accurate. It is also important to be aware of just how much data is necessary to collect in order to establish the idea that is attempting to be formulated. One important idea to understand is that statistics usually deal with a specific **model**, **hypothesis**, or **theory** that is being attempted to be proven. One should be aware that a theory can never actually be proved correct it can only really be corroborated. (**Corroboration** means that the data presented is more consistent with this theory than with any other theory, so it makes sense to use this theory.) One should also be aware that **correlation** (the joint movement of various data points) does not infer **causation** (the change in one of those data points caused the other data points to change). It is important that one take these aspects into account so that one can be in a better position to appreciate what the collected data is really saying

Once collected, data must then be arranged, tabulated, and presented to permit ready and meaningful analysis and interpretation. Often tables, charts or graphs will be used to present the information in a concise easy to see manner, with the information sometimes presented in raw numerical order as well. **Tests of reliability** are used, bearing in mind the manner in which the data has been collected and the inherent biases of any artificially created model to be used to explain real world events. Indeed the methods used and the inherent biases and reasons actually for doing the study by the individual(s) involved, must never be discounted.

So one should always remember that statistical methods can and have been used to prove or disprove historically just about anything. While statistics are a good and important empirical research tool, too much reliance on them alone, without any other information or data, can be misleading and statistics should only be used with other empirical methods of research. As the saying goes, *"Figures don't lie, but liars always figure.* "

Skill 11.5 Identify how events of the past affect present human characteristics of places, such as wealth and poverty, land tenure, exploitation, colonialism, and independence.

Human communities subsisted initially as gatherers – gathering berries, leaves, etc. With the invention of tools it became possible to dig for roots, hunt small animals, and catch fish from rivers and oceans. Humans observed their environments and soon learned to plant seeds and harvest crops. As people migrated to areas in which game and fertile soil were abundant, communities began to develop. When people had the knowledge to grow crops and the skills to hunt game, they began to understand division of labor. Some of the people in the community tended to agricultural needs while others hunted game.

As habitats attracted larger numbers of people, environments became crowded and there was competition. Experience led to the development of skills and of knowledge that make the work easier. Farmers began to develop new plant species and hunters began to protect animal species from other predators for their own use. This ability to manage the environment led people to settle down, to guard their resources, and to manage them.

Camps soon became villages and villages became year-round settlements. Animals were domesticated and gathered into herds that met the needs of the village. With the settled life it was no longer necessary to travel light. Pottery was developed for storing and cooking food.

By 8000 BCE, culture was beginning to evolve in these villages. Agriculture was developed for the production of grain crops, which led to a decreased reliance on wild plants. Domesticating animals for various purposes decreased the need to hunt wild game. Life became more settled. It was then possible to turn attention to such matters as managing water supplies, producing tools, making cloth, etc. There was both the social interaction and the opportunity to reflect upon existence. Mythologies arose and various kinds of belief systems. Rituals arose that re-enacted the mythologies that gave meaning to life.

As farming and animal husbandry skills increased, the dependence upon wild game and food gathering declined. With this change came the realization that a larger number of people could be supported on the produce of farming and animal husbandry.

Two things seem to have come together to produce cultures and civilizations: a society and culture based on agriculture and the development of centers of the community with literate social and religious structures. The members of these hierarchies then managed water supply and irrigation, ritual and religious life, and exerted their own right to use a portion of the goods produced by the community for their own subsistence in return for their management.

Sharpened skills, development of more sophisticated tools, commerce with other communities, and increasing knowledge of their environment, the resources available to them, and responses to the needs to share good, order community life, and protect their possessions from outsiders led to further division of labor and community development.

As trade routes developed and travel between cities became easier, trade led to specialization. Trade enables a people to obtain the goods they desire in exchange for the goods they are able to produce. This, in turn, leads to increased attention to refinements of technique and the sharing of ideas. The knowledge of a new discovery or invention provides knowledge and technology that increases the ability to produce goods for trade.

As each community learns the value of the goods it produces and improves its ability to produce the goods in greater quantity, industry is born.

The Agricultural Revolution, initiated by the invention of the plow, led to a thoroughgoing transformation of human society by making large-scale agricultural production possible and facilitating the development of agrarian societies. During the period during which the plow was invented, the wheel, numbers, and writing were also invented. Coinciding with the shift from hunting wild game to the domestication of animals, this period was one of dramatic social and economic change.

Numerous changes in lifestyle and thinking accompanied the development of stable agricultural communities. Rather than gathering a wide variety of plants as hunter-gatherers, agricultural communities become dependent on a limited number of plants or harvest crops. Subsistence becomes vulnerable to the weather and dependent upon planting and harvesting times. Agriculture also required a great deal of physical labor and the development of a sense of discipline. Agricultural communities become sedentary or stable in terms of location. This makes the construction of dwellings appropriate. These tend to be built relatively close together, creating villages or towns. Stable communities also free people from the need to carry everything with them and the move from hunting ground to hunting ground. This facilitates the invention of larger, more complex tools. As new tools are envisioned and developed it begins to make sense to have some specialization within the society.

Skills begin to have greater value, and people begin to do work on behalf of the community that utilizes their particular skills and abilities. Settled community life also gives rise to the notion of wealth. It is now possible to keep possessions.

The Industrial Revolution of the eighteenth and nineteenth centuries resulted in even greater changes in human civilization and even greater opportunities for trade, increased production, and the exchange of ideas and knowledge.

The first phase of the Industrial Revolution (1750-1830) saw the mechanization of the textile industry, vast improvements in mining, with the invention of the steam engine, and numerous improvements in transportation, with the development and improvement of turnpikes, canals, and the invention of the railroad.

The second phase (1830-1910) resulted in vast improvements in a number of industries that had already been mechanized through such inventions as the Bessemer steel process and the invention of steam ships. New industries arose as a result of the new technological advances, such as photography, electricity, and chemical processes. New sources of power were harnessed and applied, including petroleum and hydroelectric power. Precision instruments were developed and engineering was launched. It was during this second phase that the industrial revolution spread to other European countries, to Japan, and to the United States.

The direct results of the Industrial Revolution, particularly as they affected industry, commerce, and agriculture, included:

- Enormous increase in productivity
- Huge increase in world trade
- Specialization and division of labor
- Standardization of parts and mass production
- Growth of giant business conglomerates and monopolies
- A new revolution in agriculture facilitated by the steam engine, machinery, chemical fertilizers, processing, canning, and refrigeration

The political results included:

- Growth of complex government by technical experts
- Centralization of government, including regulatory administrative agencies
- Advantages to democratic development, including extension of franchise to the middle class, and later to all elements of the population, mass education to meet the needs of an industrial society, the development of media of public communication, including radio, television, and cheap newspapers
- Dangers to democracy included the risk of manipulation of the media of mass communication, facilitation of dictatorial centralization and totalitarian control, subordination of the legislative function to administrative directives, efforts to achieve uniformity and conformity, and social impersonalization.

The economic results were numerous:

- The conflict between free trade and low tariffs and protectionism
- The issue of free enterprise against government regulation
- Struggles between labor and capital, including the trade-union movement
- The rise of socialism
- The rise of the utopian socialists
- The rise of Marxian or scientific socialism

The social results of the Industrial Revolution include:

- Increase of population, especially in industrial centers
- Advances in science applied to agriculture, sanitation and medicine
- Growth of great cities
- Disappearance of the difference between city dwellers and farmers
- Faster tempo of life and increased stress from the monotony of the work routine
- The emancipation of women
- The decline of religion
- Rise of scientific materialism
- Darwin's theory of evolution

Increased mobility produced a rapid diffusion of knowledge and ideas. Increased mobility also resulted in wide-scale immigration to industrialized countries. Cultures clashed and cultures melded.

Skill 11.6 Identify ways in which people adapt to an environment through the production and use of clothing, food, and shelter

Food, clothing and shelter are the three basic needs of human beings. As early humans increased in number and moved into new parts of the world, they had to adapt to their new environments by adopting new ways to obtain these needs.

Early humans hunted animals and gathered food from wild sources. Taking their basic support from nature like this required them to move with their food sources. Game animals might migrate, and seasonal food sources might require groups to travel to the regions where the food could be had. To take full advantage of varying areas where food could be found, portable methods of shelter were developed such as the Native American teepee or the Mongolian yurt. These shelters could be carried from place to place, allowing a greater range.

Clothing allowed humans to adapt to the wider range of climates they discovered as they moved from place to place, both in their annual circuit and as they moved into new wilderness areas that had lower average temperatures.

Clothing protects the body from cold, sun exposure, and the elements. In very hot climates, little or no clothing was worn by early humans. The advantages of having an extra layer of protection were soon realized, however, and basic coverings were fashioned from animal skin. Foot coverings were developed to protect the feet from rough ground and sharp rocks. In colder climates, clothing was crucial for survival. Animal pelts with the fur attached provided warmth. Foot coverings could also be fur-lined or stuffed with grass. Mittens or gloves kept vulnerable fingers warm and protected.

As humans moved away from hunting and gathering into agricultural pursuits, other materials for clothing became available. Wool-bearing animals were domesticated and plant fibers were woven into cloth. During the Industrial Revolution, cloth weaving methods took a great stride forward, greatly expanding the use of woven cloth clothing.

Agriculture also expanded the types of food that were available, Grains and fruits could be grown in place and meat could be had from domesticated animals. Not all climates are suitable for all crops, however, and humans have had to adapt varieties and methods to successfully produce food.

Just as their environment shaped their needs, so did the environment provide the means to meet those needs. For thousands of years, food and shelter had to be obtained from local resources, or from resources that could be grown locally. Human technology has reached a point now, however, that we are able to supply food to any location on the planet and adapt clothing and shelter to any environment, even outer space.

Skill 11.7 Identify physical, cultural, economic, and political reasons for the movement of people in the world, nation, or state.

Human communities subsisted initially as gatherers – gathering berries, leaves, etc. With the invention of tools it became possible to dig for roots, hunt small animals, and catch fish from rivers and oceans. Humans observed their environments and soon learned to plant seeds and harvest crops. As people migrated to areas in which game and fertile soil were abundant, communities began to develop. When people had the knowledge to grow crops and the skills to hunt game, they began to understand division of labor. Some of the people in the community tended to agricultural needs while others hunted game.

As habitats attracted larger numbers of people, environments became crowded and there was competition. The concept of division of labor and sharing of food soon came, in more heavily populated areas, to be managed. Groups of people focused on growing crops while others concentrated on hunting. Experience led to the development of skills and of knowledge that make the work easier. Farmers began to develop new plant species and hunters began to protect animal species from other predators for their own use. This ability to manage the environment led people to settle down, to guard their resources, and to manage them.

Camps soon became villages. Villages became year-round settlements. Animals were domesticated and gathered into herds that met the needs of the village. With the settled life it was no longer necessary to "travel light." Pottery was developed for storing and cooking food.

By 8000 BCE, culture was beginning to evolve in these villages. Agriculture was developed for the production of grain crops, which led to a decreased reliance on wild plants. Domesticating animals for various purposes decreased the need to hunt wild game. Life became more settled. It was then possible to turn attention to such matters as managing water supplies, producing tools, making cloth, etc. There was both the social interaction and the opportunity to reflect upon existence. Mythologies arose and various kinds of belief systems. Rituals arose that re-enacted the mythologies that gave meaning to life.

As farming and animal husbandry skills increased, the dependence upon wild game and food gathering declined. With this change came the realization that a larger number of people could be supported on the produce of farming and animal husbandry.

Two things seem to have come together to produce cultures and civilizations: a society and culture based on agriculture and the development of centers of the community with literate social and religious structures. The members of these hierarchies then managed water supply and irrigation, ritual and religious life, and exerted their own right to use a portion of the goods produced by the community for their own subsistence in return for their management.

Sharpened skills, development of more sophisticated tools, commerce with other communities, and increasing knowledge of their environment, the resources available to them, and responses to the needs to share good, order community life, and protect their possessions from outsiders led to further division of labor and community development.

As trade routes developed and travel between cities became easier, trade led to specialization. Trade enables a people to obtain the goods they desire in exchange for the goods they are able to produce. This, in turn, leads to increased attention to refinements of technique and the sharing of ideas. The knowledge of a new discovery or invention provides knowledge and technology that increases the ability to produce goods for trade.

Industry is born as each community learns the value of the goods it produces and improves its ability to produce the goods in greater quantity.

Skill 11.8 Identify physical and cultural characteristics that define and differentiate the major regions of the world.

The earth's surface is made up of 70% water and 30% land. Physical features of the land surface include mountains, hills, plateaus, valleys, and plains. Other minor landforms include deserts, deltas, canyons, mesas, basins, foothills, marshes and swamps. Earth's water features include oceans, seas, lakes, rivers, and canals.

Mountains are landforms with rather steep slopes at least 2,000 feet or more above sea level. Mountains are found in groups called mountain chains or mountain ranges. At least one range can be found on six of the earth's seven continents. North America has the Appalachian and Rocky Mountains; South America the Andes; Asia the Himalayas; Australia the Great Dividing Range; Europe the Alps; and Africa the Atlas, Ahaggar, and Drakensburg Mountains.

Hills are elevated landforms rising to an elevation of about 500 to 2000 feet. They are found everywhere on earth including Antarctica where they are covered by ice.

Plains are areas of flat or slightly rolling land, usually lower than the landforms next to them. Sometimes called lowlands (and sometimes located along **seacoasts)** they support the majority of the world's people. Some are found inland and many have been formed by large rivers. This results in extremely fertile soil for successful cultivation of crops and numerous large settlements of people. In North America, the vast plains areas extend from the Gulf of Mexico north to the Arctic Ocean and between the Appalachian and Rocky Mountains. In Europe, rich plains extend east from Great Britain into central Europe on into the Siberian region of Russia. Plains in river valleys are found in China (the Yangtze River valley), India (the Ganges River valley), and Southeast Asia (the Mekong River valley).

Valleys are land areas found between hills and mountains. Some have gentle slopes containing trees and plants; others have steep walls and are referred to as canyons. One example is Arizona's Grand Canyon of the Colorado River.

Deserts are large dry areas of land receiving ten inches or less of rainfall each year. Among the larger deserts are Africa's large Sahara Desert, the Arabian Desert on the Arabian Peninsula, and the desert Outback covering roughly one third of Australia.

Deltas are areas of lowlands formed by soil and sediment deposited at the mouths of rivers. The soil is generally very fertile and most fertile river deltas are important crop-growing areas. One well-known example is the delta of Egypt's Nile River, known for its production of cotton.

Mesas are the flat tops of hills or mountains usually with steep sides. Sometimes plateaus are also called mesas. Basins are considered to be low areas drained by rivers or low spots in mountains. Foothills are generally considered a low series of hills found between a plain and a mountain range. Marshes and swamps are wet lowlands providing habitat for such plants as rushes and reeds.

Oceans are the largest bodies of water on the planet. The four oceans of the earth are the **Atlantic Ocean**, one-half the size of the Pacific and separating North and South America from Africa and Europe; the **Pacific Ocean**, covering almost one-third of the entire surface of the earth and separating North and South America from Asia and Australia; the **Indian Ocean**, touching Africa, Asia, and Australia; and the ice-filled **Arctic Ocean,** extending from North America and Europe to the North Pole. The waters of the Atlantic, Pacific, and Indian Oceans also touch the shores of Antarctica.

Seas are smaller than oceans and are surrounded by land. Some examples include the Mediterranean Sea found between Europe, Asia, and Africa; and the Caribbean Sea, touching the West Indies, South and Central America. A **lake** is a body of water surrounded by land. The Great Lakes in North America are a good example.

Rivers, considered a nation's lifeblood, usually begin as very small streams, formed by melting snow and rainfall, flowing from higher to lower land, emptying into a larger body of water, usually a sea or an ocean. Examples of important rivers for the people and countries affected by and/or dependent on them include the Nile, Niger, and Zaire Rivers of Africa; the Rhine, Danube, and Thames Rivers of Europe; the Yangtze, Ganges, Mekong, Hwang He, and Irrawaddy Rivers of Asia; the Murray-Darling in Australia; and the Orinoco in South America. River systems are made up of large rivers and numerous smaller rivers or tributaries flowing into them. Examples include the vast Amazon Rivers system in South America and the Mississippi River system in the United States.

Canals are man-made water passages constructed to connect two larger bodies of water. Famous examples include the **Panama Canal** across Panama's isthmus connecting the Atlantic and Pacific Oceans and the **Suez Canal** in the Middle East between Africa and the Arabian Peninsula connecting the Red and Mediterranean Seas.

Climate is average weather or daily weather conditions for a specific region or location over a long or extended period of time. Studying the climate of an area includes information gathered on the area's monthly and yearly temperatures and its monthly and yearly amounts of precipitation. In addition, a characteristic of an area's climate is the length of its growing season. Four reasons for the different climate regions on the earth are differences in:

- Latitude,
- The amount of moisture,
- Temperatures in land and water, and
- The earth's land surface.

There are many different climates throughout the earth. It is most unusual if a country contains just one kind of climate. Regions of climates are divided according to latitudes:

0 - 23 1 /2 degrees are the "low latitudes"
23 1/2 - 66 1/2 degrees are the "middle latitudes"
66 1/2 degrees to the Poles are the "high latitudes"

The **low latitudes** are comprised of the rainforest, savanna, and desert climates. The tropical rainforest climate is found in equatorial lowlands and is hot and wet. There is sun, extreme heat and rain--everyday. Although daily temperatures rarely rise above 90 degrees F, the daily humidity is always high, leaving everything sticky and damp. North and south of the tropical rainforests are the tropical grasslands called "savannas," the "lands of two seasons"--a winter dry season and a summer wet season. Further north and south of the tropical grasslands or savannas are the deserts. These areas are the hottest and driest parts of the earth receiving less than 10 inches of rain a year. These areas have extreme temperatures between night and day. After the sun sets, the land cools quickly dropping the temperature as much as 50 degrees F.

The **middle latitudes** contain the Mediterranean, humid-subtropical, humid-continental, marine, steppe, and desert climates. Lands containing the Mediterranean climate are considered "sunny" lands found in six areas of the world: lands bordering the Mediterranean Sea, a small portion of southwestern Africa, areas in southern and southwestern Australia, a small part of the Ukraine near the Black Sea, central Chile, and Southern California. Summers are hot and dry with mild winters. The growing season usually lasts all year and what little rain falls are during the winter months. The Mediterranean climate is often found between 30 and 40 degrees north and south latitude on the western coasts of countries.

The humid **subtropical climate** is found north and south of the tropics and is very moist. The areas having this type of climate are found on the eastern side of the continents and include Japan, mainland China, Australia, Africa, South America, and the United States, where warm ocean currents are found. The winds that blow across these currents bring in warm moist air all year round. Long, warm summers, short, mild winters and a long growing season allow for different crops to be grown several times a year. All contribute to the productivity of this climate type which supports more people than any of the other climates.

The **marine climate** is found in Western Europe, the British Isles, the U.S. Pacific Northwest, the western coast of Canada and southern Chile, along with southern New Zealand and southeastern Australia. A common characteristic of these lands is that they are either near water or surrounded by it. The ocean winds are wet and warm bringing a mild, rainy climate to these areas. In the summer, the daily temperatures average at or below 70 degrees F. During the winter, because of the warming effect of the ocean waters, the temperatures rarely fall below freezing.

In northern and central United States, northern China, south central and southeastern Canada, and the western and southeastern parts of the former Soviet Union is found the **"climate of four seasons,"** the **humid continental climate**. Cold winters, hot summers, and enough rainfall to grow a variety of crops are the major characteristics of this climate. In areas where the humid continental climate is found are some of the world's best farmlands as well as important activities such as trading and mining. Differences in temperatures throughout the year are determined by the distance a place is inland, away from the coasts.

The **steppe or prairie climate** is located in the interiors of large continents like Asia and North America. These dry flatlands are far from ocean breezes and are called prairies or the Great Plains in Canada and the United States and steppes in Asia. Although the summers are hot and the winters are cold as in the humid continental climate, the big difference is rainfall. In the steppe climate, rainfall is light and uncertain, 10 to 20 inches a year mainly in spring and summer and is considered normal. Where rain is more plentiful, grass grows; in areas of less, the steppes or prairies gradually become deserts.

Desert climates are found in the Gobi Desert of Asia, central and western Australia, southwestern United States, and in the smaller deserts in Pakistan, Argentina, and Africa south of the Equator.

The two major climates found in the high latitudes are **"tundra"** and **"taiga."** The word "tundra" meaning "marshy plain" is a Russian word and aptly describes the climatic conditions in the northern areas of Russia, Europe, and Canada. Winters are extremely cold and very long. Most of the year the ground is frozen, but becomes mushy during the very short summer months. Surprisingly, less snow falls in the area of the tundra than in the eastern part of the United States. However, due to the harshness of the extreme cold, very few people live there and no crops can be raised. Despite having a small human population, many plants and animals are found there.

The **"taiga"** is the northern forest region and is located south of the tundra. In fact, the Russian word "taiga" means 'forest." The world's largest forestlands are found here along with vast mineral wealth and forbearing animals. The climate is extreme that very few people live here, not being able to raise crops due to the extremely short growing season. The winter temperatures are colder and the summer temperatures are hotter than those in the tundra are because the taiga climate region is farther from the waters of the Arctic Ocean. The taiga is found in the northern parts of Russia, Sweden, Norway, Finland, Canada, and Alaska with most of their lands covered with marshes and swamps.

In certain areas of the earth there exists a type of climate unique to areas with high mountains, usually different from their surroundings. This type of climate is called a **"vertical climate"** because the temperatures, crops, vegetation, and human activities change and become different as one ascends the different levels of elevation. At the foot of the mountain, a hot and rainy climate is found with the cultivation of many lowland crops. As one climbs higher, the air becomes cooler, the climate changes sharply and different economic activities change, such as grazing sheep and growing corn. At the top of many mountains, snow is found year round.

COMPETENCY 12.0 KNOWLEDGE OF GOVERNMENT, ECONOMICS, AND OTHER SOCIAL SCIENCES

Skill 12.1 Identify various societies' purposes and methods for establishing and maintaining governments.

Government ultimately began as a form of protection. A strong person, usually one of the best warriors or someone who had the support of many strong men, assumed command of a people or a city or a land. The power to rule those people rested in his hands. (The vast majority of rulers throughout history have been male.) Laws existed, but as the pronouncements and decision of the ruler were often not written down, they were inconsistent. Religious leaders had a strong hand in governing the lives of people, and in many instances the political leader was also the primary religious figure.

The idea of government by more than one person or more than just a handful came developed first in Greece, then Rome and spread to other areas of the world. Even though more people were involved, the purpose of government had not changed. These governments still existed to keep the peace and protect their people from encroachments by both inside and outside forces.

Through the Middle Ages and on into even the twentieth century, many countries still had **monarchs** as their heads of state. These monarchs made and upheld laws but the laws were still designed to protect the welfare of the people and the state.

In the modern day, people are subject to **laws** made by many levels of government. Local governments such as city and county bodies are allowed to pass ordinances covering certain local matters, such as property taxation, school districting, civil infractions and business licensing. These local bodies have perhaps the least political power in the governmental hierarchy, but being small and relatively accessible, they are often the level at which many citizens become directly involved with government. Funding for local governments often comes from property and sales taxes.

State governments in the United States are mainly patterned after the federal government, with an elected legislative body, a judicial system, and a governor who oversees the executive branch. Like the federal government, state governments derive their authority from **constitutions**. State legislation applies to all residents of that state, and local laws must conform. State government funding is frequently from state income tax and sales taxes.

The national or federal government of the United States derives its power from the US Constitution and has three branches, the legislative, executive and judicial. The federal government exists to make national policy and to legislate matters that affect the residents of all states, and to settle matters between states. National income tax is the primary source for federal funding.

The US Constitution also provides the federal government with the authority to make treaties and enter agreements with foreign countries, creating a body of international law. While there is no authoritative international government, organizations such as the United Nations, the European Union and other smaller groups exist to promote economic and political cooperation between nations.

Skill 12.2 Demonstrate knowledge of the rights and responsibilities of a citizen in the world, nation, state, and/or community.

Citizenship in a democracy bestows on an individual certain rights, foremost being the right to participate in one's own government. Along with these rights come responsibilities, including the responsibility of a citizen to participate.

The most basic form of participation is the vote. Those who have reached the age of 18 in the US are eligible to vote in public elections. With this right comes the responsibility to be informed before voting, and not to sell or otherwise give away one's vote. Citizens are also eligible to run for public office. Along with the right to run for office comes the responsibility to represent the electors as fairly as possible and to perform the duties expected of a government representative.

In the United States, citizens are guaranteed the right to free speech; the right to express an opinion on public issues. In turn, citizens have the responsibility to allow others to speak freely. At the community level, this might mean speaking at a city council hearing while allowing others with different or opposing viewpoints to have their say without interruption or comment.

The US Constitution also guarantees freedom of religion. This means that the government may not impose an official religion on its citizens, and that people are free to practice their religion. Citizens are also responsible for allowing those of other religions to practice freely without obstruction. Occasionally, religious issues will be put before the public at the state level in the form of ballot measures or initiatives. To what extent it should be acceptable for religious beliefs to be expressed in a public setting, such as a public school, is an issue that has been debated recently.

In making decisions on matters like these, the citizen is expected to take responsibility to become informed of the issues involved and to make his vote based on his own opinion. Being informed of how one's government works and what the effects of new legislation will be is an essential part of being a good citizen.

The US Constitution also guarantees that all citizens be treated equally by the law. In addition, federal and state laws make it a crime to discriminate against citizens based on their sex, race, religion and other factors. To ensure that all people are treated equally, citizens have the responsibility to follow these laws.

These rights and responsibilities are essentially the same whether one is voting in a local school board race, for the passage of a new state law, or for the President of the United States. Being a good citizen means exercising one's own rights while allowing others to do the same.

Almost all representative democracies in the world guarantee similar rights to their citizens, and expect them to take similar responsibilities to respect the rights of others. As a citizen of the world one is expected to respect the rights of other nations, and the people of those nations, in the same way.

Skill 12.3 Identify major concepts of the U.S. Constitution.

Within a few months from the adoption of the Articles of Confederation, it became apparent that there were serious defects in the system of government established for the new republic. There was a need for change that would create a national government with adequate powers to replace the Confederation, which was actually only a league of sovereign states. In 1786, an effort to regulate interstate commerce ended in what is known as the **Annapolis Convention**. Because only five states were represented, this Convention was not able to accomplish definitive results. The debates, however, made it clear that a government with as little authority as the government established by the Confederation could not regulate foreign and interstate commerce. Congress was therefore asked to call a convention to provide a constitution that would address the emerging needs of the new nation. The convention met under the presidency of George Washington, with fifty-five of the sixty-five appointed members present. A constitution was written in four months.

The Constitution of the United States is the fundamental law of the republic. It is a precise, formal, written document of the *extraordinary*, or *supreme*, type of constitution. The founders of the Union established it as the highest governmental authority. There is no national power superior to it. The foundations were so broadly laid as to provide for the expansion of national life and to make it an instrument which would last for all time. To maintain its stability, the framers created a difficult process for making any changes to it. No amendment can become valid until it is ratified by three-fourths of all of the states.

The Constitution binds the states in a governmental unity in everything that affects the welfare of all. At the same time, it recognizes the right of the people of each state to independence of action in matters that relate only to them. Since the Federal Constitution is the law of the land, all other laws must conform to it.

The debates conducted during the Constitutional Congress represent the issues and the arguments that led to the compromises in the final document. The debates also reflect the concerns of the Founding Fathers that the rights of the people be protected from abrogation by the government itself and the determination that no branch of government should have enough power to continually dominate the others. There is, therefore, a system of checks and balances.

Bill Of Rights - The first ten amendments to the United States Constitution dealing with civil liberties and civil rights. They were written mostly by James Madison. They are in brief:

1. Freedom of Religion.
2. Right To Bear Arms.
3. Security from the quartering of troops in homes.
4. Right against unreasonable search and seizures.
5. Right against self-incrimination.
6. Right to trial by jury, right to legal council.
7. Right to jury trial for civil actions.
8. No cruel or unusual punishment allowed.
9. These rights shall not deny other rights the people enjoy.
10. Powers not mentioned in the Constitution shall be retained by the states or the people.

An amendment is a change or addition to the United States Constitution. Two-thirds of both houses of Congress must propose and then pass one. Or two-thirds of the state legislatures must call a convention to propose one and then it must be ratified by three-fourths of the state legislatures. To date there are only 27 Amendments to the Constitution that have passed. An amendment may be used to cancel out a previous one such as the 18th Amendment (1919) known as Prohibition, canceled by the 21st Amendment (1933). Amending the United States Constitution is an extremely difficult thing to do.

An Amendment must start in Congress. One or more lawmakers propose it, and then each house votes on it in turn. The Amendment must have the support of two-thirds of each house separately in order to progress on its path to ratification. (It should be noted here that this two-thirds need be only two-thirds of a quorum, which is just a simple majority. Thus, it is theoretically possible for an Amendment to be passed and be legal even though it has been approved by less than half of one or both houses.)

The final and most difficult step for an Amendment is the ratification by state legislatures. A total of three-fourths of the states must approve the Amendment. Approvals need be only by a simple majority, but the number of states that must approve the Amendment is 38. Hundreds of Amendments have been proposed through the years, but only 27 have become part of the Constitution.

A key element in some of those failures has been the time limit that Congress has the option to put on Amendment proposals. A famous example of an Amendment that got close but did not reach the threshold before the deadline expired was the Equal Rights Amendment, which was proposed in 1972 but which couldn't muster enough support for passage, even though its deadline was extended from seven to 10 years.

The first ten Amendments are called the Bill of Rights and were approved shortly after the Constitution was ratified. The 11th and 12th Amendments were ratified around the turn of the nineteenth century and, respectively, voided foreign suits against states and revised the method of presidential election. The 13th, 14th, and 15th Amendments were passed in succession after the end of the Civil War. Slavery was outlawed by the 13th Amendment. The 14th & 15th Amendments provided for equal protection and for voting rights without consideration of skin color, respectively.

The first twentieth century Amendment was Number 16, which provided for a federal income tax. Providing for direct election to the Senate was the 17th Amendment. Up till then, Senators were appointed by state leaders, not elected by the public at large.

The 18th Amendment prohibited the use or sale of alcohol across the country. The long battle for voting rights for women ended in success with the passage of the 19th Amendment. The date for the beginning of terms for the President and the Congress was changed from March to January by the 20th Amendment. With the 21st Amendment came the only instance in which an Amendment was repealed. In this case, it was the 18th Amendment and its prohibition of alcohol consumption or sale.

The 22nd Amendment limited the number of terms that a President could serve to two. Presidents since George Washington had followed Washington's practice of not running for a third term; this changed when Franklin D. Roosevelt ran for re-election a second time, in 1940. He was re-elected that time and a third time, too, four years later. He didn't live out his fourth term, but he did convince Congress and most of the state legislature that some sort of term limit should be in place.

The 23rd Amendment provided for representation of Washington, D.C., in the Electoral College. The 24th Amendment prohibited poll taxes, which people had had to pay in order to vote.

Presidential succession is the focus of the 25th Amendment, which provides a blueprint of what to do if the president is incapacitated or dies while in office. The 26th Amendment lowered the legal voting age for Americans from 21 to 18. The 27th Amendment prohibits members of Congress from substantially raising their own salaries. This Amendment was one of 12 originally proposed in the late eighteenth century. Ten of those 12 became the Bill of Rights, and one has yet to become law.

A host of potential Amendments have made news headlines in recent years. A total of six Amendments have been proposed by Congress and passed muster in both houses but have not been ratified by enough state legislatures. The aforementioned Equal Rights Amendment is one. Another one, which would grant the District of Columbia full voting rights equivalent to states, has not passed; like the Equal Rights Amendment, its deadline has expired. A handful of others remain on the books without expiration dates, including an amendment to regulate child labor.

Skill 12.4 Compare and contrast the various political systems in the world, such as democracy, constitutional monarchy, socialism, and communism.

A person who lives in a democratic society theoretically is granted a wide spectrum of civil rights. Among these very important rights in the United States are:

- the right to speak out in public
- the right to pursue any religion
- the right for a group of people to gather in
- the right *not* to have soldiers stationed in your home
- the right *not* to be forced to testify against yourself in a court of law
- the right to a speedy and public trial by a jury of your peers
- the right *not* to be the victim of cruel and unusual punishment
- and the right to avoid unreasonable search and seizure of your person, your house, and your vehicle

The average citizen of an authoritarian country has little if any of these rights and must watch his or her words and actions to avoid disobeying one of the many oppressive laws that help the government govern its people.

In both democratic and authoritarian societies citizens can serve in government. They can even run for election and can be voted in by their peers. One large difference exists, however: In an authoritarian society, the members of government will most likely be of the same political party. A country with this setup, like China, will have a government that includes representatives elected by the Chinese people, but all of those elected representatives will belong to the Communist Party, which runs the government and the country. When the voters vote, they see only Communist Party members on the ballot. In many cases, only one candidate is on the ballot for each office. China chooses its head of government through a meeting of the Party leaders. In effect, the Party is higher in the governmental hierarchy than the leader of the country. Efforts to change this governmental structure and practice are clamped down and discouraged.

On the other side of this spectrum is the citizen of the democratic society, who can vote for whomever he or she wants to and can run for any office he or she wants to. On those ballots will appear names and political parties that run the spectrum, including the Communist Party. Theoretically, *any* political party can get its candidates on ballots locally, statewide, or nationwide; varying degrees of effort have to be put in to do this, of course. Building on the First Amendment freedom to peaceful assembly, American citizens can have political party meetings, fund-raisers, and even conventions without fearing reprisals from the Government.

Anarchism - Political movement believing in the elimination of all government and its replacement by a cooperative community of individuals. Sometimes it has involved political violence such as assassinations of important political or governmental figures. The historical banner of the movement is a black flag.

Communism - A belief as well as a political system, characterized by the ideology of class conflict and revolution, one party state and dictatorship, repressive police apparatus, and government ownership of the means of production and distribution of goods and services. A revolutionary ideology that preaches the eventual overthrow of all other political orders and the establishment of a world Communist government and is basically the same as Marxism. The historical banner of the movement is a red flag and variation of stars, hammer and sickles, representing the various types of workers.

Dictatorship - The rule by an individual or small group of individuals (Oligarchy) that centralizes all political control in itself and enforces its will with a terrorist police force.

Fascism - A belief as well as a political system, opposed ideologically to Communism, though similar in basic structure, with a one party state, centralized political control and a repressive police system. It tolerates private ownership of the means of production, though it maintains tight overall control. Central to its belief is the idolization of the Leader, a "Cult of the Personality," and most often an expansionist ideology. Examples have been German Nazism and Italian Fascism.

Monarchy - The rule of a nation by a Monarch, (a non-elected usually hereditary leader), most often a king or queen. It may or may not be accompanied by some measure of democratic open institutions and elections at various levels. A modern example is Great Britain, where it is called a Constitutional Monarchy.

Parliamentary System - A system of government with a legislature, usually involving a multiplicity of political parties and often coalition politics. There is division between the head of state and head of government. Head of government is usually known as a Prime Minister who is also usually the head of the largest party. The head of government and cabinet usually both sit and vote in the parliament. Head of state is most often an elected president, (though in the case of a constitutional monarchy, like Great Britain, the sovereign may take the place of a president as head of state). A government may fall when a majority in parliament votes "no confidence" in the government.

Presidential System - A system of government with a legislature, can involve few or many political parties, no division between head of state and head of government. The President serves in both capacities. The President is elected either by direct or indirect election. A President and cabinet usually do not sit or vote in the legislature and the President may or may not be the head of the largest political party. A President can thus rule even without a majority in the legislature. He can only be removed from office before an election for major infractions of the law.

Socialism - Political belief and system in which the state takes a guiding role in the national economy and provides extensive social services to its population. It may or may not own outright means of production, but even where it does not, it exercises tight control. It usually promotes democracy, (Democratic Socialism), though the heavy state involvement produces excessive bureaucracy and usually inefficiency. Taken to an extreme it may lead to Communism as government control increases and democratic practice decreases. Ideologically the two movements are very similar in both belief and practice.

Skill 12.5 Differentiate the structures and functions of U.S. federal, state, and local governments.

At the United States federal level

Legislative – Article I of the Constitution established the legislative or law-making branch of the government called the Congress. It is made up of two houses, the House of Representatives and the Senate. Voters in all states elect the members who serve in each respective House of Congress. The Legislative branch is responsible for making laws, raising and printing money, regulating trade, establishing the postal service and federal courts, approving the President's appointments, declaring war and supporting the armed forces. The Congress also has the power to change the Constitution itself, and to *impeach* (bring charges against) the President. Charges for impeachment are brought by the House of Representatives, and the trial is in the Senate.

Executive – Article II of the Constitution created the Executive branch of the government, headed by the President, who leads the country, recommends new laws, and can veto bills passed by the Legislative branch. As the chief of state, the President is responsible for carrying out the laws of the country and the treaties and declarations of war passed by the Legislative branch. The President also appoints federal judges and is commander-in-chief of the military when it is called into service. Other members of the Executive branch include the Vice-President, also elected, and various cabinet members as he might appoint: ambassadors, presidential advisors, members of the armed forces, and other appointed and civil servants of government agencies, departments and bureaus. Though the President appoints them, they must be approved by the Legislative branch.

Judicial – Article III of the Constitution established the Judicial branch of government headed by the Supreme Court. The Supreme Court has the power to rule that a law passed by the legislature, or an act of the Executive branch is illegal and unconstitutional. Citizens, businesses, and government officials can in an appeal capacity, ask the Supreme Court to review a decision made in a lower court if someone believes that the ruling by a judge is unconstitutional. The Judicial branch also includes lower federal courts known as federal district courts that have been established by the Congress. These courts try lawbreakers and review cases referred from other courts.

Powers delegated to the federal government:

1. To tax.
2. To borrow and coin money
3. To establish postal service
4. To grant patents and copyrights
5. To regulate interstate & foreign commerce
6. To establish courts
7. To declare war
8. To raise and support the armed forces
9. To govern territories
10. To define and punish felonies and piracy on the high seas
11. To fix standards of weights and measures
12. To conduct foreign affairs

Powers reserved to the states:

1. To regulate intrastate trade
2. To establish local governments
3. To protect general welfare
4. To protect life and property
5. To ratify amendments
6. To conduct elections
7. To make state and local laws

<u>Concurrent powers of the federal government and states</u>.
1. Both Congress and the states may tax
2. Both may borrow money
3. Both may charter banks and corporations
4. Both may establish courts
5. Both may make and enforce laws
6. Both may take property for public purposes
7. Both may spend money to provide for the public welfare

<u>Implied powers of the federal government</u>.
1. To establish banks or other corporations implied from delegated powers to tax, borrow, and to regulate commerce
2. To spend money for roads, schools, health, insurance, etc. implied from powers, to establish post roads, to tax to provide for general welfare and defense, and to regulate commerce
3. To create military academies, implied from powers to raise and support an armed force
4. To locate and generate sources of power and sell surplus implied from powers to dispose of government property, commerce, and war powers
5. To assist and regulate agriculture implied from power to tax and spend for general welfare and regulate commerce

State governments are mirror images of the federal government, with a few important exceptions: Governors are not technically commanders in chief of armed forces; state supreme court decisions can be appealed to federal courts; terms of state representatives and senators vary; judges, even of the state supreme courts, are elected by popular vote; governors and legislators have term limits that vary by state.

Local governments vary widely across the country, although none of them has a judicial branch per se. Some local governments consist of a city council, of which the mayor is a member and has limited powers; in other cities, the mayor is the head of the government and the city council are the chief lawmakers. Local governments also have less strict requirements for people running for office than do the state and federal governments.

The format of the governments of the various Native American tribes varies as well. Most tribes have governments along the lines of the U.S. federal or state governments. An example is the Cherokee Nation, which has a 15-member Tribal Council as the head of the legislative branch, a Principal Chief and Deputy Chief who head up the executive branch and carry out the laws passed by the Tribal Council, and a judicial branch made up of the Judicial Appeals Tribunal and the Cherokee Nation District Court. Members of the Tribunal are appointed by the Principal Chief. Members of the other two branches are elected by popular vote of the Cherokee nation.

State of Florida level

Politics and state government in Florida tend to resemble and follow the patterns of other rapid-growth states as opposed to the traditional pattern of other southern states. Both major political parties are very active in the state and in recent years other smaller parties have also emerged. **State government,** of course, follows the United States federal system and it is similar to other states in the Union. Florida has had six state constitutions. The current state constitution was adapted in 1968 and it has been changed by over thirty amendments since. The first Florida constitution was created to permit Florida to enter the Union as a new state in 1845. The second was adapted in 1861 when Florida joined the Confederacy. A new constitution to allow Florida to rejoin the Union was attempted after the defeat of the Confederacy in 1865, but Florida was denied admission. Finally it was readmitted to the Union with a Reconstruction constitution in 1868. That constitution was heavily revised in 1885. In 1968 a new constitution was prepared by a constitution revision commission and it replaced the 1885 constitution.

Overall, as compared with other state constitutions the length and style of the constitution is standard, but it is subject to frequent amendments because it does contain many detailed and specific provisions. The Florida constitution has for the most part functioned well and it has helped to facilitate Florida's modernization of its government processes. This process of modernization has been given a boost due to the changing nature of urban problems and interest in improving local administration is providing many new ideas. Florida's counties and cities, thus, appear to be better prepared to resolve different conflicts they encounter. This is in part due to the traditionally close ties of local government to the state government.

Florida is divided into 67 counties giving local Florida government a well-structured organization for the state to reach its citizens through these county governments. The counties themselves are mandated to establish a Sheriff, a Tax Collector, a Property Appraiser, a Supervisor of Elections, and a Clerk of the Circuit Court. In addition, some statutory provisions assign to counties larger responsibilities in road construction and maintenance, public health and welfare and agricultural extension services. In fact, with its numerous and ever-expanding responsibilities county government is becoming more and more similar to city government. The fact is that cities and counties are continually engaged in the process of sorting out the various municipal functions in an attempt to decide which services are better provided and managed by one or the other. In some specific instances some functions may be removed from both city and county jurisdiction and be placed under "special" administrative districts. In other cases, all city functions are transferred to a county this is called "consolidation". The Jacksonville-Duval County and Miami-Dade experiments are such examples. The cities in those counties thus have limited powers of administration.

The cities themselves are also undergoing massive changes. Migrants from the north and new immigrants are changing both the shape and style of many Florida cities.

The traditional form of city government in the United States is known as the **Mayor-Council**, based on the federal government's executive-legislative division with the chief executive of a city being the mayor and the legislative branch being a unicameral council. Other types less widely used are the City Commission Plan in which the executive power is dispersed among five commissioners, each of whom have shared executive functions over separate commissions which handle most day to day city services. There is, thus, no distinction between executive and legislative functions as in the mayor-council system.

There is also the **Commission-Manager** form that has been used in Florida in some medium-sized cities. Under it, an elected commission serves only part time, with administration of laws carried out by a city-manager selected by the commission. The official selected is supposed to have had some previous city management experience.

Florida has long been a leader in local government reform. As such it has shown itself willing to experiment with various non-traditional forms of government management if they can be found to be effective in addressing local problems and issues. One type of local administration that has gained wide acceptance over more traditional forms in Florida in recent years is the Council Manager plan for city government. This-form of city government dates from the early years of this century and was supposed to deal in a more efficient manner with the growing urbanization taking place throughout the country, especially in areas where urbanization was more recent like the west and south.

This type of city administration is supposed to eliminate the problems of political patronage and fiscal waste. A trained, professional manager is chosen by the city council to be the executive officer of the city. The manager is under the overall direction of the council who ensures that a professionally created and maintained bureaucracy replaces a staff of political appointees and that professionalism and commitment replaces political favoritism. The ideals and principles of corporate management are thus transferred from the private business sector to the public sector.

Florida had much early interest in the Council-Manager idea and that interest has increased over the years. The first Council-Manager charter was created in 1913 in Largo. By 1920, there were five other cities, West Palm Beach, Tallahassee, St. Augustine, Lakeland, and Ocala that had also adapted this system. The greatest growth in the Council-Manager system was in the 1950s with the increasing urbanization that was occurring at that time. Support for the Council-Manager government has continued to the present day. Although some cities have since dropped it, there has been a corresponding growth in the old Mayor-Council system as well. The greatest prevalence in Council-Manager government has been in the larger cities

Overall, Florida has fairly well defined areas of responsibilities for its various counties and cities, no matter what their particular administrative system may be. School education is completely controlled by the local school boards. Welfare and hospital responsibility are county or state functions as cities rarely have welfare or medical activities. The biggest problem has been who will provide public transportation facilities as most mass transit is concentrated in the cities.

Florida also has been a leader in the pioneering of different alternatives to the traditional dominance of counties and cities in local government. These include such variations as *Special Districts, Metro Government, Councils of Government (or regional planning councils), Regional Regulatory Commissions* and *Corporate Advocates.* One of the best known type of alternative government and is unique to Florida is **Metro-Government**, such as Jacksonville-Dual and Miami Metro-Dade.

City Commission

Commissioner of Public Safety

Police **Fire**

Commissioner of Public Works **Commissioner of Finance** **Commissioner of Recreation** **Commissioner of Sanitation**

Voters

Miami-Dade Metro

Metro-Government involves a variation of the Council-Manager system. This entails a consolidation of the entire county, in which it would then be exercising control in specific areas of agreement between the various cities and municipalities within the county. Thus Metro-Government is like the federal system, gaining specific administrative functions when and where the different municipalities agree to it.

Council members at the county level are known as commissioners. There are nine commissioners, each one from each of eight electoral brackets, plus a mayor. The executive functions of the Metro-Government belong to an appointed county manager, rather than to the mayor who simply presides at commission meetings. This structure was designed to lessen political conflict in the area under its control. Overall this type of system has been successful where it has managed to be instituted. Miami-Dade, the most well known, has been consolidated as a Metro-Government since 1957.

There are also *special districts* in Florida in which areas of land are given over to various concerns to develop independently of state control, though in cooperation with it. *Walt Disney World* and the adjacent land under its control is one of these in the state.

So in conclusion, though Florida has become a national leader in local government reform, it still faces the same problems as elsewhere in the country in trying to ensure that its government is responsive to the people. Properly responding to their wants and needs, and whether it can still be a leader while solving these basic problems in a fast changing environment, will continue to occupy political discourse in Florida for the foreseeable future.

Skill 12.6 Predict how limited resources affect the choices made by governments and individuals.

The scarcity of resources is the basis for the existence of economics. Economics is defined as a study of how scarce resources are allocated to satisfy unlimited wants. Resources refer to the **four factors of production**: labor, capital, land and entrepreneurs. Labor refers to anyone who sells his ability to produce goods and services. Capital is anything that is manufactured to be used in the production process. Land refers to the land itself and everything occurring naturally on it, like oil, minerals, lumber, etc. Entrepreneurship is the ability of an individual to combine the three inputs with his own talents to produce a viable good or service. The entrepreneur takes the risk and experiences the losses or profits.

The fact that the supply of these resources is finite means that society cannot have as much of everything that it wants. There is a constraint on production and consumption and on the kinds of goods and services that can be produced and consumed. **Scarcity** means that choices have to be made. If society decides to produce more of one good, this means that there are fewer resources available for the production of other goods. Assume a society can produce two goods, good X and good Y. The society uses resources in the production of each good. If producing one unit of good X results in an amount of resources used to produce three units of good Y then producing one more unit of good X results in a decrease in 3 units of good Y. In effect, one unit of good X "costs" three units of good Y. This cost is referred to as **opportunity cost**. Opportunity cost is the value of the sacrificed alternative, the value of what had to be given up in order to have the output of good X. Opportunity cost does not just refer to production. Your opportunity cost of studying with this guide is the value of what you are not doing because you are studying, whether it is watching TV, spending time with family, working, or whatever. Every **choice** has an opportunity cost.

If wants were limited and/or if resources were unlimited then the concepts of choice and opportunity cost would not exist, and neither would the field of economics. There would be enough resources to satisfy the wants of consumers, businesses and governments. The allocation of resources wouldn't be a problem. Society could have more of both good X and good Y without having to give up anything. There would be no opportunity cost. But this isn't the situation that societies are faced with.

Because resources are scarce society doesn't want to waste them. Society wants to obtain the most satisfaction it can from the consumption of the goods and services produced with its scarce resources. The members of the society don't want their scarce resources wasted through inefficiency. This indicates producers must choose an efficient production process, which is the lowest cost means of production. High costs mean wasted resources and we then have the situation given above with good X and good Y. Consumers also don't want society's resources wasted by producing goods that they don't want.

How do producers know what goods consumers want? Consumers buy the goods they want and vote with their dollar spending. A desirable good, one that consumers want, earns profits. A good that incurs losses is a good that society doesn't want its resources wasted on. This signals the producer that society wants their resources used in another way.

Government policies, whether they are federal, state or local, affect economic decision-making and in many cases, the distribution of resources. This is the purpose of most economic policies imposed at the federal level. Governments don't implement monetary and fiscal policy at the state or local level, only at the national level. Most state and local laws that affect economic decision-making and the distribution of resources have to do with taxation. If taxes are imposed or raised at the state or local level, the effect is less spending. The purpose of these taxes is to raise revenues for the state and local government, not to affect the level of aggregate demand and inflation. At the federal level, the major purpose of these policies is to affect the level of aggregate demand and the inflation rate or the unemployment rate.

Governments at all three levels affect the distribution of resources and economic decision-making through transfer payments. This is an attempt to bring about a redistribution of income and to correct the problem of income inequality. Programs like Food Stamps, AFDC (welfare), unemployment compensation, Medicaid all fall into this category. Technically, these government transfer programs result in a rearrangement of private consumption, not a real reallocation of resources. Price support programs in agriculture also result in a redistribution of income and a misallocation of resources. The imposition of artificially high prices results in too many resources going into agriculture and leads to product surpluses.

Laws can be enacted at all three levels to correct for the problem of externalities. An externality occurs when uninvolved third parties are affected by some market activity, like pollution. Dumping obnoxious and sometimes poisonous wastes into the air and water means that the air and water are being treated as a free input by the firm. The market does not register all of the costs of production because the firm does not have to pay to use the air or water. The result of the free inputs is lower production costs for the firm and an over allocation of resources into the production of the good the firm is producing. The role for government here is to cause a redistribution of resources by somehow shifting all or part of the cost on to the offending firm. They can impose fines, taxes, require pollution abatement equipment, sell pollution permits, etc. Whatever method they choose, this raises the costs of production for the firms and forces them to bear some of the cost.

Policies can be enacted in order to encourage labor to migrate from one sector of the economy to another. This is primarily done at the national level. The United States economy is so large that it is possible to have unemployment in different areas while the economy is at full employment. State unemployment and labor agencies provide the information for these people.

Skill 12.7 Compare and contrast the characteristics of various economic systems.

The **traditional economy** is one based on custom and usually exists in less developed countries. The people do things the way their ancestors did so they are not too technologically advanced. Technology and equipment are viewed as a threat to the old way of doing things and to their tradition. There is very little upward mobility for the same reason. The model of capitalism is based on private ownership of the means of production and operates on the basis of free markets, on both the input and output side. The free markets function to coordinate market activity and to achieve an efficient allocation of resources. **Laissez-faire capitalism** is based on the premise of no government intervention in the economy. The market will eliminate any unemployment or inflation that occurs. Government needs only to provide the framework for the functioning of the economy and to protect private property. A **command economy** is almost the exact opposite of a market economy. A command economy is based on government ownership of the means of production and the use of planning to take the place of the market. Instead of the market determining the output mix and the allocation of resources, the bureaucracy fulfills this role by determining the output mix and establishing production target for the enterprises, which are publicly owned. The result is inefficiency. A **mixed economy** uses a combination of markets and planning, with the degree of each varying according to country. Actual real world economies are best described as mixed economies.

Skill 12.8 Identify the role of markets from production, through distribution, to consumption.

Economic systems refer to the arrangements a society has devised to answer what are known as the Three Questions: What goods to produce, How to produce the goods, and For whom are the goods being produced, or how is the allocation of the output determined. Different economic systems answer these questions in different ways. These are the different "isms" that exist that define the method of resource and output allocation.

A market economy answers these questions in terms of **demand and supply** and the use of markets. Consumers vote for the products they want with their dollar spending. Goods acquiring enough dollar votes are profitable, signaling to the producers that society wants their scarce resources used in this way. This is how the "What" question is answered. The producer then hires inputs in accordance with the goods consumers want, looking for the most efficient or lowest cost method of production. The lower the firm's costs for any given level of revenue, the higher the firm's profits. This is the way in which the "How" question is answered in a market economy.

The "For Whom" question is answered in the marketplace by the determination of the equilibrium price. Price serves to ration the good to those that can and will transact at the market price of better. Those who can't or won't are excluded from the market. The United States has a market economy.

The opposite of the market economy is called the centrally planned economy. This used to be called Communism, even though the term is not correct in a strict Marxian sense. In a planned economy, the means of production are publicly owned with little, if any public ownership. Instead of the Three Questions being solved by markets, they have a planning authority that makes the decisions in place of markets. The planning authority decides what will be produced and how. Since most planned economies directed resources into the production of capital and military goods, there was little remaining for consumer goods and the result was chronic shortages. Price functioned as an accounting measure and did not reflect scarcity. The former Soviet Union and most of the Eastern Bloc countries were planned economies of this sort.

In between the two extremes is market socialism. This is a mixed economic system that uses both markets and planning. Planning is usually used to direct resources at the upper levels of the economy, with markets being used to determine prices of consumer goods and wages. This kind of economic system answers the three questions with planning and markets. The former Yugoslavia was a market socialist economy.

Skill 12.9 Identify concepts relative to psychology, sociology, and anthropology.

PSYCHOLOGY involves scientifically studying behavior and mental processes. The ways people and animals relate to each other are observed and recorded. Psychologists scrutinize specific patterns, which will enable them to discern and predict certain behaviors, using scientific methods to verify their ideas. In this way they have been able to learn how to help people fulfill their individual human potential and strengthen understanding between individuals as well as groups and in nations and cultures. The results of the research of psychologists have deepened our understanding of the reasons for people's behavior.

Psychology is not only closely connected to the natural science of biology and the medical field of psychiatry but it is also connected to the social science areas of anthropology and sociology which have to do with people in society. Along with the sociologists and anthropologists, psychologists also study humans in their social settings, analyzing their attitudes and relationships. The disciplines of anthropology psychology and sociology often research the same kinds of problems but from different points of view, with the emphasis in psychology on individual behavior, how an individual's actions are influenced by feelings and beliefs.

Aristotle is the Greek philosopher often credited with the beginnings of psychology. He was mainly interested in the human mind's accomplishments. He believed that the body was separate from the mind or soul, which the Greeks referred to as the "psyche". He believed that the highest human virtues came from the psyche, which helped people to reason.

Rene Descartes was a French philosopher who described the strong influence of the body and mind on each other because of their being separate and suggested that the pineal gland in the brain was where this interaction took place. He developed the doctrine of "nativism," the beliefs that people were born able to think and reason.

Thomas Hobbes, John Locke, David Hume, and George Berkeley were called "empiricists", a name given to those who rejected Descartes' doctrine of nativism. These four men believed that at birth a person's mind is empty, that one gains knowledge of the outside world through the senses, and that people get ideas from their life experiences.

Johannes P. Muller and Hermann L.F. von Hemholtz, were two German scientists pioneered the first organized studies of perception and sensation, showing the feasibility of the scientific study of the physical processes that support mental activity.

William James started what became the first psychology laboratory in the world.

William Wundt was a German philosopher trained in physiology and medicine who published the first journal dealing with experimental psychology.

It should be noted that the work of Wundt **and James** put psychology in a field by itself, separate from philosophy. Their work, along with others, led to the method of research called "introspection," training their subjects to observe and as accurately as possible record their feelings, experiences, and mental processes.

John B. Watson an American psychologist who introduced the research technique of "behaviorism", the belief that the only reliable source of information was observable behavior, not inner experiences.

Ivan Pavlov and B.F. Skinner made significant contributions to this school of behaviorism, a reaction to the emphasis on introspection. The behaviorists believed that the environment was the important influence on one's behavior and looked for any correlation between environmental stimuli and observable behavior.

Max Wertheimer started the school of Gestalt psychology. The word "Gestalt" is German and means a shape, pattern, or form. The proponents of this form of research studied behavior, not as different incidents of response to stimuli but as an organized pattern.

Sigmund Freud was an Austrian physician who founded the school of psychoanalysis, the theory that repressed inner forces buried in the subconscious determined behavior and that these repressed feelings possibly affected personality problems, self-destructive behavior, and possibly physical symptoms. Freud developed a number of techniques to treat repression, including free association.

The practice of modern psychology includes the teachings of the earlier schools as well as the development of additional ones such as stimulus-response, cognitive, and humanistic psychology.

In their research, psychologists develop hypotheses, and then test them using the scientific method. These methods used in psychological research include:

naturalistic observation which includes observing the behavior of animals and humans in their natural surroundings or environment,

systematic assessment, which describes assorted ways to measure the feelings, thoughts, and personality traits of people using case histories, public opinion polls or surveys, and standardized tests. These three types of assessments enable psychologists to acquire information not available through naturalistic observations,

experimentation enables psychologists to find and corroborate the cause-and-effect relationships in behavior, usually by randomly dividing the subjects into two groups: an experimental group and a control group.

SOCIOLOGY is the study of the individuals, groups, and institutions making up human society. It includes every feature of human social conditions. It deals with the predominant behaviors, attitudes, and types of relationships within a society, which is defined as a group of people with a similar cultural background living in a specific geographical area. It is closely related to anthropology, especially applied to groups outside of one's region, nation, or hemisphere. History puts it in perspective with an historical background. Political Science is tied to sociology with the impact of political and governmental regulation of activities. Awareness of, influence of, and use of the physical environment as studied in geography also contributes to understanding. Economic activities are a part of human society. The field of psychology is also related.

Sociology is divided into five major areas of study:

Population studies: General social patterns of groups of people living in a certain geographical area,
Social behaviors: Changes in attitudes, morale, leadership, conformity and others,
Social institutions: Organized groups of people performing specific functions within a society such as churches, schools, hospitals, business organizations, and governments
Cultural influences: Including customs, knowledge, arts, religious beliefs, and language, and
Social change: Such as wars, revolutions, inventions, fashions, and other events or activities.

Sociologists use three major methods to test and verify theories:

(1) Surveys;
(2) Controlled experiments; and
(3) Field observation.

Auguste Comte, the French philosopher who coined the term "sociology" and developed the theory called "positivism," which stated that social behavior and events could be measured scientifically.

Karl Marx and Friedrich Engels supported the theory of "economic determinism" which stated that all social patterns and institutions were controlled by economic factors, which formed much of the basis of Communism.

Herbert Spencer stated that human society's development was a process occurring gradually, evolving from lower to higher forms, very much like biological evolution.

Emile Durkheim was the French sociologist who was one of the first to use scientific research methods.

Max Weber stated that sociological theories are probably generalizations.

ANTHROPOLOGY

Margaret Mead, in the 1920s lived among the Samoans, observing their ways of life, resulting in the book "Coming of Age in Samoa."

The Leakey family, Louis, his wife Mary, and son Richard, all of whom did much field work to further the study of human origins.

ANTHROPOLOGY is the scientific study of human culture and humanity, and the relationship between man and his culture. Anthropologists study different groups, how they relate to other cultures, and patterns of behavior, similarities and differences. Their research is two fold: cross-cultural and comparative. The major method of study is referred to as "participant observation." The anthropologist studies and learns about the people being studied by living among them and participating with them in their daily lives. Other methods may be used but this is the most characteristic method used.

Socialization is the process by which humans learn the expectations their society has for their behavior, in order that they might successfully function within that society.

Socialization takes place primarily in children as they learn and are taught the rules and norms of their culture. Children grow up eating the common foods of a culture, and develop a "taste" for these foods, for example. By observing adults and older children, they learn about gender roles, and appropriate ways to interact.

Socialization also takes place among adults who change their environment and are expected to adopt new behaviors. Joining the military, for example, requires a different type of dress and behavior than civilian culture. Taking a new job or going to a new school are other examples of situations where adults must re-socialize.

Two primary ways that socialization takes place are through positive and negative sanctions. Positive sanctions are rewards for appropriate or desirable behavior, and negative sanctions are punishments for inappropriate behavior. Recognition from peers and praise from a parent are examples of positive sanctions that reinforce expected social behaviors. Negative sanctions might include teasing by peers for unusual behavior, or punishment by a parent.

Sanctions can be either formal or informal. Public awards and prizes are ways a society formally reinforces positive behaviors. Laws that provide for punishment of specific infractions are formal negative sanctions.

Sociologists have identified three main types of norms, or ways that cultures define behavioral expectations, each associated with different consequences if they are violated. These norms are called folkways, mores and laws.

Folkways are the informal rules of etiquette and behaviors that a society follows in day-to-day practice. Forming a line at a shop counter or holding a door open for an elderly person are examples of folkways in many societies. Someone who violates a folkway - by pushing to the front of a line, for instance - might be seen as rude, but is not thought to have done anything immoral or illegal.

Mores are stronger than folkways in the consequences they carry for not observing them. Examples of mores might include honesty and integrity. Cheating on a test or lying might violate a social more, and a person who does so may be considered immoral.

Laws are formal adoptions of norms by a society with formal punishment for their violation. Laws are usually based on the mores of a society. The more that it is wrong to kill is codified in a law against murder, for example. Laws are the most formal types of social norm, as their enforcement is specifically provided for. Folkways and mores, on the other hand, are primarily enforced informally by the fellow members of a society.

The folkways, mores and laws of a society are based on the prevailing beliefs and values of that society. Beliefs and values are similar and interrelated systems.

Beliefs are those things that are thought to be true. Beliefs are often associated with religion, but beliefs can also be based on political or ideological philosophies. "All men are created equal," is an example of an ideological belief.

Values are what a society thinks are right and wrong, and are often based on and shaped by beliefs. The value that every member of the society has a right to participate in his government might be considered to be based on the belief that "All mean are created equal," for instance.

Sample Test: Social Science

1. **The leader of the Protestant Revolution began with which individual?** ***(Average) (Skill 10.1)***

   A. King George

   B. Martin Luther

   C. Calvin

   D. Zwingli

2. **For the historian studying ancient Egypt, which of the following would be least useful?** ***(Easy) (Skill 10.2)***

A. The record of an ancient Greek historian on Greek-Egyptian interaction

B. Letters from an Egyptian ruler to his/her regional governors

C. Inscriptions on stele of the Fourteenth Egyptian Dynasty

D. Letters from a nineteenth century Egyptologist to his wife

3. **The Tigris-Euphrates Valley was the site of which two primary ancient civilizations?** ***(Rigorous) (Skill 10.3)***

   A. Babylonian and Assyrian

   B. Sumerian and Egyptian

   C. Hyksos and Hurrian

   D. Persian and Phoenician

4. **The first ancient civilization to introduce and practice monotheism was:** ***(Easy) (Skill 10.4)***

   A. Sumerians

   B. Hebrews

   C. Phoenicians

   D. Minoans

5. **Of all the major causes of both World Wars I and II, the most significant one is considered to be:** ***(Average) (Skill 10.4)***

   A. Extreme nationalism

   B. Military buildup and aggression

   C. Political unrest

   D. Agreements and alliances

6. **Which of the following was NOT a factor in the United States' entry into World War I? *(Average) (Skill 10.4)***

   A. The closeness of the Presidential Election of 1916

   B. The German threat to sink all allied ships, including merchant ships

   C. The desire to preserve democracy as practiced in Britain and France as compared to the totalitarianism of Germany

   D. The sinking of the Lusitania and the Sussex

7. **The world religion which includes a caste system is: *(Easy) (Skill 10.4)***

   A. Buddhism

   B. Hinduism

   C. Sikhism

   D. Jainism

8. **The native metaphysical outlook of Japan, usually characterized as a religion, is: *(Rigorous) (Skill 10.4)***

   A. Tao

   B. Shinto

   C. Nichiren Shoju

   D. Shaolin

9. **One tribe of Indians formed a representative government referred to as the _________ Confederacy. *(Average) (Skill 10.5)***

   A. Cherokee

   B. Seminole

   C. Wampanoag

   D. Iroquois

10. **The year 1619 was a memorable year for the colony of Virginia. Three important events occurred resulting in lasting effects on US history. Which one of the following was not one of the events? *(Rigorous) (Skill 10.5)***

    A. Twenty African slaves arrived.

    B. The London Company granted the colony a charter making it independent.

    C. The colonists were given the right by the London Company to govern themselves through representative government in the Virginia House of Burgesses

    D. The London Company sent to the colony 60 women who were quickly married, establishing families and stability in the colony.

11. What was a major source of contention between American settlers in Texas and the Mexican government in the 1830s and 1840s? ***(Rigorous) (Skill 10.5)***

A. The Americans wished to retain slavery, which had been outlawed in Mexico

B. The Americans had agreed to learn Spanish and become Roman Catholic, but failed to do so

C. The Americans retained ties to the United States, and Santa Anna feared the power of the U.S.

D. All of the above were contentious issues between American settlers and the Mexican government

12. What doctrine stated that the states have the right to declare invalid any act of Congress they believed to be unjust or unconstitutional? ***(Average) (Skill 10.5)***

A. Nullification

B. Secession

C. Separate but equal

D. Powers reserved to the states

13. Abraham Lincoln won re-election in 1864 chiefly through: ***(Rigorous) (Skill 10.5)***

A. His overwhelming force of personality and appeal to all segments of the electorate

B. His reputation as the Great Emancipator

C. The fact that people felt sorry for him because of his difficulties

D. His shrewd political manipulation, clever use of patronage jobs, and wide-appeal selection of cabinet members

14. Of the following groups of states, which were slave states? ***(Rigorous) (Skill 10.5)***

A. Delaware, Maryland, Missouri

B. California, Texas, Florida

C. Kansas, Missouri, Kentucky

D. Virginia, West Virginia, Indiana

15. Which of the following most closely characterizes the geopolitical events of the USSR in 1991-92: ***(Rigorous) (Skill 10.5)***

A. The USSR established greater military and economic control over the fifteen Soviet republics

B. The Baltic States (Estonia, Latvia, Lithuania) declared independence, while the remainder of the USSR remained intact.

C. Fourteen of fifteen Soviet republics declared some degree of autonomy; the USSR was officially dissolved; the Supreme Soviet rescinded the Soviet Treaty of 1922

D. All fifteen Soviet republics simultaneously declared immediate and full independence from the USSR, with no provisions for a transitional form of government

16. The economic practices under President Ronald Reagan ("Reaganomics") were characterized by: ***(Rigorous) (Skill 10.5)***

A. Low inflation, high unemployment, high interest rates, high national debt

B. High inflation, low unemployment, low interest rates, low national debt

C. Low inflation, high unemployment, low interest rates, depletion of national debt

D. High inflation, low unemployment, high interest rates, low national debt

17. The first territorial governor of Florida after Florida's purchase by the United States was: ***(Average) (Skill 10.6)***

A. Napoleon B. Broward

B. William P. Duval

C. Andrew Jackson

D. Davy Crockett

18. Which of the following is most descriptive of the conflict between the U.S. government and the Seminoles between 1818 and 1858? *(Average) (Skill 10.6)*

A. There was constant armed conflict between the Seminoles and the U.S. during these years

B. Historians discern three separate phases of hostilities (1818, 1835-42, 1855-58), known collectively as the Seminole Wars

C. On May 7, 1858, the Seminoles admitted defeat, signed a peace treaty with the U.S., and left for Oklahoma, except for fifty-one individuals

D. The former Seminole chief Osceola helped the U.S. defeat the Seminoles and effect their removal to Oklahoma

19. Who was the first governor of the state of Florida? *(Rigorous) (Skill 10.6)*

A. Andrew Jackson

B. David Levy

C. William Moseley

D. Colonel James Moore

20. Match the railroad entrepreneur with the correct area of development: *(Rigorous) (Skill 10.6)*

A. Henry Plant: Tampa and the West Coast

B. Cornelius Vanderbilt: Jacksonville and the Northeast

C. Henry Flagler: Orlando and the Central Highlands

D. J.P. Morgan: Pensacola and the Northwest

21. Florida's space exploration industry is centered in: *(Rigorous) (Skill 10.6)*

A. Baker County

B. Broward County

C. Brevard County

D. Bradford County

22. **If geography is the study of how human beings live in relationship to the earth on which they live, why do geographers include physical geography within the discipline? *(Rigorous) (Skill 11.1, 10.3)***

    A. The physical environment serves as the location for the activities of human beings

    B. No other branch of the natural or social sciences studies the same topics

    C. The physical environment is more important than the activities carried out by human beings

    D. It is important to be able to subdue natural processes for the advancement of humankind

23. **A geographer wishes to study the effects of a flood on subsequent settlement patterns. Which might he or she find most useful? *(Average) (Skill 11.2, 12.9)***

    A. A film clip of the floodwaters

    B. An aerial photograph of the river's source

    C. Census data taken after the flood

    D. A soil map of the A and B horizons beneath the flood area

24. **A physical geographer would be concerned with which of the following groups of terms? *(Easy) (Skill 11.3, 11.8)***

    A. Landform, biome, precipitation

    B. Scarcity, goods, services

    C. Nation, state, administrative subdivision

    D. Cause and effect, innovation, exploration

25. An economist might engage in which of the following activities? ***(Average) (Skill 11.4, 11.7, 12.1)***

A. An observation of the historical effects of a nation's banking practices

B. The application of a statistical test to a series of data

C. Introduction of an experimental factor into a specified population to measure the effect of the factor

D. An economist might engage in all of these

26. Which of the following is NOT considered to be an economic need: ***(Easy) (Skill 11.6)***

A. Food

B. Transportation

C. Shelter

D. Clothing

27. A cultural geographer is investigating the implications of <u>The Return of the Native</u> by Thomas Hardy. He or she is most likely concentrating on:

(Rigorous) (Skill 11.7)

A. The reactions of British city-dwellers to the in-migration of French professionals

B. The activities of persons in relation to poorly-drained, coarse-soiled land with low-lying vegetation

C. The capacity of riverine lands to sustain a population of edible amphibians

D. The propagation of new crops introduced by settlers from North America

28. Which location may be found in Canada? ***(Rigorous) (Skill 11.8)***

A. 27 N 93 W

B. 41 N 93 E

C. 50 N 111 W

D. 18 N 120 W

29. The Mediterranean type climate is characterized by: ***(Rigorous) (Skill 11.8)***

A. Hot, dry summers and mild, relatively wet winters

B. Cool, relatively wet summers and cold winters

C. Mild summers and winters, with moisture throughout the year

D. Hot, wet summers and cool, dry winters

30. The climate of Southern Florida is the ________________ type. ***(Average) (Skill 11.8)***

A. Humid subtropical

B. Marine West Coast

C. Humid continental

D. Tropical wet-dry

31. The Bill of Rights was mostly written by: ***(Rigorous) (Skill 12.3)***

A. Thomas Jefferson

B. James Madison

C. George Washington

D. Alexander Hamilton

32. In the United States government, the power of coining money is: ***(Rigorous) (Skill 12.4)***

A. Implied or suggested

B. Concurrent or shared

C. Delegated or expressed

D. Reserved

33. Which branch is responsible for carrying out the laws of the country? ***(Average) (Skill 12.4)***

A. Judicial

B. Executive

C. Legislative

D. Supreme Court

34. Which branch established the power of the Supreme Court? ***(Average) (Skill 12.4)***

A. Judicial

B. Executive

C. Legislative

D. House of Representatives

35. The ________ branch of government is made up of House of Representatives and the Senate. ***(Average) (Skill 12.4)***

A. Judicial

B. Executive

C. Legislative

D. Supreme Court

36. An economist investigates the spending patterns of low income individuals. Which of the following would yield the most pertinent information? ***(Average) (Skill 12.6)***

A. Prime lending rates of neighborhood banks

B. The federal discount rate

C. City-wide wholesale distribution figures

D. Census data and retail sales figures

37. As your income rises, you tend to spend more money on entertainment. This is an expression of the: ***(Rigorous) (Skill 12.6, 12.8)***

A. Marginal propensity to consume

B. Allocative efficiency

C. Compensating differential

D. Marginal propensity to save

38. Economics is best described as: ***(Average) (Skill 12.6)***

A. The study of how money is used in different societies

B. The study of how different political systems produce goods and services

C. The study of how human beings use limited resources to supply their necessities and wants

D. The study of how human beings have developed trading practices through the years

39. Capitalism and communism are alike in that they are both: *(Average) (Skill 12.7, 12.4)*

A. Organic systems

B. Political systems

C. Centrally planned systems

D. Economic systems

40. If the price of Good G increases, what is likely to happen with regard to comparable Good H? *(Rigorous) (Skill 12.8)*

A. The demand for Good G will stay the same

B. The demand for Good G will increase

C. The demand for Good H will increase

D. The demand for Good H will decrease

41. During the latter part of the 20th century, the centrally planned economy was more commonly known as what? *(Rigorous) (Skill 12.8)*

A. Consumerism

B. Market economy

C. Market socialism

D. Communism

42. A historian would be interested in: *(Average) (Skill 12.9)*

A. The manner in which scientific knowledge is advanced

B. The effects of the French Revolution on world colonial policy

C. The viewpoint of persons who have written previous "history"

D. All of the above

43. The sub-discipline of linguistics is usually studied under: *(Average) (Skill 12.9)*

A. Geography

B. History

C. Anthropology

D. Economics

44. Which of the following is not generally considered to be a discipline within the social sciences? *(Easy) (Skill 12.9)*

A. Geometry

B. Anthropology

C. Geography

D. Sociology

45. **Psychology is a social science because:** ***(Easy) (Skill 12.9)***

    A. It focuses on the biological development of individuals

    B. It focuses on the behavior of individual persons and small groups of persons

    C. It bridges the gap between the natural and the social sciences

    D. It studies the behavioral habits of lower animals

46. **Which of the following is most reasonably studied under the social sciences?** ***(Easy) (Skill 12.9)***

    A. Political science

    B. Geometry

    C. Physics

    D. Grammar

47. **A social scientist observes how individual persons react to the presence or absence of noise. This scientist is most likely a:** ***(Easy) (Skill 12.9)***

    A. Geographer

    B. Political Scientist

    C. Economist

    D. Psychologist

48. **As a sociologist, you would be most likely to observe:** ***(Easy) (Skill 12.9)***

    A. The effects of an earthquake on farmland

    B. The behavior of rats in sensory-deprivation experiments

    C. The change over time in Babylonian obelisk styles

    D. The behavior of human beings in television focus groups

49. **Which of the following is most closely identified as a sociologist?** ***(Rigorous) (Skill 12.9)***

    A. Herodotus

    B. John Maynard Keynes

    C. Emile Durkheim

    D. Arnold Toynbee

50. **Political science is primarily concerned with ________________**

    (Average) (Skill 12.9)

    A. Elections

    B. Economic Systems

    C. Boundaries

    D. Public Policy

Answer Key: Social Science

1. B
2. D
3 A
4. B
5. A
6. A
7. B
8. B
9. D
10. B
11. D
12. A
13. D
14. A
15. C
16. A
17. C
18. B
19. C
20. A
21. C
22. A
23. C
24. A
25. D
26. B
27. B
28. C
29. A
30. A
31. B
32. C
33. B
34. A
35. C
36. D
37. A
38. C
39. D
40. C
41. D
42. D
43. C
44. A
45. B
46. A
47. D
48. D
49. C
50. D

Rigor Table: Social Studies

	Easy 20%	Average Rigor 40%	Rigorous 40%
Question #	2,4,7,24,26,44,45, 46,47,48	1,5,6,9,2,17,18,23,25,30,33, 34,35,36,38,39,42,43,50	3,8,10,11,13,14,15,16, 19,20,21,22,27,28,29, 31,32,37,40,41,49

Rationales with Sample Questions: Social Science

1. The leader of the Protestant Revolution began with which individual? *(Average) (Skill 10.1)*

A. King Henry

B. Martin Luther

C. John Calvin

D. Zwingli

Answer: B Martin Luther

The Protestant Revolution began in Germany with the revolt of (B) Martin Luther against Church abuses. It spread to Switzerland where it was led by (C) John Calvin. It began in England with the efforts of (A) King Henry VIII to have his marriage to Catherine of Aragon annulled so he could wed another and have a male heir. The results were the increasing support given not only by the people but also by nobles and some rulers, and of course, the attempts of the Church to stop it. (D) Zwingli was a contemporary of Luther's and led the reforms in Switzerland.

2. For the historian studying ancient Egypt, which of the following would be least useful? *(Easy) (Skill 10.2)*

A. The record of an ancient Greek historian on Greek-Egyptian interaction

B. Letters from an Egyptian ruler to his/her regional governors

C. Inscriptions on stele of the Fourteenth Egyptian Dynasty

D. Letters from a nineteenth century Egyptologist to his wife

Answer: D Letters from a nineteenth century Egyptologist to his wife

Historians use primary sources from the actual time they are studying whenever possible. (A) Ancient Greek records of interaction with Egypt, (B) letters from an Egyptian ruler to regional governors, and (C) inscriptions from the Fourteenth Egyptian Dynasty are all primary sources created at or near the actual time being studied. (D) Letters from a nineteenth century Egyptologist would not be considered primary sources, as they were created thousands of years after the fact and may not actually be about the subject being studied.

3. The Tigris-Euphrates Valley was the site of which two primary ancient civilizations? ***(Rigorous) (Skill 10.3)***

A. Babylonian and Assyrian

B. Sumerian and Egyptian

C. Hyksos and Hurrian

D. Persian and Phoenician

Answer: A Babylonian and Assyrian

(B) While the Sumerians also lived in the southern Tigris-Euphrates valley, Egyptian civilization grew up in the Nile delta (3500BC-30 BC). (C) The Hyksos were an Asiatic people who controlled the Nile Delta during the 15th and 16th Dynasties (1674BC-1548BC). The Hurrians (2500BC-1000BC) came from the Khabur River Valley in northern Mesopotamia, where they spread out to establish various small kingdoms in the region. (D) The Persians (648BC- early 19th century AD) had a succession of empires based in the area known as modern-day Iran. The Phoenicians were a seafaring people who dominated the Mediterranean during the first century BC.

4. The first ancient civilization to introduce and practice monotheism was the: ***(Easy) (Skill 10.4)***

A. Sumerians

B. Hebrews

C. Phoenicians

D. Minoans

Answer: B. Hebrews

The (A) Sumerians and (C) Phoenicians both practiced religions in which many gods and goddesses were worshipped. Often these Gods/Goddesses were based on a feature of nature such as a sun, moon, weather, rocks, water, etc. The (D) Minoan culture shared many religious practices with the Ancient Egyptians. It seems that the king was somewhat of a god figure and the queen, a goddess. Much of the Minoan art points to the worship of multiple gods. Therefore, only the (B) Hebrews introduced and fully practiced monotheism, or the belief in one god.

5. Of all the major causes of both World Wars I and II, the most significant one is considered to be: ***(Average) (Skill 10.4)***

A. Extreme nationalism

B. Military buildup and aggression

C. Political unrest

D. Agreements and alliances

Answer: A. Extreme nationalism

Although military buildup and aggression, political unrest, and agreements and alliances were all characteristic of the world climate before and during World War I and World War II, the most significant cause of both wars was extreme nationalism. Nationalism is the idea that the interests and needs of a particular nation are of the utmost and primary importance above all else. Some nationalist movements could be liberation movements while others were oppressive regimes, much depends on their degree of nationalism. The nationalism that sparked WWI included a rejection of German, Austro-Hungarian, and Ottoman imperialism by Serbs, Slavs and others culminating in the assassination of Archduke Ferdinand by a Serb nationalist in 1914. Following WWI and the Treaty of Versailles, many Germans and others in the Central Alliance Nations, malcontent at the concessions and reparations of the treaty started a new form of nationalism. Adolf Hitler and the Nazi regime led this extreme nationalism. Hitler's ideas were an example of extreme, oppressive nationalism combined with political, social and economic scapegoating and were the primary cause of WWII.

6. Which of the following was NOT a factor in the United States' entry into World War I? ***(Average) (Skill 10.4)***

A. The closeness of the Presidential Election of 1916

B. The German threat to sink all allied ships, including merchant ships

C. The desire to preserve democracy as practiced in Britain and France as compared to the totalitarianism of Germany

D. The sinking of the Lusitania and the Sussex

Answer: A The closeness of the Presidential Election of 1916
President Woodrow Wilson was narrowly re-elected in 1916, but this was not a factor in the United State's entry into World War I. All the other answers were indeed factors.

7. The world religion which includes a caste system is: ***(Easy) (Skill 10.4)***

A. Buddhism

B. Hinduism

C. Sikhism

D. Jainism

Answer: B. Hinduism

(A) Buddhism, (C) Sikhism, and (D) Jainism all rose out of protest against Hinduism and its practices of sacrifice and the caste system. The caste system, in which people were born into castes, would determine their class for life including who they could marry, what jobs they could perform, and their overall quality of life.

8. The native metaphysical outlook of Japan, usually characterized as a religion, is: ***(Rigorous) (Skill 10.4)***

A. Tao

B. Shinto

C. Nichiren Shoju

D. Shaolin

Answer: B Shinto

(A) Tao is the Chinese philosophical work that inspired Taoism, the religious tradition sourced in China. (B) Shinto is the system of rituals and beliefs honoring the deities and spirits believed to be native to the landscape and inhabitants of Japan. (C) Nichiren Shoju is a strand of Nichiren Buddhism, a tradition started by a Japanese Buddhist monk, Nichiren (1222-1282). (D) The Shaolin temple (originally built in 497 AD) is the Chinese Buddhist monastery considered to be the source of Zen Buddhism and its subsequent martial arts.

9. One tribe of Indians formed a representative government referred to as the _________ Confederacy. ***(Average) (Skill 10.5)***

A. Cherokee

B. Seminole

C. Wampanoag

D. Iroquois

Answer: D Iroquois

Five of the (D) Iroquois tribes formed a Confederacy, a shared form of government. Living in the Southeast were the (B) Seminoles and Creeks, a huge collection of people who are best known, however, for their struggle against Spanish and English settlers, especially led by the great Osceola. The (A) Cherokee also lived in the Southeast. They were one of the most advanced tribes, living in domed houses and wearing deerskin and rabbit fur. Accomplished hunters, farmers, and fishermen, the Cherokee were known the continent over for their intricate and beautiful basketry and clay pottery. They also played a game called lacrosse, which survives to this day in countries around the world. The (C) Wampanoag tribe was found mainly in Massachusetts.

10. The year 1619 was a memorable year for the colony of Virginia. Three important events occurred resulting in lasting effects on US history. Which one of the following was not one of the events? ***(Rigorous) (Skill 10.5)***

A. Twenty African slaves arrived.

B. The London Company granted the colony a charter making it independent.

C. The colonists were given the right by the London Company to govern themselves through representative government in the Virginia House of Burgesses

D. The London Company sent to the colony 60 women who were quickly married, establishing families and stability in the colony.

Answer: B. The London Company granted the colony a charter making it independent.

In the year 1619, the Southern colony of Virginia had an eventful year including the first arrival of twenty African slaves, the right to self-governance through representative government in the Virginia House of Burgesses (their own legislative body), and the arrival of sixty women sent to marry and establish families in the colony. The London Company did not, however, grant the colony a charter in 1619.

11. What was a major source of contention between American settlers in Texas and the Mexican government in the 1830s and 1840s? ***(Rigorous) (Skill 10.5)***

A. The Americans wished to retain slavery, which had been outlawed in Mexico

B. The Americans had agreed to learn Spanish and become Roman Catholic, but failed to do so

C. The Americans retained ties to the United States, and Santa Anna feared the power of the U.S.

D. All of the above were contentious issues between American settlers and the Mexican government

Answer: D All of the above were contentious issues between American settlers and the Mexican government.

The American settlers simply were not willing to assimilate into Mexican society but maintained their prior commitments to slave holding, the English language, Protestantism, and the United States government.

12. What doctrine stated that the states have the right to declare invalid any act of Congress they believed to be unjust or unconstitutional? ***(Average) (Skill 10.5)***

A. Nullification

B. Secession

C. Separate but equal

D. Powers reserved to the states

Answer: A Nullification

(A) The doctrine of nullification states that the states have the right to "nullify" – declare invalid – any act of Congress they believed to be unjust or unconstitutional. The nullification crisis of the mid-nineteenth century climaxed over a new tariff on imported manufactured goods that was enacted by the Congress in 1828. (B) Secession is the act of withdrawing from an organization, union or political entity. (C) Separate but equal is not a doctrine. (D) Powers reserved to the state are powers that are not given to the federal government under the U.S. Constitution.

13. Abraham Lincoln won re-election in 1864 chiefly through: ***(Rigorous) (Skill 10.5)***

A. His overwhelming force of personality and appeal to all segments of the electorate

B. His reputation as the Great Emancipator

C. The fact that people felt sorry for him because of his difficulties

D. His shrewd political manipulation, clever use of patronage jobs, and wide-appeal selection of cabinet members

Answer: D His shrewd political manipulation, clever use of patronage jobs, and wide-appeal selection of cabinet members

President Lincoln in his own lifetime was a hugely divisive figure, even in the North. He did not appeal to all segments of the electorate, his reputation as the Great Emancipator really developed after the war, and few felt sorry for him for his personal and political difficulties. Rather, Lincoln constantly maneuvered to maintain the advantage, using all the powers of the Presidency to win re-election despite his own unpopularity.

14. Of the following groups of states, which were slave states? ***(Rigorous) (Skill 10.5)***

A. Delaware, Maryland, Missouri

B. California, Texas, Florida

C. Kansas, Missouri, Kentucky

D. Virginia, West Virginia, Indiana

Answer: A Delaware, Maryland, Missouri.

(A) Delaware, Maryland and Missouri were all slave states at the time of the Civil War. (B) Florida and Texas were slave states, while California was a free state. (C) Kansas, Missouri, and Kentucky were all originally slave territories, and Missouri and Kentucky were admitted to the Union as such. However, Kansas' petition to join the union in 1858 was blocked in order to preserve the balance between slave and free states. Kansas was admitted as a free state in 1861. (D) Indiana was a free state.

15. Which of the following most closely characterizes the geopolitical events of the USSR in 1991-92: ***(Rigorous) (Skill 10.5)***

A. The USSR established greater military and economic control over the fifteen Soviet republics

B. The Baltic States (Estonia, Latvia, Lithuania) declared independence, while the remainder of the USSR remained intact.

C. Fourteen of fifteen Soviet republics declared some degree of autonomy; the USSR was officially dissolved; the Supreme Soviet rescinded the Soviet Treaty of 1922

D. All fifteen Soviet republics simultaneously declared immediate and full independence from the USSR, with no provisions for a transitional form of government

Answer: C Fourteen of fifteen Soviet republics declared some degree of autonomy; the USSR was officially dissolved; the Supreme Soviet rescinded the Soviet Treaty of 1922.

The unraveling of the USSR in 1991-92 and the establishment of independent republics in its wake was a complex if relatively peaceful end to its existence. After a succession of declarations of autonomy by constituent states forced the dissolution of the central government, the Baltic States of Latvia, Lithuania, and Estonia immediately declared their independence. Other republics took longer to reconfigure their relationships to one another. There was no serious attempt by the central government to resist these changes militarily or economically.

16. The economic practices under President Ronald Reagan ("Reaganomics") were characterized by: ***(Rigorous) (Skill 10.5)***

A. Low inflation, high unemployment, high interest rates, high national debt

B. High inflation, low unemployment, low interest rates, low national debt

C. Low inflation, high unemployment, low interest rates, depletion of national debt

D. High inflation, low unemployment, high interest rates, low national debt

Answer: A High inflation, low unemployment, high interest rates, high national debt.

President Reagan was an advocate of “trickle-down” economics, which espoused cutting social programs to save money and decrease the tax burden on the wealthy and corporations, believing that largesse for the top tier of the population would eventually trickle down to the lower income strata of workers. Ronald Reagan was a strong supporter of de-regulation, insisting that private sector corporations could do oversight and self-policing better, which was contradicted by the high level of corporate abuse for safety, health and environmental concerns. Although the Reagan Era (Reaganomics) was a period of great wealth and financial boom times, the unprecedented level of military spending increased the national debt to its highest levels to date during peacetime.

17. The first territorial governor of Florida after Florida's purchase by the United States was: ***(Average) (Skill 10.6)***

A. Napoleon B. Broward

B. William P. Duval

C. Andrew Jackson

D. Davy Crockett

Answer: C Andrew Jackson

18. Which of the following is most descriptive of the conflict between the U.S. government and the Seminoles between 1818 and 1858? ***(Average) (Skill 10.6)***

A. There was constant armed conflict between the Seminoles and the U.S. during these years

B. Historians discern three separate phases of hostilities (1818, 1835-42, 1855-58), known collectively as the Seminole Wars

C. On May 7, 1858, the Seminoles admitted defeat, signed a peace treaty with the U.S., and left for Oklahoma, except for fifty-one individuals

D. The former Seminole chief Osceola helped the U.S. defeat the Seminoles and effect their removal to Oklahoma

Answer: B Historians discern three separate phases of hostilities (1818, 1835-42, 1855-58), known collectively as the Seminole Wars.

(A) Intermittent conflicts between the U.S. government and the Seminole Native Americans can be classified into (B) three separate phases of hostilities.

19. Who was the first governor of the state of Florida? ***(Rigorous) (Skill 10.6)***

A. Andrew Jackson

B. David Levy

C. William Moseley

D. Colonel James Moore

Answer: C William Moseley

Florida became the twenty-seventh state in the United States on March 3, 1845. (C) William D. Moseley was elected the new state's first governor, and(B) David Levy Yulee, one of Florida's leading proponents for statehood, became a U.S. Senator. By 1850, the population had grown to 87,445, including about 39,000 African American slaves and 1,000 free blacks. (A) Andrew Jackson was the military governor before Florida became a state. (D) Colonel James Moore led the Carolinians and their Creek Indian allies in an attack on Spanish Florida in 1702 and destroyed the town of St. Augustine.

20. Match the railroad entrepreneur with the correct area of development: ***(Rigorous) (Skill 10.6)***

A. Henry Plant: Tampa and the West Coast

B. Cornelius Vanderbilt: Jacksonville and the Northeast

C. Henry Flagler: Orlando and the Central Highlands

D. J.P. Morgan: Pensacola and the Northwest

Answer: A Henry Plant: Tampa and the West Coast

(A) Henry Plant (1819-1899) was responsible for building railroad along the West Coast of Florida, making Tampa the end of the line. (B) Cornelius Vanderbilt (1794-1877), transportation mogul, concentrated his efforts in the Northeast of the country and was largely uninvolved in Florida. (C) Henry Flagler (1830-1913) was a Floridian involved in railways and oil production but is more closely associated with Miami than Orlando. (D) J.P. Morgan (1837-1913) was a New York-based banker.

21. Florida's space exploration industry is centered in: ***(Rigorous) (Skill 10.6)***

A. Baker County

B. Broward County

C. Brevard County

D. Bradford County

Answer: C Brevard County

(C) Florida's Kennedy Space complex is on Cape Canaveral in Brevard County.

22. If geography is the study of how human beings live in relationship to the earth on which they live, why do geographers include physical geography within the discipline? ***(Rigorous) (Skill 11.1, 10.3)***

A. The physical environment serves as the location for the activities of human beings

B. No other branch of the natural or social sciences studies the same topics

C. The physical environment is more important than the activities carried out by human beings

D. It is important to be able to subdue natural processes for the advancement of humankind

Answer: A The physical environment serves as the location for the activities of human beings.

Cultures will develop different practices depending on the predominant geographical features of the area in which they live. Cultures that live along a river will have a different kind of relationship to the surrounding land than those who live in the mountains, for instance. Answer (A) best describes why physical geography is included in the social science of geography. Answer (B) is false, as physical geography is also studied under other natural sciences (such as geology.) Answers (C) and (D) are matters of opinion and do not pertain to the definition of geography as a social science.

23. A geographer wishes to study the effects of a flood on subsequent settlement patterns. Which might he or she find most useful? *(Average) (Skill 11.2, 12.9)*

A. A film clip of the floodwaters

B. An aerial photograph of the river's source

C. Census data taken after the flood

D. A soil map of the A and B horizons beneath the flood area

Answer: C

C. Census data taken after the flood

(A) A film clip of the flood waters may be of most interest to a historian, (B) an aerial photograph of the river's source, and (D) soil maps tell little about the behavior of the individuals affected by the flood. (C) Census surveys record the population for certain areas on a regular basis, allowing a geographer to tell if more or less people are living in an area over time. These would be of most use to a geographer undertaking this study.

24. A physical geographer would be concerned with which of the following groups of terms? *(Easy) (Skill 11.3, 11.8)*

A. Landform, biome, precipitation

B. Scarcity, goods, services

C. Nation, state, administrative subdivision

D. Cause and effect, innovation, exploration

Answer: A

A. Landform, biome, precipitation.

(A) Landform, biome, and precipitation are all terms used in the study of geography. A landform is a physical feature of the earth, such as a hill or valley. A biome is a large community of plants or animals, such as a forest. Precipitation is the moisture that falls to earth as rain or snow. (B) Scarcity, goods and services are terms encountered in economics. (C) Nation, state and administrative subdivision are terms used in political science. (D) Cause and effect, innovation and exploration are terms in developmental psychology.

25. An economist might engage in which of the following activities?
(Average) (Skill 11.4, 11.7, 12.1)

A. An observation of the historical effects of a nation's banking practices

B. The application of a statistical test to a series of data

C. Introduction of an experimental factor into a specified population to measure the effect of the factor

D. An economist might engage in all of these

Answer: D An economist might engage in all of these

Economists use statistical analysis of economic data, controlled experimentation as well as historical research in their field of social science.

26. Which of the following is NOT considered to be an economic need:
(Easy) (Skill 11.7)

A. Food

B. Transportation

C. Shelter

D. Clothing

Answer: B

B. Transportation

An economic need is something that a person absolutely must have to survive. (A) Food, (C) shelter and (D) clothing are examples of these needs. While an individual may also require (B) transportation to participate in an economy, it is not considered an absolute need.

27. A cultural geographer is investigating the implications of The Return of the Native by Thomas Hardy. He or she is most likely concentrating on: ***(Rigorous) (Skill 11.7)***

A. The reactions of British city-dwellers to the in-migration of French professionals

B. The activities of persons in relation to poorly-drained, coarse-soiled land with low-lying vegetation

C. The capacity of riverine lands to sustain a population of edible amphibians

D. The propagation of new crops introduced by settlers from North America

Answer: B

B. The activities of persons in relation to poorly-drained, coarse-soiled land with low-lying vegetation

Thomas Hardy's novel The Return of the Native takes place in England, in a fictional region based on Hardy's home area, Dorset. Hardy describes the people and landscape of this area, which is primarily heath. A heath is a poorly drained, coarse-soiled land with low-lying vegetation, as described in answer (B). This is the most likely concentration for a cultural geographer studying Hardy's novel.

28. Which location may be found in Canada? ***(Rigorous) (Skill 11.8)***

A. 27 N 93 W

B. 41 N 93 E

C. 50 N 111 W

D. 18 N 120 W

Answer: C 50 N 111 W

(A) 27 North latitude, 93 West longitude is located in the Gulf of Mexico. (B) 41 N 93 E is located in northwest China. (D) 18 N 120 W is in the Pacific Ocean, off the coast of Mexico. (C) 50 N 120 W is located near the town of Medicine Hat in the province of Alberta, in Canada.

29. The Mediterranean type climate is characterized by: ***(Rigorous) (Skill 11.8)***

A. Hot, dry summers and mild, relatively wet winters

B. Cool, relatively wet summers and cold winters

C. Mild summers and winters, with moisture throughout the year

D. Hot, wet summers and cool, dry winters

Answer: A Hot, dry summers and mild, relatively wet winters

Westerly winds and nearby bodies of water create stable weather patterns along the west coasts of several continents, and along the coast of the Mediterranean Sea, after which this type of climate is named. Temperatures rarely fall below the freezing point and have a mean between 70 and 80 degrees F. in the summer. Stable conditions make for little rain during the summer months.

30. The climate of Southern Florida is the ________________ type. ***(Average) (Skill 11.8)***

A. Humid subtropical

B. Marine West Coast

C. Humid continental

D. Tropical wet-dry

Answer: A Humid subtropical

The (B) marine west coast climate is found on the western coasts of continents. Florida is on the eastern side of North America. The (C) humid continental climate is found over large land masses, such as Europe and the American Midwest, not along coasts such as where Florida is situated. The (D) tropical wet-dry climate occurs within about 15 degrees of the equator, in the tropics. Florida is sub-tropical. Florida is in a (A) humid subtropical climate, which extends along the East Coast of the United States to about Maryland, and along the gulf coast to northeastern Texas.

31. The Bill of Rights was mostly written by: ***(Rigorous) (Skill 12.3)***

A. Thomas Jefferson

B. James Madison

C. George Washington

D. Alexander Hamilton

Answer: B. James Madison

The Bill of Rights, along with the majority of the Constitution, was mostly written by James Madison. Thomas Jefferson wrote the Declaration of Independence. Washington and Hamilton were present at the Constitutional Convention of 1787 in Philadelphia and they were advocates of federalism or increasing the power of the federal government.

32. In the United States government, the power of coining money is: ***(Rigorous) (Skill 3.1d)***

A. Implied or suggested

B. Concurrent or shared

C. Delegated or expressed

D. Reserved

Answer: C. Delegated or expressed

In the United States government, the power of coining money is delegated or expressed. Therefore, only the United States government may coin money, the states may not coin money for themselves.

33. Which branch is responsible for carrying out the laws of the country? ***(Average) (Skill 12.4)***

A. Judicial

B. Executive

C. Legislative

D. Supreme Court

Answer: B. Executive

In the United States, the three branches of the federal government mentioned earlier, the **Executive**, the **Legislative**, and the **Judicial**, divide up their powers thus:

Article 2 of the Constitution created the (B) Executive branch of the government, headed by the President, who leads the country, recommends new laws, and can veto bills passed by the legislative branch. As the chief of state, the President is responsible for carrying out the laws of the country and the treaties and declarations of war passed by the legislative branch.

34. Which branch established the power of the Supreme Court? ***(Average) (Skill 12.4)***

A. Judicial

B. Executive

C. Legislative

D. House of Representatives

Answer: A. Judicial

In the United States, the three branches of the federal government mentioned earlier, the **Executive**, the **Legislative**, and the **Judicial**, divide up their powers thus:

Article 3 of the Constitution established the (A) judicial branch of government headed by the Supreme Court. The Supreme Court has the power to rule that a law passed by the legislature or an act of the Executive branch is illegal and unconstitutional.

35. The ________ branch of government is made up of House of Representatives and the Senate. ***(Average) (Skill 12.4)***

A. Judicial

B. Executive

C. Legislative

D. Supreme Court

Answer: C Legislative

In the United States, the three branches of the federal government mentioned earlier, the **Executive**, the **Legislative**, and the **Judicial**, divide up their powers thus:

Article 1 of the Constitution established the (C) legislative, or law-making branch of the government called the Congress. It is made up of two houses, the House of Representatives and the Senate.

36. An economist investigates the spending patterns of low-income individuals. Which of the following would yield the most pertinent information? ***(Average) (Skill 12.6)***

A. Prime lending rates of neighborhood banks

B. The federal discount rate

C. City-wide wholesale distribution figures

D. Census data and retail sales figures

Answer: D

D. Census data and retail sales figures

(A) Local lending rates and (B) the federal discount rate might provide information on borrowing habits, but not necessarily spending habits, and give no information on income levels. (C) Citywide wholesale distribution figures would provide information on the business activity of a city, but tell nothing about consumer activities. (D) Census data records the income levels of households within a certain area and retail sales figures for that area would give an economist data on spending, which can be compared to income levels, making this the most pertinent source.

37. As your income rises, you tend to spend more money on entertainment. This is an expression of the: ***(Rigorous) (Skill 12.6, 12.8)***

A. Marginal propensity to consume

B. Allocative efficiency

C. Compensating differential

D. Marginal propensity to save

Answer: A

A. Marginal propensity to consume

The (A) marginal propensity to consume is a measurement of how much consumption changes compared to how much disposable income changes. Entertainment expenses are an example of disposable income. Dividing your change in entertainment spending by your total change in disposable income will give you your marginal propensity to consume.

38. Economics is best described as: ***(Average) (Skill 12.6)***

A. The study of how money is used in different societies

B. The study of how different political systems produce goods and services

C. The study of how human beings use limited resources to supply their necessities and wants

D. The study of how human beings have developed trading practices through the years

Answer: C The study of how human beings use limited resources to supply their necessities and wants

(A) How money is used in different societies might be of interest to a sociologist or anthropologist. (B) The study of how different political systems produce goods and services is a topic of study that could be included under the field of political science. (D) The study of historical trading practices could fall under the study of history. Only (C) is the best general description of the social science of economics as a whole.

39. Capitalism and communism are alike in that they are both: ***(Average) (Skill 12.7, 12.4)***

A. Organic systems

B. Political systems

C. Centrally planned systems

D. Economic systems

Answer: D Economic systems

While economic and (B) political systems are often closely connected, capitalism and communism are primarily (D) economic systems. Capitalism is a system of economics that allows the open market to determine the relative value of goods and services. Communism is an economic system where the market is planned by a central state. While communism is a (C) centrally planned system, this is not true of capitalism. (A) Organic systems are studied in biology, a natural science.

40. If the price of Good G increases, what is likely to happen with regard to comparable Good H? ***(Rigorous) (Skill 12.8)***

A. The demand for Good G will stay the same

B. The demand for Good G will increase

C. The demand for Good H will increase

D. The demand for Good H will decrease

Answer: C The demand for Good H will increase.

If Good G and Good H are viewed by consumers as equal in value, but then the cost of Good G increases, it follows that consumers will now choose Good H at a higher rate, increasing the demand.

41. During the latter part of the 20th century, the centrally planned economy was more commonly known as what? ***(Rigorous) (Skill 12.8)***

A. Consumerism

B. Market economy

C. Market socialism

D. Communism

Answer: D. Communism

(A) Consumerism refers to economic policies that emphasize purchasing material possessions and consumption. A (B) market economy answers these questions in terms of demand and supply and the use of markets. The opposite of the market economy is called the centrally planned economy. This used to be called (D) Communism, even though the term is not correct in a strict Marxian sense. In a planned economy, the means of production are publicly owned with little, if any public ownership. In between the two extremes is (C) market socialism. This is a mixed economic system that uses both markets and planning. Planning is usually used to direct resources at the upper levels of the economy, with markets being used to determine prices of consumer goods and wages. This kind of economic system answers the three questions with planning and markets.

42.A historian would be interested in: ***(Average) (Skill 12.9)***

A. The manner in which scientific knowledge is advanced

B. The effects of the French Revolution on world colonial policy

C. The viewpoint of persons who have written previous "history"

D. All of the above

Answer: D All of the above

Historians are interested in broad developments through history (A), as well as how individual events affected the time in which they happened (B). Knowing the viewpoint of earlier historians can also help explain the common thinking among historical cultures and groups (C), so all of these answers are correct (D).

43. The sub-discipline of linguistics is usually studied under: ***(Average) (Skill 12.9)***

A. Geography

B. History

C. Anthropology

D. Economics

Answer: C Anthropology

The fields of (A) Geography, (B) History and (D) Economics may study language as part of other subjects that affect these fields of study, but taken by itself, language is a defining characteristic of a culture. (C) Anthropology studies human culture and the relationships between cultures, so linguistics is included under this social science.

44. Which of the following is not generally considered a discipline within the social sciences? ***(Easy) (Skill 12.9)***

A. Geometry

B. Anthropology

C. Geography

D. Sociology

Answer:

A. Geometry

(B) Anthropology studies the culture of groups of people. (C) Geography examines the relationship between societies and the physical place on earth where they live. (D) Sociology studies the predominant attitudes, beliefs and behaviors of a society. All three of these fields are related to the social interactions of humans, and so are considered social sciences. (A) Geometry is a field of mathematics and does not relate to the social interactions of people, so it is not considered a social science.

45. Psychology is a social science because: ***(Easy) (Skill 12.9)***

A. It focuses on the biological development of individuals

B. It focuses on the behavior of individual persons and small groups of persons

C. It bridges the gap between the natural and the social sciences

D. It studies the behavioral habits of lower animals

Answer: B

B. It focuses on the behavior of individual persons and small groups of persons

While it is true that (C) psychology draws from natural sciences, it is (B) the study of the behavior of individual persons and small groups that defines psychology as a social science. (A) The biological development of human beings and (D) the behavioral habits of lower animals are studied in the developmental and behavioral branches of psychology.

46. Which of the following is most reasonably studied under the social sciences? ***(Easy) (Skill 12.9)***

A. Political science

B. Geometry

C. Physics

D. Grammar

Answer: A

A. Political science

Social sciences deal with the social interactions of people. (B) Geometry is a branch of mathematics. (C) Physics is a natural science that studies the physical world. Although it may be studied as part of linguistics, (D) grammar is not recognized as a scientific field of study in itself. Only (A) political science is considered a general field of the social sciences.

47. A social scientist observes how individual persons react to the presence or absence of noise. This scientist is most likely a: ***(Easy) (Skill 12.9)***

A. Geographer

B. Political Scientist

C. Economist

D. Psychologist

Answer: D

D. Psychologist

(D) Psychologists scientifically study the behavior and mental processes of individuals. Studying how individuals react to changes in their environment falls under this social science. (A) Geographers, (B) political scientists and (C) economists are more likely to study the reactions of groups rather than individual reactions.

48. As a sociologist, you would be most likely to observe: ***(Easy) (Skill 12.9)***

A. The effects of an earthquake on farmland

B. The behavior of rats in sensory-deprivation experiments

C. The change over time in Babylonian obelisk styles

D. The behavior of human beings in television focus groups

Answer: D The behavior of human beings in television focus groups.

Predominant beliefs and attitudes within human society are studied in the field of sociology. (A) The effects of an earthquake on farmland might be studied by a geographer. (B) The behavior of rats in an experiment falls under the field of behavioral psychology. (C) Changes in Babylonian obelisk styles might interest a historian. None of these answers fit easily within the definition of sociology. (D) A focus group, where people are asked to discuss their reactions to a certain product or topic, would be the most likely method for a sociologist of observing and discovering attitudes among a selected group.

49. Which of the following is most closely identified as a sociologist? ***(Rigorous) (Skill 12.9)***

A. Herodotus

B. John Maynard Keynes

C. Emile Durkheim

D. Arnold Toynbee

Answer: C Emile Durkheim

(A) Durkheim (1858-1917) was the founder of the first sociological journal in France, and the first to apply scientific methods of research to the study of human society. (A) Herodotus (ca. 484-425 BC) was an early Greek historian. (B) John Maynard Keynes (1883-1946) was a British economist who developed the field of modern theoretical macroeconomics. (D) Arnold Toynbee (1882-1853) was also a British economist who took a historical approach to the field.

50. Political science is primarily concerned with ____________. *(Average)* *(Skill 12.9)*

A. Elections

B. Economic Systems

C. Boundaries

D. Public Policy

Answer: D

D. Public policy

Political science studies the actions and policies of the government of a society. (D) Public policy is the official stance of a government on an issue, and is a primary source for studying a society's dominant political beliefs. (A) Elections are also an interest of political scientists, but are not a primary field of study. (B) Economic systems are of interest to an economist, and (C) boundaries to a geographer.

COMPETENCY 13.0 KNOWLEDGE OF WRITTEN AND ORAL LANGUAGE

Skill 13.1 Select language that is appropriate for a specific purpose.

Often, people assume that written language is simply a codified oral language. In other words, it is oral language put into symbols on a page. This is far from the truth. Consider, first, how children can speak fluently before they can communicate fluently in writing. Consider also how it is easy for most adults to orally discuss issues, yet how often adults struggle when putting words on paper.

A significant difference between oral and written language is the level of formality. Oral language tends to be informal while written language is more formal. Highly formalized oral language sounds unnatural to many listeners.

Another difference between oral and written language is that written language tends to not be affected by the diversity of oral dialects whereas regional dialects and other features such as social class have an impact on oral language. Generally, accent, word choice, tone, and other elements distinguish oral language from written language.

Finally, written language is much more uniform than oral language. In oral communication, people regularly exhibit run-on sentences, fragment sentences, and other grammatical errors that typically go unnoticed by listeners. People can add emphasis in oral speech through repeated phrases, volume, tone, hand gestures, and other elements unavailable in written language.

Understanding the difference between oral and written language is important for teachers because both skills need to be developed separately. Often teachers assume that oral language develops naturally and that no specific work needs to be done in the classroom to enhance it. This is not true, however. Even though informality and unevenness is accepted more readily in oral language, students need to learn and practice the skills needed to express themselves competently in oral language (both in formal presentations and informal discussions).

Often, modeling good oral language and having students practice it through classroom discussions, oral presentations, and group discussions will provide students good outlets in which to improve their oral language skills. Teaching writing skills is different from teaching oral communication

Skill Identify standard English usage, grammar, and punctuation.

Syntax

Language is made up of a systematic orderly arrangement and the grammatical arrangement of words. The syntax of English, reflective of its Germanic origins, relies on word order rather than inflection.

Sentence completeness

Avoid fragments and run-on sentences. Knowing the sentence elements, including independent and dependent clauses (see *Use correct coordination and subordination*) and proper punctuation, will eliminate fragments and run-on sentences.

Sentence structure

Recognize simple, compound, complex, and compound-complex sentences. Using dependent (subordinate) and independent clauses correctly is essential for creating these sentence structures.

Simple Joyce wrote a letter.
Compound Joyce wrote a letter, and Dot drew a picture.
Complex While Joyce wrote a letter, Dot drew a picture.
Compound-complex When Mother asked the girls to demonstrate their new-found skills, Joyce wrote a letter, and Dot drew a picture.

Note: Do **not** confuse compound sentence elements with compound sentences.

Simple sentence with compound subject
Joyce and Dot wrote letters.
The girl in row three and the boy next to her were passing notes across the aisle.

Simple sentence with compound predicate
Joyce wrote letters and drew pictures.
The captain of the high school debate team graduated with honors and studied broadcast journalism in college.

Simple sentence with compound object of preposition
Coleen graded the students' essays for style and mechanical accuracy.

Parallelism

Recognize parallel structures. Using phrases (prepositional, gerund, participial, and infinitive) and omissions from sentences can create a lack of parallelism.

Prepositional phrase/single modifier

Incorrect: Coleen ate the ice cream with enthusiasm and hurriedly.
Correct: Coleen ate the ice cream with enthusiasm and in a hurry.
Correct: Coleen ate the ice cream enthusiastically and hurriedly.

Participial phrase/infinitive phrase

Incorrect: After hiking for hours and to sweat profusely, Joe sat down to rest and drinking water.
Correct: After hiking for hours and sweating profusely, Joe sat down to rest and drink water.

Recognition of dangling modifiers

Dangling phrases can be placed incorrectly and thus create ambiguity and unintended meaning.

Participial phrase

Incorrect: Hanging from her skirt, Dot tugged at a loose thread.
Correct: Dot tugged at a loose thread hanging from her skirt.

Incorrect: Relaxing in the bathtub, the telephone rang.
Correct: While I was relaxing in the bathtub, the telephone rang.

Infinitive phrase

Incorrect: To improve his behavior, the dean warned Fred.
Correct: The dean warned Fred to improve his behavior.

Prepositional phrase

Incorrect: On the floor, Father saw the dog eating table scraps.
Correct: Father saw the dog eating table scraps on the floor.

Recognition of syntactic redundancy or omission

These errors occur when superfluous words have been added to a sentence or key words have been omitted from a sentence.

Redundancy

Incorrect: Joyce made sure that when her plane arrived that she retrieved all of her luggage.
Correct: Joyce made sure that when her plane arrived she retrieved all of her luggage.

Incorrect: He was a mere skeleton of his former self.
Correct: He was a skeleton of his former self.

Omission

Incorrect: Dot opened her book, recited her textbook, and answered the teacher's subsequent question.
Correct: Dot opened her book, recited from the textbook, and answered the teacher's subsequent question.

Avoidance of double negatives

This error occurs from positioning two negatives that, in fact, cancel each other in meaning.

Incorrect: Dot didn't have no double negatives in her paper.
Correct: Dot didn't have any double negatives in her paper.
Or Correct: Dot had not double negatives in her paper.

Incorrect: I didn't have hardly any bills this month.
Correct: I had hardly any bills this month.

Types of Clauses

Clauses are connected word groups composed of *at least* one subject and one verb. (A subject is the doer of an action or the element that is being joined. A verb conveys either the action or the link.)

Students are waiting for the start of the assembly.
Subject Verb

At the end of the play, students wait for the curtain to come down.
Subject Verb

Clauses can be independent or dependent.

Independent clauses can stand alone or can be joined to other clauses.

Independent clause	for and nor	
Independent clause,	but or yet so	Independent clause
Independent clause	;	Independent clause
Dependent clause	,	Independent clause
Independent clause		Dependent clause

Dependent clauses, by definition, contain at least one subject and one verb. However, they cannot stand alone as a complete sentence. They are structurally dependent on the main clause.

There are two types of dependent clauses: (1) those with a subordinating conjunction, and (2) those with a relative pronoun

Sample coordinating conjunctions:
Although
When
If
Unless
Because

Unless a cure is discovered, many more people will die of the disease.
Dependent clause + Independent clause

Sample relative pronouns:
Who
Whom
Which
That

The White House has an official website, which contains press releases, news updates, and biographies of the President and Vice-President.
(Independent clause + relative pronoun + relative dependent clause)

Misplaced and Dangling Modifiers

Particular phrases need to be placed near the word they're modifying or they are "misplaced modifiers." A modifying phrase that doesn't relate to what it is modifying is called a "dangling modifier."

Error: Weighing the options carefully, a decision was made regarding the punishment of the convicted murderer.

Problem: Who is weighing the options? No one capable of weighing is named in the sentence; thus, the participle phrase "weighing the options carefully" dangles. This problem can be corrected by adding a subject of the sentence capable of doing the action.

Correction: Weighing the options carefully, the judge made a decision regarding the punishment of the convicted murderer.

Error: One damaged house stood only to remind townspeople of the hurricane.

Problem: The placement of the misplaced modifier only suggests that the sole reason the house remained was to serve as a reminder. The faulty modifier creates ambiguity.

Correction: Only one damaged house stood, reminding townspeople of the hurricane.

Spelling

Concentration in this section is on the spelling of plurals and possessives. The multiplicity and complexity of spelling rules based on phonics, letter doubling, and exceptions to rules make a good dictionary essential.

Most plurals of nouns that end in hard consonants or hard consonant sounds followed by a silent *e* are made by adding *s*. Some words ending with a vowel add *s*.

fingers, numerals, banks, bugs, riots, homes, gates, radios, bananas

Nouns that end in soft consonant sounds *s, j, x, z, ch,* and *sh*, add *es*. Some nouns ending in *o* add *es*.

dresses, waxes, churches, brushes, tomatoes, potatoes

Nouns ending in *y* preceded by a vowel add *s*.

boys, alleys

Nouns ending in *y* preceded by a consonant change the *y* to *i* and add *es.*

babies, corollaries, frugalities, poppies

Some plurals of nouns are formed irregularly or remain the same.

sheep, deer, children, leaves, oxen

Some nouns derived from foreign words, especially Latin, may make their plurals in two different ways -- one of them Anglicized. Sometimes, the meanings are the same; other times, the two plurals are used in slightly different contexts. It is always wise to consult the dictionary.

appendices, appendixes criteria
indexes, indices crises

Make the plurals of closed (solid) compound words in the usual way.

timelines, hairpins, cupfuls

Make the plurals of open or hyphenated compounds by adding the change to the part of the word that changes in number.

fathers-in-law, courts-martial, masters of art, doctors of medicine

Make the plurals of letters, numbers, and abbreviations by adding *s.*

fives and tens, IBMs, 1990s, *P*s and Qs.

Capitalization

Capitalize all proper names of persons (including specific organizations or agencies of government); places (countries, states, cities, parks, and specific geographical areas); things (political parties, structures, historical and cultural terms, and calendar and time designations); and religious terms (any deity, revered person or group, sacred writings).

Percy Bysshe Shelley, Argentina, Mount Rainier National Park, Grand Canyon, League of Nations, the Sears Tower, Birmingham, Lyric Theater, Americans, Midwesterners, Democrats, Renaissance, Boy Scouts of America, Easter, God, Bible, Dead Sea Scrolls, Koran

Capitalize proper adjectives and titles used with proper names.

California Gold Rush, President John Adams, French fries, Homeric epic, Romanesque architecture, Senator John Glenn

Note: Some words that represent titles and offices are not capitalized unless used with a proper name.

Capitalized	Not Capitalized
Congressman McKay	the congressman from Florida
Commander Alger	commander of the Pacific Fleet
Queen Elizabeth	the queen of England

Capitalize all main words in titles of works of literature, art, and music. (See “Using Italics” in the Punctuation section.)

The candidate should be cognizant of proper rules and conventions of punctuation, capitalization, and spelling. Competency exams will generally test the ability to apply the more advanced skills; thus, a limited number of more frustrating rules is presented here. Rules should be applied according to the American style of English, i.e., spelling *theater* instead of *theatre* and placing terminal marks of punctuation almost exclusively within other marks of punctuation.

Punctuation

Using terminal punctuation in relation to quotation marks

In a quoted statement that is either declarative or imperative, place the period inside the closing quotation marks.

> “The airplane crashed on the runway during takeoff.”

If the quotation is followed by other words in the sentence, place a comma inside the closing quotation marks and a period at the end of the sentence.

> “The airplane crashed on the runway during takeoff,” said the announcer.

In most instances, when a quoted title or expression occurs at the end of a sentence, the period is placed before either the single or double quotation marks.

> “The middle school readers were unprepared to understand Bryant’s poem ‘Thanatopsis.’“

> Early book-length adventure stories such as *Don Quixote* and *The Three Musketeers* were known as “picaresque novels.”

There is an instance in which the final quotation mark would precede the period: the content of the sentence regards a speech or quote and the understanding of the meaning would be confused by the placement of the period.

The first thing out of his mouth was "Hi, I'm home."
but
The first line of his speech began "I arrived home to an empty house".

In interrogatory or exclamatory sentences, the question mark or exclamation point should be positioned *outside* the closing quotation marks if the quote itself is a statement, command, or cited title.

Who decided to lead us in the recitation of the "Pledge of Allegiance"?

Why was Tillie shaking as she began her recitation, "Once upon a midnight dreary..."?

I was embarrassed when Mrs. White said, "Your slip is showing"!

In declarative sentences, when the quotation is a question or an exclamation, place the question mark or exclamation point inside the quotation marks.

The hall monitor yelled, "Fire! Fire!"

"Fire! Fire!" yelled the hall monitor.

Cory shrieked, "Is there a mouse in the room?" (In this instance, the question supersedes the exclamation.)

Using periods with parentheses or brackets

If a complete sentence, independent of the surrounding sentences, is enclosed by brackets or parentheses, it is concluded with a period and the closing parenthesis or bracket.

Stephen Crane was a confirmed alcohol and drug addict. (He admitted as much to other journalists in Cuba.)

If the parenthetical expression is a statement inserted into another statement, the period in the enclosure is omitted.

Mark Twain used the character Injun Joe (He also appeared in *The Adventures of Tom Sawyer*) as a foil for Jim in *The Adventures of Huckleberry Finn*.

When an enclosed word or words come at the end of a sentence requiring quotation marks, place the period outside the concluding parenthesis or bracket.

"The Secretary of State consulted with the ambassador [Albright]."

Using commas

Use commas in lists separating two or more coordinate adjectives that modify the same word or three or more nouns, phrases, or clauses in a list.

Maggie's hair was dull, dirty, and lice-ridden.

Dickens portrayed the Artful Dodger as a skillful pickpocket, a loyal follower of Fagin, and a defender of Oliver Twist.

Ellen daydreamed about getting out of the rain, taking a shower, and eating a hot dinner.

In Elizabethan England, Ben Johnson wrote comedy, Christopher Marlowe wrote tragedies, and William Shakespeare composed both.

Use commas to separate antithetical or complementary expressions from the rest of the sentence.

The veterinarian, not his assistant, would perform the delicate surgery.

The more he knew about her, the less he wished he had known.

Randy hopes to, and probably will, get an appointment to the Naval Academy.

His thorough, though esoteric, scientific research could not easily be understood by high school students.

Using double quotation marks with other punctuation

Quotations - whether words, phrases, or clauses - should be punctuated according to the rules of the grammatical function they serve in the sentence.

> The works of Shakespeare, "the bard of Avon," have been contested as originating with other authors.
>
> "You'll get my money," the old man warned, "when 'Hell freezes over'."
>
> Sheila cited the passage that began "Four score and seven years ago . . . . " (Note the ellipsis followed by an enclosed period.)
>
> "Old Ironsides" inspired the preservation of the U.S.S. Constitution.

Use quotation marks to enclose the titles of shorter works: songs, short poems, short stories, essays, and chapters of books. (See "Using Italics" for punctuating longer works.)

> "The Tell-Tale Heart" "Casey at the Bat" "America the Beautiful"

Using semicolons

Use semicolons to separate independent clauses when the second clause is introduced by a transitional adverb. (These clauses may also be written as separate sentences, preferably by placing the adverb into the second sentence.)

> The Elizabethans modified the rhyme scheme of the sonnet; thus, it was called the English sonnet.
>
> *or*
>
> The Elizabethans modified the rhyme scheme of the sonnet. It thus was called the English sonnet.
>
> *Or*
>
> The Elizabethans modified the rhyme scheme of the sonnet. Thus it was called the English sonnet.

Use semicolons to separate items in a series that are long and complex or have internal punctuation.

> The Italian Renaissance produced masters in the fine arts: Dante Alighieri, author of the *Divine Comedy;* Leonardo da Vinci, painter of *The Last Supper;* and Donatello, sculptor of the *Quattro Coronati*, the four saints.
>
> The leading scorers in the WNBA were Haizhaw Zheng, averaging 23.9 points per game; Lisa Leslie, 22; and Cynthia Cooper, 19.5.

Using colons

Place a colon at the beginning of a list of items. (Note its use in the sentence about Renaissance Italians on the previous page.)

> The teacher directed us to compare Faulkner's three symbolic novels: *Absalom, Absalom; As I Lay Dying;* and *Light in August*.

Do **not** use a comma if the list is preceded by a verb.

> Three of Faulkner's symbolic novels are *Absalom, Absalom; As I Lay Dying,* and *Light in August*.

Using dashes

Place dashes to denote sudden breaks in thought.

> Some periods in literature - the Romantic Age, for example - spanned different time periods in different countries.

Use dashes instead of commas if commas are already used elsewhere in the sentence.

> The Fireside Poets included three Brahmans - James Russell Lowell, Henry David Wadsworth, and Oliver Wendell Holmes.

Using italics

Use italics to punctuate the titles of long works of literature, names of periodical publications, musical scores, works of art and motion picture television, and radio programs. (When unable to write in italics, students should be instructed to underline the words that would be italicized.)

The Idylls of the King	*Hiawatha*	*The Sound and the Fury*
Mary Poppins	*Newsweek*	*The Nutcracker Suite*

Skill 13.3 Select statements that best develop and support a thesis.

Supporting a thesis involves providing the reasons behind the thesis, offering examples that illustrate these reasons, and giving details that show how these examples support the conclusion.

The presentation of a prosecutor in a court trial is a good example of how a thesis is developed and supported.

The **thesis** of the prosecutor may be: John O'Hara stole construction materials from a house being built at 223 Hudson Ave. by the Jones Construction Company. As a **reason**, he might cite the following: He is building his own home on Green Street and needs materials and tools. This will answer the question why. He might give **examples**: 20 bags of concrete disappeared the night before Mr. O'Hara poured the basement for his house on Green Street. The electronic nail-setter disappeared from the building site on Hudson Ave. the day before Mr. O'Hara began to erect the frame of his house on Green Street. He might fill in the **details**: Mr. O'Hara's truck was observed by a witness on Hudson Ave. in the vicinity of the Jones Construction Company site the night the concrete disappeared. Mr. O'Hara's truck was observed again on that street by a witness the night the nail-setter disappeared.

Another example of a trial might be: **Thesis**, Adam Andrews murdered Joan Rogers in cold blood on the night of December 20. **Reason #1**: She was about to reveal their affair to his wife. **Reason #2**: Andrews' wife would inherit half of his sizeable estate in case of a divorce since there is no prenuptial agreement. **Example #1**: Rogers has demonstrated that he is capable of violence in an incident with a partner in his firm. **Example #2**: Rogers has had previous affairs where he was accused of violence. **Detail #1**: Andrews' wife once called the police and signed a warrant. **Detail #2**: A previous lover sought police protection from Andrews.

An **opinion** as a thesis requires support. The support may require reasons, examples, and details.

For example:

Opinion: Our borders must be protected.

Reason #1: Terrorists can get into the country undetected. **Example #1**: An Iranian national was able to cross the Mexican border and live in this country for years before being detected. **Detail**: The Iranian national came up through Central America to Mexico then followed the route that Mexican illegal immigrants regularly took. **Example #2**: A group of Middle Eastern terrorists were arrested in Oregon after they had crossed the Canadian border. **Detail**: There was no screening at that border.

Reason #2: Illegal aliens are an enormous drain on resources such as health care. **Example**: The states of California and Texas bear enormous burdens for health care and education for illegal immigrants. **Detail**: Legal citizens are often denied care in those states because resources are stretched so thin.

Skill 13.4 Choose an organizational strategy for a specific purpose.

Authors must choose a particular organizational structure to best present the concepts that they are writing about. Teaching students to recognize organizational structures helps them to understand authors' literary intentions and helps them in deciding which structure to use in their own writing.

Cause and Effect: When writing about *why* things happen as well as *what* happens, authors commonly use the cause and effect structure. For example, when writing about how he became so successful, a CEO might talk about how he excelled in math in high school, moved to New York after college, and stuck to his goals even after multiple failures. These are all *causes* that led to the *effect*, or result, of his becoming a wealthy and powerful businessman.

Compare and Contrast: When examining the merits of multiple concepts or products, "compare and contrast" lends itself easily to organization of ideas. For example, a person writing about foreign policy in different countries will show the differences and similarities, easily highlighting the concepts the author wishes to emphasize.

Problem and Solution: This structure is used in many handbooks and manuals. Writing that is organized around procedure-oriented tasks, such as computer repair, gravitates toward a problem and solution format because it offers such clear, sequential text organization.

Skill 13.5 Identify appropriate modes to create effective discourse.

The successful conversationalist is a person who keeps up with what's going on in the world both far and near and ponders the meanings of events and developments. That person also usually reads about the topics that are of the most interest to him, both in printed materials and online. In addition, the effective conversationalist has certain areas of particular interest that have been probed in some depth. An interest in human behavior, for example, is usually one of this person's most particular interests. Why do people behave as they do? Why do some succeed and some fail? This person may also be interested in and concerned about social issues, in the immediate community and the world at large and will have ideas for solving associated problems.

The most important thing a good conversationalist can do is to *listen*, not just wait until another person quits speaking so the conversationalist can take the floor again but carefully listen to learn what the other person has to say and learn more about the other person.

It is acceptable to be passionate about one's convictions in polite conversation; it is *not* acceptable to be overbearing or unwilling to hear and consider another's point of view. It's important to keep one's emotions under control in these circumstances even if the other person does not.

Skill 13.6 Select appropriate strategies and resources, including technological resources, for teaching written and oral language in all areas of the curriculum.

Media's impact on today's society is immense and ever-increasing. Children watch programs on television that are amazingly fast-paced and visually rich. Parents' roles as verbal and moral teachers are diminishing in response to the much more stimulating guidance of the television set. Adolescence, which used to be the time for going out and exploring the world firsthand, is now consumed by the allure of television, popular music, and video games. =Young adults are exposed to uncensored sex and violence.

Media's effect on society is beneficial and progressive at the same time. Its effect on education in particular provides special challenges and opportunities for teachers and students.

Thanks to satellite technology, instructional radio and television programs can be received by urban classrooms and rural villages. CD-ROMs enable students to learn information through a virtual reality experience. The Internet allows instant access to unlimited data and connects people across all cultures through shared interests. Educational media, when used in a productive way, enriches instruction and makes it more individualized, accessible, and economical.

Multimedia Teaching Model

Step 1. DIAGNOSE
- Figure out what students need to know.
- Assess what students already know.

Step 2. DESIGN
- Design tests of learning achievement.
- Identify effective instructional strategies.
- Select suitable media.
- Sequence learning activities within program.
- Plan introductory activities.
- Plan follow-up activities.

Step 3. PROCURE
- Secure materials at hand.
- Obtain new materials.

Step 4. PRODUCE
- Modify existing materials.
- Craft new materials.

Step 5. REFINE
- Conduct small-scale test of program.
- Evaluate procedures and achievements.
- Revise program accordingly.
- Conduct classroom test of program.
- Evaluate procedures and achievements.
- Revise in anticipation of next school term.

Tips for using print media and visual aids
- Use pictures instead of words whenever possible.
- Present one key point per visual.
- Use no more than 3-4 colors per visual to avoid clutter and confusion.
- Use contrasting colors such as dark blue and bright yellow.
- Use a maximum of 25-35 numbers per visual aid.
- Use bullets instead of paragraphs when possible.
- Make sure a presentation is student-centered, not media-centered. Delivery is just as important as the media presented.

Tips for using film and television

- Study programs in advance.
- Obtain supplementary materials such as printed transcripts of the narrative or study guides.
- Provide your students with background information, explain unfamiliar concepts, and anticipate outcomes.
- Assign outside readings based on their viewing.
- Ask cuing questions.
- Watch along with students.
- Observe students' reactions.
- Follow up viewing with discussions and related activities.

Research is beginning to document the ways cultural minority parents interact with their children that support learning, yet differ from more mainstream approaches. The strategies of research reflect the cultural practices of the home that support success in school. One recent study explored the nontraditional ways Hispanic parents tend to be involved in their children's education, ways not necessarily recognized by educators as parent involvement. Further research is needed to delve deeply into the connections that diverse families create that traditional indicators do not recognize. Building a body of knowledge about the specific practices of various cultural groups may support the validation of those practices by school personnel and may support the sharing of effective practices across cultural groups.

Interactive homework assignments: The development of interactive homework assignments (homework that requires parent-child interaction as part of the activity) has shown promise as a way of supporting parent involvement and student achievement. Homework activities explicitly designed to encourage interaction between parents and children have shown positive results for increasing achievement in several subject areas, including science and language arts. Well-designed interactive assignments can have a number of positive outcomes: they can help students practice study skills, prepare for class, participate in learning activities, and develop personal responsibility for homework, as well as promote parent-child relations, develop parent-teacher communication, and fulfill policy directives from administrators.

School support of parental homework help: Although parents express positive feelings about homework, they have concerns about homework, including their personal limitations in subject-matter knowledge and effective helping strategies. More research is needed on how school personnel can effectively support parental homework help.

Teachers have a critical role to play in encouraging multicultural experiences. They have an opportunity to incorporate activities that reflect our nation's increasing diversity and allow students to share their similarities, develop a positive cultural identity, and appreciate the unique contributions of all cultures. The best way to incorporate multicultural literature, depicting African-American, Asian, Arabic, Native American, and Hispanic heritage, is to integrate it into the established reading program rather than as a separate or distinct area of study.

Reading Workshops
In reading workshops, students select from a variety of reading materials such as novels, biographies, encyclopedias, and magazines. Students share their responses to the literature by writing or talking with teachers and classmates. It allows students to take ownership of their reading by choosing their own reading material. Teachers need to have a large supply of multicultural literature to choose from that is sensitive to and reflective of students' diverse cultural backgrounds. When reading these materials, students can learn that most people have similar emotions, needs and dreams. During reading workshops, students usually engage in reading, responding, sharing, and reading aloud.

Reading. Students usually spend an hour independently reading books and other written materials that include material on diverse cultures. Classrooms should have a variety of instructional materials representing diverse cultures.

Responding. After students read a multicultural storybook, teachers should direct the students to reflect on the meaning of the story in their own lives. In this process, students interpret meanings and draw inferences based upon their own cultural perspectives and experiences. Students might keep journals in which they write their initial responses to the materials they are reading. They may also talk with the teacher about their books. Teachers should help students move beyond simply writing summaries and toward reflecting and making connections between literature and their own lives.

Sharing. Sharing differences of diverse families heightens a child's sensitivity to issues involving prejudice, racism, and intolerance toward students of different cultures. Exposing students to culturally diverse literature provides them with a means to become global citizens who can perform more effectively in a culturally diverse society.

Reading Aloud. Teachers read aloud when they wish to present literature that students might not be able to read themselves, such as classics. Students should participate in a class discussion about the literature, share the reading experience, and respond to the story together as a community of learners, not as individuals.

Writing Workshops

Teachers can encourage students to write stories depicting the lives of persons around the world as they imagine a setting and characters with foreign names. In a writing workshop, students can make a box containing cultural items of a country or several countries such as ornaments, clothing, pictures, or audio materials associated with the storyline they create. Another way of integrating multicultural activities in a writing workshop is to involve students in a multicultural pen-pal project. Students can compose group letters to partner classes in other nations about their school, their lives, or a favorite part of the books they have read about the partner's country. Copies of these books and thank-you notes from partner classes can be displayed in the school by posting them on bulletin boards. From this activity, students learn that there are interesting books to read from different countries and nice kids from all around the world to share ideas with. As students engage in these writing activities, they expand their views about other cultures by sharing language, beliefs, religion, heritage, and their school and home life.

Teachers can also invite guest speakers available in their local area by contacting a minority community center. Speakers might be a director of an international program at a local university, a minister, or a person from the community with knowledge of a different culture. It is useful for the students to prepare questions in advance. Students should write the invitation and follow-up letter of appreciation to the speaker.

Oral Communication

Preparing to speak on a topic should be seen as a process that has stages: **Discovery**, **Organization**, and **Editing**.

Discovery: There are many possible sources for the information that will be used to create an oral presentation. The first step in the discovery process is to decide upon a topic or subject. Answer the question, "What is the speech going to be about?" In the discovery stage, one's own knowledge, experience, and beliefs should be the first source, and notes should be taken as the speaker probes the topic. The second source can very well be interviews with friends or possibly experts. The third source will be research: what has been written or said publicly on this topic? This stage can get out of hand very quickly, so a plan for the collecting of source information should be well-organized with time limits set for each part.

Organization: At this point, several decisions need to be made. The first is what the *purpose* of the speech is. Does the speaker want to persuade the audience to believe something or to act on something, or does the speaker simply want to present information that the audience might not have? Once that decision is made, a thesis should be developed. What *point* does the speaker want to make? And what are the points that will support that point? And in what order will those points be arranged? Introductions may well be written last. The purpose of the introduction is to draw the audience into the topic. The purpose of the conclusion is to polish off the speech, making sure the thesis is clear, reinforcing the thesis, or summarizing the points that have been made.

Editing: This is the most important stage in preparing a speech. Once decisions have been made in the discovery and organization stages, it's good to allow time to let the speech rest for awhile and to go back to it with "fresh eyes." Objectivity is extremely important, and the speaker should be willing to make drastic changes if they are needed. It's difficult to turn loose of one's own composition, but good speech-makers are able to do that. On the other hand, this can also get out of hand, and it should be limited. The speaker must recognize that at some point, the decisions must be made, the die must be cast, and commitment to the speech as it stands must be made if the speaker is to deliver the message with conviction.

The concept of recursiveness is useful to one who writes speeches. That is, everything must be written at the onset with full knowledge that it can be changed. The willingness to go backward, even to the discovery stage, is what makes a good speechwriter.

COMPETENCY 14.0 KNOWLEDGE OF READING

Skill 14.1 Identify purpose.

The questions to be asked first when approaching a reading task are: What is my objective? What do I want to achieve from this reading? How will I use the information I gain from this reading? Do I need only to grasp the gist of the piece? Do I need to know the line of reasoning—not only the thesis but the subpoints? Will I be reporting important and significant details orally or in a written document?

A written document can be expected to have a thesis—either expressed or derived. To discover the thesis, the reader needs to ask what point the writer intended to make. The writing can also be expected to be organized in some logical way and to have subpoints that support or establish that the thesis is valid. It is also reasonable to expect that there will be details or examples that will support the subpoints. Knowing this, the reader can make a decision about reading techniques required for the purpose that has already been established.

If the reader needs only to know the gist of a written document, speed-reading or skimming techniques may be sufficient, using the forefinger, moving the eyes down the page, picking up the important statements in each paragraph and deducing mentally that this piece is about such-and-such. If the reader needs to a little better grasp of how the writer achieved his/her purpose in the document, a quick and cursory glance—a skimming—of each paragraph will yield what the subpoints are, the topic sentences of the paragraphs, and how the thesis is developed, yielding a greater understanding of the author's purpose and method of development.

In-depth reading requires the scrutiny of each phrase and sentence with care, looking for the thesis first of all and then the topic sentences in the paragraphs that provide the development of the thesis, also looking for connections such as transitional devices that provide clues to the direction the reasoning is taking.

Sometimes rereading is necessary in order to make use of a piece of writing for an oral or written report. If this is the purpose of reading it, the first reading should provide a map for the second reading. The second time through should follow this map, and those points that are going to be used in the report or analysis will be focused upon on more carefully. Some new understandings may occur in this rereading, and it may become apparent that the "map" derived from the first reading will need to be adjusted. If this rereading is for the purpose of writing an analysis or using material for a report, either highlighting or note-taking is advisable.

Skill 14.2 Identify inferences and conclusions.

Conclusions are drawn as a result of reasoning. Inductive reasoning begins with particulars and reasons to a generality. For example: "When I was a child, I bit into a green apple from my grandfather's orchard, and it was sour" (specific fact #1). "I once bought green apples from a roadside vendor, and when I bit into one, it was sour" (specific fact #2). "My grocery store had a sale on green Granny Smith apples last week, and I bought several only to find that they were sour when I bit into one" (specific fact #3). Conclusion: All green apples are sour. While this is an example of inductive reasoning, it is also an example of the weakness of such reasoning. The speaker has not tasted all the green apples in the world, and there very well may be some apples that are green that are not sour.

Deductive reasoning begins with the generalization: "Green apples are sour" and supports that generalization with the specifics.

An inference is drawn from an inductive line of reasoning. The most famous one is "all men are mortal," which is drawn from the observation that everyone a person knows has died or will die and that everyone else concurs in that judgment. It is assumed to be true and for that reason can be used as proof of another conclusion: "Socrates is a man; therefore, he will die."

Sometimes the inference is assumed to be proven when it is not reliably true in all cases, such as "aging brings physical and mental infirmity." Reasoning from that *inference*, many companies will not hire anyone above a certain age. Actually, being old does not necessarily imply physical and/or mental impairment. There are many instances where elderly people have made important contributions that require exceptional ability.

Skill 14.3 Identify main idea.

It's very difficult to understand the reason for the inclusion of certain details in a text until you understand the main idea—what point the writer intended to make. Sometimes a writer will be helpful when he or she states the thesis or point of the piece of writing first. This is an approach often used by professional writers. It is used particularly frequently in speeches. Another place where the thesis often appears is at the end of the first paragraph, particularly if the paragraph is laying a background for the information that is being developed. Sometimes a writer will delay the statement of the point until the conclusion— sometimes until the very last sentence. Occasionally, a writer will not actually state the thesis directly.

In searching for the main idea, then, the piece should be read thoroughly from beginning to end. The reader can then ask what point the writing makes. The answer may be very clear.

Text-book reading—as well as the reading of other informative material—should be approached with a plan:

- Survey the material, looking at headings and quickly determining what the gist of the paragraphs is, and devise a map (either mental or on paper) for the second reading.
- The second time through will follow this preliminary map and will be a close reading, giving the most important points the greatest attention. Some new understandings may occur in this rereading, and it may become apparent that the "map" derived from the first reading will need to be adjusted. Underlining or highlighting is useful at this time. If the text will be passed on after the class is over, the material can be photocopied, so highlighting or underlining can be done.
- The final reading will be a review of the major points, sub-points, supporting ideas, and conclusions regarding what the point of the document is, what is important to commit to memory, and what will be useful later. If the reading is preparation for a test, making an outline is useful. If the reading is for a report, more careful notes are needed. If the reading is simply for a classroom where discussion will take place, a brief outline might be useful.

Skill 14.4 Distinguish fact from opinion.

Facts are statements that are verifiable. Opinions are statements that must be supported in order to be accepted. Facts are used to support opinions. For example, "Jane is a bad girl" is an opinion. However, "Jane hit her sister with a baseball bat" is a *fact* upon which the opinion is based. Judgments are opinions—decisions or declarations based on observation or reasoning that express approval or disapproval. Facts report what has happened or exists and come from observation, measurement, or calculation. Facts can be tested and verified whereas opinions and judgments cannot. They can only be supported with facts.

Most statements cannot be so clearly distinguished. "I believe that Jane is a bad girl" is a fact. The speaker knows what he/she believes. However, it obviously includes a judgment that could be disputed by another person who might believe otherwise. Judgments are not usually so firm. They are, rather, plausible opinions that provoke thought or lead to factual development.

Skill 14.5 Identify valid and invalid arguments.

An argument is a generalization that is proven or supported with facts. If the facts are not accurate, the generalization remains unproven. Using inaccurate "facts" to support an argument is called a *fallacy* in reasoning. Some factors to consider in judging whether the facts used to support an argument are relevant:

1. Are the facts current, or are they out of date? For example, if the proposition "Birth defects in babies born to drug-using mothers are increasing," then the data must include the latest that is available.
2. Where was the data obtained, and is that source reliable?
3. The calculations on which the facts are based may be unreliable. It's a good idea to run one's own calculations before using a piece of derived information.

Even facts that are true and have a sharp impact on the argument may not be relevant to the case at hand.

1. Health statistics from an entire state may have no relevance, or little relevance, to a particular county or zip code. Statistics from an entire country cannot be used to prove very much about a particular state or county.
2. An analogy can be useful in making a point, but the comparison must match up in all characteristics or it will not be relevant. Analogy should be used very carefully. It is often just as likely to destroy an argument as it is to strengthen it.

The importance or significance of a fact may not be sufficient to strengthen an argument. For example, with regard to the millions of immigrants in the U.S., using a single family to support a solution to the immigration problem, will not make much difference overall even though those single-example arguments are often used to support one approach or another. They may achieve a positive reaction, but they will not prove that one solution is better than another. If enough cases were cited from a variety of geographical locations, the information might be significant.

How much is enough? Generally speaking, three strong supporting facts are sufficient to establish the thesis of an argument. For example:

Conclusion: All green apples are sour.

- When I was a child, I bit into a green apple from my grandfather's orchard, and it was sour.
- I once bought green apples from a roadside vendor, and when I bit into one, it was sour.
- My grocery store had a sale on green Granny Smith apples last week, and I bought several only to find that they were sour when I bit into one.

The fallacy in the above argument is that the sample was insufficient. A more exhaustive search of literature, etc., will probably turn up some green apples that are not sour.

Sometimes more than three arguments are too many. On the other hand, it's not unusual to hear public speakers, particularly politicians, who will cite a long litany of facts to support their positions.

A good example of the omission of facts in an argument might be the resumé of an applicant for a job. The applicant is arguing that he/she should be chosen to be awarded a particular job. The application form will ask for information about past employment, and unfavorable dismissals from jobs in the past may just be omitted. Employers are usually suspicious of periods of time when the applicant has not listed an employer.

A writer makes choices about which facts will be used and which will be discarded in developing an argument. Those choices may exclude anything that is not supportive of the point of view the arguer is taking. It's always a good idea for the reader to do some research to spot the omissions and to ask whether they have impact on acceptance of the point of view presented in the argument.

No judgment is either black or white. If the argument seems too neat or too compelling, there are probably facts that might be relevant that have not been included.

Skill 14.6 Determine cause and effect.

Linking cause to effect seems to be ingrained in human thinking. We get chilled and then the next day come down with a cold; therefore, getting chilled caused the cold even though medical experts tell us that the virus that causes colds must be communicated by another human being. Socrates and the other Greek orators did a lot of thinking about this kind of thinking and developed a whole system for analyzing the links between causes and their effects and when they are valid—that is, when such and such a cause did, in fact, bring about a particular effect—and spelled out ways to determine whether or not the reasoning is reliable— or whether it is not reliable, in which case it is called a fallacy.

A common fallacy in reasoning is the *post hoc ergo propter hoc* ("after this, therefore because of this") or the false-cause fallacy. These occur in cause/effect reasoning, which may either go from cause to effect or effect to cause. They happen when an inadequate cause is offered for a particular effect; when the possibility of more than one cause is ignored; and when a connection between a particular cause and a particular effect is not made.

An example of a *post hoc*: Our sales shot up thirty-five percent after we ran that television campaign; therefore, the campaign caused the increase in sales. It might have been a cause, of course, but more evidence is needed to prove it.

An example of an inadequate cause for a particular effect: An Iraqi truck driver reported that Saddam Hussein had nuclear weapons; therefore, Saddam Hussein is a threat to world security. More causes were needed to prove the conclusion.

An example of failing to make a connection between a particular cause and an effect assigned to it: Anna fell into a putrid pond on Saturday; on Monday she came down with polio; therefore, the polio was caused by the water in the pond. This, of course, is not acceptable unless the polio virus is found in a sample of water from the pond. A connection must be proven.

Skill 14.7 Select appropriate strategies and resources, including technological resources, for teaching reading.

See Skill 13.6.

Morphemes are the smallest units of language that have an associated meaning and cannot be subdivided into smaller units that have meaning. The purpose of morphemic analysis is to study the morphemes of words to help in understanding the meaning of those words.

Literal questions are based on the facts in the reading. The student can put his finger right on the answer and prove that he is correct.

Inferential questions are based on inferring from interpretations.

Semantic mapping is a visual strategy to expand vocabulary and build knowledge by putting words into categories words related to one another.

Word mapping is a visual strategy for building vocabulary by arranging a diagram with the definition of a word, its synonyms and antonyms, and the use of the word in a sentence.

Graphic organizers include webbing, mapping, Venn diagrams, storyboards, and flow charts. Differentiating the processes means varying learning activities or strategies to provide appropriate methods for students to explore the concepts. It is important to give students alternative paths to manipulate the ideas embedded within the concept. For example, students may use graphic organizers, maps, diagrams, or charts to display their comprehension of concepts covered. Varying the complexity of the graphic organizer can very effectively facilitate differing levels of cognitive processing for students of differing ability.

Metacognition refers to higher order thinking in learning and involves active control over the cognitive processes..

COMPETENCY 15.0 KNOWLEDGE OF LITERATURE

Skill 15.1 Identify selections from literature, including folklore and mythology, for a variety of student interests and needs.

Literary allusions are drawn from classic mythology, national folklore, and religious writings that are supposed to have such familiarity to the reader that he can recognize the comparison between the subject of the allusion and the person, place, or event in the current reading. Children and adolescents who have knowledge of proverbs, fables, myths, epics, and the *Bible* can understand these allusions and thereby appreciate their reading to a greater degree than those who cannot recognize them.

Fables and folktales

This literary group of stories and legends was originally orally transmitted to the common populace to provide models of exemplary behavior or deeds worthy of recognition and homage.

In fables, animals talk, feel, and behave like human beings. The fable always has a moral and the animals illustrate specific people or groups without directly identifying them. For example, in Aesop's *Fables,* the lion is the "King" and the wolf is the cruel, often unfeeling, "noble class." In the fable of "The Lion and the Mouse" the moral is that "Little friends may prove to be great friends." In "The Lion's Share" it is "Might makes right." Many British folktales—*How RobinBecame an Outlaw* and *St. George-Slaying of the Dragon*—stress the correlation between power and right.

Classical mythology

Much of the mythology alluded to in modern English writing is a product of ancient Greece and Rome. Some Norse myths are also well known. Children are fond of myths because those ancient people were seeking explanations for those elements in their lives that predated scientific knowledge just as children seek explanations for the occurrences in their lives. These stories provide insight into the order and ethics of life as ancient heroes overcome the terrors of the unknown and bring meaning to the thunder and lightning, to the changing of the seasons, to the magical creatures of the forests and seas, and to the myriad of natural phenomena that can frighten mankind. There is often a childlike quality in the emotions of supernatural beings with which children can identify. Many good translations of myths exist for readers of varying abilities, but Edith Hamilton's *Mythology* is the most definitive reading for adolescents.

Fairy tales

Fairy tales are lively fictional stories involving children or animals that come in contact with super-beings via magic. They provide happy solutions to human dilemmas. The fairy tales of many nations are peopled by trolls, elves, dwarfs, and pixies—child-sized beings capable of fantastic accomplishments.

Among the most famous fairy tales are "Beauty and the Beast," "Cinderella," "Hansel and Gretel," "Snow White and the Seven Dwarfs," "Rumplestiltskin," and "Tom Thumb." In each tale, the protagonist survives prejudice, imprisonment, ridicule, and even death to receive justice in a cruel world.

Older readers encounter a kind of fairy-tale world in Shakespeare's *The Tempest* and *A Midsummer Night's Dream*, in which pixies and fairies are characters. Adolescent readers today are as fascinated by the creations of fantasy realms in the works of Piers Anthony, Ursula LeGuin, and Anne McCaffrey. An extension of interest in the supernatural is the popularity of science fiction that allows us to use current knowledge to imagine the possible course of the future.

Angels (or sometimes fairy godmothers) play a role in some fairy tales, and Milton in *Paradise Lost* and *Paradise Regained* also used symbolic angels and devils.

Biblical stories provide many allusions. Parables are moralistic like fables but have human characters, and include the stories of the Good Samaritan and the Prodigal Son. References to the treachery of Cain and the betrayal of Christ by Judas Iscariot are oft-cited examples.

American folk tales

American folktales are divided into two categories.

Imaginary tales, also called tall tales (humorous tales based on non-existent, fictional characters developed through blatant exaggeration)

> John Henry is a two-fisted steel driver who beats out a steam drill in competition.
>
> Rip Van Winkle sleeps for twenty years in the Catskill Mountains and upon awakening cannot understand why no one recognizes him.
>
> Paul Bunyan, a giant lumberjack, owns a great blue ox named Babe and has extraordinary physical strength. He is said to have plowed the Mississippi River while the impression of Babe's hoof prints created the Great Lakes.

Real tales, also called legends (based on real persons who accomplished the feats that are attributed to them even if they are slightly exaggerated)

For more than forty years, Johnny Appleseed (John Chapman) roamed Ohio and Indiana planting apple seeds.

Daniel Boone - scout, adventurer, and pioneer - blazed the Wilderness Trail and made Kentucky safe for settlers.

Paul Revere, a colonial patriot, rode through the New England countryside warning of the approach of British troops.

George Washington cut down a cherry tree, which he could not deny, or did he?

Native American writings often focus on the hardiness of the human body and soul and sorrow for the loss of the old ways of life. It would be rare to find Native American writing that encourages multi-cultural assimilation.

Skill 15.2 Interpret fictional and non-fictional texts representative of diverse cultures and historical periods.

Young children tend to rely heavily on an either "that is me" or a "that is not me" mentality when evaluating literature. A modern, diverse classroom has the potential to break down those rigid barriers and open students' minds to redefine "what *could* be me" or "what I'd *like* to learn more about." Differences should be seen as valuable assets to the classroom.

The teacher should be careful though, when selecting material that emphasizes diversity, to not pick works that perpetuate stereotypes. The following books are great resources for enhancing diversity in the classroom:

- *Indian Winter* by Russell Freeman, illustrated by Karl Bodmer (Holiday House, 1992). In 1833, German Prince Alexander Philipp Maximilian and Karl Bodmer, a Swiss painter, journeyed up the Missouri River and spent the winter among the Mandan Indians. Russell Freeman draws upon the prince's diary and Bodmer's detailed paintings to create an incredible account of their adventure.
- *¡Viva México!*: The Story of Benito Juárez and Cinco de Mayo by Argentina Palacios (Steck-Vaughn, 1993). Inspire kids to have faith against all odds with the story of Zapotec Indian Benito Juárez, who became president of Mexico. The author provides information on Cinco de Mayo, a major holiday celebrated by Mexicans and Mexican-Americans.
- *Alvin Ailey* by Andrea Davis Pinkney, illustrated by Brian Pinkney (Hyperion, 1993). This insightful biography about dancer/choreographer Ailey provides children with a model of an important 20th-century African-American.

- *The Devil's Arithmetic* by Jane Yolen (Viking, 1988). In this compelling novel, a young girl is mystically transported from present-day New York to Poland during World War II, where she goes into a gas chamber to save the life of another.
- *Older Brother, Younger Brother* retold by Nina Jaffe, illustrated by Wenhai Ma (Viking, 1995). This traditional Korean folktale explores the universal theme that if good is returned for ill treatment, good will triumph over evil.

Holidays provide a fun and interesting outlet to learn about other cultures. Choose books that explore Kwanzaa, Chinese New Year, Cinco de Mayo, or Ramadan. Focusing on how other cultures have fun is likely to foster interest in those cultures.

Skill 15.3 Identify common literary elements.

Essential terminology and literary devices germane to literary analysis include alliteration, allusion, antithesis, aphorism, apostrophe, assonance, blank verse, caesura, conceit, connotation, consonance, couplet, denotation, diction, epiphany, exposition, figurative language, free verse, hyperbole, iambic pentameter, inversion, irony, kenning, metaphor, metaphysical poetry, metonymy, motif, onomatopoeia, octava rima, oxymoron, paradox, parallelism personification, quatrain, scansion, simile, soliloquy, Spenserian stanza, synecdoche, terza rima, tone, and wit.

The more basic terms and devices, such as alliteration, allusion, analogy, aside, assonance, atmosphere, climax, consonance, denouement, elegy, foil, foreshadowing, metaphor, simile, setting, symbol, and theme are defined and exemplified in the* English 5-9 Study Guide*.

Antithesis: Balanced writing about conflicting ideas, usually expressed in sentence form. Some examples are expanding from the center, shedding old habits, and searching never finding.

Aphorism: A focused, succinct expression about life from a sagacious viewpoint. Writings by Ben Franklin, Sir Francis Bacon, and Alexander Pope contain many aphorisms. "Whatever is begun in anger ends in shame" is an aphorism.

Apostrophe: Literary device of addressing an absent or dead person, an abstract idea, or an inanimate object. Sonneteers, such as Sir Thomas Wyatt, John Keats, and William Wordsworth, address the moon, stars, and the dead Milton. For example, in William Shakespeare's *Julius Caesar*, Mark Antony addresses the corpse of Caesar in the speech that begins: "O, pardon me, thou bleeding piece of earth/ That I am meek and gentle with these butchers! Thou art the ruins of the noblest man/ That ever lived in the tide of times. Woe to the hand that shed this costly blood!"

Ballad: A ballad is an *in media res* story told or sung, usually in verse and accompanied by music, and usually with a refrain—a repeated section. Typically, ballads are based on folk stories. The Rime of the Ancient Mariner by Samuel Coleridge is an example.

Bildungsroman: the story of a protagonist who undergoes development and growth, often from youth into or through adulthood.

Blank Verse: Poetry written in iambic pentameter but unrhymed. Works by Shakespeare and Milton are epitomes of blank verse. Milton's *Paradise Lost* states, "Illumine, what is low raise and support/ That to the highth of this great argument/ I may assert Eternal Providence,/ And justify the ways of God to men."

Caesura: A pause, usually signaled by punctuation, in a line of poetry. The earliest usage occurs in *Beowulf*, the first English epic dating from the Anglo-Saxon era. 'To err is human, // to forgive, divine' (Pope).

Conceit: A comparison, usually in verse, between seemingly disparate objects or concepts. John Donne's metaphysical poetry contains many clever conceits. For instance, Donne's "The Flea" (1633) compares a flea bite to the act of love; and in "A Valediction: Forbidding Mourning" (1633) separated lovers are likened to the legs of a compass, the leg drawing the circle eventually returning home to "the fixed foot."

Connotation: The ripple effect surrounding the implications and associations of a given word, distinct from the denotative, or literal meaning. For example, "Good night, sweet prince, and flights of angels sing thee to thy rest," refers to a burial.

Consonance: The repeated usage of similar consonant sounds, most often used in poetry. "Sally sat sifting seashells by the seashore" is a familiar example.

Couplet: Two rhyming lines of poetry. Shakespeare's sonnets end in heroic couplets written in iambic pentameter. Pope is also a master of the couplet. His *Rape of the Lock* is written entirely in heroic couplets.

Denotation: What a word literally means, as opposed to its connotative meaning. Sleep means to take a rest. Connotative meanings would be associated with "a sleep over", "sleeping with", or "put to sleep."

Diction: The right word in the right spot for the right purpose. The hallmark of a great writer is precise, unusual, and memorable diction.

Dramatic monologue: Literary character revealing inner thoughts and feelings in his or her own voice, and this lets the audience know the character's deepest thoughts and feelings.

Epic Poem: A long narrative poem about a hero's adventures

Epiphany: The moment when the proverbial light bulb goes off in one's head and comprehension sets in.

Euphemism: A mild term that substitutes for one people may find harsh

Exposition: Fill-in or background information about characters meant to clarify and add to the narrative; the initial plot element which precedes the buildup of conflict.

Figurative Language: Language not meant in a literal sense, but interpreted through symbolism. Figurative language is made up of such literary devices as hyperbole, metonymy, synecdoche, and oxymoron. A synecdoche is a figure of speech in which the word for part of something is used to mean the whole; for example, "sail" for "boat. "or “wheels” for car..

Free Verse: Poetry that does not have any predictable meter or patterning. Margaret Atwood, e. e. Cummings, and Ted Hughes write in this form.

Hyperbole: Exaggeration for a specific effect. For example, "I’m so hungry that I could eat a million of these."

Iambic Pentameter: The two elements in a set five-foot line of poetry. An iamb is two syllables, stressed and unstressed, per foot or measure. Pentameter means five stresses per line.

Inversion: Ssentence order to create a given effect or interest. Bacon and Milton used inversion successfully. Emily Dickinson was fond of arranging words outside of their familiar order. For example in "Chartless" she writes "Yet know I how the heather looks" and "Yet certain am I of the spot." Instead of saying "Yet I know" and "Yet I am certain" she reverses the usual order and shifts the emphasis to the more important words.

Irony: An unexpected disparity between what is written or stated and what is really meant or implied by the author. Verbal, situational, and dramatic are the three literary ironies. Verbal irony is when an author says one thing and means something else. Dramatic irony is when an audience perceives something that a character in the literature does not know. Irony of situation is a discrepancy between the expected result and actual results. Shakespeare's plays contain a frequent and highly effective use of irony. O. Henry’s short stories have ironic endings.

Kenning: Another way to describe a person, place, or thing so as to avoid prosaic repetition. The earliest examples can be found in Anglo-Saxon literature such as *Beowulf* and "The Seafarer." Instead of writing King Hrothgar, the anonymous monk wrote, great Ring-Giver, or Father of his people. A lake becomes the swans' way, and the ocean or sea becomes the great whale's way. In ancient Greek literature, this device was called an “epithet.”

Metaphysical Poetry: Verse characterization by ingenious wit, unparalleled imagery, and clever conceits. The greatest metaphysical poet is John Donne. Henry Vaughn and other 17th century British poets contributed to this movement as in *Words*, "I saw eternity the other night,/ like a great being of pure and endless light."

Metonymy: Use of an object or idea closely identified with another object or idea to represent it.. "Hit the books" means "to study." Washington, D.C. means the U.S. government, and the White House means the U.S. President.

Motif: A key, oft-repeated phrase, name, or idea in a literary work. Dorset/Wessex in Hardy's novels and the moors and the harsh weather in the Bronte sisters' novels are effective use of motifs.
Narrative: A collection of events that tells a story. The story may be true (such as a news story) or not (fiction or poetry), and the events are arranged in a particular order and answer the questions of who, what, where, when, why..

Onomatopoeia: Word used to evoke the sound in its meaning. The early Batman series used *pow*, *zap*, *whop*, *zonk* and *eek* in an onomatopoeic way.

Octava rima: A specific eight-line stanza of poetry whose rhyme scheme is abababcc. Lord Byron's mock epic, *Don Juan*, is written in this poetic way.

Oxymoron: A contradictory form of speech, such as jumbo shrimp, unkindly kind, or singer John Mellencamp's "It hurts so good."

Paradox: Seemingly untrue statement, which when examined more closely proves to be true. John Donne's sonnet "Death Be Not Proud" postulates that death shall die and humans will triumph over death, at first thought not true, but ultimately explained in this sonnet.

Parallelism: A type of close repetition of clauses or phrases that emphasize key topics or ideas in writing. The psalms in the Bible contain many examples because parallelism is integral to Hebrew poetry.

Personification: Giving human characteristics to inanimate objects or concepts.

Quatrain: A poetic stanza composed of four lines. A Shakespearean or Elizabethan sonnet is made up of three quatrains and ends with a heroic couplet.

Scansion: The two-part analysis of a poetic line. Count the number of syllables per line and determine where the accents fall. Divide the line into metric feet. Name the meter by the type and number of feet. Much is written about scanning poetry. Try not to inundate your students with this jargon; rather allow them to feel the power of the poets' words, ideas, and images instead.

Soliloquy: A highlighted speech, in drama, usually delivered by a major character expounding on the author's philosophy or expressing, at times, universal truths. This is done with the character alone on the stage.

Spenserian Stanza: Invented by Sir Edmund Spenser for usage in *The Fairie Queene*, his epic poem honoring Queen Elizabeth I. Each stanza consists of nine lines, eight in iambic parameter. The ninth line, called an alexandrine, has two extra syllables or one additional foot.

Sprung Rhythm: Invented and used extensively by the poet, Gerard Manley Hopkins. It consists of variable meter, which combines stressed and unstressed syllables fashioned by the author. See "Pied Beauty" or "God's Grandeur."

Stream of Consciousness: A style of writing which reflects the mental processes of the characters, at times expressing jumbled memories, feelings, and dreams. Some authors using this type of expression are James Joyce, Virginia Woolf, and William Faulkner.

Terza Rima: A series of poetic stanzas utilizing the recurrent rhyme scheme of aba, bcb, cdc, ded, and so forth. The second-generation Romantic poets—Keats, Byron, Shelley, and, to a lesser degree, Yeats—used this Italian verse form, especially in their odes. Dante used this stanza in *The Divine Comedy.*

Tone: The discernible attitude inherent in an author's work regarding the subject, readership, or characters. Swift's and Pope's tones are satirical. James Boswell's tone toward Samuel Johnson is admiring.

Wit: Writing of genius, keenness, and sagacity expressed through clever use of language.

Skill 15.4 Evaluate strategies that provide for a variety of responses to literature.

Reading literature involves a reciprocal interaction between the reader and the text.

<u>**Types of Responses**</u>
In an **emotional response**, the reader can identify with the characters and situations so as to project himself into the story. The reader feels a sense of satisfaction by associating aspects of his own life with the people, places, and events in the literature. Emotional responses are observed in a reader's verbal and non-verbal reactions —laughter, comments on its effects, and retelling or dramatizing the action.
Interpretive

Interpretive responses result in inferences about character development, setting, or plot; analysis of style elements —metaphor, simile, allusion, rhythm, tone; outcomes derivable from information provided in the narrative; and assessment of the author's intent. Interpretive responses are made verbally or in writing.

Critical responses offer reactions to the writer's style and language as well as making a claim about the literature and supporting the claim with evidence from the literature or related disciplines, such as history or economics.

Evaluative response expresses whether an author should have or should not have done something based on a standard. Compare/contrast is often used for this response. "This book was better than that book because . . ."

Middle school readers will exhibit both emotional and interpretive responses. Naturally, making interpretive responses depends on the degree of knowledge the student has of literary elements. A child's being able to say why a particular book was boring or why a particular poem made him sad evidences critical reactions on a fundamental level. Adolescents in ninth and tenth grades should begin to make critical responses by addressing the specific language and genre characteristics of literature. Evaluative responses are harder to detect and are rarely made by any but a few advanced high school students. However, if the teacher knows what to listen for, she can recognize evaluative responses and incorporate them into discussions.

For example, if a student says, "I don't understand why that character is doing that," he is making an interpretive response to character motivation. However, if he goes on to say, "What good is that action?" he is giving an evaluative response that should be explored in terms of "What good should it do and why isn't that positive action happening?"

At the emotional level, the student says, "I almost broke into a sweat when he was describing the heat in the burning house." An interpretive response says, "The author used descriptive adjectives to bring his setting to life." Critically, the student adds, "The author's use of descriptive language contributes to the success of the narrative and maintains reader interest through the whole story." If he goes on to wonder why the author allowed the grandmother in the story to die in the fire, he is making an evaluative response.

Levels of Response The levels of reader response will depend largely on the reader's level of social, psychological, and intellectual development. Most middle school students have progressed beyond merely involving themselves in the story enough to be able to retell the events in some logical sequence or describe the feeling that the story evoked. They are aware to some degree that the feeling evoked was the result of a careful manipulation of good elements of fiction writing. They may not explain that awareness as successfully as a high school student might, but they are beginning to grasp the concepts and not just their personal reactions. They are beginning to differentiate between responding to the story itself and responding a literary creation.

Fostering self-esteem and empathy for others and the world in which one lives

All-important is *bibliotherapy*, which allows the reader to identify with others and become aware of alternatives, yet not feelidirectly betrayed or threatened. For the high school student, the ability to empathize is an evaluative response, a much desired outcome of literature studies. Use of these books, either individually or as a thematic unit of study, allows for discussion or writing. The titles are grouped by theme, not by reading level.

ABUSE:

Blair, Maury and Brendel, Doug. *Maury, Wednesday's Child*

Dizenzo, Patricia. *Why Me*?

Parrot, Andrea. *Coping with Date Rape and Acquaintance Rape*

NATURAL WORLD CONCERNS:

Caduto, M. and Bruchac, J. *Keepers of Earth*

Gay, Kathlyn. *Greenhouse Effect*

Johnson, Daenis. *Fiskadaro*

Madison, Arnold. *It Can't Happen to Me*

EATING DISORDERS:

Arnold, Caroline. *Too Fat, Too Thin, Do I Have a Choice?*

DeClements, Barthe. *Nothing's Fair in Fifth Grade*

Snyder, Anne. *Goodbye, Paper Doll*

FAMILY

Chopin, Kate. *The Runner*

Cormier, Robert. *Tunes for Bears to Dance to*

Danzinger, Paula. *The Divorce Express*

Neufield, John. *Sunday Father*

Okimoto, Jean Davies. *Molly by any Other Name*

Peck, Richard. *Don't Look and It Won't Hurt*

Zindel, Paul. *I Never Loved Your Mind*

STEREOTYPING:

Baklanov, Grigory. (Trans. by Antonina W. Bouis) *Forever Nineteen*

Kerr, M.E. *Gentle Hands*

Greene, Betty. *Summer of My German Soldier*

Reiss, Johanna. *The Upstairs Room*

Taylor, Mildred D. *Roll of Thunder, Hear Me Cry*

Wakatsuki-Houston, Jeanne and Houston, James D. *Farewell to Manzanar*

SUICIDE AND DEATH:

Blume, Judy. *Tiger Eyes*

Bunting, Eve. *If I Asked You, Would You Stay?*

Gunther, John. *Death Be Not Proud*

Mazer, Harry. *When the Phone Rings*

Peck, Richard. *Remembering the Good Times*

Richter, Elizabeth. *Losing Someone You Love*

Strasser, Todd. *Friends Till the End*

Cautions

There is always a caution when reading materials of a sensitive or controversial nature. The teacher must be cognizant of the happenings in the school and outside community to spare students undue suffering. A child who has known a recent death in his family or circle of friends may need to distance himself from classroom discussion. Whenever open discussion of a topic brings pain or embarrassment, the child should not be further subjected. Older children and young adults will be able to discuss issues with greater objectivity and without making blurted, insensitive comments. The teacher must be able to gauge the level of emotional development of her students when selecting subject matter and the strategies for studying it. The student or his parents may consider some material objectionable. Should a student choose not to read an assigned material, it is the teacher's responsibility to allow the student to select an alternate title. It is always advisable to notify parents if a particularly sensitive piece is to be studied.

Skill 15.5 Select appropriate strategies and resources, including technological resources, for teaching literature.

Multimedia refers to a technology for presenting material in both visual and verbal forms. This format is especially conducive to the classroom, since it reaches both visual and auditory learners.

Knowing how to select effective teaching software is the first step in efficient multi-media education. First, decide what you need the software for (creating spreadsheets, making diagrams, creating slideshows, etc.) Consult magazines such as *Popular Computing, PC World, MacWorld,* and *Multimedia World* to learn about the newest programs available. Go to a local computer store and ask a customer service representative to help you find the exact equipment you need. If possible, test the programs you are interested in. Check reviews in magazines such as *Consumer Reports, PCWorld, Electronic Learning* or *MultiMedia Schools* to ensure the software's quality.

Software programs useful for producing teaching material

- Adobe Photoshop
- Aldus Freehand
- CorelDRAW!
- DrawPerfect
- Claris Works
- PC Paintbrush
- Harvard Graphics
- Visio
- Microsoft Word
- Microsoft Powerpoint

Also, see Skill 13.6.

COMPETENCY 16.0 KNOWLEDGE OF TEACHING LANGUAGE ARTS TO MIDDLE GRADES STUDENTS

Skill 16.1 Demonstrate knowledge of the characteristics of middle grades students.

Most middle school students have reached the concrete operations level. By this time they have left behind their egocentrism for a need to understand the physical and social world around them. They become more interested in ways to relate to other people. Their favorite stories become those about real people rather than animals or fairy tale characters. The conflicts in their literature are internal as well as external. Books such as Paula Fox's *The Stone-Faced Boy*, Betsy Byards' *The Midnight Fox*, and Lois Lenski's *Strawberry Girl* deal with a child's loneliness, confusion about identity or loyalty, and poverty. Pre-adolescents are becoming more cognizant of and interested in the past, thus their love of adventure stories about national heroes such as Davy Crockett, Daniel Boone, and Abe Lincoln and biographies/autobiographies of real life heroes, such as Jackie Robinson and Cesar Chavez. At this level, children also become interested in the future; thus, their love of both fantasy (often medieval in spirit) and science fiction.

The seven- to eleven-year-olds also internalize moral values. They are concerned with their sense of self and are willing to question rules and adult authority. In books such as Beverly Cleary's *Henry Huggins* and *Mitch and Amy*, the protagonists are children pursuing their own desires with the same frustrations as other children. When these books were written in the 1960s, returning a found pet or overcoming a reading disability were considered representative problems.

Skill 16.2 Apply interdisciplinary techniques within the middle grade classrooms.

Gone are the days when students engage in skill practice with grammar worksheets. Grammar needs to be taught in the context of the students' own work. Listed below is a series of classroom practices that encourage meaningful context-based grammar instruction, combined with occasional mini-lessons and other language strategies that can be used on a daily basis.

* Connect grammar with the student's own writing while emphasizing grammar as a significant aspect of effective writing.

* Emphasize the importance of editing and proofreading as an essential part of classroom activities.

* Provide students with an opportunity to practice editing and proofreading cooperatively.

* Give instruction in the form of 15-20 minute mini-lessons.

* Emphasize the sound of punctuation by connecting it to pitch, stress, and pause.

* Involve students in all facets of learning English, including reading, writing, listening, speaking, and thinking. Good use of language comes from exploring all forms of it on a regular basis.

There are a number of approaches that involve grammar instruction in the context of the writing.

1. Sentence combining - try to use the student's own writing as much as possible. The theory behind combining ideas and the correct punctuation should be emphasized.

2. Sentence and paragraph modeling - provide students with the opportunity to practice imitating the style and syntax of professional writers.

3. Sentence transforming - give students an opportunity to change sentences from one form to another, i.e., from passive to active, inverting the sentence order, or changing forms of the words used.

4. Daily Language Practice - introduce or clarify common errors using daily language activities. Use actual student examples whenever possible. Correct and discuss the problems with grammar and usage.

Ideas for Interdisciplinary Classroom Activities:

- Have students produce a newspaper that incorporates many different subject areas (sports, weather, crossword puzzles, books reviews, pictures, poetry, advertisements, etc.).
- Connect each student with an "adoptive grandparent" at a nearby nursing home. Have students write their "grandparent" letters and stories, make timelines of the "grandparents'" lives, and learn about life during the time period they grew up in.
- Have students create a Powerpoint presentation on a career they are interested in pursuing. Research pros and cons, salary information, skills necessary for the job, etc.
- Using a book the whole class is reading, have students pick out any words they are unfamiliar with. Research the origin of those words and their definitions, and then have them write a creative story using each word.

Sample Test: English

1. **Which of the following is a ballad? (Skill 15.1) (Rigorous)**

   A. "The Knight's Tale"

   B. *Julius Caesar*

   C. *Paradise Lost*

   D. "The Rime of the Ancient Mariner"

2. **Which of the following is an epic? (Skill 15.1) (Rigorous)**

   A. *On the Choice of Books*

   B. *The Faerie Queene*

   C. *Northanger Abbey*

   D. *A Doll's House*

3. **Which of the following is an example of alliteration? (Skill 15.3) (Average)**

   A. "The City's voice itself is soft like Solitude."

   B. "Both in one faith unanimous; though sad"

   C. "By all their country's wishes blest!"

   D. "In earliest Greece to thee with partial choice"

4. **Which of the following is a definition of *bildungsroman*? (Skill 15.3) (Average)**

   A. A true story about the life of a person.

   B. A true story about the life of a person written by the subject, himself or herself.

   C. A novel that traces the spiritual, moral, psychological, or social development and growth of the main character.

   D. A work of fiction telling the story of a brave, noble hero, who, because of some tragic character flaw, brings ruin upon himself.

5. **In a drama, what is a dramatic monologue? (Skill 15.3) (Average)**

   A. Satire or parody.

   B. An exchange between the protagonist and antagonist.

   C. An offstage voice.

   D. A speech that is directed at the actor, himself or herself, but also intended for the audience.

6. Our borders must be protected from illegal immigrants. Which of the following does *not* support this thesis? (Skill 13.3) (Average)

A. Terrorists can get across the border undetected.

B. Illegal drugs flow across the unprotected borders.

C. Illegal aliens are a drain on the American economy.

D. Illegal aliens make good citizens.

7. Which of the following are good choices for supporting a thesis? (Skill 13.3) (Average)

A. Reasons

B. Examples

C. Answer to the question why

D. All of the above.

8. Which of the following is a good definition of the *purpose* for an essay? (Skill 13.3) (Rigorous)

A. To get a good grade.

B. To fulfill an assignment.

C. To change the minds of the readers.

D. The point of the writing.

9. Which of the following is a valid conclusion? (Skill 14.2) (Average)

A. Based on the evidence, I believe John Jones stole the car.

B. I suspect that John Jones stole the car.

C. John Jones looks guilty, so he must have stolen the car.

D. Of the two suspects, John Jones' cynical expression makes me think he's guilty.

10. Which of the following is a fact? (Skill 14.4) (Easy)

A. It's going to rain.

B. John is close-minded.

C. Joe said he believes John is close-minded.

D. The world is going to the dogs.

11. Which of the following is an opinion? (Skill 14.4) (Easy)

A. Subjective evaluation based upon personal bias.

B. A statement that is readily provable by objective empirical data.

C. The sky is blue.

D. Airplanes flew into the World Trade Center on September 11, 2001.

12. Which of the following best describes the structure of English? (Skill 13.2) (Average)

A. Syntax based on word order

B. Inflected

C. Romantic

D. Orthography is phonetic

13. Which of the following sentences contains an error in agreement? (Skill 13.2) (Easy)

A. Jennifer and Jill are two of the women who writes for the magazine.

B. Each one of their sons plays a different sport.

C. This band has performed at the Odeum many times.

D. The data are available online at the listed website.

14. All of the following are research-based strategies that support reading, EXCEPT: (Skill 14.7) (Rigorous)

A. reading more

B. reading along with a more proficient reader

C. reading a passage no more than twice

D. self-monitoring progress

15. Use the table below to answer the question that follows.

	Math Usage	General Usage
bi (two)	bilinear	bicycle
	bimodal	biplane
	binomial	bifocals
cent (hundred)	centimeter	century
	centigram	centigrade
	percent	centipede
circum (around)	circumference	circumnavigate
	circumradius	circumstance
	circumcenter	circumspect

The table above is an example of which vocabulary strategy? (Skill 14.7) (Rigorous)

A. Frayer method

B. morphemic analysis

C. semantic mapping

D. word mapping

16. The student has been given a story to read after which he is to answer a series of questions, all of which begin with "who," "what," "where," or "how." What type of comprehension will these questions assess? (Skill 14.7) (Rigorous)

A. Evaluative

B. Inferential

C. Literal

D. narrative

17. A teacher has taught his students several strategies to monitor their reading comprehension. These strategies include identifying where in the passage they are having difficulty, identifying what the difficulty is, and restating the difficult sentence or passage in their own words. These strategies are examples of: (Skill 14.7) (Rigorous)

A. graphic and semantic organizers

B. metacognition

C. recognizing story structure

D. summarizing

18. A teacher has given her students an anticipation guide with a list of statements related to the topic of their reading. Before reading, the students are asked to indicate for each statement whether they agree or disagree with it. The primary purpose(s) of this guide are to: (Skill 14.7) (Rigorous)

A. elicit students' prior knowledge of the topic and set a purpose for reading

B. identify the main ideas and supporting details in the text

C. synthesize information from the text

D. visualize the concepts and terms in the text

19. Varying the complexity of a graphic organizer would be an example of differentiating: (Skill 14.7) (Rigorous)

A. content/topic

B. environment

C. process

D. product

20. All of the following are examples of ongoing informal assessment techniques used to observe student progress EXCEPT (Skill 13.6) (Rigorous0

A. analyses of student work product

B. collection of data from assessment tests

C. effective questioning

D. observation of students

21. A sixth-grade science teacher has given her class a paper to read on the relationship between food and weight gain. The writing contains signal words such as "because," "consequently," "this is how," and "due to." This paper has which text structure? (Skill 13.4) (Average)

A. cause & effect

B. compare & contrast

C. description

D. sequencing

22. A student has written a paper with the following characteristics: written in first person; characters, setting, and plot; some dialogue; events organized in chronological sequence with some flashbacks. In what genre has the student written? (Skill 13.5) (Rigorous)

A. expository writing

B. narrative writing

C. persuasive writing

D. technical writing

23. Which of the following does not constitute a sentence? (Skill 13.2) (Rigorous)

A. In keeping with the graduation tradition in spite of the rain, the students standing in the cafeteria tossing their mortarboards.

B. Rosa Parks, who refused to give up her seat on the bus, will be forever remembered for her courage.

C. Taking advantage of the goalie's being out of the net, we scored our last and winning goal.

D. When it began to rain, we gathered our possessions and ran for the pavilion.

24. In which of the following sentences is there an error that a word processing spellchecker would not likely pick up? (Skill 13.2) (Average)

A. He took the horse by the rains and led it back to the stable.

B. The vilage is adding a park on the west side of town.

C. George works in a glas factory near the railroad tracks.

D. We will be going to Tenessee this summer for vacation.

25. If a student uses inappropriate language that includes slang and expletives, what is the best course of action to take in order to influence the student's formal communication skills? (Skill 13.6) (Average)

A. ask the student to paraphrase the writing, that is, translate it into language appropriate for the school principal to read.

B. refuse to read the student's papers until he conforms to a more literate style.

C. ask the student to read his work aloud to the class for peer evaluation.

D. rewrite the flagrant passages to show the student the right form of expression.

26. Which of the following is not a theme of Native American writing? (Skill 15.1) (Rigorous)

A. Emphasis on the hardiness of the human body and soul

B. The strength of multi-cultural assimilation

C. Contrition for the genocide of native peoples

D. Sorrow for the destruction of the Indian way of life

27. Oral debate is most closely associated with which form of discourse? (Skill 13.5) (Rigorous)

A. Description

B. Exposition

C. Narration

D. Persuasion

28. What is the prevailing form of discourse in this passage?

"It would have been hard to find a passer-by more wretched in appearance. He was a man of middle height, stout and hardy, in the strength of maturity; he might have been forty-six or seven. A slouched leather cap hid half his face, bronzed by the sun and wind, and dripping with sweat." (Skill 13.5) (Average)

A. Description

B. Narration

C. Exposition

D. Persuasion

29. Which of the following should not be included in the opening paragraph of an informative essay? (Skill 13.5) (Average)

A. Thesis sentence

B. Details and examples supporting the main idea

C. broad general introduction to the topic

D. A style and tone that grabs the reader's attention

30. Identify the sentence that has an error in parallel structure. (Skill 132.) (Average)

A. In order to help your favorite cause, you should contribute your time or money, raise awareness, and write to your congressman.

B. Many people envision scientists working alone in a laboratory and discovering scientific breakthroughs.

C. Some students prefer watching videos to textbooks because they are used to visual presentation.

D. Tom Hanks, who has won two Academy Awards, is celebrated as an actor, director, and producer.

31. Mr. Brown is a school volunteer <u>with a reputation and twenty years service</u>. (Skill 13.2) (Average)

A. with a reputation for twenty years' service

B. with a reputation for twenty year's service

C. who has served twenty years

D. with a service reputation of twenty years

32. Joe didn't hardly know his cousin Fred, who'd had a surgery. (Skill 13.2) (Easy)

A. hardly did know his cousin Fred

B. didn't know his cousin Fred hardly

C. hardly knew his cousin Fred

D. didn't know his cousin Fred

33. The literary device of personification is used in which example below? (Skill 15.4) (Average)

A. "Beg me no beggary by soul or parents, whining dog!"

B. "Happiness sped through the halls cajoling as it went."

C. "O wind thy horn, thou proud fellow."

D "And that one talent which Is a death to hide."

34. What is the form of the following poem?

My name is John Wellington Wells,
I'm a dealer in magic and spells,
In blessings and curses,
And ever-fill'd purses,
In prophecies, witches, and knells. (Skill 15.1) (Easy)

A. Sonnet

B. Haiku

C. Limerick

D. cinquain

35. Which of the following is *not* a figure of speech (figurative language)? (Skill 15.3) (Easy)

A. Simile

B. Euphemism

C. Onomatopoeia

D. Allusion

36. Modeling is a practice that allows students to: (Skill 13.6) (Average)

A. create a style unique to their own language capabilities.

B. emulate the writing of professionals.

C. paraphrase passages from good literature.

D. peer evaluate the writings of other students.

37. Who was the principal writer of *The Declaration of Independence*? (Skill 15.1) (Easy)

A. Patrick Henry

B. Thomas Jefferson

C. Ben Franklin

D. George Washington

38. **Which of the following indicates that a student is a fluent reader? (Skill 14.7) (Rigorous)**

A. reads texts with expression or prosody.

B. reads word-to-word and haltingly.

C. must intentionally decode a majority of the words.

D. in a writing assignment, sentences are poorly-organized structurally.

39. When should reading assessment take place? (Skill 14.7) (Rigorous)

A. At the end of the semester.

B. At the end of a unit.

C. All the time—ongoing.

D. All of the above.

40. Which of the following is an essential characteristic of effective assessment? (Skill 13.6) (Average)

A. Students are the ones being tested; they are not involved in the assessment process.

B. Testing activities are kept separate from the teaching activities.

C. Assessment should reflect the actual reading the classroom instruction has prepared the student for.

D. Tests should use entirely different materials than those used in teaching so the result will be reliable.

41. Which of the following is an essential characteristic of effective assessment? (Skill 13.6) (Rigorous)

A. When it comes to assessment, age and culture are irrelevant.

B. Teaching should be aimed at a student's weaknesses.

C. Assessment focuses only on the students' reading skills.

D. Assessment should be a natural part of the instruction and not intrusive.

42. Which of the following activities is *not* useful in the assessment process for slower or immature readers? (Skill 14.7) (Average)

A. Repeated readings.

B. Echo reading.

C. Wide reading.

D. Reading content that is more difficult than their skill levels in order to "stretch" their abilities.

43. Of the following situations, which would *not* require referral to another resource? (Skill 13.6) (Rigorous)

A. Auditory trauma.

B. Ear infection.

C. Vision problems.

D. Underdeveloped vocabulary.

44. Of the following, which one is the Middle-School student most likely to be encountering for the first time? (Skill 16.1) (Rigorous)

A. Phonics.

B. Phonemics.

C. Textbook reading assignments.

D. Stories read by the teacher.

45. Which of the following is *not* recommended for reading an assignment for comprehension. (Skill 14.7) (Easy)

A. Read it through only once, but read slowly and carefully.

B. Read it through more than once according to a plan.

C. Create a map for the next reading.

D. Highlight or take notes.

Answer Key: English

1. D
2. B
3 A
4. C
5. D
6. D
7. D
8. C
9. A
10. C
11. A
12. A
13. A
14. C
15. B
16. C
17. B
18. A
19. C
20. B
21. A
22. B
23. A
24. A
25. A
26. B
27. D
28. A
29. B
30. C
31. D
32. C
33. B
34. C
35. D
36. B
37. B
38. A
39. D
40. C
41. D
42. D
43. D
44. C
45. A

Rigor Table: English

Easy (20%)	Average (40%)	Rigorous (40%)
8,11,12,14,33,35,36,37,39,50	3,4,5, 10, 13, 19, 20, 22, 24, 25,26, 29, 30, 31, 32, 34, 38, 41,42, 47	1,2,6,7,9,15,16,17,18,21,23,27,28, 40,43,44,45,46,48,49

Rationales with Sample Questions: English

1. Which of the following is a ballad? (Skill 15.1) (Rigorous)

A. "The Knight's Tale"
B. *Julius Caesar*
C. *Paradise Lost*
D. *The Rime of the Ancient Mariner*

Answer:

D. *The Rime of the Ancient Mariner*

The answer is D. "The Knight's Tale" is a Romantic poem from the longer *Canterbury Tales* by Chaucer. *Julius Caesar* is a Shakespearian play. *Paradise Lost* is an epic poem in blank verse. A ballad is an *in media res* story told or sung, usually in verse and accompanied by music, and usually with a refrain—a repeated section. Typically, ballads are based on folk stories

2. Which of the following is an epic? (Skill 15.1) (Rigorous*

A. *On the Choice of Books*
B. *The Faerie Queene*
C. *Northanger Abbey*
D. *A Doll's House*

Answer:

B. *The Faerie Queene*

The correct answer is B. An epic is a long poem, usually of book length, reflecting the values of the society in which it was produced. *On the Choice of Books* is an essay by Thomas Carlyle. *Northanger Abbey* is a novel written by Jane Austen, and *A Doll's House* is a play written by Henrik Ibsen.

3. Which of the following is an example of alliteration? (Skill 15.3) (Average)

A. "The City's voice itself is soft like Solitude."
B. "Both in one faith unanimous; though sad"
C. "By all their country's wishes blest!"
D. "In earliest Greece to thee with partial choice"

Answer:

A. "The City's voice itself is soft like Solitude"

The correct answer is A. Alliteration is the repetition of consonant sounds in two or more neighboring words or syllables, usually the beginning sound but not always. This line from Shelley's *Stanzas Written in Dejection Near Naples* is an especially effective use of alliteration using the sibilant *s* not only at the beginning of words but also within words. Alliteration usually appears in prosody; however, effective use of alliteration can be found in other genres.

4. Which of the following is a definition of *bildungsroman*? (Skill 15.3) (Average)

A. A true story about the life of a person.
B. A true story about the life of a person written by the subject, himself or herself.
C. A novel that traces the spiritual, moral, psychological, or social development and growth of the main character.
D. A work of fiction telling the story of a brave, noble hero, who, because of some tragic character flaw, brings ruin upon himself.

Answer:

C. A novel that traces the spiritual, moral, psychological, or social development and growth of the main character.

The correct answer is C. A true story about the life of a person is a biography; a biography written by the subject, himself or herself, is an autobiography. A fictional work that tells the story of a brave and noble hero who brings ruin upon himself is a tragedy. *Bildungsroman*, from the German, tells the story of a protagonist who undergoes development and growth, often from youth into or through adulthood.

5. In a drama, what is a dramatic monologue? (Skill 15.3) (Average)

A. Satire or parody.
B. An exchange between the protagonist and antagonist.
C. An offstage voice.
D. A speech that is directed at the actor, himself or herself, but also intended for the audience.

Answer:

D. A speech that is directed at the actor, himself or herself, but also intended for the audience.

The correct answer is D. When an actor is talking and obviously addressing his inmost self, the speech is also intended for the audience as silent listener, who will pass judgment and, perhaps, feel sympathy.

6. Our borders must be protected from illegal immigrants. Which of the following does *not* support this thesis? (Skill 13.3) (Average)

A. Terrorists can get across the border undetected.
B. Illegal drugs flow across the unprotected borders.
C. Illegal aliens are a drain on the American economy
D. Illegal aliens make good citizens.

Answer:

D. Illegal aliens make good citizens.

The correct answer is D. It does not support the thesis statement. Good questions to ask to determine whether a point supports the statement are "how?" and "why?" For example: Our borders must be protected from illegal immigrants. Why? Terrorists can get across the border undetected.

7. Which of the following are good choices for supporting a thesis? (Skill 13.3) (Easy)

A. Reasons
B. Examples
C. Answer to the question why
D. All of the above.

Answer:

D. All of the above.

The correct answer is D. When answering "why," you are giving reasons, but those reasons need to be supported with examples.

8. Which of the following is a good definition of the *purpose* for an essay? (Skill 13.3) (Rigorous)

A. To get a good grade.
B. To fulfill an assignment.
C. To change the minds of the readers.
D. The point of the writing.

Answer:

C. To change the minds of the readers.

The purpose is what you want your writing to achieve. It is based on the four forms of discourse: expository, descriptive, narrative, and persuasive.

9. Which of the following is a valid conclusion? (Skill 14.2) (Average)

A. Based on the evidence, I believe John Jones stole the car.
B. I suspect that John Jones stole the car.
C. John Jones looks guilty, so he must have stolen the car.
D. Of the two suspects, John Jones' cynical expression makes me think he's guilty.

Answer:

A. Based on the evidence, I believe John Jones stole the car.

Valid conclusions are based on evidence.

10. Which of the following is a fact? (Skill 14.4) (Easy)

A. It's going to rain.
B. John is a close-minded
C. Joe said he believes John is close-minded.
D. The world is going to the dogs.

Answer:

C. Joe said he believes John is close-minded.

The only answer that is a fact is C. Joe said he believes John is close-minded. It's a fact that he *said* it, even though what he said may not be a fact.

11. Which of the following is an opinion? (Skill 14.4) (Easy)

A. Subjective evaluation based upon personal bias.
B. A statement that is readily provable by objective empirical data.
C. The sky is blue.
D. Airplanes flew into the World Trade Center on September 11, 2001.

Answer:

A. Subjective evaluation based upon personal bias.

The correct answer is A. An opinion is a subjective evaluation based upon personal bias.

12. Which of the following best describes the structure of English? (Skill 13.2) (Average)

A. Syntax based on word order
B. Inflected
C. Romantic
D. Orthography is phonetic

Answer:

A. Syntax based on word order.

The syntax of English, reflective of its Germanic origins, relies on word order rather than inflection. Because of this, combined with the many influences of other languages, particularly with regard to vocabulary, the orthography is not phonetic, which complicates the teaching of standardized spelling.

13. Which of the following sentences contains an error in agreement? (Skill 13.2) (Easy)

A. Jennifer and Jill are two of the women who writes for the magazine.
B. Each one of their sons plays a different sport.
C. This band has performed at the Odeum many times.
D. The data are available online at the listed website.

Answer:

A. Jennifer and Jill are two of the women who writes for the magazine.

"Jennifer and Jill" is the plural subject of the verb. The verb should be "write."

14. All of the following are research-based strategies that support reading, EXCEPT: (Skill 14.7) (Rigorous)

A. reading more
B. reading along with a more proficient reader
C. reading a passage no more than twice
D. self-monitoring progress

Answer:

C. reading a passage no more than twice

Actually, research shows that reading a passage several times improves fluency.

15. Use the table below to answer the question that follows.

	Math Usage	General Usage
bi (two)	bilinear	bicycle
	bimodal	biplane
	binomial	bifocals
cent (hundred)	centimeter	century
	centigram	centigrade
	percent	centipede
circum (around)	circumference	circumnavigate
	circumradius	circumstance
	circumcenter	circumspect

The table above is an example of which vocabulary strategy? (Skill 14.7) (Rigorous)

A. Frayer method
B. morphemic analysis
C. semantic mapping
D. word mapping

Answer:

B. morphemic analysis

Morphemes are the smallest units of language that have an associated meaning and cannot be subdivided into smaller units that have meaning. The purpose of morphemic analysis is to study the morphemes of words to help in understanding the meaning of those words.

16. The student has been given a story to read after which he is to answer a series of questions, all of which begin with "who," "what," "where," or "how." What type of comprehension will these questions assess? (Skill 14.7) (Rigorous)

A. evaluative
B. inferential
C. literal
D. narrative

Answer:

C. literal

Literal questions are based on the facts in the reading. The student can put his finger right on the answer and prove that he is correct. These questions are sometimes referred to as "right there" questions.

17. A teacher has taught his students several strategies to monitor their reading comprehension. These strategies include identifying where in the passage they are having difficulty, identifying what the difficulty is, and restating the difficult sentence or passage in their own words. These strategies are examples of: (Skill 14.7) (Rigorous)

A. graphic and semantic organizers
B. metacognition
C. recognizing story structure
D. summarizing

Answer:

B. metacognition

Metacognition may be defined as "thinking about thinking." Good readers use metacognitive strategies to think about and have control over their reading. Before reading, they might clarify their purpose for reading and preview the text. During reading, they might monitor their understanding, adjusting their reading speed to fit the difficulty of the text and fixing any comprehension problems they have. After reading, they check their understanding of what they read.

18. A teacher has given her students an anticipation guide with a list of statements related to the topic of their reading. Before reading, the students are asked to indicate for each statement whether they agree or disagree with it. The primary purpose(s) of this guide are to: (Skill 14.7) (Average)

A. elicit students' prior knowledge of the topic and set a purpose for reading
B. identify the main ideas and supporting details in the text
C. synthesize information from the text
D. visualize the concepts and terms in the text

Answer:

A. elicit students' prior knowledge of the topic and set a purpose for reading

In most assignments, student will bring at least some prior knowledge, and they need to begin exploring that source now that they are in Middle School. Using prior knowledge to work toward a purpose for reading is a skill that will continue to be very useful to them.

19. Varying the complexity of a graphic organizer would be an example of differentiating: (Skill 14.7) (Average)

A. content/topic
B. environment
C. process
D. product

Answer:

C. process

Differentiating the processes means varying learning activities or strategies to provide appropriate methods for students to explore the concepts. It is important to give students alternative paths to manipulate the ideas embedded within the concept. For example, students may use graphic organizers, maps, diagrams, or charts to display their comprehension of concepts covered. Varying the complexity of the graphic organizer can very effectively facilitate differing levels of cognitive processing for students of differing ability.

20. All of the following are examples of ongoing informal assessment techniques used to observe student progress EXCEPT (Skill 13.6) (Rigorous)

A. analyses of student work product
B. collection of data from assessment tests
C. effective questioning
D. observation of students

Answer:

B. collection of data from assessment tests

Assessment tests are formal progress-monitoring measures.

21. A sixth-grade science teacher has given her class a paper to read on the relationship between food and weight gain. The writing contains signal words such as "because," "consequently," "this is how," and "due to." This paper has which text structure? (Skill 13.4) (Average)

A. cause & effect
B. compare & contrast
C. description
D. sequencing

Answer:

A. cause & effect

Cause and effect is the relationship between two things when one thing makes something else happen. Writers use this text structure to show order, inform, speculate, and change behavior. This text structure uses the process of identifying potential causes of a problem or issue in an orderly way. It is often used to teach social studies and science concepts. It is characterized by signal words such as because, so, so that, if ___ then, consequently, thus, since, for, for this reason, as a result of, therefore, due to, this is how, nevertheless, and accordingly.

22. A student has written a paper with the following characteristics: written in first person; characters, setting, and plot; some dialogue; events organized in chronological sequence with some flashbacks. In what genre has the student written? (Skill 13.5) (Rigorous)

A. expository writing
B. narrative writing
C. persuasive writing
D. technical writing

Answer:

B. narrative writing

These are all characteristics of narrative writing. Expository writing is intended to give information such as an explanation or directions, and the information is logically organized. Persuasive writing gives an opinion in an attempt to convince the reader that this point of view is valid or tries to persuade the reader to take a specific action. The goal of technical writing is to clearly communicate a select piece of information to a targeted reader or group of readers for a particular purpose in such a way that the subject can readily be understood. It is persuasive writing that anticipates a response from the reader.

23. Which of the following does not constitute a sentence? (Skill 13.2) (Average)

A. In keeping with the graduation tradition in spite of the rain, the students standing in the cafeteria tossing their mortarboards.
B. Rosa Parks, who refused to give up her seat on the bus, will be forever remembered for her courage.
C. Taking advantage of the goalie's being out of the net, we scored our last and winning goal.
D. When it began to rain, we gathered our possessions and ran for the pavilion.

Answer:

A. In keeping with the graduation tradition in spite of the rain, the students standing in the cafeteria tossing their mortarboards.

This is a sentence fragment. Verbs ending in "ing" require a helping verb.This phrasing does not have a helping verb. Change "the students standing" to "the students were standing."

24. In which of the following sentences is there an error that a word processing spellchecker would not likely pick up? (Skill 13.2) (Average)

A. He took the horse by the rains and led it back to the stable.
B. The village is adding a park on the west side of town.
C. George works in a glass factory near the railroad tracks.
D. We will be going to Tennessee this summer for vacation.

Answer:

A. He took the horse by the rains and led it back to the stable.

Only those words that violate standards of conventional modern English spelling are identified by a spellchecker. A spellchecker cannot distinguish between homophones or account for usage.

25. If a student uses inappropriate language that includes slang and expletives, what is the best course of action to take in order to influence the student's formal communication skills? (Skill 13.6) (Average)

A. ask the student to paraphrase the writing, that is, translate it into language appropriate for the school principal to read.
B. refuse to read the student's papers until he conforms to a more literate style.
C. ask the student to read his work aloud to the class for peer evaluation.
D. rewrite the flagrant passages to show the student the right form of expression.

Answer:

A. ask the student to paraphrase the writing, that is, translate it into language appropriate for the school principal to read.

Asking the student to write for a specific audience will help him become more involved in his writing. If he continues writing to the same audience—the teacher—he will continue seeing writing as just another assignment and he will not apply grammar, vocabulary, and syntax appropriately. By paraphrasing his own writing, the student will learn to write for a different audience.

26. Which of the following is not a theme of Native American writing? (Skill 15.1) (Rigorous)

A. Emphasis on the hardiness of the human body and soul
B. The strength of multi-cultural assimilation
C. Contrition for the genocide of native peoples
D. Sorrow for the destruction of the Indian way of life

Answer:

B. The strength of multi-cultural assimilation.

Native American literature was first a vast body of oral traditions from as early as before the fifteenth century. The characteristics include reverence for and awe of nature and the interconnectedness of the elements in the life cycle. The themes often reflect the hardiness of body and soul, sadness for the destruction of the Native American way of life, and the genocide of many tribes by the encroaching settlements of European Americans. These themes are still present in today's contemporary Native American literature, such as in the works of Duane Niatum, Gunn Allen, Louise Erdrich and N. Scott Momaday.

27. Oral debate is most closely associated with which form of discourse? (Skill 13.5) (Rigorous)

A. Description
B. Exposition
C. Narration
D. Persuasion

Answer:

D. Persuasion

It is extremely important to be convincing in an oral debate. This is why persuasion is so important because this is the way you can influence an audience and affect the outcome of a debate.

28. What is the prevailing form of discourse in this passage?

"It would have been hard to find a passer-by more wretched in appearance. He was a man of middle height, stout and hardy, in the strength of maturity; he might have been forty-six or seven. A slouched leather cap hid half his face, bronzed by the sun and wind, and dripping with sweat." (Skill 13.5) (Average)

A. Description
B. Narration
C. Exposition
D. Persuasion

Answer:

A. Description

A description presents a thing or a person in detail, and tells the reader about the appearance of whatever it is presenting. Narration relates a sequence of events (the story) told through a process of narration (discourse), in which events are recounted in a certain order (the plot). Narration implies a narrator, who can be the reader, another character, or the public in a theater. Exposition is an explanation or an argument within the narration. It can also be the introduction to a play or a story. Persuasion strives to convince either a character in the story or the reader.

29. Which of the following should not be included in the opening paragraph of an informative essay? (Skill 13.5) (Average)

A. Thesis sentence
B. Details and examples supporting the main idea
C. Broad general introduction to the topic
D. A style and tone that grabs the reader's attention

Answer:

B. Details and examples supporting the main idea

The introductory paragraph should introduce the topic, capture the reader's interest, state the thesis and prepare the reader for the main points in the essay. Details and examples, however, should be given in the second part of the essay so as to help develop the thesis presented at the end of the introductory paragraph, following the inverted triangle method consisting of a broad general statement followed by some information, and then the thesis at the end of the paragraph.

30. Identify the sentence that has an error in parallel structure. (Skill 13.2) (Average)

A. In order to help your favorite cause, you should contribute your time or money, raise awareness, and write to your congressman.
B. Many people envision scientists working alone in a laboratory and discovering scientific breakthroughs.
C. Some students prefer watching videos to textbooks because they are used to visual presentation.
D. Tom Hanks, who has won two Academy Awards, is celebrated as an actor, director, and producer.

Answer:

C. Some students prefer watching videos to textbooks because they are used to visual presentation.

In order for the structure to be parallel, the sentence should read "Some students prefer watching videos to **reading** textbooks because they are used to visual presentation."

31. Mr. Brown is a school volunteer <u>with a reputation and twenty years service</u>. (Skill 13.2) (Average)

A. with a reputation for twenty years' service
B. with a reputation for twenty year's service
C. who has served twenty years
D. with a service reputation of twenty years

Answer:

D. with a service reputation of twenty years

32. Joe <u>didn't hardly know his cousin Fred</u>, who'd had a surgery. (Skill 13.2) (Easy)

A. hardly did know his cousin Fred
B. didn't know his cousin Fred hardly
C. hardly knew his cousin Fred
D. didn't know his cousin Fred

Answer:

C. hardly knew his cousin Fred

33. The literary device of personification is used in which example below? (Skill 15.4) (Average)

A. "Beg me no beggary by soul or parents, whining dog!"
B. "Happiness sped through the halls cajoling as it went."
C. "O wind thy horn, thou proud fellow."
D. "And that one talent which is death to hide."

Answer:

B. "Happiness sped through the halls cajoling as it went".

Personification is defined as giving human characteristics to inanimate objects or concepts. Happiness, an inanimate object, is "speeding through the halls" and "cajoling," both of which are human behaviors.

34. What is the form of the following poem?

> **My name is John Wellington Wells,**
> **I'm a dealer in magic and spells,**
> **In blessings and curses,**
> **And ever-fill'd purses,**
> **In prophecies, witches, and knells. (Skill 15.1) (Easy)**

A. sonnet
B. haiku
C. limerick
D. cinquain

Answer:

C. limerick

The limerick is a form of short, humorous verse, often nonsensical. The rhyme scheme is strictly aabbaa with three feet in all lines except the third and fourth, which have only two. Although some may break with the traditional form, this usually happens only for purposes of impact.

35.Which of the following is *not* a figure of speech (figurative language)? (Skill 15.3) (Easy)

A. Simile
B. Euphemism
C. Onomatopoeia
D. Allusion

Answer:

D. Allusion

Allusion is an implied reference to a person, event, thing, or a part of another text. A simile is a direct comparison between two things. Euphemism is the substitution of an agreeable or inoffensive term for one that might offend. Onomatopoeia is a word that vocally imitates the sound associated with it.

36.Modeling is a practice that allows students to (Skill 13.6) (Average)

A. create a style unique to their own language capabilities.
B. emulate the writing of professionals.
C. paraphrase passages from good literature.
D. peer evaluate the writings of other students.

Answer:

B. emulate the writing of professionals.

The answer is B. Modeling has students analyze the writing of a professional writer, and try to reach the same level of syntactical, grammatical and stylistic mastery as the author whom they are studying.

37. Who was the principal writer of *The Declaration of Independence*?(Skill 15.1) (Easy)

A. Patrick Henry
B. Thomas Jefferson
C. Ben Franklin
D. George Washington

Answer:

B. Thomas Jefferson

The correct answer is Thomas Jefferson. Although Benjamin Franklin was responsible for editing it and making it the prime example of neoclassical writing that it is, *The Declaration of Independence* came directly from the mind and pen of Jefferson. Patrick Henry was a great orator and his speeches played an important role in bringing on the revolution; and while George Washington's oration, *Farewell to the Army of the Potomac*, is an important piece of writing from that era, it was Jefferson whose genius produced the *Declaration.*

38. Which of the following indicates that a student is a fluent reader? (Skill 14.7) (Rigorous)

A. reads texts with expression or prosody.
B. reads word-to-word and haltingly.
C. must intentionally decode a majority of the words.
D. in a writing assignment, sentences are poorly-organized structurally.

Answer:

A. reads texts with expression or prosody

The correct answer is A. The teacher should listen to the children read aloud, but there are also clues to reading levels in their writing.

39. When should reading assessment take place? (Skill 14.7) (Rigorous)

A. At the end of the semester.
B. At the end of a unit.
C. All the time—ongoing.
D. All of the above.

Answer:

D. All of the above.

End-of-unit and end-of-semester measurements yield important information regarding achievement of course objectives and the evaluating of students' growth; however, assessment should be going on all the time. The teacher should be observing and taking notes that will serve as a guide to class activities.

40. Which of the following is an essential characteristic of effective assessment? (Skill 13.6) (Average)

A. Students are the ones being tested; they are not involved in the assessment process.
B. Testing activities are kept separate from the teaching activities.
C. Assessment should reflect the actual reading the classroom instruction has prepared the student for.
D. Tests should use entirely different materials than those used in teaching so the result will be reliable.

Answer:

C. Assessment should reflect the actual reading the classroom instruction has prepared the student for.

The correct answer is C. The only reliable measure of the success of a unit will be based on the reading the instruction has focused on.

41. Which of the following is an essential characteristic of effective assessment? (Skill 13.6) (Rigorous)

A. When it comes to assessment, age and culture are irrelevant.
B. Teaching should be aimed at a student's weaknesses.
C. Assessment focuses only on the students' reading skills.
D. Assessment should be a natural part of the instruction and not intrusive.

Answer:

D. Assessment should be a natural part of the instruction and not intrusive.

The correct answer is D. If assessment is to be effective, it must be ongoing and must not interfere with instruction and practice.

42. Which of the following activities is *not* useful in the assessment process for slower or immature readers? (Skill 14.7) (Average)

A. Repeated readings.
B. Echo reading.
C. Wide reading.
D. Reading content that is more difficult than their skill levels in order to "stretch" their abilities.

Answer:

D. Reading content that is more difficult than their skill levels in order to "stretch" their abilities.

Reading content should be at a level where students cannot only read and understand the words but grasp meaning and nuances.

43. Of the following situations, which would *not* require referral to another resource? (Skill 16.1) (Rigorous)

A. Auditory trauma.
B. Ear infection.
C. Vision problems.
D. Underdeveloped vocabulary.

Answer:

D. Underdeveloped vocabulary

The *teacher* is the expert in vocabulary development.